A BIBLIOGRAPHY OF
THE MUSICAL WORKS
PUBLISHED BY
JOHN WALSH
1695–1720

√10/98

THE THEATRE ROYALL

Vivitur Ingenio

See Nos. 19a, 20a, and 29a

A BIBLIOGRAPHY OF THE MUSICAL WORKS PUBLISHED BY JOHN WALSH

during the years

1695—1720

BY

WILLIAM C. SMITH

LONDON

PRINTED FOR THE BIBLIOGRAPHICAL SOCIETY
AT THE UNIVERSITY PRESS, OXFORD

1948

BIBLIOGRAPHICAL SOCIETY PUBLICATION
FOR THE YEAR 1941
PUBLISHED 1948

PRINTED IN GREAT BRITAIN

CONTENTS

i

LIST OF ILLUSTRATIONS

List of Illustrations

Music

INTRODUCTION

OF the music published in England during the Elizabethan period very little remains unknown to the musician of to-day or is unrecorded by the authorities on the subject. In addition to existing copies of many of the works, there is a comprehensive summary of the output of professional and art music, as distinct from whatever existed of folk-music, in *A Catalogue of all the Musick-Bookes That have been Printed in England, either for Voyce or Instruments*, printed by John Playford in 1653.

From an examination of the catalogue, which consists mainly of an Elizabethan section up to about 1620,[1] it is easy to see that the practised and professional musicians of the day had definite and limited spheres for the exercise of their art, and that there was very little published music for the amateur and less skilled performers, such as was offered to them in increasing quantities in the developments of music and music-publishing of the later seventeenth and early eighteenth centuries. In the Playford catalogue there is little to indicate the existence of music amongst the ordinary folk—few tutors or instruction books, no popular songs or dance books, no theatre music. This is not to be wondered at, as these branches of music were largely subsequent developments of the art, and appear much more frequently in the later catalogues and publications.

For some twenty years or so after 1620 music publishing in England suffered an eclipse until the foundation of the historic house of the Playfords, who, pre-eminent among a number of less important publishers, were responsible for much of the music issued until the end of the seventeenth century, the firm continuing until 1707.

From the various Playford and other seventeenth-century catalogues, and from available copies of published works, many of which have other works advertised in them, it is possible, as in the case of Elizabethan music, to obtain a fairly complete idea of what was published, the kinds of music practised, the spread and evolution of the art, both professional and amateur, and public and private. The works recorded show the steady development of music from religious, scholastic, and highly cultured forms to the more popular and intimate music of the wealthy and leisured folk, who were

---

[1] A fuller description and examination of the catalogue and others was given in the *Musical Times*, July and August 1926.

becoming more interested in singing and playing in the family circle, in taverns, and other places of assembly and association.

In view of the existing knowledge of Elizabethan and later seventeenth-century music it is surprising that the eighteenth century has been treated so inadequately, except for the works of a few composers. Pepusch, Arne, Lampe, Burney, Greene, Boyce, Arnold, Carey, Hasse, Eccles, Daniel Purcell, G. B. Bononcini, Leveridge, and many other well-known musicians, English and foreign, who played important parts in the musical life of this country in the eighteenth century, are still awaiting attention, and adequate biographies and bibliographies of their works would be extremely useful.[1] As for the publishers of the period, except for a few well-known ones, there is little available information about them apart from what is contained in Frank Kidson's admirable work on the subject, and his statements need considerable amendment and expansion in the light of recent investigation.

The purpose of the present study is to make accessible for the first time a detailed bibliography of the publications of John Walsh the elder during the first twenty-five years of his career as a music publisher, including all the works advertised or published by him alone or in conjunction with other publishers from July 1695 until the end of 1720, from information existing in certain libraries and elsewhere as indicated later on.

The business of John Walsh and his successors was one of the greatest in music-publishing history, and this becomes more obvious as the conditions of music and music-publishing in the eighteenth century are investigated.

John Walsh, like many another figure eminent in history and art, was fortunate in the time of his arrival. Music was rapidly changing in form, substance, and performance. It was becoming much more the concern of everyday folk. The flute, the harpsichord, the violin, were being developed, manufactured, and used much more widely than hitherto. Foreign music in increasing quantities, more particularly instrumental and chamber music, was coming into England from famous firms of music engravers and publishers like Roger of Amsterdam, who had their established agents here; and amongst the imported works, the great musicians of the Continent, like Corelli and others, were widely represented. The development of opera in England after Purcell, and its easy transition to Italian Opera, which held the field for so long, provided many new works for publication. One thing

---

[1] Dr. Percy Scholes has recently published an exhaustive biography of Burney, and works are in preparation on some of the other composers named, but there is still a wide field awaiting research and investigation.

that contributed very largely to Walsh's success was the development of a popular press, with facilities for continuous advertisement, of which this enterprising publisher took the fullest advantage. Another point, to which greater consideration is given later on, is the fact that Walsh departed from the sixteenth- and seventeenth-century practice of printing music from type, and almost invariably used engraved music plates, which provided a comparatively cheap and easy method of printing and reproduction over many years.

All these features played their part in the establishment of the firm of Walsh, and as the eighteenth century progressed, advantage was derived from subsequent developments in music, which cannot be enlarged on here except to mention the unprecedented benefit and publicity given to the publisher by Handel, who, as the great figure of Italian Opera in England, as producer of what was virtually a new English art form, the Oratorio, and as composer of popular keyboard and other instrumental music, created a demand for the many editions of his works that were issued by Walsh and his successors. It is a matter for satisfaction that in the flood-tide of music and musicians which swept over England from the Continent, a British publisher was ingenious enough to take full advantage of what came from abroad, and at the same time to assist actively in the development and distribution of so many works by British composers.

John Walsh advertised and issued his first work in July 1695. All that appears to be known of him prior to that date is officially recorded in the reference in the Lord Chamberlain's papers under the date June 24, 1692: 'Warrant to swear and admit John Walsh musicall instrument maker in ordinary to his Majesty, in place of John Shaw, surrendered.' Shaw held his royal appointment as early as February 1688; but he had been making and repairing instruments long before that date. Of Walsh as an instrument-maker the present writer has no information, and is unaware of any instruments that may have been made by him.

Shaw's premises were 'The Goulden Harp and Hoboy neere the Maypole in the Strand'. The site of the Maypole is now covered by the church of St. Mary-le-Strand, which was erected in Walsh's time, as the foundation stone was laid in February 1714, and the consecration was in January 1723. Another maypole erected a little to the west of the earlier one was removed in 1718. Walsh may have been associated with St. Mary's; at any rate he was buried there, in March 1736, as it is recorded in the *Gazetteer and New Daily Advertiser*, January 23, 1766, that the remains of his son 'were interred with great funeral pomp in a new vault, in St. Mary's le Strand church yard. The remains of his father and mother were dug up and carefully put in the vault along with his corpse.' Kidson could not find any 'tablet or other memorial in the building to remind the modern world of one of the most energetic business men of his time'.

Apart from what can be learned from his advertisements and publications, and from the brief reports of his early appointment and of his death, little is known about Walsh. He was of sufficient importance for his death to be recorded in a number of the newspapers of the day. Some of these notices, not previously indicated in the writings of Kidson and others, are transcribed here and provide some important facts about Walsh and his family not otherwise available. Kidson pointed out that he died on March 13, and, according to the *Gentleman's Magazine*, left £30,000.

Daily Post, Monday, March 15, 1736:

The same morning (Saturday, March 13) died at his House in Catharine-street in the Strand, Mr. John Walsh, late Musick Printer and Instrument Maker to his Majesty, which Place he had resign'd some Time since to his Son, Mr. John Walsh, who succeeds him in his Business.

Daily Journal, Monday, March 15, 1736:

On Saturday last died, in the 71st Year of his Age, at his House in Catherine-street, Mr. John Walsh, late Musick Printer and Instrument Maker to his Majesty; which Place on his Resignation, was given to his Son, who succeeds him in his Business. (This notice also appeared in other papers.)

London Daily Post and General Advertiser, Monday, March 15, 1736:

Last Saturday Morning died at his House in Catherine street in the Strand, Mr. Walsh, late Musical Instrument-maker to his Majesty, which place he resigned some time ago to his Son. He is said to have died worth £20,000 which he hath left among his Children.

From these notices we learn for the first time of his age, that he had more than one child, that his royal appointment had been terminated some time before his decease and that his son had been appointed in his place, that he left his fortune to his children (which suggests that his wife predeceased him), and that the amount was given as £20,000, not £30,000, as in the *Gentleman's Magazine*. The latter journal gives the date of his death as March 12.

It is interesting to note that Walsh was about 30 when he started his publishing business in 1695, and that the younger Walsh probably assumed control of it some years before he actually inherited it on his father's death. In 1730, as pointed out later on, Joseph Hare ceased to collaborate with Walsh, and about the same time the firm's series of numbered works commenced. It seems apparent, therefore, that some definite changes in management and practice were made at this period, and it is not unreasonable to suppose that the younger Walsh was given his royal appointment at a time when he was really managing the business, his father being too old to do very much.

In addition to the notices quoted above, two references in the Treasury Papers are of interest, and help to confirm the opinion that the founder of the firm was a shrewd, determined, business man, not inclined to accept the official view about things without protest. The first, in 1726, evidently refers to an application of the publisher for exemption from stamp duties on some of his 'ballads and songs and other little books and papers'. The Commissioners of Stamps reported to the Lords of the Treasury that 'as musical books and papers are not within any of the exceptions of the act (Statute 10 Anne c. 19), they apprehend the duties ought to be paid'. (*Calendar of Treasury Papers, 1720–8*, p. 427.) The second reference, under date January 2, 1734, is to a 'Petition to the Treasury from John Walsh of Catherine Street, Strand, music printer, concerning a wrong entry of paper at the Custom House'. (*Calendar of Treasury Papers, 1731–4*, p. 591.)

Walsh adopted Shaw's sign; but his premises were in Catherine Street, frequently given as Catharine Street, or as in Strype's 1720 edition of Stow's *London*, Katharine and Katherine Street. This street was on the north side of the Strand and almost opposite Somerset House. It was partly demolished in the Strand-to-Holborn improvement scheme in the opening years of this century. The remaining portion, reconstructed since Walsh's day, still exists with the Strand Theatre at the bottom and Drury Lane Theatre at the top. Strype describes 'Katharine Street' as:

a very large and handsome street with good Houses, well inhabited chiefly by noted Tradesmen, especially the East side not many years since built. This Street cometh into the Strand against Somerset Yard Gate. On the West side is a pretty handsome Court, with a Free-stone Pavement, neatly kept, called Blakes Court, as built by Sir Richard Blake, the owner thereof.

John Gay in *Trivia* (1716) referred to the ladies of easy virtue 'who nightly stand where Katherine-street descends into the Strand'.

Walsh's shop, workshop, and dwelling-house were situated on the east side of Catherine Street, and presumably from these premises he and his successors issued their publications from 1695 until some time in 1801, when the business was transferred to 386 Strand. From the majority of the Walsh imprints, which are in the form 'Printed for and sold by J. Walsh', it does not appear evident that Walsh was a printer, nor is it clear if the work was actually done in Catherine Street, although Kidson goes so far as to say that it was done on the premises. 'Printed for and sold by' was a form generally used by other publishers of the period, and Walsh varied it at times with 'Engraved and printed for', reserving as a rule 'Sold by' for works of which he was merely retailer. 'Printed and sold by' is a most unusual form and has been traced in one or two notices only. To whatever extent Walsh himself was a craftsman, it seems clear that the work was done under his direction, and we have records of two of his apprentices—William Smith of Corelli's Head in the Strand and Luke Pippard; the latter, referred to under No. 334 in the bibliography, claimed to have been an apprentice of Walsh, and accused Walsh of re-printing works formerly published by him.

Before dealing more particularly with the period of the bibliography, it may be of interest to give in outline the names and approximate dates of John Walsh, his partners and successors, throughout the history of the firm:

John Walsh the elder alone, or more frequently in association with John Hare and sometimes with others (P. Randall, November 1706–December 1710), carried on from 1695 until December 1721.

From January 1722 until September 1725 Walsh was generally in association with John and Joseph Hare.

After the death of John Hare (September 1725), until about November 1730, the popular forms of imprint included John Walsh and Joseph Hare or J. Hare.

From 1730 until 1766 the firm published and advertised as John Walsh, this form covering John Walsh the elder, who died as stated on March 13, 1736, and the younger, who succeeded his father and carried on until his death on January 15, 1766. The royal appointment of the elder Walsh as musical-instrument-maker in ordinary to the King was mentioned as a rule in one form or another in his imprints and advertisements. The younger Walsh continued in the appointment, but except in a few cases in the earlier years of his control of the business, it is not mentioned on the works or in the advertisements, so it must be assumed that the appointment had ceased or was not of much consequence as time went on.

The younger Walsh was succeeded by William Randall and Abell, whose name appears on one or two works as I. Abell. They probably took over the business immediately following the death of Walsh, but the first notice with their joint names appeared in September 1766, the few earlier notices of the year usually reading, 'printed and sold at the late Mr. J. Walsh's'.

From August 1768 to January 1776, Abell having died at the end of July, 1768, William Randall carried on alone, as announced in the *Public Advertiser*, August 3, 1768: 'William Randall, successor to the late Mr. Walsh. . . . My Partner (Mr. Abell) being dead the business will be carried on as usual solely by me', &c. To this announcement Randall added an advertisement for an assistant: 'Wanted, as a Journeyman, a young Man who has been used to a Musick-Shop, and understands how to serve behind the counter.' It is not unreasonable to suppose that Robert Birchall or H. Wright may have entered Randall's employment as the result of this advertisement. Birchall, when commencing a business of his own at 129 New Bond Street, in February 1783, announced that he was 'from the late Mr. Randall's formerly Walsh's'. (*Morning Herald*, February 17, 1783.) Wright's connexion with the business is mentioned later on.

In January 1776 Elizabeth Randall, widow of William, took over the business, using her late husband's form of imprint as a rule, with some exceptions when she used her own name. A notice in the *Public Advertiser*, January 16, 18, 1776 states: 'Mrs. Randall most respectfully acquaints her Friends and the Public in general, that she continues the business of her late Husband for the Benefit of herself and four Children. She therefore humbly entreats the Continuance of their favours, and further informs them that the Old Stock is selling off considerably under Prime Cost, that a fresh Assortment will immediately be laid in, and the business carried on upon Terms equal to any Shop in Town'. Both William and Elizabeth Randall issued reprints from Walsh's plates without altering the Walsh imprints, consequently there is difficulty in definitely dating copies of some works.

Wright and Wilkinson succeeded Elizabeth Randall in or before April 1783, and advertised themselves as 'Successors to Mr. Walsh'.

In June 1784, the form was 'Wright & Co.' and from February 1785 or thereabouts, it was 'H. Wright, No. 13 Catherine Street, Strand'. The number may have been added to the premises during Randall's time; but it has not been traced in his imprints and is not regularly given in the directories until 1789 (*see* p. xxv). It is assumed that the same premises, probably with modifications, were occupied during the whole of the eighteenth century; but there may be a little doubt about this as Lowndes's *London Directory*,

1784, gives Wright and Wilkinson at No. 12 Catherine Street, and one imprint at least (Gawler's *Harmonia Sacra*, 1781) is 'Randall's Music Shop, No. 10 Catharine Street'. These differences, however, may be considered as probable misprints for No. 13, which is given in the advertisement of Gawler's work.

In 1801–3, H. Wright was at No. 386 Strand, and after that there is no record of him. With his disappearance, the business founded by John Walsh can be considered to have come to an end, but there is an interesting footnote to this outline story. Some of the Walsh plates were used in turn by Randall and Abell, Elizabeth Randall, and Wright and Wilkinson. After Wright ceased publishing, his entire stock of plates was purchased by Thomas Preston, music publisher of 97 Strand, who had succeeded his father, John, and who was later at 71 Dean Street, Soho (1823–*c*. 1833). Coventry and Hollier succeeded Thomas Preston, and were in business until 1848–9, and at the sale of their effects in December 1849 J. Alfred Novello acquired a number of the Walsh and Randall plates and issued Handel works from them, with modifications. Some of these plates were still in existence a few years ago, and it should be pointed out that the Novello reprints from them, without Novello's outer title-pages, sometimes get mistaken for early Walsh editions.

The bibliography of the first twenty-five years contains 642[1] items in chronological order as far as possible, but in some cases no advertisement has been traced and the date assigned is speculative. The work is based almost entirely on contemporary newspaper advertisements found in the British Museum, on Walsh catalogues and copies of the works that are available in the British Museum (Department of Printed Books, excluding the Hirsch Collection), The King's Music Library (British Museum), the Royal College of Music, and a few other places, with some details from the Term Catalogues (*Ed*. Arber) and Day and Murrie's *English Song-Books*. Other libraries, collections, and sources that contain additional works and notices could be mentioned, but to have made a comprehensive survey of them would have seriously delayed publication, and although some unrecorded copies would have been located, the results would not have increased the total number of items by very many. The annual lists of his publications, which Walsh

---

[1] Numbered 1–622, with additional items that have been traced during the revision of the proofs entered in correct chronological order with a letter as well as a number. (Nos. 19*a*, 20*a*, 20*b*, &c.) When it has been necessary to remove an item to another place the original number given to that item has been left vacant. (Nos. 56, 200, 225, &c.)

issued from time to time (Nos. 258, 282*a*, 331, and 370), containing an average of about 25–30 items, are additional evidence that the bibliography would not be very much longer even if we had all the facts at our disposal.

Wherever possible, transcriptions of the title-pages have been given, dates of advertisements and locations of copies being added where possible. When no copy has been available, or the details of the title-page are not known, the title has been taken from the earliest Walsh advertisement or catalogue, or from some other work. The advertisements can be distinguished from the transcribed titles as a rule by the absence of pressmarks, and the supplementary notes that accompany many of the items should prevent any confusion between advertisements and actual titles. As a general rule, the Walsh newspaper advertisements followed the title-pages fairly accurately, at least sufficiently so to enable the works to be identified, and in many cases, the advertisements as transcribed will need only slight revision if copies subsequently come to light for examination. In some cases, however, it has been quite impossible to identify a notice with any listed work or to be sure which edition is referred to, and it has therefore been considered advisable to enter every notice that appears to refer to a work or an edition not previously listed. Consequently there may be some doubtful entries, and some works and editions may be entered more than once. Further research may clear up such doubtful cases. In some instances, for special reasons, notices about the same work appearing on different dates have been included, but obvious re-advertisements of the same edition of a work have been omitted. It should be pointed out that it was customary to make two or three issues of the *London Gazette* under the same date, each being differently set up. No attempt has been made to indicate in the bibliography from which issue any particular notice has been copied, or to draw attention to any of the slight variations in the form of the notices as they occur in different issues. When the year given in the newspaper is according to the Old Calendar it has been altered to agree with the later practice, but only in some cases are these changes indicated.[1]

Besides works that contain a date as part of the title ('Twenty Four New Country Dances for the year 1711', &c.) only twenty-four of the items in the bibliography are dated and few of these occur after 1706. Of the total number of items recorded in the bibliography copies of about 230 are in the British Museum Library, 90 or so in the Royal College of Music, and less

---

[1] As a special example of the difficulties involved in the matter of identification, the reader is referred to the many entries of Corelli's works and notices of them.

than a dozen in The King's Music Library. These are only approximate figures, owing to the difficulties of identification in some cases, but it can be stated with reasonable certainty that well over 300 of the items are not represented in the collections examined, thus leaving a good deal for further investigation in collections elsewhere.

The bibliography of Walsh after 1720 is as important as his bibliography before that date, and the materials for it have been largely prepared by the present writer; but the first twenty-five years were considered sufficient for a first volume, and enabled a break to be made before Walsh and his son got into their stride as publishers of the works of Handel, although a few of these were issued before the end of 1720.

Over 240 of the works listed in the bibliography are included in a Walsh catalogue issued with *Astartus*, *c.* 1721 (BM. 7897. y. 12. (1.) *See* illustrations Nos. 27 and 28), and a considerable number of them, doubtless from the early plates with some modifications, are included in later Walsh catalogues and the catalogue of William Randall dated 1776. The 1721 catalogue, of which there were later editions, can be considered a reasonably complete one of Walsh's stock-in-trade at the time, and like the Randall catalogue, provides material for some interesting speculations. How many of the works that were not in stock had disappeared because they had been sold out, or were not in demand? How many copies of a work were printed and what was a reasonable sale? How many copies could be printed from a single plate? From what we know of musical works issued by subscription, and many such appeared in the eighteenth century, two or three hundred copies was a good edition, even for composers as important as Handel. But the subscription lists were usually associated with major instrumental works, operas, oratorios, &c., and are not much guide to the number of copies issued of the smaller, inexpensive works—tutors, sets of dances, and small books of arrangements for the flute, harpsichord, violin, &c., that were very popular.

The elder Walsh, as already mentioned, is reported to have left twenty or thirty thousand pounds, a very considerable fortune to have been made by anyone in those days out of retail trade, and it is not unreasonable to suppose that in addition to his profits as a music publisher and dealer, Walsh may have received a considerable amount from other sources—his business as a musical-instrument-maker, his royal appointment, or from some wise or fortunate speculations. Kidson says that Walsh's publications of Handel's works must have brought much of the £30,000, but it should be remembered that it

was not until about 1730 that Walsh settled down as Handel's regular publisher. Up to the end of 1720, *Rinaldo* and a few less important works were
the only ones published by Walsh; *Floridante, Ottone,* and *Flavio* (1722–3)
were 'Publish'd by the Author' (Handel) but printed and sold by Walsh;
and John Cluer published most of the Handel operas of the years 1724–9.
From 1730 onwards, the Walshes, father and son, had an unbroken business
association with Handel until his death. During that time, in addition to
publishing works of most of the contemporary composers, the firm issued
Handel works and editions of them in rapid succession. When the younger
Walsh died in 1766, he was reported to have left £40,000 (*The Gazetteer,*
January 23, 1766), not very much more than his father, which is surprising
when it is remembered that his business appears to have been on a much
larger scale, and was concerned with much more expensive works.

Everybody is familiar with the popular story that Walsh the elder made
£1,500 out of the sale of Handel's *Rinaldo*. The absurdity of this is apparent
when it is pointed out that even if all the copies were produced and sold
without cost to the publisher, more than 3,000 must have been issued to
produce such a sum. This number must be considered fantastic, in view of
what we know of music purchasing by the opera-goer, and in view of the
scarcity of copies to-day. It is true that we know little about the arrangements made by Walsh with the composers of the works he published, about
the payments they received, and about the terms of publication, and whether
he drew fees for the use of copies supplied by him to the theatres and elsewhere. Some evidence exists that twenty or twenty-five guineas were paid
by Walsh to Handel for each of a number of his operas; but the whole
subject is one for further investigation and cannot be pursued here.

The works included in the bibliography range in price from 6*d.* to 9*s.* or
so, three or four shillings being a good average. If the latter price is taken,
£30,000 represents the sale of 150,000 copies of works of various kinds
during the life of Walsh the elder, without allowing anything for payment
to the composers, or for production and sale, to cover which many more
than the 150,000 would have to be sold. An annual estimated cost of running
the business at £500 would mean in 40 years another 100,000 copies at
4*s.* each. The question naturally arises—What has happened to all these
copies?[1]

---

[1] The prices of some of Walsh's works were slightly increased in later editions (3*s.* to 4*s.*;
9*s.* to 10*s.* 6*d.*) and more than once he announced reductions in price due to competition.
(Nos. 251, 299, 334, 505, and 519.)

Walsh was not without rivals, indeed they were fairly numerous, as indicated in the late Frank Kidson's article on John Walsh in the *Musical Quarterly*, July 1920. None of them, however, were competitors on a very large or increasing scale. The combined newspaper advertisements of all of them are approximately equivalent in number to only one quarter of the notices put out by Walsh. The most serious rivals for about ten years from 1720 onwards were John Cluer and his successors, who published a number of Handel's works, but who were quite unable to prevent Walsh from ultimately capturing the market and putting his firm securely at the head of the British music publishers for the best part of a century.

Walsh has been accused sometimes of copying other publishers' works without authority; but from the evidence existing in notices in the press, it seems clear that the practice of music piracy was not uncommon and that Walsh had good reason for complaint against others. It is quite certain that he kept a sharp eye on the publications of his contemporaries, particularly the finely engraved works issued by Estienne Roger of Amsterdam, which were first introduced into England at the end of the seventeenth century. From 1701 onwards these works were advertised and sold by Francis Vaillant, a French bookseller in the Strand 'three doors from the West Corner of Catherine Street', and a near neighbour of Walsh's. Francis Vaillant was succeeded (*c.* 1706–7) by Isaac Vaillant 'Book and Mapseller at the Bishops Head in the Strand'. On October 4, 1711, the following notice appeared in the *Post Man*:

Notice is hereby given that all the Musick which was formerly sold by Messieurs Vaillant Booksellers, is now to be sold by Henry Riboteau Bookseller, at the Crown over against Exeter Exchange in the Strand. NB. Care is taken by the said H. Ribotteau to have all the new pieces of Musick that shall hereafter come out beyond Sea, like-wise all the New Books in all Faculties.

Riboteau went on advertising until towards the end of 1715 at least, and a steady stream of the Amsterdam publications continued to flow into the country, spurring Walsh on to produce the same or similar kinds of works in competition with them to such an extent that Walsh editions followed Amsterdam editions with almost clock-work regularity.

From about 1716 agents' notices of Roger's publications ceased to appear in the press, and one work at least (No. 610), apparently issued by Walsh, has on the title-page 'Sur l'Edition d Amsterdam par Etienne Roger', which suggests that Walsh had some friendly relationship with Roger at the time, or could afford to copy his work with impunity. Later on, publications of Roger are found with a Walsh label over Roger's imprint, and sometimes Walsh used the Roger plates with modifications, substituting his own imprint in place of Roger's on the title-page. This was the case with 'VI Sonates à deux Violons, deux haubois ou deux Flutes traversieres & Basse Continue Composées Par G. F. Handel Second ouvrage'. Copies of this work with Roger's imprint covered by Walsh's label were sold about 1731–2, and Walsh's own edition from the Roger plates with Walsh's imprint was issued *c.* 1733.

It is clear that it was customary for some of the music publishers to stock the works of other publishers, and in his advertisements Walsh distinguishes between works 'Printed for and sold by J. Walsh' and works 'Sold by J. Walsh'. In 1732 he advertised a number of the Handel operas that had been originally published by John Cluer, as works 'by Mr. Handel which may be had where these are sold', and copies exist of these Cluer editions with the Walsh labels over the original imprints. I do not know if this was an accepted practice amongst publishers selling works by other firms, although a number of similar cases could be mentioned. Walsh's name and those of other publishers appear in many of the lists of subscribers to works of the period.

It is difficult to estimate the full extent to which unlawful or unlicensed copies of other publishers' works were issued by Walsh and his contemporaries, but the following items in the bibliography provide evidence on the questions of piracy and competitive editions, on works taken over by one publisher from another, and on works of which the advertising publisher may have been acting as a selling agent only:

Nos. 6, 7, 15, 22, 28, 29, 31, 49, 82*a*, 83, 84, 88, 89, 102, 103, 108, 119, 125, 144, 162, 167, 174, 177, 179, 181, 190, 195, 214, 221, 230, 234, 235, 248, 251, 264*a*, 277, 280, 293, 296, 299, 303, 324, 334, 336, 343*a*, 349, 350, 351, 358, 400, 403, 434, 458, 461, 466, 469, 479, 480, 499, 505, 506, 510, 511, 513, 515, 517, 518, 519, 522, 528, 536, 537, 539, 546, 547, 549, 550, 551, 555, 570, 572, 573, 575, 576, 577, 579, 595, 602, 610, and 611.[1]

One of Walsh's contemporaries who was particularly active in issuing works that were also advertised by Walsh was Daniel Wright the elder, who was in business from about 1709 to 1734. From his advertisements in the press and a catalogue which he issued in 1734, it is quite clear that he had

---

[1] This list does not indicate all of the Walsh works editions of which were issued or advertised by other publishers.

no scruples about publishing unauthorized editions, and his works contradict the popular opinion that Walsh was *the* rascally publisher of the time.[1]

As already indicated, Walsh's publications were printed almost invariably from plates. A few works in type, mostly taken over from other publishers, were issued by him (Nos. 8, 195, 208, 248, 427, 485, 533, and 558), but throughout the whole career of the firm the works were generally printed from plates, engraved, or partly engraved and partly stamped.

The practice of issuing music from engraved copper plates was established long before John Walsh set up in business, and he is generally supposed to have adopted the method and material then in vogue, which there is no reason to doubt. Whether he was an engraver or not we do not know, and who engraved his works is not generally indicated on them except in the case of some of the illustrated title-pages that are referred to later on. Either before the end of the seventeeth century, or early in the eighteenth, two changes were made: punches were used to stamp the notes on the plates, the staves, ties, and other details being engraved by hand, and pewter as a softer metal and more easily punched was substituted for copper. Who really instituted these changes is not definitely known. Thomas Cross, the chief music-engraver in England, and who worked from about 1683 until well on into the eighteenth century, is said to have been responsible for using a softer metal, probably pewter, while the practice of stamping the notes is supposed to have originated with Estienne Roger of Amsterdam, who was established before the end of the seventeenth century and who certainly worked in copper. Walsh and Hare are credited with combining the two changes by stamping the notes and completing the engraving by hand on pewter or soft metal plates, some authorities giving the date of the introduction of their process as 1710 (Hawkins) and others as 1724 or thereabouts.

An examination of works by Cross, Roger, and Walsh and Hare does not entirely clear up the doubts. Cross's work is generally most distinctive and is beautifully engraved without evidence of punching. Roger's editions, as Kidson says, 'give the suggestion of pure engraving'. It is impossible to sort out accurately the purely engraved works published by Walsh from the partly punched ones, nor is there much definite indication as to which are from copper plates and which from pewter. Walsh frequently used the

[1] The Corelli items, Nos. 31 and 181, provide some very interesting information about the publication of these works by rival firms, and No. 334 (William Topham's Sonatas, Op. 3) is of more than ordinary interest in the story of Walsh.

terms, 'The whole engraven', 'Fully engraven', 'Fairly engraven', and 'Engraven', suggesting that the works in question were not from type or stamped plates; but many engraved works are not so described. In a few cases only are the works advertised as being on copper, and these notices are mostly confined to the earlier years of the firm. (Nos. 1, 2, 4, 5, 10, 14, 20*a*, 29*a*, 55, 64, 71, 181 (Portrait), 287, 348, 379, and 478.) Later on, particularly in the editions of Randall and his successors, it is quite easy to recognize additions to the old plates and also new plates that had been punched. Changes were frequently made in the plates of Handel's works; but the subject of Walsh and his connexion with Handel is outside the scope of this work.

Without attempting to fix the date of the earliest work of Walsh engraved on pewter, it can be definitely stated that Chrysander was wrong in claiming that John Cluer preceded Walsh in this respect by issuing Handel's *Julius Cæsar* from pewter plates in July 1724. (*Musical Times,* December 1877.) The notices (*London Journal,* May 2, June 6, 1724), which Chrysander misread, indicate quite clearly that Cluer's edition was from copper plates and the 'incorrect pirated Editions done on large Pewter Plates' which preceded the Cluer edition although without Walsh's imprint were doubtless issued by him. Having mistaken the facts, Chrysander adopted most ingenious and plausible explanations to justify his false conclusions about the size of paper used, and to maintain that Walsh copied the idea of pewter from Cluer, and that Cluer did the subsequent Handel work of *Tamerlane* on copper because of the difficulties he encountered in using pewter. Considering that Cluer quite clearly advertised *Julius Cæsar* and other works as 'Engrav'd on copper plates', and warned the public against 'spurious editions stampt on large folio pewter plates', it is remarkable that any mistake should have been made. One work (No. 16) was 'cut on steel and cast'; but Walsh and Hare were probably only the selling agents and had no part in its production.

On the whole, Walsh's works were better engraved than those of any of his English competitors, with the exception of those by Thomas Cross, but, apart from the title-pages, they were only moderately well done and showed no marked improvement as time went on, although some were better than others. (No. 366.) A few of the early works (Nos. 6, 12, and 35) are superior to many of the later ones, and differ considerably from the average Walsh work in the quality of the engraving. Specimen pages of music are reproduced as examples from different times during the period of the bibliography (*see* Ills. 29–38), but they represent only a few works and are not to be accepted as conclusive evidence in dating other works, especially as Walsh was anything but consistent in working very closely to a style or through any well-known engravers. The finely engraved originals of his various illustrated title-pages, that justly deserve the highest commendation, were nearly all made in the early days of his career and fall within the limits of this bibliography. Roger's works have as a rule much more character, and the layout is more artistic than in original works by Walsh, who, however, endeavoured to follow very closely the style of some of the Amsterdam editions that he copied.

Considerable economy in plates was achieved by Walsh the elder and his successors by the use of a single plate for the title-pages of different works, such title-pages being sometimes described as *passe-partout* title-pages. These were frequently finely illustrated during the period of the elder Walsh; but the son continued the practice with plain title-pages. The substitution of the new title on such plates was usually done by blocking out the old title or part of it with a supplementary plate on which the new title or matter was engraved. Sometimes the old title was blocked out with a blank supplementary plate, the new title being supplied in manuscript after the title-page had been printed off. (No. 298.) In other cases (Nos. 404–15, 430–33) the plate was engraved with a general title which could be used for a number of works, with a blank space left on the plate so that the particular part of the title could be written in by hand. Imprints had the necessary corrections made to them by erasion, alteration, and addition. For instance, a plate used for Walsh and Hare and required for a later work without Hare, would have Hare's named erased, although the correction was in many cases very carelessly done and the earlier form remained still recognizable. Walsh was most careful to alter 'His Majesty' to 'Her Majesty', and *vice versa* as changes in the Monarchy occurred; these alterations are a very useful help in arriving at the earliest or latest possible date of particular copies.

The bibliography contains a number of illustrations of plates; the necessary particulars of origin, &c., are recorded under the appropriate items referring to the first use of each plate by Walsh. A few of the most interesting are referred to more fully here.

The extremely rare and very interesting illustration of a stage scene, reproduced as frontispiece to the bibliography, is the earliest example of a Walsh illustration that has been traced.[1] It was published in *Theater Musick*

[1] A detached copy of the illustration in the Bodleian Library has not been recognized hitherto

(Nos. 19*a*, 20*a*, and 29*a*), and the words 'The Theatre Royall' at the top of the design can be accepted as referring to Drury Lane. The title-page of the first book of *Theater Musick*, describes the collection as 'perform'd at both Theaters', and mentions the *Opera of Rinaldo & Armida*. This was a play by John Dennis, with music by John Eccles, produced at 'Little-Lincoln's-Inn-Fields' in 1698. The Third Book of *Theater Musick* includes airs from *Ephigenia, & yᵉ Trip to the Iubilee*. The former was a play by John Dennis, produced at 'Little-Lincoln's-Inn-Fields' in 1699; the latter, better known as *The Constant Couple*, by George Farquhar with music by D. Purcell, was produced at Drury Lane in 1699.[1]

Usually the plates in their original form were designed for Walsh, but sometimes he took over a plate that had been first used by another publisher. This was the case with the well-known Collins design, which was used for many works during a long period. It is a finely designed and executed example of contemporary engraving, and with its original title gives a balanced and harmonious effect. It was first issued (*c.* 1690–2) for *Songs for One Two and Three Voices Composed to a Through Basse For yᵉ Organ or Harpsicord By R King*. (BM. K.8. h. 19. *See Ill.* 4.) This work was published, without imprint, by Robert King himself, but another issue, a little later (*c.* 1692) has an added imprint: 'Sold by Iohn Crouch att yᵉ 3 Lutes in Princes Street in Drury Lane'. (Day and Murrie, No. 117.)[2] Apparently Walsh did not use the plate until June 1698 (No. 15. *See* Ill. 3), but how or when he obtained possession of it is not known. Is it unreasonable to suppose that as an apprentice or in some other capacity he worked with Crouch before setting up in business for himself, or that Collins went over to work for Walsh and took the plate with him? Some later Walsh plates although not signed by Collins are very much in his style.

Another title-page, used by Walsh for a number of works (*see* Ills. 8 and 20), was first issued with Godfry Finger's *VI Sonatas or Solo's. Three for a Violin & Three for a Flute wᵗʰ. a Thorough Bass for yᵉ Harpsychord, &c.*, which

as belonging to a Walsh work, and the question of its identification was raised in *Theatre Notebook*, vol. 1, no. 3, April 1946.

[1] As Walsh's business was only a step or two away from Drury Lane Theatre he was probably well acquainted with the managers and thus able to acquire the right to publish the music used in various productions. Soon after the publication of *Theater Musick* he commenced the long series of music to dramatic works that ran from 1700 to 1706, and appears in the bibliography under the separate titles (Nos. 32, 42, &c.) and as collected volumes with the title *Harmonia Anglicana*. (Nos. 48, 75, &c.) These publications must have contributed largely to the early success of Walsh as a publisher.

[2] Crouch was publishing *c.* 1683–1704 or later.

was dedicated to the Earl of Manchester, and published privately without imprint in 1690. When Walsh took over the work he added his imprint below the design of the title-page. (No. 82*a*.) In the subsequent use of the plate for other works (Nos. 293, 296, &c.) he substituted the arms of Queen Anne for those of the Earl of Manchester, Baron Kimbolton, in the medallion of the design.

The earliest original *passe-partout* plate issued by Walsh was either No. 12 or No. 13 in the bibliography. These two works, which are each dated 1697, are amongst the very few works dated by Walsh. The two title-pages, though plainly designed, are finely lettered and spaced; the subsequent changes made in them are recorded in the bibliography. (*See* Ills. 1 and 2.)

The attractive plate engraved by M. Van de Gucht for Walsh's edition of D. Purcell's *The Judgment of Paris* (No. 89. *See* Ill. 10)[1] was also used for John Eccles's work of the same name. (No. 102.) Walsh's use of this plate is a good illustration of his shrewd business capacity and of the attention he paid to detail, a quality not usually associated with him by some of his critics who prefer to consider him generally careless and inaccurate. In 1706 Walsh published Saggione's *Songs in the Opera Call'd the Temple of Love* (No. 222) and *The Judgment of Paris* plate was cleverly adapted for this work, the new title being engraved in place of the old one at the top and bottom of the design, and a temple very appropriately added in the centre background. (*See* Ill. 17.) The plate was used again for *The Monthly Mask of Vocal Musick*, July 1717. (No. 517.)

The finely designed canopied title-page of Pepusch's *Six English Cantatas, &c.*, 1710 (No. 353. *See* Ill. 22) was the first impression from a plate which was afterwards used extensively by Walsh for operas and other works. It has the distinction of having been used for Handel's *Rinaldo* (No. 385) which marked the beginning of Walsh's association with the composer.

The Monthly Mask of Vocal Music, a periodical that ran from November 1702 until September 1711, and then again from July 1717 until July 1724, had an illustrated title-page to each monthly part from plates generally engraved by Hulsbergh, some plates being used for a number of parts, with the necessary correction of dates. They are not listed in detail in the bibliography, which only records the beginning of the series (No. 103), and essential entries after that. (*See* Ill. 11.)

In 1700 Corelli's *Sonate a Violino e Violone o Cimbalo . . . Opera Quinta*

---

[1] The original drawing for this plate is in the collection of Edward Croft-Murray at Richmond.

was issued at Rome 'Incisa da Gasparo Pietra Santa', with an illustrated frontispiece designed by Antonio Meloni, and engraved by Girolamo Frezza. (*See* Ill. 5.) Walsh used another engraving from Meloni's design by P. P. Bouche as a frontispiece to his edition of Corelli's Opera Quinta in 1700. (No. 31.) In September 1701 the Bouche plate was used as an outer title-page for William Topham's *Six Sonata's or Solos, for the Flute. With a Through Bass* (No. 60. *See* Ill. 6), the title being added from a supplementary plate to the shield which in the Frezza and Bouche engravings contained the arms of the Electress of Brandenburg, to whom the Corelli work was dedicated.

Before dealing with some points that may help in the use of the bibliography, a word may be permitted with regard to Walsh's practice of numbering his publications. Existing records show that there were nearly 700 works in the series, and there has been much speculation as to the date when the scheme first commenced. Information on the matter is still far from complete, but from available evidence at the moment, it seems fairly certain that the series started after the period covered by the bibliography, probably about 1727, or a little later, maybe in 1730 when Joseph Hare ceased to collaborate with Walsh. The numbered series included some works that had appeared before the series commenced, and when Walsh incorporated any of these earlier works in the series he added the number to the old plate of the title-page, or in manuscript to the copies of the work in stock. The first editions of such works are therefore without this enumeration, but in the absence of earlier copies the particulars given in the bibliography have been taken in some instances from the later numbered copies. Works in the bibliography that subsequently appeared in the numerical series are indicated accordingly. (Nos. 63, 85, 176, 181, 198, 211, 308, 429, 460, 465, 466, 468, 474, 476, 480, 491, 495, 501, 505, 511, 513, 522, 531, 539, 552, 553, 556, 564, 572, 593, 597, 610, 611, and 612.)

Probably a year or two prior to the establishment of this well-known numerical series Walsh advertised a list of 'Choice Musick by the most Celebrated Authors in Europe Printed for John Walsh'. This catalogue, which is arranged alphabetically, according to composers, followed by collections, occurs at the end of an edition of *Apollo's Feast, 3ᵈ. Book*, 1729, a copy of which is in my possession. It seems likely, however, that the catalogue was originally issued in an earlier edition, *c.* 1726–7, as it is evident that additions had been made to it. Each composer is given a number and under it are listed the works published by Walsh. These serial numbers have nothing to do with, and should not be confused with, those of the series referred to above. Numbers also occur, either in manuscript or stamped on the title-pages of much later Walsh works, which in some cases have not been fully investigated, but are at any rate outside the period of the bibliography and appear to have no connexion with earlier Walsh series.

In transcribing the newspaper notices and the title-pages of the works examined, initial capitals, punctuation, and spelling, have been generally copied, with a few exceptions; in some cases the capitals and punctuation are uncertain. No attempt has been made to indicate the lining and layout of the title-pages or to give variations in the style of lettering, except in the case of initial capitals, which have always been given as they occur at the beginning of words or if the whole word is in capitals and is of sufficient importance. The title of each work is in every case completed with a full stop, whether it occurs on the work or not, the whole title being transcribed without a break until the imprint, which always commences a new line and is always completed with a full stop. The imprints are given in full wherever necessary; always on the first appearance of a particular form of imprint or of changes in the names. When a variation occurs that is worth recording in order to help identification, the new imprint is given in full, but in subsequent works with the same imprint the particulars are abbreviated as necessary. The form of imprint is a rough guide to the dating of a work, or the placing of it within a certain period, but in the absence of a definite advertisement or other evidence of publication much must be left to speculation.

Walsh published some works alone, but more often than not other publishers' names are given with his in the advertisements and imprints (Hare, Randall, &c.) during the period under review. The extent to which Walsh was in partnership with these other publishers, or whether they were only acting as selling agents, is not very clear, but it appears that Walsh was entirely in control of his own firm as the signed notices in the press were issued above his name only. Works advertised or published by any of his collaborators without any mention of Walsh are not included in the bibliography, which is confined to works with which Walsh was associated in any way, and, therefore, works advertised or published by Hare alone or without Walsh's name are omitted. An examination of many title-pages gives convincing proof that, as a rule, Walsh did not include the names of other publishers unless they were actually associated with him in the work at the time, and he was most particular to eliminate from, and add to imprints other names as his business relationships changed. In spite of this, the reissue of earlier works with imprints erased, added to, and re-engraved in part, was so common, that it is quite easy to be misled.

The following particulars, which give in chronological order the principal changes in the form and composition of the imprints and advertisements, may help as a rough guide in the identification and placing of other works not included in the bibliography, but it must be remembered that the various forms overlapped, and were not always used in strict chronological order, partly owing to the Walsh practice of adapting old plates with earlier imprints for later works.

The address of Walsh, first given as 'The Golden Harp and Hautboy in Catherine-street in the Strand' appeared from the earliest days of the firm in various forms: 'The Golden Harp and Hoboy', 'The Harp and Hoboy', 'The Harp and Hautboy', and with 'Katharine' and 'Catharine street'. After a few years the word 'Golden' was gradually dropped, and the form, 'The Harp and Hoboy', with modifications in spelling, remained until No. 13 was added to Catherine Street probably in the W. Randall period; it occurs on Elizabeth Randall's Catalogue. 'Catherine-street' and its various forms appear with and without the hyphen, which was ultimately dropped.

The first seven works in the bibliography with their variations of matter and form in the imprints and advertisements indicate the difficulty in dating works from such particulars, but from 1697 onwards the Walsh and Hare imprints more or less conform to 'J. Walsh Musical Instrument-maker in Ordinary to his Majesty at the Golden Harp and Hoboy (or Hautboy) in Catherine (or Katharine, Katherine, &c.) street in the Strand and J. Hare Musical Instrument seller (or maker) at the Golden Viol in St. Pauls Church-yard and at his Shop in Freemans-yard in Cornhill,' &c.

After the accession of Queen Anne (March 1702) Walsh is given as 'Servant to her Majesty'.

During 1702–3, Hare sometimes used 'Golden Violin' in place of 'Golden Viol', especially in the newspaper notices.

During 1704 Walsh changed to the more regular form of 'Golden Harp and Hautboy', and 'Katherine-street' became more common than 'Catherine-street' for some time, although both of these forms as well as 'Catharine-street' were used during the period of the bibliography.

In April 1706 Hare gave up the St. Paul's Church Yard and Freeman's Yard addresses, and was established 'at the Golden Viol and Flute in Corn-hill near the Royal Exchange'; the combined forms of Walsh and Hare being 'Printed for J. Walsh Servant to her Majesty at the Golden Harp and Hautboy in Katherine-street near Somerset House in the Strand, and J. Hare at the Golden Viol and Flute in Cornhill near the Royal Exchange'. This remained fairly consistent until November 1706, when 'and P. Randall (or Randal) at the Violin and Lute by Paulsgrave Hand (or head) Court without Temple-Bar', or other forms of this, were added to the imprints of Walsh and Hare. From January 1707, Randall's address was sometimes given in the shortened form: 'At the Violin and Lute without Temple Bar', or 'At the Viol and Lute by Paulsgrave head Court', &c.

In October 1708 the order of names appeared as 'J. Walsh and P. Randal (or Randall) at the Harp and Hoboy in Catherine-street . . . and the Violin and Lute by Paulsgrave Court without Temple Bar, and J. Hare', &c. This suggests a closer business association of Walsh with Randall, probably a partnership, as by July 1709 the 'Violin and Lute' address was omitted, and Walsh and Randall are both given together 'at the Harp and Hoboy in Catherine-street', &c. It is not unreasonable to suppose that Randall was a relative of Walsh or became so by marriage, and an ancestor of the William Randall who came on the scene in 1766.

From December 1710 Randall's name was omitted, except for a few reissues and re-advertisements, and the popular form was 'J. Walsh, Servant in Ordinary to Her Majesty, at the Harp and Hoboy . . . and J. Hare at the Viol and Flute,' &c. After the death of Queen Anne (August 1714) 'Her Majesty' became 'His Majesty', and except for variations of 'Hautboy' for 'Hoboy', 'Katherine' for 'Catherine', there was no particular change until January 1722, when Joseph Hare joined his father, and the announcements were made in the names of J. Walsh, John and Joseph Hare.

As a general rule throughout the bibliography, the various issues of the same work have been referred to as 'editions', but occasionally to avoid repetition as 'issues', and no attempt has been made to distinguish between issues, editions, reprints with slight variations, other copies with new title-pages, &c. This may not commend itself to the meticulous bibliographer, but it is offered as a practical solution to a very difficult problem and serves the main purposes of the work—a list of what was published and the identification of copies. To attempt to describe musical works in the same detailed terms as are applied to books can only be done after a page by page, bar by bar, examination. Every item listed, therefore, is different in some way from other entries of the same work, and the differences as indicated should be sufficient to identify and distinguish copies. The apparently trivial minor variations in the imprints that occur so frequently in Walsh works have been considered sufficient to justify the inclusion of such copies as separate items, although there may have been quite a number of copies with such slight variations that have escaped notice.

Sizes have not been given except in one or two instances, as the works can be readily identified otherwise. Walsh used various sized plates for his larger works, usually described by cataloguers as folio, and this is sufficient for all practical purposes. The actual sizes of the plates are not of much conse-quence, but they were roughly anything from about $6\frac{1}{2}$ in. × 11 in. to 7 in. × 12 in. or thereabouts, during the period of the bibliography. Any attempt to apply to Walsh's music the usual rules based on the foldings of paper, directions of lines, or position of watermarks is out of the question, as it is clear that he used and cut his paper without regard to such, and as it suited his purpose at the time.

Walsh did not, as a rule, give any information as to the binding or covers of his works as issued. In a few cases they were advertised as bound, especi-ally collections of operas, oratorios, &c., or issued in volumes (Nos. 114, 142c, 156, 238, 268, 297, &c.), but it is quite safe to conclude that most of the early works, especially the small and inexpensive ones, were issued with paper wrappers, usually blue, sewn through with the leaves of the work. A number of works with these original paper wrappers still exist. Heavier works were done in a similar way with stouter paper or thin cardboard. Such works as may have been sold bound were most likely issued in marbled boards with leather backs and corners. There are plenty of Walsh works existing to-day covered in this way, but it would be quite unsafe to assume that they were issued in that condition. Later on in the history of the firm, it is pretty certain that the oratorios and other large works were issued inexpensively bound, with leather backs and paper-covered boards.

Some works were advertised and issued 'in quires', evidently unbound (Nos. 138 and 596), and the first part of *Thomyris* was sold at '1s. the book, or the Songs single for 1d. a piece'. (No. 251.)

A number of single-sheet songs of the period exist in the British Museum and elsewhere without any indication of publisher, but many of these are obviously extracts from vocal scores, from collections of songs from operas, or from *The Monthly Mask of Vocal Music,* originally published by Walsh. No general attempt has been made to include these extracts, although some with Walsh imprints have been mentioned.

Material supplied by the compiler to the titles from other sources than the works or notices is given in square brackets [ ], and words of single songs

e   xxvii

not given in the titles are supplied in round brackets ( ). Pressmarks of works in the British Museum Library, The King's Music Library, and the Royal College of Music are indicated respectively as: BM, RM, and RCM; the Term Catalogues by TC, and the National Library of Scotland by NLS.

It is unnecessary to analyse here the contents of the bibliography, or to give the numbers of the various classes of music included in it. Walsh took advantage of every opportunity to expand and develop his business in keeping with the musical evolution of the time. As the flute, violin, harpsichord, the song, the play, the opera, and chamber music became more generally accepted and appreciated Walsh was always at hand with his advertisements in the press of the latest additions to his stock. He imitated and copied others, with or without their permission, but there is plenty of evidence to show that he experimented with and speculated in new ideas—musical periodicals, gratis copies, subscription issues, economy in the use of plates, and fine title-pages are all indicative of his business skill and technical ability. He was unquestionably a great figure in the history of music in England, who did much for the spread and practice of the art by publishing the works of so many composers of the time. He is entitled to be placed side by side with the most important publishers of the Continent. His work and character must be judged according to the standards of the day, and with this in mind the quality of his publications must be considered very good on the whole, and there is little reason for thinking that his business methods were bad in principle or practice.

The conditions under which this bibliography has been prepared for publication have made it impossible to cross-check some details, but apart from mistakes that may be attributed to this cause, a work of this kind under any circumstances is almost bound to have errors and cannot possibly be complete. It is not the last word to be spoken on John Walsh, but rather a supplement to the first word so ably said by Frank Kidson, who concluded his article in the *Musical Quarterly*, July 1920, by pointing out the importance of a Walsh bibliography, the compilation of which would be a great task and not unpleasant to those who delight in such work, and he wondered whether any bold spirit or spirits would ever undertake it.

In offering this first contribution to a complete bibliography of the amazing Mr. Walsh and his successors, the compiler can register his keen enjoyment in the preparation of the work, in spite of the difficulties entailed, but is unable to lay claim to any boldness of spirit. This quality was certainly characteristic of Frank Kidson in all that he did on the subject of British music publishers, and has been emulated in the quiet, unobtrusive, and de-tailed work carried on for many years by Mr. Charles Humphries of the Music Department, British Museum. He is responsible for the tracing and transcription of many of the newspaper notices, and in numerous ways has been of invaluable assistance to an old colleague and friend. Sincere apprecia-tion is also due to Sir George Dyson for his kindness in allowing the Walsh works in the Royal College of Music to be examined. In addition to giving other helpful assistance, Richard Newton, of Henley-in-Arden, produced from his own collection a fine copy of Finger's Sonatas (No. 82a) with the illus-trated title-page, adapted by Walsh for a number of works, the original of which was not generally known (*see* Ill. 8), and also brought to the writer's notice besides other works, the rare copy of *Theater Musick*. (Nos. 19*a,* 20*a,* and 29*a*.) Through the kindness of Canon S. L. Greenslade, M.A., and with the permission of the Dean and Chapter of Durham Cathedral, it has been possible to include the details of this work in the bibliography, and also a reproduction of the interesting Walsh illustration. (*See* Frontispiece.) Dr. H. W. Meikle, formerly Librarian of the National Library of Scotland, and W. Beattie, M.A., Keeper of Printed Books in the same library, kindly provided the illustration and details of No. 166. L. W. Hanson, of the Department of Printed Books, British Museum, pointed out the Walsh notices in the Treasury Papers; and amongst others who have been helpful in various ways are Edmund J. Rees, F.L.A., Librarian, Cardiff Public Libraries, Gerald Coke, P. H. Muir, Dr. O. E. Deutsch, Paul Hirsch, and Dr. A. Loewenberg. A special word of thanks is due to F. C. Francis, of the British Museum and Honorary Secretary of the Bibliographical Society, who has always been ready with helpful suggestions and advice. The compiler is also deeply grateful to the Society for undertaking publication, and to the authorities of the British Museum for permission to make the reproductions for most of the illustrations, so essential to the work.

CATALOGUES ISSUED BY JOHN WALSH
AND HIS SUCCESSORS

In addition to advertisements in the press, John Walsh used two other means for making his publications known—priced sheet catalogues and lists on the title-pages or elsewhere in some of the works. The latter of these methods was cheap and effective, costing nothing after the engraving of the plates; and the younger Walsh used it extensively, particularly in the case of Handel. The notices vary from one or two items to quite considerable lists, some of which give the output for a whole year. (Nos. 258, 282a, and 331.) Works containing such advertisements are indicated in the bibliography in about forty cases, and it is unnecessary to give further details here; but particulars of the principal sheet catalogues issued by the firm up to 1783 are given below; copies of them being extremely rare. It is impossible to say whether they were issued in every copy of the particular works in which some of them are found to-day, or whether they were included in other works from which they have now disappeared. Doubtless, in some instances, they were treated as unimportant advertisement matter and were consequently destroyed when the volumes were bound; and it is quite certain that some of the copies available to-day in sheet form were issued attached to works.

Two or more issues, with modifications and additions, were sometimes made from the same plate; in some cases the variations being very few, and in others quite considerable. A change in the style of engraving and the absence of prices generally indicate later additions to the plates.

Particulars of catalogues issued during the period of the bibliography are recorded in their appropriate places and some are reproduced as illustrations: Nos. 7, 9, 27, and 28.

1. The Overture's and Ayrs, in four Parts, made for the Opera's, Tragedy's, and Comedy's of the Theater's, Printed for I. Walsh.

> [1701.] Single sheet, oblong folio, 26 items, in 2 columns. (No. 60. *See* Ill. 7.) *See also* No. 3a.

2. The Setts of Aires in 4 parts contain'd in yᵉ Several Collections of yᵉ Musick of yᵉ English Stage.

> [1702.] Single sheet, folio, 20 items. (No. 89. *See* Ill. 9.)

3a. The Overture's and Ayrs, in four Parts, made for the Opera's, Tragedy's, and Comedy's of the Theater's, Printed for I. Walsh.

> [1703.] Single sheet, oblong folio, 44 items. From the same plate as No. 1, with alterations and additional items. (No. 140.)

Verso:

3*b*. A Catalogue of English and Itallian Musick for all sorts of Instruments printed for J. Walsh.

>   Folio, 48 items, in four groups. (No. 140.)

4*a*. A Catalogue of English & Italian Musick, Vocal & Instrumental Printed for Iohn Walsh.

>   [*c.* 1721.] Single sheet, folio, 152 items, in four columns. (*See* Ill. 27.)

> *Verso*:

4*b*. A Catalogue of English and Italian Musick for Flutes Printed for Iohn Walsh.

>   88 items, in four columns. (*See* Ill. 28.)
>   BM. 7897. y. 12. (1.); Hirsch Catalogue, Vol. II, No. 90, 'Astartus'; RCM. XXXII. B. 11. (2.), 'Astartus'.
>   The first edition of this two-paged catalogue was probably issued early in 1720, and contained 10 items less than in the *c.* 1721 edition. *See also* Nos. 6*a* and 6*b*.

5. Choice Musick by the most Celebrated Authors in Europe Printed for John Walsh.

> *Verso*:

Choice Musick by the most Celebrated Authors.

>   Single sheet folio, in four columns. The composers are given in alphabetical order, each with a number under which their works are listed but not separately numbered, with anonymous works and collections at the end of the catalogue.
>   [*c.* 1726–7.] The first edition, probably with Nos. 1–75 only.
>   [*c.* 1729 and later.] Other editions: with Nos. 1–82; Nos. 1–84, Hirsch Catalogue, Vol. IV, No. 1116; with additional works under some of the numbers 1–75.
>   The catalogue was issued at the end of volumes of 'Apollo's Feast'; a copy of Vol. III of that work, *c.* 1729, containing the catalogue with Nos. 1–82, *c.* 1733, is referred to in the bibliography.

6*a*. A Catalogue of English & Italian Musick Vocal & Instrumental Printed for Inᵒ. Walsh.

>   [*c.* 1733 or earlier.] Single sheet folio, 291 items, in four columns. Based on No. 4*a*, but from a new plate containing many more works.

> *Verso*:

6*b*. A Catalogue of English and Italian Musick for Flutes Printed for Iohn Walsh.

>   138 items, in four columns. A later edition of No. 4*b*, from the same plate. Gerald Coke Collection, 'Apollo's Feast', Book III.

>   [*c.* 1733.] A later edition of No. 6*a* with 298 items and of No. 6*b* with 148 items. Hirsch Catalogue, Vol. IV, No. 1115.

7. Musick Printed for Iohn Walsh in Catherine Street in the Strand.

>   [*c.* 1743.] Single sheet folio, containing probably 122 items, in three columns, and three lines of other items at the bottom. No copy available for examination.
>   [*c.* 1744.] From the same plate containing 128 items, &c. A copy exists in Gasparo Fritz's 'Sei Sonate . . . Opera Prima, 1742' (Hirsch Catalogue, Vol. III, No. 208); but the catalogue is certainly later than 1742.

The items at the bottom include 'other Pieces which may be seen in the Great Catalogue Printed for I. Walsh'. No catalogue has been traced with the title 'Great Catalogue', but in the *Daily Advertiser*, Oct. 3, 1743, Walsh advertised:

'A Complete Catalogue of all the Musick printed in England Price 6d;'
and in the *London Evening Post*, Oct. 18–20, 1743:

'A Compleat Catalogue of Musick for all Instruments by the best Masters.'

No contemporary catalogue agreeing with these notices has been identified; but the work listed as No. 9 is probably a later edition of the 'Great Catalogue'.

See also No. 12.

8. Divine Musick, Just Publish'd by I Walsh, in Catherine Street, in the Strand.

[1743.] Single sheet folio, 21 items in a single column: 'Handel's Coronation Anthems Vol. 1st . . . Dr. Greene's 40 Select Anthems', followed by: 'N.B. Great variety of new Concertos . . . Vocal Musick by all the Eminent Masters.'

BM. 7897. y. 12. (2.) With signs that an item after 'Greene's Anthems' had been erased from the plate, which may have been first issued earlier than 1743. Advertisements by Walsh of 'Divine Musick' were put out in 1731, 1735, &c. A later edition of the catalogue is listed as No. 11.

9. A Catalogue of Vocal and Instrumental Musick, Printed for and Sold by I. Walsh in Catharine Street in the Strand.

Verso:

A Catalogue of Instrumental and Vocal Musick Printed for and Sold by I. Walsh in Catharine Street in the Strand.

[*c.* 1747.] Single sheet folio, 2 pp., 380 items, in four columns. Hirsch Catalogue, Vol. IV, No. 1115a.

Slightly later editions containing 386 and 391 items were issued early in 1748, and occur in volumes of Handel's 'Joshua', and at BM. 7897. y. 12. (4.)

As all editions of this catalogue contain nearly 400 items, covering many more works, and have three times the number of items in No. 7 which advertised 'the Great Catalogue Printed for I. Walsh', it is reasonable to identify them as editions of 'the Great Catalogue'.

See also No. 12.

10. A Catalogue of New Musick, and new Editions of Musick Printed for I. Walsh in Catharine Street in the Strand.

[*c.* 1752.] Single sheet folio, 2 pp., 353 items covering many more works, in three columns.
BM. 7897. y. 12. (3.)

11. Divine Musick, Just Publish'd by I Walsh, in Catherine Street, in the Strand.

[*c.* 1752 or later.] Single sheet folio.
A later edition of No. 8, in 23 lines with additional items, and finishing with 'Pope's Ode of the Dying Christian. Set by Sig^r. Pergolesi'.
RM. 14. d. 19, 'Forty Select Anthems . . . by Dr. Maurice Greene'.

12. A Compleat Catalogue of Vocal and Instrumental Music. Price 6d.

Public Advertiser, Nov. 17, &c., 1760; July 14, &c., 1761; Sept. 23, 1763; Jan. 20, &c., 1764. Not identified.
See also Nos. 7 and 9.

13. A Catalogue of Vocal and Instrumental Music, For the Year 1776. Printed for, and sold by William Randall, Successor to the late Mr. John Walsh, in Catherine-Street, in the Strand. N.B. The greatest Choice of all Kinds of Music printed in England.

> 1776. Folio, 4 pp., 721 items, in three columns.
> The most comprehensive catalogue issued by the firm up to date, evidently representing the stock-in-trade at the time, including many works listed in the bibliography. Copies were issued in 'Le Delizie dell'Opere' (BM. G. 159.) and other works.
> Hirsch Catalogue, Vol. IV, No. 1113.

14. A Catalogue of Vocal and Instrumental Music, Printed for, and Sold by Elizabeth Randall, No. 13, Catharine-Street, in the Strand. N.B. The greatest Choice of all Kinds of Music printed in England.

> [*c.* 1782–3.] Folio, 4 pp., 769 items, in three columns.
> A similar list to No. 13, but differently set up and with new items.
> BM. 1879. cc. 13. (22.); RM. 7. f. 1, Wright and Wilkinson's edition of the 'Chandos Anthems'; Hirsch Catalogue, Vol. IV, No. 1112.

A BIBLIOGRAPHY OF THE MUSICAL WORKS
PUBLISHED BY JOHN WALSH DURING THE YEARS 1695–1720

At the appropriate places in the Bibliography attention is called to changes in the imprints and notices that are of sufficient importance to help in the identification and dating of particular works; but such information does not record in detail every change or variation and must only be accepted as a general indication of the practice at the time.

1. The Self-Instructor on the Violin: Or, The Art of playing on that Instrument Improv'd and made easie, by plain Rules and Directions: Together with a choice Collection of the newest Tunes and Ayres composed by the ablest Masters. To which is added, an excellent Solo of Mr. Courtiville's fairly engraven on Copper.

Printed for J. Walsh (His Majesty's Instrument-Maker in Ordinary) at the Golden Harp and Hautboy in Catherine-street in the Strand, and for J. Miller at the Violin and Haut-boy on London-bridge, and J. Hare in Freeman's Yard in Cornhill, Musical Instrument-Sellers. Price 1s. 6d.

July 15–18, 1695, *London Gazette.*

See No. 10.

2. The Compleat Flute-Master: Or, the whole Art of playing on the Recorder laid open, in such easie and plain Instructions, that by them the meanest capacity may arrive to a perfection on that Instrument: With a Collection of the newest and best Tunes, composed by the most able Masters. To which is added, an admirable Solo, fairly Engraven on Copper Plates.

Sold by John Walsh, Musical Instrument-Maker in Ordinary to His Majesty at the Harp and Hoboy in Catherine-street in the Strand, and John Hare, Musical Instrument-Seller in Freemans Yard in Cornhill, near the Royal Exchange. Price 1s. 6d.

Aug. 19–22, 1695, *London Gazette.*

See Nos. 3, 9, 236, 240, 421, and 423.

3. The Complete Flute Master . . . The Second Edition, with Additions of several new Lessons, made by the late Famous Mr. Henry Purcell.

Sold by John Walsh, Musical Instrument Maker in Ordinary to His Majesty, at the Golden Harp and Hoboy in Katharine-street near Somerset-house in the Strand; and John Hare, Musical Instrument Seller, at the Golden Violin in St. Pauls Church-yard, and at his Shop in Freemans-yard in Cornhill near the Royal Exchange.

Feb. 27–Mar. 2, 1695 [i.e. 1696], *London Gazette.*

See Nos. 2, 9, 236, 240, 421, and 423.

I

4. A Collection of new Songs Set by Mr. Nicola Matteis made purposely for the use of his Scholers, with a thorough Bass to each Song, for the Harpsichord Theorboe or Bass Viol; to which is added some new Airs for the Violin and Bass by the same Author, as allso Simphony's for two Flutes by a person of Qualyty: fairly engrav'd on Copper plates The 1st. Book. Price One Shilling Six Pence.

London, Printed for and Sold by John Walsh Musical Instrument maker in ordinary to his Majesty at the Harp and Ho-boy in Catherine street nere Somerset House in the Strand. and likewise to be had at Mr. Hare's Shop in Freemans yard in Cornhill near the Royal Exchange. 1696.

> May 7–11, 1696, *London Gazette.*
>> Hirsch Collection, BM.
>> Day and Murrie, No. 143.
>> TC. II. 589. June 1696.
>> With dedication: To the Right Honoble: Wm. Lord Biron
>> My Lord

The following Songs (whose excellency can never be doubted by those that have any knowledge of the Author) were not design'd to be made publick, had not the importunities of some Gentlemen, (from whom Mr. Nicola had receiv'd particular obligations) prevail'd upon him to let e'm be publish'd. Gratitude obliges me in the highest degree to present e'm to your Lordship; & Mr. Nicola's as well as my own Interest makes me presume to beg your Honour's Patronage of e'm: for your Lordship's approbation is like the Royal Assent that empowers e'm with an almost irresistible force and efficacy, and your name is ye Sterling-mark that will make e'm pass currant in all Countrys and Ages. Musick has in all times been esteem'd for diverting Mankind with its charms and beauty's; but when persons of your Lordships rank think some hours not ill spent in the Study of it, certainly it ought to be had in the highest Honour (I had almost said Adoration) yet how many Gentlemen attempt it, and how few arrive to such perfection as your Lordship, to whom the best Masters need not blush to yeild; and in composition as well as performance own themselves equall'd, if not out done.

But Panegyrick is not my Province: my business is to beg pardon for this presumption, and eternally to acknowledge the innumerable favours confer'd upon (my Lord)

Your Lordship's most obliged
and entirely devoted Servant.
JOHN WALSH.

> The 'Simphony's for two Flutes' were presumably by Lord Byron.
> *See* No. 20.

5. A Collection of New Songs, Set by several eminent Masters; with a Through-Bass to each Song, for the Harpsichord, Theorbo, or Bass-Viol: Engraven on Copper-Plates.

Sold by J. Walsh, Musical-Instrument-maker in Ordinary to His Majesty, at the Golden Harp and Hautboy in Catherine-street, against Somerset-house Water-gate, in the Strand; and J. Hare, Musical-Instrument-seller, in Freeman's-yard in Cornhill, and at his Shop in St. Paul's Church-yard. Price 1s.

> Nov. 23–6, 1696, *London Gazette.*
>> Day and Murrie, No. 144.
>> *See* No. 39.

6. A new Song Sung in the Spanish Frier, [words by John Dryden] set by M^r: Henry Purcell.

    Engraven for I: Walsh.

    (Whils't I with greif did on you look.)

    [*c.* 1696.]

        BM. G. 304. (182.) *See* Ill. 29.
        Another edition was engraved, printed, and sold by Thomas Cross. (BM. H. 1601. c.(4.))

7. A Song in the Play call'd the Cornish Comedy Set by M^r: Clarke, Sung by Mr. Leveredge.

    Grav'd and Printed for H Playford I Walsh and I. Hare.

    (When maids live to thirty.)

    [*c.* 1696.]

        RCM. II. B. 2. (31.) With Hare's name almost illegible.
        Other editions, without imprints, were also published. (BM. H. 1601. (486.); G. 316. g. (71.))

From 1697 onwards the Walsh and Hare imprints and notices conform, more or less, to:

    J. Walsh Musical Instrument-maker in Ordinary to His Majesty at the Golden Harp and Hoboy, or simply Harp and Hoboy, in Catherine-street in the Strand and J. Hare Musical Instrument Seller (or Instrument-maker) at the Golden Viol in St. Paul's Church-Yard and at his Shop in Freemans-Yard in Cornhill.

No one form was adhered to, and the spelling and other details show continual variation.

----

8. Single Songs, and Dialogues, in the Musical Play of Mars & Venus. [Words by Peter Anthony Motteux.] Perform'd with the Anatomist, or the Sham Doctor. Set to Musick by Mr. Finger, and Mr. John Eccles.

    London, Printed by J. Heptinstall, for the Authors, and Sold by John Hare Musical Instrument Seller, at the Golden Viol in St. Paul's Church-Yard, and at his Shop in Freeman's-Yard in Cornhill. And by John Welch Musical Instrument-maker in Ordinary to His Majesty, at the Golden Harp and Hautboy in Catharine-street against Somerset-house Water-Gate in the Strand. 1697.

    Dec. 31, 1696–Jan. 2, 1697, *Post Boy.*

        BM. G. 119.
        RCM. I.G. 13. (7.) With title supplied in manuscript.
        Day and Murrie, No. 157.
        Not a Walsh publication. Printed from type, Walsh acting as a selling agent with others.

9. The Second Book of the Compleat Flute Master; Or, The Art of Playing on the Recorder, laid open in easie and plain instructions, that the meanest Capacity may arrive to a perfection of that Instrument; With a Collection of the newest Ayres and Song Tunes by the best Masters; To which is added an easie Scale, shewing

how to transpose any Tune to the Flute, that is set for Violin or Voice; as also a Sonata for two Flutes by Mr. Morgan.

Printed, and sold by J. Walsh, Musical Instrument maker to His Majesty, at the Harp and Hautboy in Catherine-street in the Strand, J. Hare at the Viol in St. Pauls Church-Yard, and at his Shop in Freemans-yard near the Royal-Exchange; and J. Miller at the Violin and Hautboy on London Bridge. Pr. 1s. 6d.

Apr. 1–5, 1697, *London Gazette.*

See Nos. 2, 3, 236, 240, 421, and 423.

10. The Second Book of the Self-Instructer on the Violin, or, The Art of playing on that Instrument, by plain Rules and Directions, together with a Collection of the newest Aires and Song Tunes, by the most able Masters, to which is added a Collection of the newest Country Dances now in use, with Rules how to Dance them, which will be continued by the Authors in every Addition, in order to compleat a Volume, all fairly Engraven on Copper.

Printed; and sold by J. Walsh Musical Instrument-maker in Ordinary to His Majesty at the Harp and Hautboy in Catherine-street in the Strand; J. Hare at the Viol in St. Pauls Church Yard, and at his Shop in Freemans-Yard in Cornhil; and J. Miller at the Violin and Hautboy on London Bridge. Price 1s. 6d.

May 20–4, 1697, *London Gazette.*

See No. 1.

11. A New Book of Songs, with a Thorough Bass to each Song. Composed by Mr. Leveridge.

Printed and sold by J. Walsh, Instrument maker in Ordinary to His Majesty, at the Golden Harp and Hautboy in Catherine-street near Summerset house in the Strand; and J. Hare, Musical Instrument seller at the Golden-Viol in St. Pauls Church-Yard, and at his Shop in Freemans-yard in Cornhil.

May 31–June 3, 1697, *London Gazette.*

Day and Murrie, No. 156.
See Nos. 23 and 24.

12. Songs In The New Opera, Call'd the World in the Moon. [Words by Elkanah Settle. Music by Jeremiah Clarke and Daniel Purcell.]

Sould by I: Walsh Musicall Instrument maker in Or=/=dinary to his Majesty, at the Golden Harpe and Ho=boy, in Catherine=Street near Summersett House in the Strand, and I: Hare Musicall Instrument Seller at y^e Golden Violl in S^t. Paules Church=yard, and at his Shopp in Freemans=Yard in Cornhill, 1697.

July 12–15, 1697, *London Gazette.*

BM. G. 120.
Day and Murrie, No. 159.
This title-page or the next is from the earliest of the numerous plates engraved for Walsh that he used at different times for different works, by making the necessary alterations on the plates or by superimposing other plates containing the new titles.
See Ills. 1 and 30.

4

13. A Collection of new Songs With a Through Bass to each Song, and a Sonata for two Flutes, Compos'd by M^r: Morgan.

London Sould by I: Walsh Musicall Instrument maker in Ordinary to his Majesty, at the Golden Harpe and Hoboy in Cathe=/=rine Street, near Summerset House in the Strand, and I: Hare Musicall Instrument Seller at the Golden Violl in S^t: Paules Church=Yard, and at his Shop in Freemans=Yard in Cornhill near the Royall Exchange price 1^s. 6^d 1697.

> May have been issued before No. 12.
> BM. K. 2. i. 21.
> Day and Murrie, No. 155.
> This title-page or the preceding is from the earliest of the numerous plates engraved for Walsh that he used at different times for different works, by making the necessary altera-tions on the plates or by superimposing other plates containing the new titles.
> *See* Ills. 2 and 31.

14. The Harpsicord Master. Containing plain and easy Instructions for Learners on the Spinnet or Harpsicord; written by the late famous Mr. H. Purcell, at the request of a particular Friend, and taken from his own Manuscript, never before publish'd, being the best extant, together with a choice Collection of the newest Aires and Song-Tunes, Compos'd by the best Masters, and fitted for the Harpsi-cord, Spinnet or Harp, by those that compos'd them, all graven on Copper Plates. Price 1 shilling and 6 pence.

Sold by J. Walsh . . . at the Golden Harp and Ho-boy . . . and J. Hare . . . at the Golden Viol . . . and . . . in Freeman's-yard, Cornhill.

Oct. 21-3, 1697, *Post Boy*.

TC. III. 54. [Feb.] 1698.

> Walsh used some plates from various books of *The Harpsicord Master* for *The Lady's Banquet*, and some items of *The Harpsicord Master* appear in more than one book of that series.
> *See* Nos. 27, 59, 403, 471, and 566.

15. Six Sonata's or Solos, three for a Violin, And three for the Flute, with a Through Bass for the Harpsicord, Compos'd by M^r. D. Purcell.

London Printed for & Sould by I: Walsh Musicall Instrument maker in Ordi-nary to his Majesty at the Golden Harp & Ho=boy in Catherine=street near Summer-set=house in y^e strand & I: Hare Musicall Instrument maker at y^e Golden Violl in S^t. Pauls Church=Yard & at his Shop in Freemans=Yard in Cornhill near y^e Royall Exchange.

June 2-6, 1698, *London Gazette*.

> Rowe collection, King's College, Cambridge.
> With dedication by Purcell to the Hon. Francis Roberts.
> This work is the earliest known use by Walsh of the Collins title-page (*see* Ill. 3), the plate of which was used by the publisher for many later works, the title of each work being engraved on a supplementary plate and superimposed in the medallion centre of the original

plate, or inserted in manuscript on the title-page after it had been printed off with the medallion centre blocked out by a plain supplementary plate.

The plate was first used for *Songs for One Two and Three Voices Composed to a Through Basse For yᵉ Organ or Harpsicord By R King Servant to his Majesty*. This work was published, without imprint, by King himself.

King's interesting preface is worth quoting in full:

'Haveing observ'd that most of my former Songs in the Common Printed Books about Town were not only imperfect but in a very bad Caracter, feareing least these should meet wᵗʰ. the same Fate, I was willing to publish them my self, in Regard to those perticular Lovers of Musick for whom I design'd them, And that I may doe the Authors of yᵉ words as well as my selfe the Right to have them Faire and Correct, I have bin at yᵉ Charge of Engraveing them on Copper In some of these Compositions I have imitated the Italians in their manner of Ariettas; who for there Excellence in Vocal Musick are (in my Judgment) the best Paterns; if I find them acceptable to those whose Opinions I most value, I have my end,

Non e bel quelche bel
Ma quel che piace
R K.'

A copy of this work is in the British Museum (K. 8. h. 19.), and it may be dated *c.* 1690–2. (*See* Ill. 4.) Another issue was made with the added imprint 'Sold by Iohn Crouch att yᵉ 3 Lutes in Princes Street in Drury lane'. (Christ Church, Oxford, with inscription dated 1692. Day and Murrie, No. 117.) Crouch was publishing *c.* 1683–1704.

A Second Booke of Songs . . . Composed by R King B M; Servant to his Majesty (BM. C. 411.), *c.* 1696, has a title-page in the Collins style that may have been engraved by him although his name does not occur on the work, which is without imprint. (*See* Day and Murrie, Fig. 31.) The plate of this title-page was used by Walsh for Nos. 119 and 264*a*. (*See* Ill. 19.)

The reproduction of the Collins title-page (*see* Ill. 3) is from a later use of the plate for No. 20, with Hare's name deleted from the imprint.

16. Musica Oxoniensis. A Collection of Songs: for One and Two Voices, with the Thorough-Bass. Publish'd by Francis Smith, and Peter de Walpergen Letter-Founder, by whom 'twas Cut on Steel, and Cast, by the Directions of the former.

Oxford: Printed by Leon. Lichfield: And are to be Sold by John Walsh . . . at the Golden Harp and Hoboy . . . And John Hare . . . at the Golden Viol . . . and . . . in Freeman's Yard, Cornhil, London, 1698.

> BM. K. 8. k. 12.
> Day and Murrie, No. 164.
> Another issue, probably earlier, does not include Walsh and Hare in the imprint.

17. A Collection of Ayers fitted for the new Instrument call'd the mock Trumpet, with Instructions to play on it, as also first and Second Trebles for two Trumpets: Graven price 1s.

Sold by J. Walsh . . . at the Golden Harp and Ho-boy in Catherine-street, near Summerset-house in the Strand.

Sept. 13–15, 1698, *Post Boy*.

> See Nos. 21 and 137.

6

18. A Collection of Ayers Purposely contriv'd for two Flutes, Compos'd by several Masters, to which is annexed Senior Nicolas's Trumbet Tune for 2 Flutes. Engraven. Price 1s. 6d.

Printed for John Walsh . . . at the Harp and Ho-boy in Catherine-street near Somerset-House in the Strand.

Oct. 18–20, 1698, *Post Boy*.

Nov. 3–5, 1698, *Flying Post*. (Sold by J. Walsh . . . and J. Hare.)

19. Six Sonata's of two Parts; purposely contriv'd for Two Flutes. Composed by Mr. Rogers.

Sold by J. Walsh . . . at the Golden-Harp and Hautboy . . . and J. Hare . . . at the Golden-Viol . . . and . . . in Free-man's yard in Cornhill, near the Royal-Exchange. Price 1s. 6d.

Nov. 19–22, 1698, *Flying Post*.

Jan. 12–16, 1698 [i.e. 1699], *London Gazette*. (Fairly Engraven. Price 3s.)

19a. Theater Musick Being A Collection of the newest Ayers for the Violin, with the French Dances perform'd at both Theaters, as also the new Dances at yᵉ late Ball at Kensington on yᵉ Kings Birth day and those in the new Opera of Rinaldo & Armida, with a Through Bass to each Dance, Compos'd by Mʳ: Iohn Eccles, graven price one Shilling Six pence.

London Sould by I: Walsh Musicall Instrument maker in Ordinary to his Majesty at the Golden Harpe & Ho=boy in Catherine street near Sumerset house in yᵉ strand.

Dec. 6–8, 1698, *Flying Post*. (Sold by J. Walsh . . . and J. Hare.)

   Durham Cathedral Library.
   With a frontispiece shewing a stage scene at Drury Lane Theatre headed: 'The Theatre Royall'. (*See* Frontispiece.) John Eccles was the editor, rather than the composer of the work, which includes music by Mr. Clark, Mr. Powell, and Mr. Morgan.
   See Nos. 20a, 29a, and 91.

20. A Collection of new Songs, Set by Mʳ Nicola [Matteis], with A Through Bass to each Song For the Harpsicord, Theorbo, or Bass Viol, being all teaching Songs, made for his Scholars, most of them Transpos'd for the Flute. The second Book.

London Printed for & Sould by I: Walsh Musicall Instrument maker in Ordinary to his Majesty at the Golden Harp & Ho=boy in Catherine=street near Summerset=house in yᵉ strand.

April 3–6, 1699, *London Gazette*. (Printed for J. Walsh . . . Mr. Salter at the Lute in St. Paul's Church-yard; and Mr. Livingston in Birchin-Lane near the Royal Exchange. Price 1s. 6d.)

April 8–11, 1699, *Post Boy*. (Sold by J. Walsh . . . Mr. Salter . . . and Mr. Livingston.)

TC. III. 139. June, 1699.

Day and Murrie, No. 171. Fig. 37.
Title-page from Collins plate. (No. 15. *See* Ill. 3.)
Hare's name was omitted from the imprint of the Day and Murrie copy, but it is not known whether this was so in all copies. Walsh used this form of imprint for a number of works, the title-pages of which were from the Collins plate; but Nos. 117 and 425 of the bibliography include Hare's name differently engraved on the original plate.
See No. 4.

20a. The Second Book of Theatre Musick: Containing Plain & Easie Rules with yᵉ Best Instructions for Learners on yᵉ Violin. Likewise All the New French Dances now in Vse at Publick Balls & Dancing=Schools; With Variety of yᵉ Newest Ayers, Song=Tunes & Dances, Perform'd in yᵉ late Opera's at yᵉ Theatres: All of them being proper to Play on yᵉ Hautboy, A Scale is added at yᵉ End of yᵉ Book for such as desire to Practice on yᵗ Instrument. Fairly Engrauen on Copper Plates.

London Printed for & sold by I: Walsh (Musicall Instrument maker to his Majesty) at yᵉ Golden=Harp and Hautboy in Catherine=street over against Somer-set=House in the Strand, 1699. Price one Shilling Six Pence.

June 1–3, 1699, *Flying Post.*

> Durham Cathedral Library.
> The advertisement gives: 'Sold by J. Walsh ... Mr. Salter at the Lute in St. Paul's Church-yard; Mr. Levingston's at his Shop in Birchin-lane, near the Royal-Exchange, and at most Musick-shops in Town.' With the frontispiece as in the first and third books. (*See* Frontis-piece.)
> *See* Nos. 19a, 29a, and 91.

20b. The New Flute Master: Or, the Art of Playing on the Flute Improved and made Easie to the meanest Capacity, by very plain Rules and Directions for Learners. Also, a choice Collection of new Musick, made for Mr. Banister's and Mr. King's Consort, performed by Gentlemen at Exeter Exchange. With variety of Ayres and Song-Tunes, by the best Masters. Fairly Engraven.

Sold by J. Walsh ... at the Harp and Hautboy ... Mr. Salter, at the Lute in St. Paul's Church-yard; and Mr. Levingston, at his Shop in Birchin-lane, near the Royal-Exchange. Price 1s. 6d.

June 8–10, 1699, *Post Boy.*

TC. III. 139. June, 1699.

> *See* Nos. 33, 113, 182, 305, 390, 486, 510, 563, and 578 for other books and works with similar titles. No details of the third, sixth, and eighth books of the early series finishing with No. 486 have been traced.

21. A Second Book for the new Instrument, called, The Mock Trumpet; contain-ing variety of Trumpet-tunes, Ayrs, Marches, Minuets, made purposely for that Instrument: with Instructions for Learners. Also several first and second Trebles for two Trumpets. Engraven. Price 1s.

Printed for J. Walsh, &c.
July 18–20, 1699, *Flying Post*.
TC. III. 139. June, 1699.

Four books were advertised in the Walsh Cat., *c.* 1721, Ill. 28, as: 'Books for Learners on yᵉ Mock Trumpet'. Only details of the first three books have been traced.
See Nos. 17 and 137.

22. Songs in the First and Second Part of Massianello. [i.e. The Famous History of the Rise and Fall of Massaniello. Words by Thomas D'Urfey.] Set by Mr. [Daniel] Purcell. Sung by Mr. Leveridge, Mr. Pate, and Mr. Freeman: as also the Songs in The Iland [i.e. Island] Princess. [Words by Peter Anthony Motteux. Music by Richard Leveridge, Daniel Purcell and Jeremiah Clarke?]
Printed for J. Walsh, &c.
TC. III. 139. June, 1699.

Day and Murrie, Nos. 179 and 180.
No complete copy of the work is available for examination. Some numbers by Clarke were published by William Pearson. (*See* Day and Murrie, No. 181.) Numbers from *Massaniello* and *The Island Princess* were also issued separately by Walsh (No. 26) and others. (*See* BM. catalogue under D. Purcell, R. Leveridge, and J. Clarke.)
Thomas Cross and John Young advertised, Mar. 7–9, 1699, *Post Boy*: 'The Songs and Dialogues in . . . the Island Princess', &c.
Henry Playford advertised, June 24–7, *Post Boy*, June 27–9, *Post Man*: 'The first and second collection of New Songs and Ballards in the First and Second part of Massaniella.'
Walsh Cat., Ill. 7: 'Songs and Dialogues in the Opera of the Island Princess. 3s. od', may have been the work listed above.

23. A Second Book of Songs with a Through Bass to each Song, Compos'd by Mʳ: R. Leveridge.
London Sould by I. Walsh, Musicall Instrument maker in Ordinary to his Majesty, at the Golden Harpe & Hoboy, in Catherine Street near Sumerset house in the Strand, & I. Hare Musicall Instrument maker at the Golden Violl in Sᵗ. Paules Church Yard, and at his Shopp in Freemans Yard in Cornhill, & I. Young, Musicall Instrument maker at yᵉ Dolphin & Crown, in Sᵗ Paules Church Yard.
July 1–4, 1699, *Post Boy*.

Day and Murrie, No. 176. Fig. 38.
RCM. I.G. 48. (2.)
See Nos. 11 and 24.

24. A Second Book of Songs with a Through Bass to each Song Compos'd by Mʳ: R. Leveridge.
London Sould by I. Hare Musicall Instrument maker at yᵉ Golden Viol in Sᵗ: Paules Church=yard, and at his Shopp in Freemans=Yard in Cornhill, & I. Walsh Musicall Instrument maker in Ordinary to his Majesty, at yᵉ Golden Harp & Hoboy in Catherine street near Sum̃erset house in yᵉ strand. & I. Young Musi=/=

call Instrument maker at y^e Dolphin and Crown in S^t. Paules Church=yard. price 1^s. 6^d.

> [c. 1699.]
>> Day and Murrie, No. 176.
>> Another issue of the preceding, no comma after 'Song', no stop after 'Leveridge', and with a different imprint.

25. A Collection of Songs, set to Musick, by Mr. William Robart.

> Sold by Tho. Cross, at his house in Catherine-Wheel-Court on Snow Hill; John Hare, at the Golden Viol in St. Paul's Church-Yard, and at his Shop in Freeman's-Yard in Cornhil, near the Royal Exchange; John Walsh at the Golden Harp and Haut-boy in Catherine-street in the Strand, and J. Young at the Dolphin and Crown in St. Paul's Church-Yard. And at all other Musick-Shops in Town. Price 1s. 6s. [sic.]

>> Aug. 5–8, 1699, *Flying Post*.
>> Day and Murrie, No. 172.

> *In September, 1699, Walsh commenced a series of Weekly Songs that appears to have been discontinued after a month or two, or the later issues, if any, are not identifiable or available. The series was advertised in No. 26a and on No. 28.*
> *Details of the 8 numbers that have been traced are as follows:*

---

26. The Jolly Swains A Song in the Island Princess Set by M^r. D. Purcell. The 1st Weekly Song for Thursday ye 7th of Septem^r. to be continu'd the Yeare Round.

> Printed for I: Walsh.

>> BM. G. 304. (147.)
>> *See* No. 22.

A New Scotch Song, to a Tune of M^r. Keen's. The 4th Weekly Song for Septem^r. ye 28th.

> Publish'd every Thursday Printed for I. Walsh.
> (Jemmy told his Passion.)

>> BM. G. 304. (81.)
>> RCM. II. B. 2. (43.)

The 1st. Weekly Song for Octob^r. ye 5th. a New one Publish'd every Thursday. A Song Set by M^r. John Barrett.

> Printed for I: Walsh.
> (Gloriana is engaging fair.)

>> BM. G. 304. (63.)
>> W^m. C. Smith collection.

The 2ᵈ Weekly Song for Octobʳ. the 12ᵗʰ. a New one Publish'd every Thursday. A Song Set to Musick by Mʳ. Finger.

Printed for I Walsh.

(While here for the fair Amarillis I dye.)

Wᵐ. C. Smith collection.

The 3ᵈ. Weekly Song For Octobʳ. the 19ᵗʰ a New one Publish'd every Thursday. A Song Set by Mʳ. Courtivill.

Printed for I: Walsh.

(Whilst Galatea you design.)

BM. G. 304. (174.)

Wᵐ. C. Smith collection.

The 4ᵗʰ. Weekly Song For Octobʳ. the 26ᵗʰ. a New one Publish'd every Thursday. An Enthusiastick Song in the Island Princess Set and Sung by Mʳ. Leveridge.

Printed for I Walsh.

(Oh cease, cease, urge no more the God.)

Wᵐ. C. Smith collection.

Another edition, not part of the weekly series, and without imprint is at BM. G. 310. (291.)

The 1ˢᵗ. Weekly Song For Novemʳ. yᵉ 2ᵈ. a New one Publish'd every Thursday A Song Set to Musick by Mʳ Elford.

Printed for I: Walsh.

(Once more Love's mighty chains are broak.)

Wᵐ. C. Smith collection.

The 2ᵈ Weekly Song For Novemʳ. yᵉ9ᵗʰ. a New one Published every Thursday. A Song Set by Mʳ Covrtivill.

Printed for I: Walsh.

(Racking thoughts of what is past.)

BM. G. 304. (129.)

Wᵐ. C. Smith collection.

26a. Country Dances: Being a Composition entirely New, and the whole cast Different from all that have yet been publish'd; with Base and Treble to each Dance. Also the Newest French Dances in use, Entry's, Genteel and Grotesque, Chacons, Rigodoons, Minutes and other Dancing Tunes. By Thomas Bray.

Sold by John Walsh . . . at the Golden Harp and Hautboy . . . and John Hare . . . at the Golden Viol . . . and . . . in Freeman's Court Cornhill, near the Royal Exchange. Price 2s. Where is also Sold, the Weekly Song, publish'd every Thursday.

Sept. 28–30, 1699, *Post Boy*.

Oct. 19–21, 1699, *Flying Post*, gives: 'Minuets' in place of 'Minutes', in the title.

27. The Second Book of the Harpsicord Master Containing A Choice Collection of Lessons for the Harpsicord or Spinnett as Almands, Corants, Sarabrands, Ayres, Minuetts, and Jiggs, By Dʳ: Blow Mʳ: Courtivall Mʳ: Clark Mʳ. Barrett & Mʳ

Croffts To which is added Plain & Easy Rules for Learners. The whole Fairly Engraven.

London Printed for & sold by I: Walsh Musicall instrument mak=er in ordinary to his Matie: at y^e Golden Harp & Hautboy in Katherine Street near Somerset house in y^e Strand 1700.

Jan. 1–4, 1699 [i.e. 1700], *London Gazette*.

Jan. 13–16, 1700, *Post Boy*, adds: 'Where are sold all the new Songs made for the Theatres and other Occasions.' (*See* No. 57.)

RCM. I. F. 9. (3.)
See Nos. 14, 59, 403, 471, and 566.

28. Six Sonatas or Solos Three for A Violin and Three for the Flute with a Thorough Bass for y^e Harpsicord Theorboe or Bass=Viol Compos'd by Mr Wm Crofts & an Italian M^r.

London Printed for and sold by John Walsh Musical Instrument=maker in Ordinary to his Majesty, at the Golden harp & Hautboy in Katherine Street near Somerset house in y^e Strand. & John Hare Musical instrument=maker at y^e Golden viol in St Pauls Church yard & at his shop in Freemans court Cornhill, near y^e Royall Exchange. 1700 Price 2 Shillings Where is also sold, y^e weekly song, publish'd every Thursday.

BM. g. 932.
RCM. II. B. 13.
According to an advertisement Sept. 30–Oct. 3, 1699, *Post Boy*, John Young Musical Instrument-seller at the Dolphin and Crown, at the West-end of St. Paul's Church-yard, issued an edition of the above work, 'Price 3s.'

29. Songs In The New Opera, Call'd the Grove or Love's Paradise, Compos'd by M^r: Dan: Purcell. [Words by John Oldmixon.]

Sold by I: Walsh Musicall Instrument maker in Or=/=dinary to his Majesty, at the Golden Harpe and Ho=boy, in Catherine=Street near Sommerset House in the Strand.

[1700.]

BM. G. 112.
Day and Murrie, No. 187, gives Feb. 20, 1700, *Post Boy*; but this advertisement is of an edition by J. Young.
Title-page from the plate used for No. 12 (*see* Ill. 1), the words 'Grove . . . Purcell' from a supplementary plate, the imprint partly re-engraved and shortened, Hare being omitted, and a double-line border added.
'Where, where's my Pan', a single sheet song from the collection, engraved from the original plate, was issued separately without imprint. (BM. G. 315. (134.))
Walsh Cat., Ill. 7, as: 'Songs in the Opera of the Grove, or Love's Pardice. 1s. 6d.'

29a. The Third Book of Theater Musick: Being A Collection of the newest Aires for the Violin. with y^e Trumpett=Tunes, Scotch=Tunes, & French=Dances, made for y^e Play=hous=es Particularly those in y^e new Opera, likewise in Ephigenia, &

ye Trip to the Iubilee, with severall new Cibells in two parts Treble & Bass, to which is added an Excellent Introduction for Young Beginners on ye Violin. Fairly Engraven on Copper Plates.

London Printed for & Sold by I. Walsh Musicall Instrument maker to his Majesty, at ye Golden=Harp & Hautboy in Catherine=Street against Somerset= House in ye Strand. 1700 price 1s=6d.

Mar. 19–21, 1700, *Post Boy.*

Durham Cathedral Library.
With the frontispiece as in the first and second books. (*See* Frontispiece.)
A Trip to the Jubilee, by George Farquhar was produced at Drury Lane in 1699, and *Iphigenia* by John Dennis, at Lincoln's Inn Fields, December 1699.
See Nos. 19a, 20a, and 91.

30. A Collection of new Songs With a Through Bass to each Song for the Harpsi-cord. Compos'd by Mr: Daniel Purcel. Perform'd in the Revis'd=/=Comedy call'd the Pilgrim, being the last Writeings of Mr: Dryden. 1700.

London Sould by I: Walsh . . . at the Golden Harpe and Hoboy . . . in the Strand.

June 6–8, 1700, *Post Boy.* (Printed for and sold by J. Walsh . . . Mr. Salter . . . Mr. Levingston . . . and Mr. Young.)

Day and Murrie, No. 184. Fig. 40.
Title-page from the plate used for No. 13 modified by re-engraving part of the title 'Song . . . Dryden. 1700.', deleting all after 'Strand' in the imprint, and adding a double-line border. (*See* Ill. 2.)
The same plate with necessary modifications may have been used either before or after June, 1700, for No. 36.
Walsh Cat., Ill. 7, as: 'Songs in the Comedy call'd the Pilgrim. 1s. 6d.'
See No. 96.

31. Parte Prima Sonate a Violino e Violone o Cimbalo dedicate all altezza serenis-sima Electorale di Sofia Charlotta Electrice di Brandenburgo . . . da Archangelo Corelli da Fusignano Opera Quinta. [The whole title engraved in capitals.]

Sold by Iohn Walsh Servant to his Majesty at the Harp and Hautboy in Katherine Street near Somerset House in the Strand London.

Parte Seconda Preludii Allemande Correnti Gighe Sarabande Gavotte e Follia da Archangelo Corelli. [All in capitals.]

Aug. 26–9, 1700, *London Gazette.*

TC. III. 214. [Nov.] 1700.

BM. d. 73. g.
The dedication to the Electress of Brandenburg is dated January 1, 1700, as in the earlier Italian editions published at Rome. (BM. K. 1. k. 15. and e. 682. d.) These editions have an illustrated frontispiece by Antonio Meloni, engraved by Girolamo Frezza. (*See* Ill. 5.) Walsh prefaced the second impression of his edition with a similar frontispiece engraved by P. P. Bouche from Antonio Meloni's original design, which does not exist in the BM. copy. It was also issued by Walsh in a modified form, with No. 60, this issue clearly showing that the plate had previously been used for some earlier work. (*See* Ill. 6.)

13

The advertisement in the *London Gazette,* Aug. 26–9, 1700, describes the work as 'Twelve Sonnata's in Two Parts: The First Part, Solo's for a Violin, a Bass-Violin, Viol, and Harpsichord, The Second, Preludes, Almands, Corants, Sarabands, and Jigs, with the Spanish Folly. Dedicated to the Electoress of Brandenburgh by Archangelo Corelli, being his Fifth and Last Opera. Engraven in a curious Character, being much fairer, and more correct in the Musick, than that of Amsterdam . . . Price 8s. or each Part single 5s.'

The Amsterdam edition referred to is presumably that of E. Roger. (BM. d. 73. a.)

The circumstances under which Corelli's 'Sonatas, Op. V' were introduced into England are of importance in studying the conditions of music publishing at the time, and some interesting notices of contemporary editions are transcribed here.

'The New Sonata's of the famous Signior Archangelo Corelli, curiously engraven on 70 Copper-Plates, and printed on a large Imperial Paper, being now brought from Rome, will be ready to be delivered to Subscribers on Monday next, at Mr. Banister's in Brownlow-street in Drury-lane, or at Mr. King's in York-buildings. And there remaining a few Books more than were subscribed for, those who desire to have them may send to either of the Places abovesaid.' (July 8–11, 1700, *London Gazette.*)

The instrumentalists, Banister and King (*see* No. 20*b*) evidently acted as agents for the sale of the original Rome edition (BM. K. 1. k. 15.) and had probably performed the work at their concerts. Walsh may have obtained a copy from them. Before his own edition was announced the following notice appeared:

'To all Lovers of the Symphony. Francis Vaillant French Bookseller in the Strand near Catherine Street gives notice, that he is now printing the new Solos of Corelli in Scores as well ingraven in every particular as the Roman original. Such who will know further thereof may see a Specimen of it at his Shop. The price will be 5s but as the said work thus ingraved in score is only fit for such as play a thorough bass, the said Vaillant is now ingraving the same Solos, the Treble and the Bass separately for the conveniency of such who play upon the Violin or Bass Violin, so that those, who are already provided with the original from Rome, may have the Treble and the Bass separately, that they may play them at 3.' (Aug. 24–7, 1700, *Post Man.*)

Walsh then put out his advertisement of Aug. 26–9, 1700, *London Gazette,* quoted above, and a similar notice, Aug. 29–31, 1700, *Post Boy,* to which Vaillant replied:

'Whereas it has been published in some News Papers, that 12 Sonata's or Solo's composed by Archangelo Corelli, being his fifth and last Opera, are to be sold at the sign of the Harp and Hautboy in Catherine Street, being fairer and more correct in the Musick, than that of Amsterdam, this is to give notice to all Lovers of Harmony, that the said Advertisement cannot be true, seeing the Amsterdam Edition is not yet published, 2nd if any one will be at the pains to consider the only Specimen in England at Francis Vaillants Bookseller in the Strand, he will be convinced, that the reflection past upon the Amsterdam edition is but unjust and groundless. The two parts of the said Solo's will be published by the latter end of this month, and sold at the place aforesaid for 5s. or shall be given gratis to whomsoever will buy for 30s. of other Musick at once.' (Aug. 31–Sept. 3, 1700, *Post Man.*)

Walsh replied by re-advertising his edition, Sept. 3–5, 17–19, 1700, *Flying Post;* Sept. 19–21, 1700, *Post Boy,* stating in the last notice 'The Frontispiece being now finish'd exactly from the Roman Copy, will be given gratis to those Gentlemen who have bought of the first Impression.' This refers to the Bouche engraving mentioned above.

No edition with Vaillant's imprint has been traced, and it may be assumed that the work referred to as being printed and published by him was entirely from the plates of E. Roger of Amsterdam, for whom he acted as London agent for a number of years.

The Walsh work was advertised in his Catalogue, c. 1721, Ill. 27, as: '12 Solos by Corelli, for a Violin & a Bass. 5s. od.'

See Nos. 31*a*, 41, 85, 112, 135, 205, 400, and 519.

31a. A Set of Ayres, in four Parts, by Mr. Peasable, proper for Consorts, the Tunes within Compos'd of all sorts of Instruments, being the second sett, which will be Continued with the new sets of Musick made for the Play-Houses, and other Occasions, and sold at 1s 6d. the sett, in four parts, engraven in a fair Character.

Printed for, and Sold by J. Walsh . . . at the Golden Harp and Haut-boy . . . and at most Musick Shops in Town, where are also Sold Correllis new Solos.

Oct. 24–6, 1700, *Post Boy*.

No details of the first set have been traced.

See Nos. 32, 48, &c. for 'the new sets of Musick made for the Play-Houses', advertised on the title-page, and No. 31 for the Corelli Solos.

32. All the new setts of Tunes, in four parts, at 1s. 6d. the set Engraven; being all the new Overtures and Ayres, made for the Play-houses and other Occasions.

TC. III. 214. [Nov.] 1700.

Not listed in TC. as by Walsh; but the sets were advertised by Walsh and Hare, July 17–19, 1701, *Post Boy*.

The notices refer to miscellaneous items (No. 31a, &c.) and to the series subsequently known as *Harmonia Anglicana* (No. 48, &c.) separate numbers of which were advertised in the Walsh Cat., Ill. 7, and elsewhere, and are also entered separately in the bibliography.

33. The new Flute-Master. The Second Book; containing variety of the newest Ayres for the Flute: together with the Song-Tunes, Scotch-Tunes, and other Musick made for the Play-houses by the best Masters; likewise a Solo by Mr. William Williams, and a new Sebel by Mr. Jer. Clarke. To which is added, Plain and easie Directions for Learners on the Flute.

Printed for J. Walsh . . . and J. Hare, &c.

TC. III. 214. [Nov.] 1700.

Nov. 25–8, 1700, *London Gazette*. (Sold by J. Walsh . . . and J. Hare.)

See Nos. 20b, 113, 182, 305, 390, 486, 510, 563, and 578 for other books and works with similar titles. No details of the third, sixth, and eighth books of the early series finishing with No. 486 have been traced.

34. The French Dancing Master; being a Collection of the choicest Minuets, Rigadoons, Jiggs, Entry's and Paspy's, Danced at Court, the Theatres, and publick Balls: also the Play-house Dances by Mons. Baloon, Labee, Nevelong, Cotine, La-sac, the Bohemian Woman, and others. The whole being very proper for Lovers of Musick and Dancing. The Tunes for the Violin and Haut-boy, most of them within the compass of the Flute, fairly engraven.

Printed for J. Walsh . . . and J. Hare, &c.

TC. III. 214. [Nov.] 1700.

Dec. 10–12, 1700, *Post Boy*.

See Nos. 70 and 197.

34a. Harmonia Lenis, the First Part, containing Airs and Sonata's, Composed for two Flutes by John Bishop, Organist of the College at Winton.

Printed for the Author. Sold by John Hare at the Viol in St. Paul's Church Yard, and . . . in Freeman's Yard, Cornhill; Humphrey Salter at the Lute in St. Paul's Church Yard; and John Walsh, at the Harp and Hautboy &c.

Dec. 19–21, 1700, *Post Boy*; *Flying Post*.

35. Sung by M^{ss}: Campion. (Jenny long resisted.) Set by M^r. Leveridge.

London Sold by I: Walsh Musicall Instrument maker in Ordinary to his Ma=/=jesty, at y^e Golden Harpe & Hoboy in Catherine=street near Summersett house in y^e štrand. and I: Hare Musicall Instrument maker at y^e Golden Viall in S^t: Paules Church=yard and at his Shopp in Freemans Yard in Cornhill near the Royall Exchange. & I: Young Musi=/=call Instrument maker at y^e Dolphin & Crown in S^t: Pauls Churchyard.

[*c.* 1700.]

> BM. G. 304. (85.); G. 309. (62.)
> RCM. II. B. 2. (39.)
> *See* Ill. 32.

36. A Collection of Songs by Mr Iohn Eccles 1s. 6d.

[J. Walsh and J. Hare. *c.* 1700–1.]

Walsh Cat., Ill. 7.

> A different work from Eccles's larger collection. (No. 156.)
> The title-page may have been from the same plate, modified, as No. 30. (*See* Ill. 2.)

37. A Collection of Scotch Songs. 1s. 6d.

[J. Walsh and J. Hare. *c.* 1700–1.]

Walsh Cat., Ill. 7.

> For later collections of Scotch Songs, *see* Nos. 318 and 464.

38. Ayres in the Vestal Virgins by M^r. O. 1s. 6d.

[J. Walsh and J. Hare. *c.* 1700–1.]

In four parts.

Walsh Cat., Ill. 7.

39. A Collection of Songs by Severall Masters. 1s. 6d.

[J. Walsh and J. Hare. *c.* 1700–1.]

Walsh Cat., Ill. 7.

> May be the same work as No. 5.

40. A Sett of Ayres in three Parts by M^r. Hen^r Simons the Tunes for alsorts of Instruments.

[J. Walsh.]

Jan. 14–16, 1701, *Post Boy*. (A New Set of Ayres in three Parts by Mr Symons . . . this being the Fifth Set publish'd which will be continued with the Sets of

Tunes made for the Playhouses and other Occasions. Printed and Sold by J. Walsh . . . and at most Musick Shops in Town.)

> RCM. XXIX. A. 11. (2.)
> Walsh Cat., Ill. 7, as: 'Ayres by Mr Simons, in three Parts. 1s. 6d.'
> The first four sets have not been identified. *See* No. 32.

41. Correllis, new Solos reprinted on a large Paper, and sold at reasonable rates. Printed and Sold by J. Walsh . . . and at most Musick Shops in Town.
Jan. 14–16, 1701, *Post Boy.*

> A re-advertisement of No. 31.
> *See* Nos. 31, 31a, 85, 112, 135, 205, 400, and 519.

42. A New Set of Ayres for the Consorts of the Musicall Society the Tunes for all sorts of Instruments.
[J. Walsh and J. Hare. *c.* 1701.]
In four parts.

> RCM. XXIX. A. 11. (26.); XXIX. A. 12. (5.) Imperfect.
> Included in *Harmonia Anglicana.* (First Collection, No. I; BM. b. 29; b. 29. a; *see* No. 48.)
> Walsh Cat. Ill. 9 (No. 89) as: 'A Set of Aires made for Mr Banisters Consort by Mr. Orm.'

43. M^r. Peasable Ayres in the Comedy of Loves Stratagem the Tunes for alsorts of Instruments.
[J. Walsh and J. Hare. *c.* 1701.]
In four parts.
Walsh Cat., Ill. 7.

> RCM. XXIX. A. 11. (3.)
> Included in *Harmonia Anglicana.* (First collection, No. II; BM. b. 29; b. 29. a; *see* No. 48.)
> Walsh Cat. Ill. 9. (No. 89.)

44. M^r. W^m. Croft Ayres in the Comedy [by David Crauford] of Courtship Alamode.
[J. Walsh and J. Hare. *c.* 1701.]
In four parts.
Walsh Cat., Ill. 7.

> RCM. XXIX. A. 11. (6.); XXIX. A. 12. (3.) Imperfect.
> Included in *Harmonia Anglicana.* (First collection, No. III; BM. b. 29; *see* No. 48.) Walsh Cat. Ill. 9. (No. 89.)

45. M^r. Finger's Ayres in the Comedy [by Catharine Trotter] of Love's at a Loss [i.e. Love at a Loss].
[J. Walsh and J. Hare. *c.* 1701.]
In four parts.
Walsh Cat., Ill. 7.

> RCM. XXIX. A. 11. (4.); XXIX. A. 12. (4.) Imperfect.
> Included in *Harmonia Anglicana.* (First collection, No. IV; BM. b. 29; b. 29. a; *see* No. 48.)
> Walsh Cat. Ill. 9. (No. 89.)

46. M^r. Lenton's Ayres in the Tragedy [by Nicholas Rowe] of the Ambitious stepmother.
    [J. Walsh and J. Hare.]
    In four parts.
    Feb. 8–11, 1701, *Post Boy.*

        BM. d. 24. (4.) Imperfect.
        RCM. XXIX. A. 11. (5.)
        Advertised (*Post Boy*) as the '6th Set printed of the Play-house Musick', but included in *Harmonia Anglicana* (as first collection, No. V; B.M. b. 29; *see* No. 48), the separate edition of the parts bearing the No. VI. Walsh Cat. Ill. 9 (No. 89) as: 'First Collection, No. V.'

47. M^r. D: Purcells Ayrs in the Tragedy [by Catharine Trotter] of the unhappy Penitent.
    [J. Walsh and J. Hare.]
    In four parts.
    Feb. 20–2, 1701, *Post Boy.*

        BM. d. 24. (3.) Imperfect.
        RCM. XXIX. A. 11. (9.); XXIX. A. 12. (2.) Imperfect.
        Included in *Harmonia Anglicana.* (First collection, No. VI; BM. b. 29; *see* No. 48.) Walsh Cat. Ill. 9. (No. 89.)

48. Harmonia Anglicana or The Musick of the English Stage, Containing Six sets of Ayers and Tunes in 4 Parts, made for the Operas Tragedys and Comedyes of the Theater Royal, The first Collection Which will be continued with the sets of Tunes made for the Play Houses and other occasions, Engraven in a fair Character.
    London Printed & Sold by I: Walsh . . . & I: Hare . . . at the Golden Viol . . . & . . . in Freemans yard, etc.
    Mar. 6–8, 1701, *Post Boy.*

        BM. b. 29; b. 29. a. Imperfect.
        Durham Cathedral Library.
        A collected edition of six numbers previously published separately. (Nos. 42, 43, 44, 45, 46, and 47.) Walsh Cat. Ill. 9. (No. 89.)
        See Nos. 75, 90, 106, 121, and index.

49. Ayres in ye Opera [Words by Peter Anthony Motteux] call'd ye Mad Lover Compos'd by M^r. Iohn Eccles Master of his Majesty's Musick.
    [J. Walsh and J. Hare.]
    In four parts.
    Mar. 27–9, 1701, *Post Boy.*

        BM. d. 24. (1.) Imperfect.
        RCM. XXIX. A. 11. (7.); XXIX. A. 12. (9.) Imperfect.
        Advertised (*Post Boy*) as 'the 8th Set', but included in *Harmonia Anglicana.* (Second collection, No. I; *see* No. 75.) Walsh Cat. Ill. 9. (No. 89.) No complete copy of the second collection of *Harmonia Anglicana* available for examination.
        Henry Playford included in *Mercurius Musicus,* Jan.–April, 1701, some of Eccles's Songs in 'The Mad Lover'.

50. A Collection of Choice Sonatas, or Salo's for a Violin and a Bass. By Basani, Corelli, Mr. Courtiville, Sen. Nicola &c. To which is Added, A plain and easy Scale, shewing how to play any Bass upon a Violin, that is made for the Bass-Violin or Harpsicord, being very Useful to all Practitioners in Consort, and never before published.

    Sold by J. Walsh . . . and J. Hare . . . at the Golden Viol . . . and . . . in Freemans-Yard and at most Musick-Shops in Town. Price 1s. 6d.

    Apr. 12–15, 1701, *Post Boy*.

51. A Collection of new Songs With a Through Bass to each Song for the Harpsicord. Compos'd by M^r. Dan: Purcell, Performed in the new Opera's, Tragedy's and Comedy's, at the Theater Royall. Price 1^s 6^d 1701.

    London Sould by I: Walsh . . . in the Strand.

    Apr. 29–May 1, 1701, *Post Boy*. (J. Walsh and J. Hare.)

    Day and Murrie, No. 190. Fig. 42.

    Title-page from the plate used for No. 30, modified by re-engraving part of the title: 'M^r. Dan: Purcell . . . 1701.' (*See* Ill. 2.)

    July 17–19, 1701, *Post Boy* advertises the work as: 'Lately published . . . A Collection of Songs in the Humours of the Age, the Fop's Fortune, Alexander the Great & other plays, Daniel Purcell.'

    Gottfried Finger contributed some of the music to *The Humours of the Age* (No. 62), *The Fop's Fortune* (No. 58), and *Alexander the Great* (No. 66).

52. A Set of Ayres for Two Flut's and a Bass by Mr Henry Simons.
    [J. Walsh and J. Hare.]
    May 10–13, 1701, *Post Boy*.

    RCM. XXIX. A. 11. (1.) Imperfect.

    The *Post Boy* gives: 'A New Set of Ayres made purposely for Two Flutes and a Bass, by Mr. Henry Simons. Price 1s. 6d. the Set.'

    Walsh Cat., Ill. 7, as: 'Ayres for two Flut's and a Bass by Mr Simons.'

    See No. 418 which appears to be a different work.

53. Lessons for a Single Flute, as Preludes, Almands, Sarabands, Corants, Minuets and Jiggs. Made purposely for the Flute by Mr. Daniel Demovire [i.e. Demoivre]. Price 1s.

    Printed for and Sold by John Walsh . . . and John Hare . . . at the Golden Viol . . . and at . . . in Freemans Yard . . . and at most Musick Shops in Town.

    May 20–2, 1701, *Post Boy*.

    July 17–19, 1701, *Post Boy* (A Collection of Tunes for a Single Flute by Mr. Demoire.)

    Walsh Cat. *c*. 1721. Ill. 28, as: 'Demoivers 1st Aires. 1s. 6d.'

    Walsh Cat., 'Apollo's Feast', third book, *c*. 1729 (W^m. C. Smith copy), as: 'Demoivers Aires for a Single Flute. Opera Prima.'

    See Nos. 148 and 473.

54. M^r. Finger's Ayres in the Opera [Words by Elkanah Settle] call'd the Virgin Prophetess or the Fate of Troy.
[J. Walsh and J. Hare.]
In four parts.
May 27–9, 1701, *Post Boy.*

> BM. d. 24. (2.) Imperfect.
> RCM. XXIX. A. 11. (8.); XXIX. A. 12. (10.) Imperfect.
> Included in *Harmonia Anglicana.* (Second collection, No. II; *see* No. 75.) Walsh Cat. III. 9. (No. 89.) No complete copy of the second collection of *Harmonia Anglicana* available for examination.

55. The Third Book of Military Musick; Or, The Art of Playing upon the Hautboys: Improv'd and made familiar to the meanest Capacity by compendious and easie Directions. Also a Collection of Ayres, Marches, Trumpet-Tunes, Minuets, &c. purposely Composed for that Instrument, by the best Masters, and fairly Engraven on Copper-Plates.
Sold by J. Hare . . . and J. Walsh, &c.
June 2–5, 1701, *London Gazette.*

> Walsh's name is not associated with this work except in the advertisement. It was presumably a Hare issue, the second book being by Hare and J. Miller in 1699, and *Military Musick,* &c., the first of the series, by Thomas Cross, of Katharine Wheel Court, Snow Hill, in 1697. *See* No. 71.

56. [Vacant. *See* Introduction p. xii.]

57. All the new Songs made for the Playhouses and other occasions in single sheet. Engraven.
Printed and Sold by J. Walsh . . . and J. Hare, &c.
July 17–19, 1701, *Post Boy.*

> A general notice covering miscellaneous single-sheet songs which Walsh and Hare issued from time to time from plates previously used in collections of songs of particular operas or other works, or from newly engraved plates, frequently without imprints. No attempt is made to include in this bibliography all of these single songs, only a few being mentioned in exceptional cases. *See* Nos. 27 and 68.

58. M^r. Fingers Ayres in the Comedye [by Colley Cibber] of Loue makes a man or ye Fops Fortune.
[J. Walsh and J. Hare.]
In four parts.
July 24–6, 1701, *Post Boy.*

> BM. d. 24. (5.) Imperfect.
> RCM. XXIX. A. 11. (10.); XXIX. A. 12. (6.)
> Included in *Harmonia Anglicana.* (Second collection, No. III; BM. b. 29. a; *see* No. 75.) Walsh Cat. III. 9. (No. 89.)
> Daniel Purcell contributed Songs to this comedy. (*See* No. 51.)

59. The Third Book of the Harpsicord Master Being A Collection of Choice Lessons with Song Tunes and Town Ayres, fitted to the Harpsicord or Spinnet. By M^r. Ier: Clark M^r: Barrett M^r: Croft and other Masters The Ayres and Lessons plac'd on five lines, it being now the Generall way of Practice, Likewise at the end of the Book is added plain and Easy Rules for Learners, made by the late famous M^r: Hen Purcell. The whole Engraven in A very fair Character.

London Printed & Sold by I. Walsh Musicall Instrument maker in Ordinary to his Majesty, at the Golden Harp & Hoboy in Catherine Street near Somerset=house in the Strand, & I. Hare Musicall Instrument maker at y^e Golden Viol in S^t. Pauls Church=Yard, & at his Shop in Freemans yard in Cornhill near the Royall Exchange. 1702 price 1^s=6^d.

Aug. 2–5, 1701, *Post Boy.*

RCM. I. F. 9. (4.)
See Nos. 14, 27, 403, 471, and 566.

60. Six Sonata's or Solos, for the Flute. With a Through Bass for the Harpsicord. Compos'd by William Topham. A.M. [All in capitals.]

London Printed & Sold by I: Walsh . . . and I: Hare . . . at y^e Viol . . . & . . . in Freemans–yard, &c.

Sept. 4–8, 1701, *London Gazette.*

With an outer illustrated title–page with title:
Six Sonata's or Solos for the Flute with a Through Bass for the Harpsicord Compos'd by W^m: Topham. A.M.

BM. c. 105. a. (5.) with illustrated title-page and catalogue; BM. d. 150. (5.) without illustrated title-page and catalogue.

The illustrated title-page (see Ill. 6) designed by Antonio Meloni and engraved by P. P. Bouche was used earlier by Walsh for the second impression of Corelli's, *Sonate . . . Opera Quinta.* (*See* No. 31.)

Walsh Cat., *c.* 1721, Ill. 28, as: 'Tophams 1st Solos, for a Flute & a Bass, 3s. od.'

The BM. copy of Topham's Sonatas (c. 105. a. (5.)) contains what is probably the earliest Walsh catalogue. (*See* Ill. 7.) This catalogue may not have been issued with the earliest copies of Topham as it contains one or two works advertised after the Sonatas.

61. M^r. Fingers Ayres in the Comedye [by George Farquhar] of S^r. Hary Wild Hair [i.e. Sir Harry Wildair].

[J. Walsh and J. Hare.]

In four parts.

Sept. 13–16, 1701, *Post Boy.*

BM. d. 24. (6.) Imperfect.
RCM. XXIX. A. 11. (25.)
Included in *Harmonia Anglicana.* (Second collection, No. IV; BM. b. 29. a; *see* No. 75.)
Walsh Cat. Ill. 9. (No. 89.)

62. M^r. Fingers Ayres in the Comedye [by Thomas Baker] call'd the Humors of the Age [i.e. Humour of the Age].

[J. Walsh and J. Hare. 1701.]
In four parts.
Walsh Cat., Ill. 7.

> RCM. XXIX. A. 11. (24.)
> Included in *Harmonia Anglicana*. (Second collection, No. V; *see* No. 75.) Walsh Cat. Ill. 9. (No. 89.) No complete copy of the second collection of *Harmonia Anglicana* available for examination.
> Daniel Purcell contributed Songs to this Comedy. (*See* No. 51.)

63. Bononcini's Ayres in 3 Parts, as Almands Corrants Preludes Gavotts Sarabands and Jiggs. With a Through Bass for the Harpsicord. [All in capitals.]
    Printed and Sold by I: Walsh . . . and I: Hare . . . at the Golden Viol . . . and
. . . in Freemans=Yard near the Royal Exchang in Cornhill. Pr. 3ˢ. [Price in ms.]
    Oct. 2–4, 1701, *Post Boy.*

> BM. d. 150. (2.); d. 20. (5.) Violino Primo and Violino Secondo parts only, not priced.
> Probably by Giovanni Maria Bononcini, but generally attributed to his son Giovanni Battista.
> This edition is for 2 Violins and Bass. An edition for 2 Flutes and Bass was issued by Walsh and Hare in 1705 (No. 178) with the same contents in a different order.
> Walsh, who did not distinguish one Bononcini from the other in his catalogues, advertised the edition for violins as: 'Bononcinis Aires, for two Violins. 3s. od.' (Walsh Cat. *c.* 1721, Ill. 27.) Walsh Cat., Ill. 7, as: 'Ayres by Bononcini in three Parts with a Through Bass.'
> Included later in Walsh's numerical series with 'No. 348' added to the plate of the title-page.

64. Musical Recreations: or The whole Art and Mystery of playing on the Violin, unfolded and practically improv'd by short and plain Rules . . . To which is added a new Collection of choice Airs and Song-Tunes, compos'd by the most skilful Professors of Musick, and accurately engrav'd on Copper-Plates, with two new French Dances and several Tunes in the Opera called the Virgin Prophetess. [Music by Gottfried Finger.]
    Sold by John Hare . . . at the Golden Viol . . . and . . . in Freeman's Yard . . . and John Walsh, &c.
    Oct. 23–5, 1701, *Flying Post.*

> *See* No. 288. The fourth book. No details of the second and third books have been traced.

65. A Collection of Original Scotch Tunes for the Flute. Price 1s.
    Printed and Sold by J. Walsh . . . John Hare, &c.
    Oct. 28–30, 1701, *Post Boy.*

> Probably the work in Walsh Cat. *c.* 1721, Ill. 28 as: 'Scotch Aires, for a Single Flute. 1s. od.'

66. Ayres in the Opera [from text by Nathaniel Lee] of Alexander the Great, Mr. Finger. 1s. 6d.
    [J. Walsh and J. Hare.]
    In four parts.

Oct. 28–30, 1701, *Post Boy.*
Walsh Cat., Ill. 7.

Included in *Harmonia Anglicana*. (Second collection, No. VI; *see* No. 75.) Walsh Cat. Ill. 9. (No. 89.) No complete copy of the second collection of *Harmonia Anglicana* available for examination.

The opera was also known as *The Rival Queens or the Death of Alexander.*

Daniel Purcell contributed Songs to this opera. (*See* Nos. 51 and 67.)

67. Songs in the Opera [from text by Nathaniel Lee] of Alexander the Great. [By Daniel Purcell and others.]
[J. Walsh and J. Hare. 1701.]
Walsh Cat., Ill. 7.

The correct title may have been: 'Songs In The New Opera, Call'd' &c. adapted from the title-page used for No. 29. (*See* Ill. 1.) The work was also known as *The Rival Queens or the Death of Alexander.*

Gottfried Finger contributed some music to this opera. (*See* No. 66.)

One number by Purcell was published separately, probably by Walsh, *c.* 1701: 'A Song set by M^r. Dan: Purcell in Alexander the Great.' (Phillis talk not more of passion. BM. G. 304. (122.))

68. Songs made for the Playhouses and other occasions, sold at fourpence the Sheet, and two-pence the halfe Sheet.
[J. Walsh and J. Hare. 1701.]
Walsh Cat., Ill. 7.

This general notice covers miscellaneous single- or double-sheet songs, a number of which exist in the British Museum and elsewhere, usually without imprint.

See Nos. 27 and 57.

69. A Set of Airs for two Flutes; with a Thorough-Bass for the Harpsicord. Composed by Mr. Frank [i.e. Johann Wolfgang Franck?], Price 1s. 6d.
Printed and Sold by J. Walsh . . . John Hare, &c.
Nov. 20–2, 1701, *Post Boy.*

70. The French Dancing Master. Price 1s. 6d.
Printed and Sold by J. Walsh . . . John Hare, &c.
Nov. 20–2, 1701, *Post Boy.*

See Nos. 34 and 197.

71. The Third Book of Military Musick; Or The Art of playing upon the Hautbois, improv'd and made familiar to the meanest Capacity by compendious and easie Directions: Also a Choice Collection of Aires, Marches, Trumpet-Tunes, Minuets, &c. purposely compos'd for that Instrument by the most able Masters, and fairly Engraven on Copper-Plates. Price 1s. 6d.
London, Printed for and sold by J. Hare . . . at the Golden Viol . . . and . . . in Freeman's Yard . . . and J. Walsh, &c.
Nov. 22–5, 1701, *Flying Post.*

A re-advertisement or another edition of No. 55.

72. Nolens Volens, The second Book for the Violin. Being an Introduction for the Instructing of young Practitioners on that Delightful Instrument, digested in a more plain and easie Method than any yet extant, together with a choice Collection of New Ayres, Compos'd by the best Masters. Also Flourishes or Preludes in every Key, with a Collection of the newest Country-Dances now in use. Price 1s. 6d.

    Printed and Sold by J. Walsh . . . and John Hare . . . 1701.

    Dec. 4–6, 1701, *Post Boy.*

      See Nos. 158, 306, 424, 442, 472, and 487 for other books. No details of the first book have been traced.

73. Mr. Peasable's Ayre's in the Comedy call'd the Humors of Sr Iohn Falstaf.

    [J. Walsh and J. Hare.]

    In four parts.

    Dec. 11–13, 1701, *Post Boy.*

      RCM. XXIX. A. 11. (12.)
      Included in *Harmonia Anglicana.* (Third collection, No. I; BM. b. 29. a; see No. 90.) Walsh Cat. Ill. 9. (No. 89.)

74. Mr Wm. Crofts Ayres in the Comedy [by Sir Richard Steele] call'd the Funeral, or Grief Allamode.

    [J. Walsh and J. Hare.]

    In four parts.

    Dec. 16–18, 1701, *Post Boy.*

      BM. d. 24. (7.) Imperfect.
      RCM. XXIX. A. 11. (11.); XXIX. A. 12. (7.) Imperfect.
      Included in *Harmonia Anglicana.* (Third collection, No. II; BM. b. 29. a; see No. 90.) Walsh Cat. Ill. 9. (No. 89.)

75. The Second Collection of Harmonia Anglicana or The Musick of the English Stage, containing Six Sets of Overtures and Aires in the Operas, Tragedies and Comedies of the Theatres.

    Printed for and Sold by J. Walsh . . . and J. Hare . . . at the Golden Viol . . . and . . . in Freeman's Yard . . . And at most Musick Shops in Town.

    Dec. 16–18, 1701, *Post Boy.*

      Durham Cathedral Library.
      A collected edition of six sets previously published separately. (Nos. 49, 54, 58, 61, 62, and 66.) Walsh Cat. Ill. 9. (No. 89.)
      The title-page may have been adapted from the plate used for the first collection. (No. 48.)
      See Nos. 48, 90, 106, 121, and index.

76. Arcangelo Corelli Opera Quarto XII Sonatas or Ayers as Preludes Almands Corrants Sarabands Gavotts and Jiggs by Arcangelo Corelli. [All in capitals.]

    London Sold by In: Walsh Servant to his Majst: . . . and I: Hare at the Golden Viol . . . and . . . in Freemans yard, &c.

    For two Violins and a Bass.

    [c. 1701–2.]

BM. d. **73**. b.; d. 20. (2.) Violino Primo and Violino Secondo parts only.
See Nos. 181, 205, 477, 512, and 596.
For complete list of Corelli items consult index.

77. Sonatas of two Parts, Composd and Purposley Contrived for two Flutes.
By M^r: Raphael Courtivill.
   London Printed and Sold by I: Walsh Musical Instrument maker in Ordinary
to his Majesty, at the Golden=Harp & Hoboy, &c.
   [*c.* 1701–2.]

> BM. c. 105. a. (3.)
> Listed on later Walsh works. (Croft, *Six Sonatas*, &c. No. 144.) Walsh Cat. *c.* 1721, Ill.
> 28, as: 'Courtivills Sonatas, for two Flutes. 3s. od.'

78. M^r. Barretts Ayres in the Tragedy [by Bevill Higgons] call'd the Generous
Conquerour or the timely Discoverry.
   [J. Walsh and J. Hare.]
   In four parts.
   Jan. 22–4, 1701 [i.e. 1702], *Post Boy.*

> BM. d. 24. (8.) Imperfect.
> RCM. XXIX. A. 12. (20.)
> Included in *Harmonia Anglicana.* (Third collection, No. III; BM. b. 29. a; *see* No. 90.)
> Walsh Cat. Ill. 9. (No. 89.)

79. Mr Lenton's Aires in the Tragedy [by Nicholas Rowe] called Tamberlain.
   [J. Walsh and J. Hare.]
   In four parts.
   Feb. 10–12, 1701 [i.e. 1702], *Post Boy.*

> RCM. XXIX. A. 11. (14.)
> Included in *Harmonia Anglicana.* (Third collection, No. IV; BM. b. 29. a; *see* No. 90.)
> Walsh Cat. Ill. 9. (No. 89.)

80. Aires in the Play [by Sir John Vanbrugh] call'd the False Friend Composed
by a Person of Quality.
   [J. Walsh and J. Hare.]
   In four parts.
   Feb. 10–12, 1701 [i.e. 1702], *Post Boy.*

> BM. d. 24. (9.) Imperfect.
> RCM. XXIX. A. 11. (13.)
> Included in *Harmonia Anglicana.* (Third collection, No. V; BM. b. 29. a; *see* No. 90.)
> Advertised as by 'L^d. B.' in Walsh Cat. Ill. 9 (No. 89), and in Walsh Cat., *c.* 1703, issued
> with No. 140.
> 'L^d. B' was William Byron, Fourth Baron Byron.
> *See* Nos. 171, 183, 498, and 601.

81. Aires in the Comedy [by George Farquhar] call'd the Inconstant or ye way
to Win him Compos'd by Mr D. Purcell.

[J. Walsh and J. Hare.]
In four parts.
March 3–5, 1701 [i.e. 1702], *Post Boy.*

    RCM. XXIX. A. 11. (20.); XXIX. A. 12. (11.) Imperfect.
Included in *Harmonia Anglicana.* (Third collection, No. VI; *see* No. 90.) **Walsh** Cat.
Ill. 9. (No. 89.) No complete copy of the third collection of *Harmonia Anglicana* available
for examination.
    In the Tenor part the play is called *Love's Contrivance.* A Song from this play (Since
Celia 'tis not in our power) was issued separately, probably by Walsh. (BM. G. 304. (134.))

82. A New Set of Airs or Lessons for the Harpsicord or Spinet by Mr. D. Purcell.
Price 6d.
    Printed and Sold by J. Walsh . . . and J. Hare, &c.
    March 3–5, 1701 [i.e. 1702], *Post Boy.*

82a. VI Sonatas or Solo's. Three for a Violin & Three for a Flute wth. a Thorough
Bass for ye Harpsychord Most humbly Dedicated To The Right Honourable
Charles Earl of Manchester Vicount Mandevil Baron Kimbolton and Lord
Lieutenant of the county of Huntingdon by ye Author Godfry Finger.
    London Printed for & Sold by Iohn Walsh Servant to his Majesty at the Harp
and Hautboy in Katherine Street near Somerset House in the Strand.
    [*c.* 1702 or earlier.]

    Details from copy in possession of Richard Newton, Henley-in-Arden. This work first
published privately, without imprint, in 1690 (Roger North, *Memoirs of Musick,* Edited by
E. F. Rimbault, 1846) has the first form of the illustrated title-page (*see* Ill. 8) afterwards
modified and used by Walsh for Nos. 293, 296, and other works. The plates of the Finger
Sonatas, including the dedication, were probably acquired by Walsh from the composer,
who left England for good, *c.* 1701. Walsh added his imprint to the illustrated title-
page, and in the later use for other works substituted the Arms of Queen Anne in place of
those of the Earl of Manchester, Baron Kimbolton, in the medallion of the design. There
is no doubt that the first use of the illustrated title-page was for Finger's Sonatas, as the
music quoted in the design is from Sonata Seconda (page 7, bar 1) of the work. (Identified
by Richard Newton.)
    The original Finger title shows signs of having been re-engraved, but the reason for this
is not evident.
    Walsh does not appear to have included the work in his various catalogues, unless it is
referred to in 'Apollo's Feast', third book, *c.* 1729 (W^m. C. Smith copy), under the two
entries: 'Fingers Solos for a Violin and a Bass', and 'Solos for a Flute & a Bass'.
    A copy of Finger's original edition is listed as being in the Henry Watson Library, Man-
chester, and another is in the Mann collection, King's College, Cambridge.

    After the death of William III, March 8, 1702, the imprints give 'Her Majesty' *in
place of* 'His Majesty'.

---

83. The Second Book of the Gentleman's Companion, being a choice Collection
of the newest Tunes for the Flute, As also several Excellent Song-Tunes fitted to

that Instrument, Compos'd by the best Masters: To which are added several new French Dances Perform'd by Mademoiselle de Subligny, the whole fairly Engraven, 1702. Price One Shilling.

Printed and Sold by John Walsh, Musical Instrument-maker in Ordinary to her Majesty . . . and J. Hare . . . at the Golden Viol . . . and . . . in Freemans Yard, &c.

April 25–8, 1702, *Post Boy.*

> The first book was issued by Hare only, in February 1699. *See* Nos. 236, 240, 421, and 423. No details of the third book have been traced.
>
> John Cullen advertised, May 5–7, 1702, *Post Boy*: 'The Flute Improved. . . . To which is added a Collection of the best Tunes . . . particularly the Dances danc'd by Mademoiselle de Subligny,' &c.

84. The first and second Books of Italian and English Songs, Compos'd and Sung in Consorts by Mr. John Abell.

Printed and Sold by John Walsh . . . and J. Hare, &c.

April 25–8, 1702, *Post Boy.*

> Henry Playford advertised, May 22–4, 1701, *Post Boy*: 'Mr Abell's two Collections of Songs, one in English, and the other in Italian, French and English that was Perform'd in Dorset Garden, last Wednesday,' &c.

85. Six Solos for a Flute and a Bass By Archangelo Corelli Being The second part of his Fifth Opera Containing Preludes Allmands Corrants Iiggs Sarabands Gavotts with the Spanish Folly The whole exactly Transpos'd and made fitt for A Flute and A Bass with the aprobation of severall Eminent Masters.

Printed for and Sold by I: Walsh Servant to her Majesty . . . and I: Hare at ye Golden Viol . . . and . . . in Freemans yard, &c.

May 28–30, 1702, *Post Boy.* (Price Four Shillings.)

> BM. e. 682.
> The BM. copy has 'N°. 111' in MS. on the title-page of each part, thus incorporating the work at a later date in Walsh's numerical series.
> Assumed to be the work in Walsh Cat., *c.* 1721, Ill. 28, as: 'Correllis Solos, for a Flute & a Bass. 4s. od.'
> *See* Nos. 31, 31*a*, 41, 112, 135, 205, 400, and 519.

86. M^r. Peasables Aires in the Play call'd King Edward the Third.

[J. Walsh and J. Hare. 1702.]

In four parts.

> RCM. XXIX. A. 11. (15.)
> Included in *Harmonia Anglicana*. (Fourth collection, No. I; *see* No. 106.) Walsh Cat. Ill. 9. (No. 89.)
> No complete copy of the fourth collection of *Harmonia Anglicana* available for examination.

87. Aires in the Play calld the Royall Captive Composed by Mr Lenton.

[J. Walsh and J. Hare. 1702.]

In four parts.

BM. d. 24. (10.) Imperfect.
Included in *Harmonia Anglicana*. (Fourth collection, No. II; *see* No. 106.) Walsh Cat. Ill. 9. (No. 89.) No complete copy of the fourth collection of *Harmonia Anglicana* available for examination.

88. A Sett of Aires Made for The Queen's Coronation by M^r. I. Eccles Master of Her Majesty's Musick.

[J. Walsh.]

In four parts.

June 6–9, 1702, *Post Man*. (A new Sett of Airs in four parts, with a Trumpet, &c.)

RCM. XXIX. A. 12. (12.) Imperfect.
Included in *Harmonia Anglicana*. (Fourth collection, No. III; BM. b. 29. a; *see* No. 106.)
At the end of the First Treble part is the following: 'Note, This makes 21 Setts of Aires in 4 Parts, besides Several Setts in 3 Parts for Violins and Flut's Engraven & Printed for I. Walsh and Sold at his Shop & Other Musick Shops in Towne.'
Hare is not associated with Walsh in the advertisement of this work, but a similar work was advertised by H. Playford and Hare (June 4–6, 1702, *Post Boy*): 'A New Set of Ayres in four parts, with a Trumpet for the Coronation of her most Sacred Majesty, Queen Anne, was Perform'd at the New Theatre. Compos'd by Mr John Eccles Master of her Majesty's Musik. Printed for H. Playford . . . and J. Hare,' &c.
No copy with this title available for examination, and there is no evidence as to why Hare was associated with Playford and not Walsh at the time, or whether one or other of the works was issued without authority.

89. The Iudgment of Paris A Pastoral Composed for the Music=Prize by M^r: D: Purcell. [Words by William Congreve.]

London Printed for I. Walsh Servt to Her Matie., at the Harp and Hoboy in Katherine Street near Somerset House. in y^e Strand.

June 13–16, 1702, *Post Boy*. (Subscrib'd to by the Nobility and Gentry, &c.)

BM. I. 325.
RCM. I. G. 15. (2.)
Day and Murrie, No. 198. Fig. 45.
With a finely illustrated title-page signed: 'M Vander Gucht Sculp.' This plate was also used for J. Eccles's *Judgment of Paris* (No. 102) and modified for Nos. 222 and 517. (*See* Ills. 10 and 17.)
The *Judgment of Paris* was subsequently reprinted, and advertised as *The Subscription Musick, &c.* (No. 114.)
The RCM. and Paul Hirsch copies include the Walsh Cat.: 'The Setts of Aires in 4 parts contained in ye Several Collections of ye Musick of ye English Stage.' (*See* Ill. 9.)
These sets are the first three collections and part of the fourth collection of *Harmonia Anglicana*. (Nos. 48, 75, 90, and 106.)
Thomas Cross published some separate numbers from *The Judgment of Paris*. (BM. K. 7. i. 2. (25.) &c.)

90. The Third Collection of Harmonia Anglicana or The Musick of the English Stage, &c.

London Printed & Sold by I: Walsh . . . & I: Hare, &c.

[1702.]

A collected edition of six sets previously published separately. (Nos. 73, 74, 78, 79, 80, and 81.) Walsh Cat. Ill. 9. (No. 89.) No copy available for examination.

The title-page of this third collection may have been adapted from the plate used for the first two collections.

See Nos. 48, 75, 106, 121, and index.

91. The 1st, 2d and 3d Books of Theatre Musick in one Volume containing variety of Airs for the Flute, Violin and Hoboy, Price 2s.

Printed and Sold by John Walsh . . . and J. Hare at the Golden Viol . . . and . . . in Freemans Yard, &c.

June 18–20, 1702, *Post Boy.* (Lately publish'd.)

A reissue in one volume of Nos. 19a, 20a, and 29a.

92. A Choice Collection of Tunes with the newest Country Dances. Price 1s. 6d.

Printed and Sold by John Walsh . . . and J. Hare, &c.

June 18–20, 1702, *Post Boy.* (Lately publish'd.)

Presumably for the Flute or Violin.

93. Select Airs for the Violin, as Preludes, Almands, Corants, Sarabands and Jigs. Price 1s. 6d.

Printed and Sold by John Walsh . . . and J. Hare, &c.

June 18–20, 1702, *Post Boy.* (Lately publish'd.)

Probably the same work as: 'Select Lessons for a single Violin', Walsh Cat., *c.* 1703, issued with No. 140; and in Walsh Cat., *c.* 1721, Ill. 27, as: 'Select Lessons 1st book. 1s. 6d.'

See No. 322.

94. [First Book of Songs by John Weldon.]

Printed and Sold by J. Walsh . . . and J. Hare, &c.

July 2–4, 1702, *Post Man.*

No copy identified.

Details of title-page uncertain. The title and title-page may have been as used for No. 124, (Collins plate, *see* Ill. 3), or as that used for No. 95. (*See* Ill. 2.) The first book may have included the dedication to Lord Conway which appears in No. 124.

Day and Murrie, No. 196.

Weldon's three books of Songs (Nos. 94, 95, and 123) in Walsh Cat., *c.* 1721, Ill. 27, as: 'Mr Weldons Songs. 10s. 0d.'

95. A Collection of new Songs With a Through Bass to each Song for the Harpsicord. Compos'd by M^r. Iohn Welldon Perform'd att his Consort in York Bildings.

London Sould by I: Walsh Musicall Instrument maker in Ordinary to her Majesty, at the Golden Harpe and Hoboy in Cathe=/=rine Street, near Summerset House in the Strand.

July 2–4, 1702, *Post Man.*

BM. G. 301. (2.)

Day and Murrie, Nos. 195 and 201. Fig. 44.

This is Weldon's second book of Songs, advertised with the first book at 1s. 6d. each.

The title-page from the plate used for No. 51 (*see* Ill. 2), modified by re-engraving and by the use of a supplementary plate. The title-page may have been used also for Weldon's first book of Songs.

See Nos. 94, 123, and 124.

96. Mr Barretts Aires in the Comedy [by Sir John Vanbrugh] call'd the Pilgrim. [J. Walsh and J. Hare. 1702.] In four parts.

BM. d. 24. (11.) Imperfect.
RCM. XXIX. A. 12. (8.) Imperfect.
Included in *Harmonia Anglicana.* (Fourth collection, No. IV; BM. b. 29. a; *see* No. 106.)
See No. 30, where the Comedy is attributed to Dryden, who contributed to Vanbrugh's revised and altered version of John Fletcher's original work.

From August 1702 Hare sometimes used 'Golden Violin' in place of 'Golden Viol', especially in the advertisements.

---

97. A new set of Airs in 4 parts: Perform'd in the Play call'd, The Faithful Bride of Granada [by William Taverner?] Compos'd by Mr Daniel Purcel This being the 23d Sett Publish'd of the Musick made for the Opera's Tragedy's and Comedy's Sold at 1s. 6d. the Sett.

Printed for and Sold by J. Walsh . . . and J. Hare at the Golden Violin in St. Paul's Church-yard, &c.

Aug. 25–7, 1702, *Post Man.*

RCM. XXIX. A. 12. (14.) Wanting Treble part with title, details of which are not known.

The work was presumably issued as No. 5 of the fourth collection of *Harmonia Anglicana* (*see* No. 106), no complete copy of which is available for examination.

98. Six Sonata's of 2 parts for 2 Violins, Composed by Mr. Courtevil. price 3s.

Printed for and Sold by J. Walsh . . . and J. Hare . . . at the Golden Violin . . . and . . . in Freeman's Yard . . . and at most Musick-shops in Town.

Oct. 3–6, 1702, *Post Man.*

Walsh Cat., *c.* 1721, Ill. 27, as: 'Courtivills Aires, for two Violins. 3s. od.'

99. Six Sonatas of two Parts For Two Flute's Composed by Mr: Finger Opera Secunda.

London Printed for I. Walsh Servt. to Her Matie. . . . and I. Hare at the Golden Viol . . . and . . . in Freemans=yard, &c.

Oct. 3–6, 1702, *Post Man.*

BM. c. 105. a. (2.)
The advertisement gives 'price 3s', and Hare's address as 'the Golden Violin'.
Presumably the work Walsh Cat., *c.* 1721, Ill. 28, as: 'Fingers Sonatas, for two Flutes. 3s. od.'

100. Mr Ier: Clarkes Aires in the Comedy [by Francis Manning] call'd all for the Better.

[J. Walsh and J. Hare.]

In four parts.

Oct. 24–7, 1702, *Post Man.*

> BM. d. 24. (12.) Imperfect.
> Included in *Harmonia Anglicana.* (Fourth collection, No. VI; BM. b. 29. a; *see* No. 106.)
> The advertisement gives Hare's address as 'the Golden Violin'.

101. Songs in the reviv'd Comedy [by John Fletcher and William Rowley] called, The Maid in the Mill.

Printed for and Sold by J. Walsh . . . and J. Hare . . . at the Golden Violin . . . and . . . in Freeman's Yard, &c.

Oct. 24–7, 1702, *Post Man.*

> The BM. contains several separate numbers from this Comedy, which may or may not have been issued by Walsh and Hare. (BM. G. 304. (4.); G. 304. (65.); G. 304. (82.); G. 306. (51.))

102. The Iudgment of Paris or the Prize Music as it was perform'd Before the Nobility and Gentry in Dorsett Garden as also att the Theatre Compos'd by M^r: I: Eccles Master of Her Majesti's Music The Words by Mr Congreve.

Londen Printed for I. Walsh Servt. to Her Matie. at the Harp and Hoboy . . . and I. Hare at the Golden Viol . . . and . . . in Freemans yard, &c.

Oct. 31–Nov. 3, 1702, *Post Man.*

Nov. 2–5, 1702, *London Gazette.*

> BM. H. 111. Without the illustrated title-page.
> RM. 11. c. 16.
> RCM. I. G. 15. (1.) With the illustrated title-page mounted as frontispiece.
> Day and Murrie, No. 197.
> With an outer illustrated title-page adapted from the plate by M. Van der Gucht used for D. Purcell's work of the same name (No. 89, *see* Ill. 10):
> The Iudgment of Paris A Pastoral Composed for the Music=Prize by M^r: I: Eccles. London Printed for I. Walsh Servt to Her Matie. at the Harp and Hoboy in Katherine Street near Somerset House. in y^e Strand.
> July 16, 1702, *Post Boy* are the advertisement details given in Day and Murrie, and the work is placed before Purcell's work of the same name, which was advertised June 13–16, 1702, *Post Boy.*
> According to a note by Julian Marshall in the BM. copy of *Songs in the Opera Calld Loves Triumph* (No. 450), the illustrated title-page used for No. 293 (*see* Ills. 8 and 20) appeared originally in *The Judgment of Paris,* by J. Eccles, but there is no other available evidence that the title-page was used for Eccles's work.
> *The Judgment of Paris* was subsequently reprinted, and advertised as: *The Subscription Musick,* &c. (No. 114.)
> Thomas Cross published some separate numbers from *The Judgment of Paris.* (BM. K. 7. i. 2. (43.) &c.)

103. The Monthly Mask of Vocal Music or the New=est Songs Made for the Theatre's & other Ocations Publish'd for November Price 6 pence These Collection's will be Continued Monthly for yᵉ Year 1703.

London Printed for and sold by I. Walsh and I. Hare and may be had at most musick shops in Town Likewise all yᵉ new Setts of Tunes in 4 parts made for yᵉ Operas, Tragedys, and Comedys of the Theatres fairly engraven sold at 1ˢ. 6ᴾ. yᵉ Sett at yᵉ places afore said.

Nov. 21–4, 1702, *Post Man*. (Thursday next will be published . . . Compos'd by Mr John Welden and Mr Dan. Purcel.)

Nov. 24–6, 1702, *Post Man*. (This day is published.)

> BM. H. 313–H. 313. j; K. 7. e. 4.
> RCM. II. A. 15.
> The first number of a very important and attractive periodical which contained many well-known works. It continued without interruption from November 1702 until September 1711 at least, after which it ceased until July 1717, when a new series commenced which continued until July 1724.
> In 1737 the younger Walsh issued 'The Monthly Mask or an Entertainment of Musick', the first number of which appeared probably in June, the series continuing irregularly until December 1737, when No. XII was advertised, 'Price 6d'. No further details of this work are known.
> Daniel Wright advertised, July 18–20, 1717, *Post-Man*, &c.: 'The Monthly Mask of New Songs', &c.
> Richard Meares also advertised 'The Monthly Mask for 1722, by Tho. Cross', a different work from that issued by Walsh; Cross presumably being the engraver.
> Each number of the early series by Walsh and Hare had a finely illustrated title-page, mostly engraved by H. Hulsbergh and bearing his name; the first title-page being used for the different numbers of the year 1703, with the necessary alteration of date made by writing the month in manuscript in the blank space left on the plate for this purpose, or by affixing a printed slip in the space as in the first number, November 1702. The monthly collections, *Mercurius Musicus*, issued for Henry Playford 1699–1702, may have given Walsh the idea of *The Monthly Mask*. No complete set of *The Monthly Mask* is known, but the BM. and the RCM. imperfect sets contain a good many numbers. It is unnecessary to give full particulars of the contents and various advertisements in this bibliography, but some notices of the annual volumes, and references to important Walsh catalogues that appear in some of them, are included. The annual volumes run from November to October inclusive and are dated with the year of the latter (e.g. November 1702 commences the year 1703). The title-page of the first number, November 1702, is reproduced as Ill. 11.
> *See* Nos. 109, 140, 160, 188, 223, 258, 282a, 331, 370, and 517.

104. A Set of Lessons for the Harpsicord or Spinnet Composed by Mr. John Eccles Master of her Majesties Musick.

Sold by J. Walsh . . . at the Golden Harp and Hoboy . . . and J. Hare . . . at the Golden Violin . . . and . . . in Freeman's-yard, &c.

Nov. 21–4, 1702, *Post Man*.

> Walsh Cat., *c.* 1703, issued with No. 140, as: 'A Collection of Aires or Lessons for the Harpsicord by Mʳ I. Eccles, &c.'

105. Mr D. Purcells Aires in the Tragedy [by Charles Gildon] call'd the Patriot or the Itallian Conspiracy.
[J. Walsh and J. Hare.]
In four parts.
Nov. 28–Dec. 1, 1702, *Post Man*.

> BM. d. 24. (13.) Imperfect.
> RCM. XXIX. A. 12. (13.) Imperfect.
> Presumably included in *Harmonia Anglicana* (Fifth collection, No. I; *see* No. 121), no complete copy of which is available for examination.

106. Harmonia Anglicana or The Musick of the English Stage, the fourth collection containing six Sets of Airs in 4 parts, made for the Tragedies and Comedies of the Theatres Composed by Mr. John Eccles, Mr. Paisible, Mr. Bartet [i.e. Barrett] Mr. Dan Purcel and Mr. Jer. Clark. Engraven in a fair character.
Printed for and Sold by J. Walsh . . . J. Hare . . . at the Golden Violin . . . and . . . in Freeman's yard, &c.
Nov. 28–Dec. 1, 1702, *Post Man*.

> BM. b. 29. a. Imperfect.
> A collected edition of six sets previously published separately. (Nos. 86, 87, 88, 96, 97, and 100.)
> The first two numbers are advertised in Walsh Cat. Ill. 9. (No. 89.)
> No copy of the title-page of this fourth collection is known, but it may have been adapted from the plate used for the first three collections.
> *See* Nos. 48, 75, 90, 121, and index.

107. Six Setts of Airs for two Flutes and a Bass. By Archangelo Correlli. Being the Choicest of his Preludes, Allemands, Sarabands, Corants, Minuets and Jiggs. Collected out of his several Opera's, exactly transpos'd and fitted to the Flute with the approbation of our eminent Masters, pr. 3s.
Printed and Sold by J. Walsh . . . and J. Hare . . . at the Golden Violin . . . and . . . in Freemans yard, &c.
Dec. 10–12, 1702, *Post Man*.

> Walsh Cat., *c.* 1721, Ill. 28, as: 'Correllis 1st Collection, for 2 Flutes & a Bass. 3s. od.'
> *See* Nos. 205, 243, and 255.

108. Mr. Henry Purcels Te Deum which was sung to the Queen, Lords and Commons, at the Cathedral Church of St Pauls, on the Thanksgiving-day for the Glorious Success of her Majesties Arms both by Land and Sea.
Printed for and Sold by J. Walsh . . . and J. Hare . . . at the Golden Violin . . . and . . . in Freemans yard &c.
Dec. 10–12, 1702, *Post Man*.

> Presumably a first Walsh issue (hitherto unrecorded) of the work first performed for St. Cecilia's Day, 1694, and published by Heptinstall, 1697 (BM. Add. MSS. 31,444.); a second Walsh announcement in April 1707 refers to a reissue of Heptinstall's edition with an additional Walsh title-page. (No. 248.)

No further details of the 1702 issue are available, and particulars of title-page or title-pages cannot be given. It is to be noted that Walsh's advertisement says 'Printed for and Sold by J. Walsh &c.', which suggests that Walsh may have by this time taken the work over from Heptinstall, or from Purcell's widow who advertised his works after his death and had a personal interest in the publication of them.

See Nos. 248, 276, and 595.

109. The Monthly Mask of Vocal Music or the New=est Songs Made for the Theatre's & other Ocations Publish'd for decem^r Price 6 pence These Collection's will be Continued Monthly for y^e Year 1703.

London Printed for and sold by I. Walsh and I. Hare, &c.

Dec. 15–17, 1702, *Post Man.* (Composed by Mr John Weldon and Mr John Barret.)

> BM. H. 313.
> Title-page from the Hulsbergh plate of the November issue (No. 103, *see* Ill. 11) with 'decem^r' supplied in MS. to the blank space left for the insertion of the month and in some copies with 'December' engraved on a separate slip. The advertisement in the *Post Man* has the following note: 'Any Gentleman whose Genius inclines to Poetry that will be pleas'd to send good Words proper for Songs, to the Publisher of these Collections, care will be taken to have them set to Musick by the best Masters.'
> *See* Nos. 103, 140, 160, 188, 223, 258, 282a, 331, 370, and 517.

110. Mr Peasables Aires in the Comedy [by Colley Cibber] call'd She wou'd and She wou'd not.

[J. Walsh and J. Hare.]

In four parts.

Dec. 15–17, 1702, *Post Man.*

> RCM. XXIX. A. 11. (16.); XXIX. A. 12. (15.) Imperfect.
> Presumably included in *Harmonia Anglicana* (Fifth collection, No. II; *see* No. 121), no complete copy of which is available for examination.
> *See* No. 448, music for a revival of this comedy.

111. Mr Croft's Aires in the Comedy [by George Farquhar] calld the twinn Rivalls.

[J. Walsh and J. Hare.]

Jan. 7–9, 1703, *Post Man.* (A new Set of Airs in 4 parts &c.)

> RCM. XXIX. A. 11. (17.); XXIX. A. 12. (16.) Imperfect.
> Presumably included in *Harmonia Anglicana* (Fifth collection, No. III; *see* No. 121), no complete copy of which is available for examination.

112. 6 New Solos for a Flute and a Bass by the same Author. [i.e. Arcangelo Corelli.] pr. 4s.

Printed for and Sold by J. Walsh . . . and J. Hare . . . at the Golden Violin . . . and . . . in Freeman's-yard, &c.

Jan. 7–9, 1703, *Post Man.*

> Presumably a re-advertisement of No. 85.
> For complete list of Corelli items consult index.

113. The fourth Book of the new Flute Master, containing the best rules and directions for learners on the Flute; as also a collection of the newest Tunes, Composed by the most eminent Masters. To which is added the new Dances performed before her Majesty at Bath, and those Danced by Mrs. Bignell at the Theatre, with the Harlequin Chaccoone and other excellent tune, never before published; likewise a scale shewing how to transpose any Tune to the Flute that is made for the Violin or Voice. Also a new set of flourishes in every key on the Flute. Composed by Mr. J. B. [i.e. Bolton?] Price 1s. 6d.

Printed for and Sold by J. Walsh . . . and J. Hare . . . at the Golden Violin . . . and . . . in Freemans-yard, &c.

Jan. 21–3, 1703, *Post Man.*

> See Nos. 20b, 33, 182, 305, 390, 486, 510, 563, and 578 for other books and works with similar titles. No details of the third, sixth, and eighth books of the early series finishing with No. 486 have been traced.

114. There is also Reprinted and Published, the Subscription Musick, which has of late so often been perform'd before the Nobility and Gentry at the Theatres. Composed by Mr. J. Eccles Master of Her Majesties Musick, and Mr. D. Purcel, in 2 vol. pr. each 10s.

Printed for and Sold by J. Walsh . . . and J. Hare . . . at the Golden Violin . . . and . . . in Freeman's yard, &c.

Jan. 30–Feb. 2, 1703, *Post Man.*

> Reissues of D. Purcell's and J. Eccles's, *The Judgment of Paris.* (Nos. 89 and 102.)

115. Mr Barretts Musick in the Comedy [by Thomas Baker] call'd Tunbridg walks or the Yeoman of Kent.

[J. Walsh and J. Hare.]

In four parts.

Feb. 9–11, 1703, *Post Man.*

> BM. d. 24. (14.) Imperfect.
> RCM. XXIX. A. 11. (18.); XXIX. A. 12. (18.) Imperfect.
> Presumably included in *Harmonia Anglicana* (Fifth collection, No. IV, BM. b. 29. a; *see* No. 121), no complete copy of which is available for examination.

116. Mr. Isacks [i.e. Isaac's] new Dances Danced at Court on her Majesties Birthday, 1703. The Tunes by Mr. Lefevre. To which is added several others of the newest French Dances. Price 6d.

Printed for and Sold by J. Walsh . . . and J. Hare . . . at the Golden Violin . . . and . . . in Freemans-yard, &c.

Feb. 9–11, 1703, *Post Man.* (On Saturday next will be published.)

Feb. 11–13, 1702 [i.e. 1703] *Post Boy.* (J. Walsh and . . . J. Hare . . . at the Golden Viol, &c.)

117. The Songs and Symphonys Perform'd before Her Majesty at her Palace of St. James, on New=years day, Compos'd by Mr. J. Eccles Master of her Majestys Musick, Published for Febrvary 1703 price 1s. 6d.

London Printed for & Sould by I: Walsh Musicall Instrument maker in Ordinary to his Majesty at the Golden Harp & Ho=boy in Catherine=street near Summerset=house in ye strand.

Feb. 11–13, 1702 [i.e. 1703], *Post Boy.* (Next week will be publish'd.)

Feb. 20–3, 1703, *Post Man.* (The Monthly Mask of Vocal Musick containing the Songs and Symphonys, &c.)

RCM. II. A. 15. Collins title-page, with Walsh imprint only.

BM. H. 111. c. With Walsh imprint with 'and I. Hare at the Golden Viol in St. Pauls Church=yard, and at his Shop in Freemans=yard near ye Royal Exchange', from a superimposed plate added below the pedestal of the design of the Collins plate. (No. 15. *See* Ill. 3.) Although issued during the reign of Queen Anne, the imprint has 'his' Majesty.

The title was printed from the plate originally engraved 'Published for January 1703', but was issued with a label engraved 'Febrvary' pasted over 'January'.

The work was issued as an exceptionally large number of *The Monthly Mask of Vocal Music.*

118. Mr Corbett's Musick in the Comedy [by Charles Burnaby] call'd the agreeable Disappointment.

[J. Walsh and J. Hare.]

In four parts.

Feb. 23–5, 1703, *Post Man.* (The new Musick performed in the Comedy called Love Betray'd or the agreeable disappointment, Composed by Mr. Wm. Corbett, pr. 1s. 6d.)

RCM. XXIX. A. 11. (19.); XXIX. A. 12. (17.)

Presumably included in *Harmonia Anglicana* (Fifth collection, No. V; *see* No. 121), no complete copy of which is available for examination.

119. Senr: Nicola's first and Second Book's of Aire's in 3 Parts Containing Preludes Allemand's Saraband's Corrant's Minuett's and Jigg's with divers Fancye's and Vollentary's in Every Key for two Violins and a Bass The Second Treble never being Printed before is now Engraven from the Authors own Manuscript which renders the whole work Compleat Composed by Nicola Matteis Napolitano Libro Primo ett Secundo.

London Printed for I. Walsh . . . and I. Hare at the Golden Viol . . . and . . . in Freemans yard near ye Royall Exchange. pr. 5.0. [Price in MS.]

Mar. 9–11, 1703, *Post Man*; Mar. 9–11, 1703, *Post Boy.*

BM. c. 66. Without the illustrated title-page, price in MS. BM. d. 20. (3.) Violino Primo, with illustrated title-page, and Violino Secondo parts only.

Outer illustrated title-page:

Senr Nicola's Aires in 3 Parts Containing Preludes Allemand's Saraband's, &c. with Fancye's and Vollentary's in Every Key for two Violins and a Bass his First and Second Book's.

London Printed for I. Walsh Servt. in ordinari to Her Matie at the Harp and Hoboy in Katherine Street near Somerset House in ye strand.

The illustrated title-page from the plate originally used for '*A Second Booke of Songs* . . . *Composed by R King*', &c. (*See* No. 15, BM. C. 411; Day and Murrie, Fig. 31.) The engraved Matteis title in the medallion centre, from a supplementary plate, and with the Walsh imprint added to the original design, which has the appearance of having been engraved by Collins although not signed by him. The plate was used again by Walsh for No. 264a. (*See* Ill. 19.)

The Violino Secondo and Bassus parts have also a separate title-page to Libro Secundo:

The Second Booke of Aire's Containing Preludes Allemand's Saraband's &c more Difficult than the Former for the Improvement of the Hand on the Violin Composed by Senr. Nicola Matteis Napolitano Libro Secundo.

The advertisements state 'There is now Reprinted' &c. The work was another edition of that issued as *Ayrs for the Violin*, &c. in 1685, without imprint. (BM. K. 1. f. 10; RCM. II. c. 26, without title-page.)

Walsh Cat., *c.* 1721, Ill. 27 as: 'Nicola Matice Aires, for 2. Violins & a Bass. 10s. od.'

The BM. copy (d. 20. (3.)) has John Young's label, dated 1702, pasted over the imprint of each part.

120. Mr Lentons Musick in the Tragedy [by Nicholas Rowe] call'd the fair Penitent.

[J. Walsh and J. Hare.]
In four parts.
March 30–April 1, 1703, *Post Man.*

BM. d. 24. a. (2.)
RCM. XXIX. A. 11. (22.) Imperfect.
Presumably included in *Harmonia Anglicana* (Fifth collection, No. VI; *see* No. 121), no complete copy of which is available for examination.
John Eccles contributed one song at least to this play. (BM. G. 311. (66.))

121. The Fifth Collection of Harmonia Anglicana or The Musick of the English Stage, &c.

London Printed & Sold by I: Walsh . . . and I: Hare, &c.
[1703.]

A collected edition of six sets previously published separately. (Presumably Nos. 105, 110, 111, 115, 118, and 120.)

No copy of the title-page of this fifth collection is known, but it may have been adapted from the plate used for the first four collections.

See Nos. 48, 75, 90, 106, and index.

122. Mr Corbetts Musick in the Comedy [by Charles Boyle, Earl of Orrery] call'd As you find it.

[J. Walsh and J. Hare.]
In four parts.
May 4–6, 1703, *Post Man.*

BM. d. 24. (15.) Imperfect.
RCM. XXIX. A. 11. (23.); XXIX. A. 12. (19.) Imperfect.
Presumably included in *Harmonia Anglicana* (Sixth collection, No. I), no complete copy of which is available for examination.
See Nos. 48, 75, 90, 106, and 121.

123. M^r. Weldon's Third Book of Songs Begining with single Songs Perform'd at the Consorts in York Buildings and at y^e Theatre^s as also Symphony Songs for Violins and Flutes never before Publish'd Carefully Corrected by y^e Author price 2^s–6^d.

  London Printed for & Sould by I: Walsh Musicall Instrument maker in Ordinary to her Majesty at the Golden Harp & Ho=boy in Catherine=street near Summerset= house in y^e strand.

    May 8–11, 1703, *Post Man.*

      BM. G. 301. a.
      RCM. II. F. 22. (3.)
      Title-page from the Collins plate. (No. 15. *See* Ill. 3.)
      See Nos. 94, 95, and 124.

124. A Collection of New Songs Songs Accompagni'd with Violins and Flutes with a Thorow Bass to Each Song for ye Organ or Harpsicord Composed by Mr John Weldon.

  London Printed for & Sould by I: Walsh . . . in ye strand. price 2 : 6^d. [Price in MS.]

    [*c.* 1703.]

      BM. G. 301. (1.)
      RCM. I. A. 11. (2.)
      This is another copy of Weldon's third book of Songs (No. 123) with another title which may have been issued for the first book (No. 94) as also the accompanying dedication to Lord Conway.
      Title-page from the Collins plate (No. 15, *see* Ill. 3) with the imprint as No. 123.

125. Gasperini's Solos for a Violin with a through Bass for the Harpsicord or Bass Violin Containing Preludes Allemands Sarabands &c. Composed by Seign^r. Gasparo Visconti Opera Prima.

  Printed for I. Walsh . . . and I. Hare at the Golden Viol . . . and . . . in Freemans= yard, &c.

    May 25–7, 1703, *Post Man.*

      BM. e. 790.
      The work was advertised as 'carefully corrected by the Author. Printed on Royal Paper.'
      The original edition was also advertised in the *Post Man*, May 25–7, as follows: 'To all Lovers of Simphony. The Original Edition of Sig. Gasparinis Solo Book for a Violin and a Base, Engraven at Amsterdam, by Stephen Rogers, and Printed on Royal Paper, is Sold by Francis Vaillant 3 doors from the West-corner of Catherine-street, by Mr Collin near Temple-bar, and by Mr. Hare in Pauls Church-yard,' &c.
      Clearly, Walsh's edition was issued in competition with the original, probably without permission, and Hare stocked both editions.

126. Six Sonata's in Three Parts. Three for Two Violins, and Three for Two Flutes. With a Part for the Base-Violin or Viol, and a Figur'd Base for the Organ, Harpsicord or Archlute. Composed by William Williams Servant to his late Majesty.

London. Printed for and Sold by John Hare . . . at the Golden Viol . . . and . . . in Freeman's Yard . . . and John Walsh, &c.

June 17–19, 1703, *Post Boy*.

127. A Collection of Airs purposely made and contriv'd for 2 Flutes, being entirely new. Composed by Signior Gasparini [i.e. Gasparo Visconti], price 2s.

Printed for and sold by J. Walsh . . . and J. Hare . . . at the Golden Viol . . . and . . . in Freeman yard, &c.

July 15–17, 1703, *Post Man*.

Advertised on No. 144 as: 'Seign^r. Gasperini's Aires for two Flutes.' Walsh Cat., *c.* 1721, Ill. 28, as: 'Gasperinis Aires, for two Flutes. 2s. od.'

128. Albinoni's Aires in 3 Parts for Two Violins and a Through Bass Containing Almand's Saraband's Corrant's Gavots and Jiggs &c Collected out of the Choisest of his works with the Apro=/bation of our Best Masters the whole Carefully Corrected and fairly Engraven.

London Printed for I. Walsh . . . and I. Hare at the Golden Viol . . . and . . . in Freemans yard, &c.

Aug. 12–14, 1703, *Post Man*.

BM. d. 20. (4.) Violino Primo and Violino Secondo parts only, with John Young's label dated 1702 pasted on both parts. *See* No. 366.

129. Arcangelo Correlli Opera Secunda XII Sonata's or Aires For Two Violins and a Through Bass, Containing Preludes Almand's Corra^nt's Saraband's Gavots and Jiggs &c. The whole Carefully Corrected.

London Printed for I. Walsh Servt. to Her Matie: at the Harp and Hoboy in Katherine Street near Somerset House in ye Strand and I. Hare at the Goldē Viol in S^t. Pauls Church yard, and at his Shop in Freemans yard near ye Royall Exchange.

Aug. 12–14, 1703, *Post Man*. (Corellis Opera Secunda, or his first Aires.)

BM. d. 20. (1.) Violino Primo and Violino Secondo parts only.
See No. 181.
For complete list of Corelli items consult index.

130. The Psalms set full for the Organ or Harpsicord, by Dr. Blow, as they are play'd in Churches or Chapels, proper for Organists or others who play on the Organ or Harpsicord, being the first Published of this kind in so compleat a manner, fairly Engraven, pr. 1s.

Printed for and sold by J. Walsh . . . and J. Hare . . . at the Golden Viol . . . and . . . in Freeman yard, &c.

Aug. 17–19, 1703, *Post Man*.

Title was probably as on p. 1 of the later edition issued as 'No 184' of Walsh's numerical series (BM. c. 93.):
The Psalms by D^r. Blow Set full for the Organ or Harpsicord as they are Play'd in Churches or Chapels.
See Nos. 176 and 537.

131. Corelli's first and second sets of Airs at 5s per set.
   Printed for and sold by J. Walsh ... and J. Hare, &c.
      Aug. 17–19, 1703, *Post Man.*
         Re-advertisements of Nos. 76 and 129.
         See No. 181.
         For complete list of Corelli items consult index.

132. Mr Corbet's Musick in the Comedy call'd Hen^r. the 4th Play'd all the time
of the Bublick [*sic*] Act in Oxford.
   [J. Walsh and J. Hare.]
   In four parts.
      Aug. 21–4, 1703, *Post Man.*
         BM. d. 24. (16.) Imperfect.
         RCM. XXIX. A. 11. (27.); XXIX. A. 12. (21.) Imperfect.
         Presumably included in *Harmonia Anglicana* (Sixth collection, No. II), no complete
copy of which is available for examination.
         See Nos. 48, 75, 90, 106, and 121.

133. Ziani's Airs, or Sonato's in 3 parts for 2 Violins, and a through Bass for the
Harpsicord or Bass Violin. Containing the most refin'd Italian Airs; Engraven
from the Manuscript, which was never before Printed: the whole carefully Corrected Opera Prima, price 4s.
   Printed for and sold by J. Walsh ... and J. Hare ... at the Golden Violin, &c.
      Aug. 26–8, 1703, *Post Man.*
         Walsh Cat., *c.* 1721, Ill. 27, as: 'Zianis Sonatas, for 2 Violins & a Bass. 4s. 0d.'

134. A Collection of Aires For two Flutes and a Bass Compos'd by M^r: J: Weldon
M^r: Hen^r: Simons and others Fairly Engraven price 3^s.
   London Printed for I. Walsh ... and I. Hare at the Golden Viol ... and ... in
Freemans yard near ye Royall Exchange.
      Sept. 23–5, 1703, *Post Man.*
         BM. d. 150. (6.)

135. The 2d part of Correllis fifth Opera, proper for the Harpsicord, consisting of
Preludes, Allemonds, Sarabrands, Gavots and Jiggs, price 3s.
   Printed for and sold by J. Walsh ... and J. Hare ... at the Golden Violin ...
and ... in Freemans yard, &c.
      Sept. 23–5, 1703, *Post Man.*
         This edition, presumably for Harpsicord alone, is not otherwise known.
         See Nos. 31, 31*a*, 41, 85, 112, 205, 400, and 519.

136. Select Lessons for the Bass Viol of 2 Parts. Collected by our best Violists
out of the works of that great Master Giovanni Schenk, being the choicest Preludes,
Allemonds, Sarabands, Courants, Minuets and Jigs, fairly Engraven, price 3s.

40

Printed for and sold by J. Walsh . . . and J. Hare . . . at the Golden Violin . . . and . . . in Freemans yard, &c.

Oct. 19–21, 1703, *Post Man.*

Walsh Cat., *c.* 1721, Ill. 27, as: 'Lessons for yᵉ Bass Viol. 3s. od.'
The title as given in H. Reeves's Catalogue No. 107, 1933, p. 23, of what appears to be a later edition, is:
Select Lessons for the Bass Viol of two Parts. Collected by our Best Viollists out of the Works of that Great Master Giovanni Schenk, being the Choisest Preludes, Allemands, Sarabands, Corrants, Minuets and Jigs. Fairly Engraven, the First Collection.
London, Walsh, *c.* 1750.

137. The 3d Book of the Mock Trumpet. Containing variety of new Trumpet Tunes, Airs and Minuets fitted to that Instrument, and very proper for the Brazen Trumpet, as also for Learners on the Violin, Flute or Hoboy, being both easy and pleasant. Likewise 1st and 2d Trebles for 2 Trumpets, with directions for Learners, price 1s.

Printed for and sold by J. Walsh . . . and J. Hare . . . at the Golden Violin . . . and . . . in Freemans-yard, &c.

Oct. 23–6, 1703, *Post Man.*

See Nos. 17 and 21.

138. Proposals for Printing a general Collection of J. Eccles Songs, where encouragement is great for those persons who shall subscribe, on or before the 1st of February next, for 12s. each they shall receive the Book in Quires, after which time no Subscription will be taken, nor the Books sold under 18s. each in Quires. Proposals at large may be had and Subscriptions taken in at the Authors House in Great Russel-street in Bloomsbury; at Mr. Walsh's Musick-shop . . . and at Mr. Hares Musick-shop at the Viol . . . and in Freemans yard, &c.

Oct. 26–8, 1703, *Post Man.*

The work was issued Oct. 1704.
See No. 156.

139. The Songs and Symphonys Perform'd before Her Majesty at her Palace at Sᵗ. Jame's on her Birth Day. 1703 Composed by Mʳ: Eccles Master of Her Majestys Musick price 1ˢ. 6ᵈ.

London Printed for & Sould by I: Walsh Musicall Instrument maker in Ordinary to her Majesty at the Golden Harp & Ho=boy in Catherine=street near Summerset=house in yᵉ strand.

Nov. 2–4, 1703, *Post Man.*

BM. H. III. b.
RCM. I. G. 16.
Title-page from the Collins plate. (No. 15. *See* Ill. 3.)

140. The Whole Volume Compleat Intituled The Monthly Masks of Vocal Musick Containing all the Choisest Songs by the Best Masters made for the

Play-houses Publick Consorts and other Occasions for the Year 1703 [i.e. Nov. 1702–Oct. 1703] with a Through Bass to Each Song and most of them with in the Composs of the Flute price 5ˢ.

London Printed for & Sould by I: Walsh Musicall Instrument maker in Ordinary to her Majesty, &c.

Dec. 2–4, 1703, *Post Man*. (The Whole Volume of Monthly Collections . . . J. Walsh and J. Hare.)

> BM. H. 313. Imperfect.
> RCM. II. A. 15. Imperfect.

The first of these yearly volumes, with title-page from the Collins plate (No. 15, *see* Ill. 3) as used for 1704 and other volumes, in addition to the illustrated title-pages issued with the monthly parts. The complete volume, of which there is a copy in the Bodleian Library, includes 'A Table of the Songs', a dedication to 'William Lord Marquiss of Hartington', and at the end of the volume an important and very rare Walsh catalogue. The dedication is as follows:

To yᵉ Right Honᵇˡᵉ. William Lord Marquiss of Hartington.
My Lord

Having compleated the Monthly Collection of Vocall Musick for the Year Seaventeen hundred & three, the first of my Vndertaking of this kind, I have made bold to shelter it under your Lordᴘᴘˢ-Protection, the Compositions are of the best Mas=/ters, & I perswade my self the Publick will approve 'em, were it onely for the Name they are inscrib'd to.

I know my Lord, the distance there is between an Author & a Publi=/sher, & therefore shall not presume to Ennumerate the particulars that Qualify you for an exact Judge of this science, nor those other high Abil=/litys that have deservedly Drawne on you the Vniversal Esteem, but must content my self with declaring by this Oppertunity, the great encourage=/ment that I have receiv'd in my Labours from your Lordᴘᴘˢ. kind Generosity, which with the utmost Gratitude shall be ever acknow=/ledgᵈ. by

                         My Lord
                            yʳ. Lordshipps most
                                 Humble & most Obedient
                                      Servant
                                           John Walsh.

The Walsh catalogue, printed on both sides of the last leaf, contains on the recto a list of theatre overtures and airs, with some miscellaneous vocal music, printed as an oblong folio, and on the verso, a catalogue of English and Italian instrumental music followed by some miscellaneous vocal and instrumental items, printed as an upright folio. The first page is from the same plate as that used by Walsh for the earlier catalogue included in Topham's, 'Six Sonata's or Solos, for the Flute', &c. (No. 60, *see* Ill. 7), but with a number of additional items and with three of the Topham list erased from the plate. The two pages of the catalogue cover some hundred or more separate works, and can therefore be reasonably accepted as a fairly complete statement of Walsh's stock-in-trade at the time.

The contents are transcribed here in detail, with some slight modifications in punctuation, &c., and with the reference numbers to the entries in the bibliography added, in order to aid identification:

The Overture's and Ayrs, in four Parts, made for the Opera's, Tragedy's, and Comedy's of the Theater's, Printed for I. Walsh.

Ayres in the Opera of the Mad Lover, by Mr. I. Eccles. 1s. 6d. (No. 49.)
Ayres in the Opera of the fate of Troy, Mr. Finger. 1s. 6d. (No. 54.)

Ayres in ye Tragedy of ye Unhapy Penitent, Mr. D. Purcell. 1s. 6d. (No. 47.)
Ayres in ye Tragedy of ye Ambisious Stepmother, Mr. Lenton. 1s. 6d. (No. 46.)
Ayres in the Comedy of Loves Stratagem, Mr. Peasable. 1s. 6d. (No. 43.)
Ayres in the Comedy of Courtship Alamode, Mr. Croft. 1s. 6d. (No. 44.)
Ayres in the Comedy of Love's at a Loss, Mr. Finger. 1s. 6d. (No. 45.)
Ayres in the Vestal Virgins by Mr. O. 1s. 6d. (No. 38.)
Ayres in the Comedy of the Fops Fortune, Mr. Finger. 1s. 6d. (No. 58.)
Ayres in the Comedy of Sr Hary Wild-Hair, Mr. Finger. 1s. 6d. (No. 61.)
Ayres in the Comedy of the Humors of ye Age, M^r. Finger. 1s. 6d. (No. 62.)
Ayres in the Opera of Alexander the Great, Mr. Finger. 1s. 6d. (No. 66.)
Aires in the Comedy call'd Sr Iohn falstaff, Mr. Peasable. 1s. 6d. (No. 73.)
Aires in the Comedy call'd the Funeral, Mr. Croft. 1s. 6d. (No. 74.)
Aires in the Tragedy of the Generous Conquerour, Mr. Barrett. 1s. 6d. (No. 78.)
Aires in the Tragedy of Tamberlain, Mr. Lenton. 1s. 6d. (No. 79.)
Aires in the Play call'd the False Friend, L^d. B. 1s. 6d. (No. 80.)
Aires in ye Comedy call'd ye Inconstant, or ye way to win him, Mr. D. Purcell. 1s. 6d. (No. 81.)
Aires in the Play call'd Edward the Third, Mr. Peasable. 1s. 6d. (No. 86.)
Aires in the Play call'd the Royall Captive, Mr. Lenton. 1s. 6d. (No. 87.)
Aires for the Queen's Coronation, Mr. I. Eccles. 1s. 6d. (No. 88.)
Aires in the Comedy call'd the Pillgrim, Mr. Barrett. 1s. 6d. (No. 96.)
Aires in the Play call'd the Faithfull Bride of Granada, Mr. Purcel. 1s. 6d. (No. 97.)
Aires in the Comedy call'd all for the Better Mr. Clarke. 1s. 6d. (No. 100.)
Aires in ye Tragedy call'd ye Itallian cospiracy, D. Purcell. 1s. 6d. (No. 105.)
Aires in the Comedy call'd She wou'd and She wou'd not, Mr. Peasable. 1s. 6d. (No. 110.)
Aires in the Comedy call'd the twinn Rivalls, Mr. Crofts. 1s. 6d. (No. 111.)
Musick in the Comedy call'd Tunbridge walks, Mr. Barrett. 1s. 6d. (No. 115.)
Musick in the Comedy call'd aGreable disapointment, Mr. Corbett. 1s. 6d. (No. 118.)
Musick in the Tragedy call'd the fair penitent, Mr. Lenton. 1s. 6d. (No. 120.)
Musick in the Comedy call'd as you find it, Mr. Corbett. 1s. 6d. (No. 122.)
Musick in the Comedy call'd Hen^r. the Fourth, Mr. Corbett. 1s. 6d. (No. 132.)
Musick in the Comedy call'd the Lying Lover, Mr. Croft. 1s. 6d. (No. 141.)

Songs made for the Playhouses and other occasions, Sold at fourpence the Sheet, and two-pence the halfe Sheet. (Nos. 57 and 68.)
A Collection of Songs by Mr. Leveridge in 2 Books price each. 1s. 6d. (Nos. 11, 23, and 24.)
A Collection of Songs by Mr. Nicola. 1s. 6d. (Nos. 4 and 20.)
Songs and Dialogues in the Opera of the Island Princess. 3s. 0d. (No. 22.)
Songs in the Opera of the Grove, or Love's Pardice. 1s. 6d. (No. 29.)
A Collection of Songs by Mr. Iohn Eccles. 1s. 6d. (No. 36.)
A Collection of Songs by Mr. Dan. Purcell. 1s. 6d. (No. 51.)
A Collection of Songs by severall Masters. 1s. 6d. (Nos. 5 and 39.)
A Collection of Scotch Songs. 1s. 6d. (No. 37.)
Songs in the Opera of Alexander the Great. 1s. 6d. (No. 67.)
Songs in the Comedy call'd the Pilgrim. 1s. 6d. (No. 30.)

A Catalogue of English and Itallian
Musick for all sorts of Instruments
printed for J. Walsh.

Books for the Violin with the best Instructions for Learners and the newest tunes. Nolens Volens. 1s. 6d. (Nos. 1, 10, 64, and 72.)

Books for the Flute containing the newest tunes and best Instructions for learners. New flute Master. 1s. 6d. (Nos. 2, 3, 9, 20b, 33, 83, and 113.)

Mr. Demoivres Collection of Aires for a single Flute. 1s. 0d. (No. 53.)

Oridginall Scotch tunes for a single Flute. 1s. 0d. (No. 65.)

Books for the Harpsicord the rules by Mr. Hen^r. Purcell with Excellent Lessons. Harpsicord Master. 1s. 6d. (Nos. 14, 27, and 59.)

Books for the Hoboy with directions for Learners and Variety of the newest Tunes. 1s. 6d. (Nos. 55 and 71.)

Books of French dances danced at Court and the Theatre continu'd with all thats new. 1s. 6d. (Nos. 34 and 70.)

Select Lessons for a single Violin. 1s. 6d. (No. 93.)

Books of Country dances continued with all thats new. 1s. 6d. (No. 92.)

Books for the mock trumpet with directions for Learners and the best Tunes. 1s. 0d. (Nos. 17, 21, and 137.)

Books for the Flagillet with directions for Learners and the Choisest Tunes. 1s. 0d. (No. 618.)

Musick in Parts for Violins.

Harmonia Anglicana or the Musick of the English stage containing 6 sets of Aires 4 parts. 8s. 0d. (Nos. 48, 75, 90, 106, and 121.)

Bononcinias Aires in 3 parts. 3s. 0d. (No. 63.)

Mr. Simons Aires in 3 parts for two Violins and a Bass. 1s. 6d. (No. 40.)

Sonatas and Solos for a Violin and a Bass by Basana Corelli and Nicola. 1s. 6d. (No. 50.)

Mr. Fingers six Solos for Violins and Fluts with a through Bass. 4s. 0d. (No. 82a.)

Mr. D. Purcells six Solos for Violins and Fluts with a through Bass. 4s. 0d. (No. 15.)

Mr. Crofts six Solos for Violins and Fluts with a through Bass. 3s. 0d. (No. 28.)

Mr. Courtivills six Sonatas for two Violins. 3s. 0d. (No. 98.)

Mr. Fingers six Sonatas for two Violins. 3s. 0d. (No. 142a.)

Senr. Nicolas First and Second books of Aires in 3 parts. 10s. 0d. (No. 119.)

Corellis First Set of Aires in 3 parts Opera Seconda. 5s. 0d. (Nos. 129 and 131.)

Corellis Second Set of Aires in 3 parts Opera Quarta. 5s. 0d. (Nos. 76 and 131.)

Corellis 12 Solos for a Violin and a Bass Opera Quinta. 5s. 0d. (Nos. 31 and 41.)

Albinones Aires in 3 parts Parte Primo. 4s. 0d. (No. 128.)

Ziani's Aires in 3 parts Parte Primo. 4s. 0d. (No. 133.)

Senr. Gasperines Solos for a Violin and a through Bass Opera Primo. 2s. 6d. (No. 125.)

Musick in Parts for Fluts.

Mr. Rodgers Six Sonatas for two Fluts. 3s. 0d. (No. 19.)

Mr. Topham Six Solos for a Flute and a through Bass. 3s. 0d. (No. 60.)

Mr. Courtivills Six Sonatas for two Flut's. 3s. 0d. (No. 77.)

Mr. Fingers Six Sonatas for two Flut's. 3s. 0d. (No. 99.)

Mr. Peasables Six Sonatas for two Flut's. 3s. 0d. (No. 142b.)

Corellis Solos for a Flute and a Bass. 4s. 0d. (Nos. 85 and 112.)

Corellis Aires for two Fluts and a Bass. 3s. 0d. (No. 107.)

Aires for two Flutes and a Bass by Mr. Welldon Mr. Simons and others. 3s. 0d. (No. 134.)

Gasperinis Aires for two Fluts. 2s. od. (No. 127.)
Aires for two Flutes by Mr. Weldon Senr Gasperini & several Masters. 1s. 6d. (No. 142.)

Vocal Musick.

The Generall Collection containing 250 of the choicest Song and Dialogaes Composed by the Eminents Masters of the Age Price Bound. £1. 10s. od. (No. 142c.)

The Prize Musick by Mr. John Eccles. 10s. od. (No. 102.)

The Prize Musick by Mr. Dan: Purcell. 10s. od. (No. 89.)

Songs in the Sham Dockter. 1s. 6d. (No. 8.)

The Monthly Mask of Vocall Musick Continu'd. 6d. (Nos. 103 and 109.)

Songs made for the Playhouses and other ocasions Sold at fourpence the Sheet and twopence the half Sheet. (Nos. 57 and 68.)

The Psalms by Dr. Blow Set full for the Organ or Harpsicord. 1s. od. (No. 130.)

Select Lessons of two parts for the Bass Violl by Giovanni Schenk. 3s. od. (No. 136.)

A Collection of Aires or Lessons for the Harpsicord by Mr. I. Eccles, &c. 1s. 6d. (No. 104.)

The whole Volume of monthly Masks Compleat for the year 1073 [i.e. 1703]. 5s. od. (No. 140.)

Mr. I. Eccles General Collection of Songs now in Subscription. 18s. od. (Nos. 138 and 156.)

See Nos. 103, 109, 160, 188, 223, 258, 282*a*, 331, 370, and 517.

141. Mr Wm Croft's Musick in the Comedy [by Sir Richard Steele] call'd the Lying Lover.
[J. Walsh and J. Hare.]
In four parts.
Dec. 21–3, 1703, *Post Man.*

BM. d. 24. a. (1.); d. 24. (17.) Imperfect.
RCM. XXIX. A. 11. (28.); XXIX. A. 12. (23.) Imperfect.
Presumably included in *Harmonia Anglicana* (Sixth collection, No. III), no complete copy of which is available for examination.
See Nos. 48, 75, 90, 106, and 121.

142. A Collection of Aires for two Flutes by Eight Eminent Masters.
[J. Walsh and J. Hare. *c.* 1703.]

Advertised on the title-page of No. 144.
Probably the work in Walsh Cat., *c.* 1703, issued with No. 140, as: 'Aires for two Flutes by Mr Weldon Senr Gasperini & several Masters.'
Walsh Cat., *c.* 1721, Ill. 28, as: 'Aires by 8 Masters, for two Flutes. 2s. od.'

142*a*. Mr Fingers six Sonatas for two Violins. 3s. od.
[J. Walsh. *c.* 1703 or earlier.]

Walsh Cat., *c.* 1703, issued with No. 140.
Walsh Cat., *c.* 1721, Ill. 27, as: 'Fingers Aires, for two Violins'; presumably the same work.

142*b*. Six Sonatas of two Parts For Two Flute's Composed by M^r: Paisible Opera Prima.

London Printed for I. Walsh . . . at the Harp & Hoboy . . . and I. Hare at the Golden Viol . . . and . . . in Freemans=yard, &c.

[*c.* 1703 or earlier.]

> BM. c. 105. a. (4.)
> Walsh Cat., *c.* 1703, issued with No. 140, as: 'Mr Peasables Six Sonatas for two Flut's. 3s. od.'
> *See* Ill. 12.

142*c*. The Generall Collection containing 250 of the choisest Song and Dialogaes Composed by the Eminents Masters of the Age Price Bound. £1. 10s. od.

[J. Walsh. *c.* 1703 or earlier.]

> Walsh Cat., *c.* 1703, issued with No. 140. Probably with similar title to No. 463.

143. That famous Sonata in Alamire [*sic*] for 2 Violins and a through Bass by Signior Torrelli [i.e. G. Torelli] perform'd by Signior Gasperini [i.e. Gasparo Visconti] and Mr Dean at the Theatre, as also a new Solo, by Signior Martino [i.e. Martino Bitti] for a Violin and a Bass, perform'd by Signior Gasperini, both Publish'd for Jan. pr. 1s. 6d. Which will be continued monthly, with the best and choicest Sonata's and Solo's by the Greatest Masters in Europe for the year 1704.

Printed for and sold by J. Walsh . . . and J. Hare . . . at the Golden Viol . . . and . . . in Freemans Yard, &c.

Jan. 22–5, 1704, *Post Man*.

> First announcement of what was intended to be a monthly periodical publication of instrumental music, the subsequent history of which is not clear, although some of the early numbers were issued in a collected form as *Harmonia Mundi*. (No. 257.) In this work Torelli's Sonata is described as: 'Torelli A♯.' The periodical was presumably the same as that referred to in later advertisements as 'The Instrumental Musick for October', &c.
> A copy of the second of the works advertised is in Durham Cathedral Library, with the following title: Violino Solo A♯ del Martino Betti Perform'd by Sig[r] Gasperini at the Theater Royall The Solo Proper for the Harpsicord or Spinnett.
> *See* Nos. 149, 150, 150*a*, 150*b*, 150*c*, 153, 155, 157, 159, 165, 172, and 178.

144. Six Sonatas of two Parts Purposely made and Contrived for Two Flutes Compos'd by M[r]: William Croft To which is added an Excellent Solo for a Flute and a Bass by Seign[r]: Papus [i.e. Pepusch] The whole Carefully Corrected and Fairly Engraven There is lately Published Seign[r]. Gasperini's Aires for two Flutes . . . a Collection of Aires for two Flutes by Eight Eminent Masters, all fairly Engraven. [Eight works listed.]

London Printed for I. Walsh . . . and I. Hare at the Golden Viol . . . and . . . in Freemans yard, &c.

Jan. 22–5, 1704, *Post Man*. (Next week will be publish'd . . . pr. 2s.)

> BM. c. 105. a. (1.)
> Another edition was issued by Walsh and Hare, a little later than the original edition, with Pepusch substituted for Papus on the title-page and on p. 9 of the parts. (BM. d. 150. (3.))
> According to an advertisement Feb. 3–7, 1703 [i.e. 1704], *London Gazette*, John Young

Musical Instrument-seller at the Dolphin and Crown, St. Paul's Church Yard, issued an edition of the above work as 'being the original and carefully corrected by the Author'.

145. The Court and Country Dances. Containing Mr. Isacks new Dances made for her Majesty's Birth-day, 1704. The Tunes by Mr. Paisible. To which is added, all that's new, both French and Country Dances, by several hands. As also the Quakers Comical Dance, the whole fairly engraven, price 1s.

Printed for and sold by J. Walsh . . . and J. Hare . . . at the Golden Viol . . . and . . . in Freeman's Yard &c.

Feb. 22–4, 1704, *Post Man.*

The same work was advertised in a different form Feb. 24–6, 1704, *Post Man*: 'There is lately published The Court and Country Dances the original and best Edition engraven, containing Mr Isacks new Dances made for her Majesty's Birth-day, 1704. The Tunes by Mr Paisible. To which is added, all that's new, both French and Country Dances, by several hands price 4d, or a Book gratis to any that buys the value of half a Crown of any other Musick.'

From this notice it appears that the second part of the work was a separate supplement.

146. Mr Barretts Musick in the Play call'd Mary Queen of Scotts.

[J. Walsh and J. Hare. *c.* 1704.]

In four parts.

BM. d. 24. (18.) Imperfect.
RCM. XXIX. A. 11. (29.); XXIX. A. 12. (22.) Imperfect.
Presumably included in *Harmonia Anglicana* (Sixth collection, No. IV; BM. b. 29. a.), no complete copy of which is available for examination.
See Nos. 48, 75, 90, 106, and 121.

147. Mr Lentons Musick in the Play call'd Liberty Asserted.

[J. Walsh and J. Hare. *c.* 1704.]

In four parts.

BM. d. 24. (19.) Imperfect.
RCM. XXIX. A. 11. (30.)
Presumably included in *Harmonia Anglicana* (Sixth collection, No. V), no complete copy of which is available for examination.
See Nos. 48, 75, 90, 106, and 121.

148. Aires for a Flute and a Bass As Preludes, Almands, Sarabands, Corants, Minuets, and Jiggs, made Purposely for a Flute and a Bass by M^r. Daniel Demoivre ye 2^d Collection Musick for Flutes lately Publish'd, M^r. Crofts 6 Sonatas . . . M^r. Topham's Solos for a Flute and a Bass. [Nine works listed.]

London Printed for I. Walsh . . . and I. Hare at the Golden Viol . . . and . . . in Freemans yard, &c.

March 2–4, 1704, *Post Man.* (Mr. Daniel Demoivrs new Airs . . . pr. 2s.)

BM. b. 1. Flute part only.
May be one of the works in Walsh Cat., *c.* 1721, Ill. 28, as: 'Demoivers 2^d. Aires, for a Single Flute. 1s. 6d.', and 'Demoivers Aires, for a Flute & a Bass. 2s. 0d.'

Walsh Cat., 'Apollo's Feast', third book, *c.* 1729 (W^m. C. Smith copy), as: 'Demoivers Solos for a Flute and a Bass. Opera Seconda.'
  See Nos. 53 and 473.

149. That Excellent Sonata in F. for Violins in 3 Parts call'd the Golden Sonata Compos'd by M^r. Henry Purcell Also M^r. Nicola's [i.e. Nicola Matteis] Favourite Solo in A♯ Publish'd for Feb^r. price 1^s–6^d to be Continu'd Monthly with the Best and Choisest Sonatas and Solos by the Greatest Masters in Europe for the Year 1704.
  [J. Walsh and J. Hare.]
  March 2–4, 1704, *Post Man.* (That Excellent piece of Musick, call'd the Golden Sonata . . . perform'd by Mr. Banister and Mr. Dean.)
    BM. g. 25. a. Imperfect.
    Durham Cathedral Library.
    The title occurs only on the Basso Continuo part, and the BM. copy contains only the Purcell Sonata, the plates of which were afterwards used for the work in *Harmonia Mundi.* (No. 257.)
    See Nos. 143 and 224.

150. A Sonata for two Violins and a thorow Bass with a Trumpet part by Arcangelo Corelli, as also a new Solo for a Violin and a Bass by Martino Beity [i.e. Bitti], neither of them before printed, price of both 1s. 6d. Publish'd for April, with the best and choicest Sonata's for April, to be continued monthly with the best and choicest Sonata's and Solo's, collected from the works of the greatest Masters in Europe, for the Year 1704.
  Printed for and sold by J. Walsh . . . and J. Hare . . . at the Golden Viol . . . and . . . in Freeman's Yard, &c.
  April 27–9, 1704, *Post Man.* (Next week will be publish'd.)
    A copy of the second of the works advertised is in Durham Cathedral Library, with the following title:
    A Solo in A♯ for a Violin by Sig^r. Martino Betti The Solo Proper for the Harpsicord or Spinnet.
    See Nos. 143 and 224.

150*a.* Sonata in D ♯ for Violins in 3 Parts by Christophoro Pez As also a Solo for a Violin by Sign^r Pepusch neither of them before Printed Publish'd for June price 1–6 to be Continu'd Monthly with the Best and Choisest Sonatas and Solos by the Greatest Masters in Europe for the Year 1704.
  [J. Walsh and J. Hare.]
    Durham Cathedral Library.
    Part of the periodical described under No. 143; included later in No. 224.

150*b.* A Solo in A♯ for a Violin by Arcangelo Corelli. The Solo Proper for the Harpsicord or Spinnet.
  [J. Walsh and J. Hare. 1704 or later.]

Durham Cathedral Library.
Part of the periodical described under No. 143; included later in No. 224.

150c. A Solo in G♭ for a Violin by Carlo Ambrogio The Solo Proper for the Harpsicord or Spinnet.
   [J. Walsh and J. Hare. 1704 or later.]
     Durham Cathedral Library.
     Part of the periodical described under No. 143; included later in No. 224.

From the summer of 1704 Walsh's address was frequently given as the 'Golden Harp and Hautboy in Katherine Street' in place of 'Golden Harp and Hoboy in Catherine Street', but both of these forms and 'Catharine Street' were used during the period of the bibliography.

---

151. The Ladies Banquet, being a choice Collection of the newest and most Airy Lessons for the Harpsicord or Spinnet, very usefull for all Practitioners and others that are Lovers of these Instruments. The Lessons are Composed by Mr Jer. Clark, Mr Courtivil, Mr Barret and Mr Croft, to be continu'd annually.
   Printed for and sold by J. Walsh . . . at the Golden Harp and Hautboy . . . and J. Hare . . . at the Golden Violin . . . and . . . in Freemans Yard, &c.
   Aug. 1–3, 1704, *Post Man.*
     See Nos. 187 and 593.
     A new series of six books was issued 1730–5, the first two of which were entirely different works from Nos. 151 and 187 in this bibliography.

152. Mʳ Lentons Musick in the Play [by Joseph Trapp] call'd Abra Mule.
   [J. Walsh and J. Hare.]
   In four parts.
   Sept. 5–7, 1704, *Post Man.*
     RCM. XXIX. A. 11. (31.); XXIX. A. 12. (24.) Imperfect.
     The advertisement states: 'There is now 38 sets of Tunes compleat in 4 parts Engraven, made for the Opera's, Tragedies and Comedies of the Theatres, and sold at 1s. 6d. per set. Printed for J. Walsh . . . at the Golden Harp and Hautboy . . . and J. Hare . . . at the Golden Violin . . . and . . . in Freemans Yard,' &c.
     Presumably included in *Harmonia Anglicana* (Sixth collection), complete contents of which have not been traced.
     See Nos. 48, 75, 90, 106, and 121.

153. A Sanato Concerta Gross [*sic*] in 5 or 6 parts for Violins, Compos'd by Signior Caldara; also a Solo for a Flute and a Bass by Mr. Wm. Williams. Publish'd for August, pr. 1s. 6d. to be continued Monthly, &c.
   Printed for J. Walsh . . . at the Golden Harp and Hautboy . . . and J. Hare . . . at the Golden Violin . . . and . . . in Freemans Yard, &c.
   Sept 26–8, 1704, *Post Man.*
     See No. 143.

154. Mr Paisibles Musick Perform'd before her Majesty and the new King of Spain. [J. Walsh and J. Hare.]

In four parts.

Oct. 17–19, 1704, *Post Man.*

> RCM. XXIX. A. 11. (32.)
> Presumably included in an unidentified collection of *Harmonia Anglicana.*
> *See* Nos. 48, 75, 90, 106, and 121.

155. A Sonata in 3 parts for Violins, with a Viol by Arcangelo Corelli, as also a Solo for a Flute, and a Bass, by Mr. Courtivil Publish'd for September, price 1s. 6d.

Printed for J. Walsh . . . at the Golden Harp and Hautboy . . . and J. Hare . . . at the Golden Violin . . . and . . . in Freemans Yard, &c.

Oct. 17–19, 1704, *Post Man.*

> *See* No. 143.

156. A Collection of Songs for One Two and Three Voices Together with such Symphonys for Violins or Flutes As were by the Author design'd for any of Them; and a Thorough-Bass to Each Song Figur'd for an Organ Harpsicord or Theorbo-Lute. Compos'd by M^r. Iohn Eccles, Master of Her Majesty's Musick.

London Printed for I. Walsh Servt. to Her Matie. at the Harp and Hoboy in Katherine Street near Somerset House in ye Strand.

Oct. 26–8, 1704, *Post Man.* (On Thursday last.)

Nov. 11–14, 1704, *Post Man.* (Price bound 18s.)

> BM. G. 300.
> RCM. II. A. 13.
> With an outer illustrated title-page, Berchet Inventor, H. Hulsbergh Sculpsit:
> M^r. In^o. Eccles General Collection of Songs.
> London Printed for I. Walsh Servt. to Her Matie. at the Harp and Hoboy in Katherine Street near Somerset House in the Strand. (*See* Ill. 13.)
> This illustrated title-page was afterwards adapted for Walsh's great collection of Handel's Songs, *Apollo's Feast.* [1726, &c.]
> The Eccles collection of Songs was issued by subscription (*see* No. 138) and some of the numbers were from plates used for earlier separate issues, and some were subsequently issued separately, printed on one side of the paper only. (BM. G. 311. (66.), &c.; RCM. II. A. 13. a.)
> *See* No. 36.

157. The Instrumental Musick for October, a Sonata for Violins in 3 parts, with a Thorow Bass for the Harpsicord, compos'd by Mr. Pepusch, likewise a Solo for a Violin or Flute by Signior Pez, price of both 1s. 6d. which will be continued monthly &c.

Printed for J. Walsh . . . at the Golden Harp and Hautboy . . . and J. Hare . . . at the Golden Violin . . . and . . . in Freemans Yard, &c.

Nov. 11–14, 1704, *Post Man.*

> The items may have been included in *Harmonia Mundi.* (No. 257.)
> *See* No. 143.

158. Nolens Volens, the Third Book for the Violin, being an Introduction for the Instructing of young Practitioners on that delightful Instrument, digested in a more plain and easy Method than any yet extant, together with a choice Collection of Italian and English Airs, by the best Masters. As also a Flourish or Prelude in every Key for the Violin, by Seignior Gasperini [i.e. Gasparo Visconti]. The whole fairly engraven.

Printed for J. Walsh . . . at the Golden Harp and Hautboy . . . and J. Hare at the Golden Viol . . . and . . . in Freeman's Yard . . . and J. Miller at the Golden Violin on London Bridge. Price 2s. 6d.

Nov. 21–3, 1704, *Post Man.*

See Nos. 72, 306, 424, 442, 472, and 487 for other books. No details of the first book have been traced.

159. The Instrumental Musick for Novemb. A Sonata for Violins in parts, by Signior Albinoni, of the choicest of his Works; also a Solo for a Violin and a Bass by Mr. Tho. Dean of the New Theatre, never before printed; the Solo proper for the Harpsicord or Spinnet. Pr. of both 1s. 6d.

Printed for J. Walsh . . . at the Golden Harp and Hautboy . . . and J. Hare, at the Golden Viol . . . and . . . in Freeman's yard, &c.

Dec. 14–16, 1704, *Post Man.*

The Albinoni item was probably Sonata, Op. 1, No. 12, afterwards included in *Harmonia Mundi* (No. 257) from the same plates.

A copy of the second of the works advertised is in Durham Cathedral Library, with the following title:

A Solo in A♯ for a Violin and a Bass by Mr Tho Dean of the New Theatre the Solo Proper for the Harpsicord or Spinnett.

See No. 143.

160. The Whole Volume Compleat Intituled The Monthly Masks of Vocal Musick Containing all the Choisest Songs by the Best Masters made for the Play-houses Publick Consorts and other Occasions for the Year 1704 [i.e. Nov. 1703–Oct. 1704] with a Through Bass to Each Song and most of them with in the Composs of the Flute price 5s.

London Printed for & Sould by I: Walsh Musicall Instrument maker in Ordinary to her Majesty &c.

Dec. 14–16, 1704, *Post Man.* (The whole Volume of Monthly Collections . . . J. Walsh . . . J. Hare.)

BM. K. 7. e. 4.

RCM. II. A. 15.

The title-page from the Collins plate (No. 15, *see* Ill. 3) as used for the annual volumes for 1703 (No. 140) and other years, with 'price 5s.' after the word Flute, the price having been erased from the BM. and RCM. copies.

The work contains the following dedication: To the most noble Wriothesly Duke of Bedford; Marquess of Tavistock; Earl of Bedford; Lord Russell; Baron Russell; of Thornhaugh; Baron Howland of Streatham; Lord Lieutenant and Custos Rotulorum of the County of Middlesex, and the City and Liberty of Westminster; Lord Lieutenant of Bedford-shire; and Cambridge-shire; And One of the Knights of the Most Noble Order of the Garter, May it please your Grace,

Musick has always been reckon'd to have as fair Pretensions to the Acquaintance of Great Men, as Poetry can boast; and like that too, is liable to the Insolencies of the Stupid, and Inharmonious Part of Mankind, This Volume there fore is Ambitious to come abroad under the Shelter of Your Grace's Protection, The Delicacy of Your Grace's Tast and Knowledge in Performances of this Nature, forbids my Saying any thing of the Excellency of this Collection; and Your Grace's Name being prefix'd to it makes it needless I shou'd give it any other Recommendation to the World, I only intreat the Liberty to profess my self with the utmost Deference,

> Your Grace's
> Most Humble, and
> Most Obedient Servant,
> Iohn Walsh.

The BM. copy, wanting the August title-page, is a finely bound volume from Woburn Abbey, and contains the bookplate of 'The most Noble John Duke of Bedford 1736'. With the exception of that for May, the monthly title-pages, which are all different, are by H. Hulsbergh.

See Nos. 103, 109, 140, 188, 223, 258, 282a, 331, 370, and 517.

161. [The Biter. Comedy by Nicholas Rowe. Music by J. Eccles. 1704.]

Some numbers from this work were included in *The Monthly Mask of Vocal Music*, Dec. 1704, Jan. and Oct. 1705, Walsh and Hare (BM. H. 313. a; *see* No. 188), and were also issued separately (BM. G. 307. (8.)), but no advertisement of the work as a whole has been traced. *The Monthly Mask of Vocal Music* for Dec. 1704 was advertised as: 'Containing the new Songs and Dialogue in the Comedy call'd the Biter. Compos'd by Mr. John Eccles.' (Dec. 21–3, 1704, *Post Man*.)

162. A Choice Collection of Lessons for the Harpsicord, Spinnet. &c. Containing four Setts, As Grounds, Almands, Corants, Sarabands, Minuets, & Jiggs, By Dᵣ. Iohn Blow.

London Printed for I. Walsh Servᵗ. to Her Maᵗⁱᵉ. at the Harp and Hoboy in Katherine Street near Somerset House in yᵉ Strand and I. Hare at the Golden Viol in Sᵗ. Pauls Church yard, and at his Shop in Freemans yard near yᵉ Royall Exchange.

[*c.* 1704.]

RCM. I. F. 50. (2.) With '1704' in MS.

Walsh Cat. *c.* 1721, Ill. 27, as: 'Dᵣ Blows Lessons, for yᵉ Harpsicord, Spinnet, or Organ. 1s. 6d.'

Henry Playford advertised, July 28–30, 1698, *Post-Boy*, 'A Choice Collection of Lessons for the Harpsicord . . . By John Blow.'

See Nos. 499 and 501.

163. A Collection of Minuets and Rigadoons several of them foreign, perform'd at most of the Princes Courts in Europe with a Bast [*sic*] to each of them, being all fit for Dancing, and very proper for Balls and dancing Schools, pr. 1s.

Printed for J. Walsh . . . at the Golden Harp and Hautboy . . . and J. Hare, at the Golden Viol . . . and . . . in Freeman's Yard, &c.

Jan. 4–6, 1705, *Post Man.*

164. A Collection of the most celebrated Jigs, Lancashire Horn-pipes, Scotch and Highland Lilts, Northern Frisks, and Cheshire Rounds. Together with several excellent new Stage Dances by Mr. Duruel, Mr. Cherier, Mr. Cotine and others, being all High Dances, fitted to the Humours of most Countries and People.

Printed for J. Walsh . . . at the Golden Harp and Hautboy . . . and J. Hare, at the Golden Viol . . . and . . . in Freeman's Yard, &c.

Jan. 4–6, 1705, *Post Man.* (Next week will be publish'd.)

Feb. 8–10, 1705, *Post Man.* (This day is publish'd A Collection of the most Celebrated Jiggs . . . Together with . . . Stage Dances by Mr. Du Ruel, Mr. Cherier, Mr. Firbank, &c.)

Walsh Cat. *c.* 1721, Ill. 27, as: 'Jiggs & Hornpipes 1st book, for a single Violin. 1s. 6d.'
The same catalogue includes: 'Jiggs & Hornpipes 2d book, for a single Violin. 1s. 6d.', of which no further details have been traced.

165. The Instrumental Musick for December, 2 Sonata's for Violins in parts by Signior Caldara and Signior Gabrielli, the choicest of their Works, also a Solo for a Violin and a Bass by Signior Torelli, the Solo proper for the Harpsicord or Spinnet. Price together 1s. 6d.

Printed for J. Walsh . . . at the Golden Harp and Hautboy . . . and J. Hare, at the Golden Viol . . . and . . . in Freeman's Yard, &c.

Jan. 13–16, 1705, *Post Man.*

A copy in Durham Cathedral Library has the following title:
Two Sonatas for Violins in Parts one by Sign^r Caldara and the other by Sign^r Gabrielli of the Choisest of their Works also a Solo for a Violin and Bass by Sign^r Torelli the Solo Pro/per for the Harpsicord or Spi/nnett Price 1^s–6^d 1704.
See Nos. 143 and 224.

166. Select Preludes & Vollentarys for the Violin being Made and Contrived for the Improvement of the Hand with Variety of Compositions by all the Greatest Masters in Europe for that Instrument.

London Printed for I. Walsh . . . at the Harp and Hoboy . . . and I. Hare at the Golden Viol . . . and . . . in Freemans yard, &c.

Jan. 20–3, 1705, *Post Man.*

NLS. (Glen collection.)
With an outer illustrated title-page (*see* Ill. 14):
Select Preludes or Volentarys for ye Violin by the most eminent Masters in Europe. printed for I. Walsh and I. Hare.
With a banner on the trumpet in the design bearing the words: 'Flourish in the Key.'
The work was advertised in the *Post Man* as:
'A Collection of select Preludes or Volentaries for the Violin being made and contrived

for the Improvement of the Hand, with variety of Compositions by the most eminent Masters in Europe for that Instrument, price 2s. 6d.

> Printed for J. Walsh . . . at the Golden Harp and Hautboy . . . and J. Hare, at the Golden Viol . . . and . . . in Freeman's Yard,' &c.

> Walsh Cat. *c.* 1721, Ill. 27, as: 'Select Preludes by all Mast^rs, for a single Violin. 2s.6d.'

> Walsh afterwards adapted the plate of the illustrated title-page for *Hasse's Comic Tunes, &c.* [1741–7] by substituting 'Handel's Works' on the banner in place of 'Flourish in the Key'. (BM. a. 149.)

> *See* No. 186; and No. 283, a similar work for the Flute.

167. The First Part of the Division Violin Containing A Collection of Divisions upon Several Excellent Grounds for the Violin The Sixth Edition Corected and enlarged with Aditions of the newest Divisions upon Grounds and Chacons by the most Eminent Masters.

> London Printed for I. Walsh Sev^t to her Matie. . . . and I Hare at ye Golden Viol . . . and . . . in Fremans yard . . . price 2^s. 6^d.

> Jan. 20–3, 1705, *Post Man.* (Reprinted and publish'd.)

> RCM. I. F. 9. (1.)

> Walsh Cat. *c.* 1721, Ill. 27, as: 'Grounds & Divisions 1st B^k, for a single Violin. 2s. 6d.'

> Earlier editions were published by John and Henry Playford.

> *See* Nos. 174 and 185.

168. Twenty four new Country Dances, with Directions to each Dance, most of the Tunes within the Compass of the Flute. The whole engraven in a fine Character price 6d.

> Printed for J. Walsh . . . at the Golden Harp and Hautboy . . . and J. Hare at the Golden Viol . . . and . . . in Freeman's Yard, &c.

> Jan. 30–Feb. 1, 1705, *Post Man.*

169. Mr Lentons Musick in the Comedy [by Susannah Centlivre] call'd ye Gamester.

> [J. Walsh and J. Hare.]

> In four parts.

> Jan. 30–Feb. 1, 1705, *Post Man.*

> BM. g. 15. (1.)

> With this work Walsh commenced to publish sets of theatre music in folio size, not oblong folio as *Harmonia Anglicana,* &c. They appear to have belonged to an unidentified series as some of them have serial numbers. *See* Nos. 229, 261, 277b, 285a, and 312.

170. The Marlborough, Mr. Isaack's new Dance, set by Mr. Paisible, danc'd at Court on her Majesty's Birth-day, 1705. To which is added several new Minuets, Rigadoons and Jiggs by Mr. Lafayer, Mr. Lane and others, danc'd at Schools and publick Entertainments, pr. 6d.

> Printed for J. Walsh . . . at the Golden Harp and Hautboy . . . and J. Hare at the Golden Viol . . . and . . . in Freeman's Yard, &c.

> Feb. 10–13, 1705, *Post Man.*

> *See* No. 375.

171. Musick in the Comedy [by Colley Cibber] call'd She Wou'd if She Cou'd Composed by a Person of Quallity.
  [J. Walsh and J. Hare.]
  In four parts.
  Mar. 17–20, 1705. *Post Man.*

> BM. d. 24. (20.) Imperfect.
> The composer was probably William Byron, Fourth Baron Byron. (*See* No. 80.)
> Presumably included in an unidentified collection of *Harmonia Anglicana.*
> *See* Nos. 48, 75, 90, 106, and 121.

172. The Instrumental Musick for January, February and March, 6 new Sonatas for two Flutes and a Bass, consisting of Preludes, Allemands, Corants, Sarabands and Jiggs Compos'd by Mr. William Corbet.
  Printed for and sold by J. Walsh . . . at the Golden Harp and Hautboy . . . and J. Hare at the Golden Viol . . . and . . . in Freeman's Yard, &c.
  Apr. 3–5, 1705, *Post Man.*
  Apr. 14–17, *Post Man.* (Mr. Corbets new Airs . . . pr. 4s.)

> Walsh Cat. *c.* 1721, Ill. 28, as: 'Corbets Sonatas, for 2 Flutes & a Bass. 4s. od.'
> *See* Nos. 143 and 244.

173. 6 Sonatas, 3 for two Flutes and 3 for two Flutes and a Bass. Compos'd by several Eminent Masters price 2s. 6d.
  Printed for and sold by J. Walsh . . . and J. Hare, at the Golden Viol . . . and . . . in Freeman's Yard, &c.
  Apr. 3–5, 1705, *Post Man.*

174. The Second Part of the Division Violin Containing the newest Divisions upon Grounds for the Violin as also seueral solos by Arcangello Corelli and others the Fourth Edition Corected and enlarged with Additions of the newest Chacons Allmands Preludes and Choice Cibells Composd by the best Masters The whole Fairly Engraven.
  London Printed for I Waish Serv[t]. to her Mai[tie]. . . . and I Hare at y[e]. Golden Viol . . . & . . . in Freemans yard . . . price 2[s]. 6[d].
  Apr. 14–17, 1705, *Post Man.*

> RCM. I. F. 9. (2.)
> Walsh Cat. *c.* 1721, Ill. 27, as: 'Grounds & Divisions 2[d] B[k], for a single Violin. 2s. 6d.'
> Earlier editions were published by John and Henry Playford.
> *See* Nos. 167 and 185.

175. Mr. Barret's new Musick, in 4 parts, perform'd in the Comedy [by Sir Richard Steele] call'd the Tender Husband, or the accomplish'd Fools, price 1s. 6d. the Set.
  Printed for and sold by J. Walsh . . . at the Golden Harp and Hautboy . . . and J. Hare, at the Golden Viol . . . and . . . in Freeman's Yard, &c.
  May 5–8, 1705, *Post Man.*

176. Dr. Blow's Psalms for the Organ or Harpsicord. The 2d. Edition. To which is added several Psalms which were omitted in the 1st, pr. 1s.

Printed for and sold by J. Walsh . . . at the Golden Harp and Hautboy . . . and J. Hare, at the Golden Viol . . . and . . . in Freeman's Yard, &c.

May 5–8, 1705, *Post Man.*

> Included later in Walsh's numerical series with 'No. 184' added to the plate of p. 1.
> See Nos. 130 and 537.

177. Mr. Fingers 12 Sonata's in 4 parts, for Violins, Opera Prima, price 7s engraven.

Printed for and sold by J. Walsh . . . at the Golden Harp and Hautboy . . . and J. Hare, at the Golden Viol . . . and . . . in Freeman's Yard, &c.

May 17–19, 1705, *Post Man.* (Reprinted and published.)

> Presumably another edition of *Sonatæ XII. pro Diversis Instrumentis* . . . *Opus Primum,* published in London in 1688, without publisher's name. (BM. K. I. i. 15.) No edition by Walsh earlier than 1705 can be traced. Walsh Cat., *c.* 1721, Ill. 27, as: 'Fingers 12 Sonatas, for 2 Violins & a Bass. 6s. 0d.'

178. Bononcini's Aires for two Flutes and a Bass or two Flutes with out a Bass the Aires Consisting of Allemands Sarabands Corants Preludes Gavots and Jiggs with a Through Bass for the Harpsicord or Bass Violin Fairly Engraven.

London Printed for I. Walsh . . . and I. Hare at the Golden Viol . . . and . . . in Freemans-yard, &c.

June 14–16, 1705, *Post Man.*

> BM. d. 150. (1.)
> Advertised as: 'The Instrumental Musick for April, May and June, being 6 Sets of Airs or Italian Arietta's for 2 Flutes and a Bass by Signior Bononcini. Price 3s.' (See No. 143.)
> An earlier edition for 2 Violins and a Bass was issued in Oct. 1701 (No. 63) with the same contents in a different order. The work was probably by G. M. Bononcini, but generally attributed to his son Giovanni Battista.

179. Select Lessons for the Harpsicord or Spinnett as Allemands Sarabands Corants Gavots Minuets and Jiggs Compos'd by M^r. Dieupart Plac'd on five lines in ye English Cliff Engraven in a fair Caracter.

London Printed for I. Walsh . . . and I. Hare at the Golden Viol . . . and . . . in Freemans-yard, &c.

June 16–19, 1705, *Post Man.*

> BM. e. 5. i. (1.)
> Roger of Amsterdam issued a work, advertised in London by Francis Vaillant, Nov. 1701, as: 'Six Suittes de Clavessin . . . Composees & mis en Concert par Mr. Dieupart'; and as: 'Suits of Lessons for the Harpsicord', &c.; again in March 1702 as: 'Mr. Dieupart's Book of Lessons, for the Harpsichord made in Consorts.'
> Walsh and Hare's edition may have been taken from Roger's work. Walsh Cat. *c.* 1721, Ill. 27, as: 'Dupars Lessons, for ye Harpsicord, Spinnet or Organ. 2s. 6d.'

180. Mr D. Purcell's Musick in the Comedy [by Richard Brome] call'd the Northern Lass.

[J. Walsh and J. Hare.]
In four parts.
Sept. 15–18, 1705, *Post Man.*

> BM. d. 24. (21.) Imperfect.
> Presumably included in an unidentified collection of *Harmonia Anglicana.*
> *See* Nos. 48, 75, 90, 106, and 121.

181. To all Lovers of Musick. There is now printed and published, a new Edition of the Works of Signior Arcangelo Correlli, viz 1st, 2d, 3d and 4th Operas, with an Addition of a Bass doubly printed to the 2d and 4th Operas, which never was to any former Edition, the whole engraven from an exact Score, and printed on Royal Paper with the Author's Effigies from a Copper Plate, each Opera carefully corrected by the Ingenious Signior Nicolini Haiam, who is very well acquainted with the Author and his Works. This Edition for its beautiful Character and Exactness excels any other Musick that hath been hitherto printed, and to shew that no Country shall outdo us in either perfection or price, they will be sold at very reasonable rates for the encouragement of Performers in Musick, and each Opera may be had single or in one Volume.

Printed for J. Walsh, Servant to her Majesty at the Golden Harp and Hautboy in Katherine street . . . and J. Hare, at the Golden Viol . . . and . . . in Freeman's yard &c.

Sept. 22–5, 1705, *Post Man.*

> This advertisement of an edition by Walsh, copies of which it is difficult to identify, was apparently rushed out in order to forestall the Amsterdam edition by Roger, as the following notice suggests:

To all Lovers of Musick. Whereas in the last Post-Man there was an Advertisement publish'd by Mr. John Walsh, that I Nicolini Haym, have corrected his Edition of Correlli's Works: I do herby give notice for my own credit, that I did not correct the same directly nor indirectly. I do acknowledge to have revis'd and corrected the Amsterdam Edition by Stephen Roger, which will be speedily published, and will excel in Beauty and Exactnes any Edition of Correlli's Works hitherto printed,

Nicolini Haym.

Sept. 25–7, 1705, *Post Man.*

> To this Walsh replied:

Whereas by an advertisement in the Post-Man of the 27th of September, 1705, it is pretended that the Works of Arcangelo Corelli, now printed by John Walsh, were not corrected by Seignior Nicolini Haym directly or indirectly, the said Advertisement being signed by Nicolini Haym, and publish'd by Mr. Vaillant, a French Bookseller, in favour of a Dutch Edition, which by this desingenious means he would impose upon the World to obstruct the Sale of mine and as far

I

as he can to lessen my Reputation: In answer to which for my own credit and for a clear Proof of the Baseness and Falshood of the said Advertisement is now attested by two Witnesses upon Affidavit before Mr. S. Keck, Master in Chancery; the one asserts that the abovesaid Edition of Corelli's Works, printed by J. Walsh were 3 months under the said Nicolini Haym's Correction, and were at times seen by him and the other Deponent correcting them; and when the said Nicolini Haym returned the Proofs of the several Operas owned them Correct, which appears more at large by the said Affidavits, which are to be seen at my Shop by all Gentlemen that desire to know the Truth thereof.

John Walsh.

For a further satisfaction to the World of the Exactness of Mr. Walsh's Edition of Corelli's Works, I do also declare to have corrected each Opera of the said Edition, who am well acquainted with the Author and his Works. having been 5 years Corelli's Scholar and that on a Review of the said Edition, I do declare them to be as Correct and Beautiful as any Musick I have yet seen Printed,

Gasparini.

Sept. 29–Oct. 2, 1705, *Post Man*; Oct. 1, 1705, *Daily Courant.*

Roger's edition was advertised by Francis Vaillant (Oct. 16–18, 1705, *Post Man*) as follows:

There is daily expected from Holland the curious Edition of Corelli's Works, viz, 1st, 2d, 3d and 4th Opera's with an Addition of a Bass doubly printed to the 2d and 4th Opera's, and both Basses figured, which is not in any former Edition. The whole engraven on Copper from an Italian Score, printed on the best Imperial Paper by Stephen Roger, the like never seen in England before, and carefully corrected by Mr. Haym. This Edition doth excell in Beauty and Exactness all the former Editions of Corelli's Works hitherto printed. Price 30s, and for encouragement, Subscriptions will be taken at 24s, till the last day of the month, Subscribers paying 10s down, and the rest on the delivery of the Books, a 7th Book gratis to those that subscribe for 6, which reduces the price to 20s. 6d. The said Books are to be seen at Francis Vaillant's near Catherine street in the Strand, where Subscriptions are taken in, and at John Cullen's at the Buck between the 2 Temple Gates in Fleet-Street.

I acknowledge to have carefully examined this Edition of Corelli's Works and have corrected a multitude of Faults that are in all the former Editions hitherto printed, having had the same above 2 years by me to correct it at leisure.

Nicolini Haym.

A copy of Roger's edition is at BM. g. 39. a. On Oct. 16, 1708 (*Daily Courant*) Isaac Vaillant, Bookseller at the Bishops-head in the Strand, advertised 'The last Edition of Corelli's Works, Corrected by Mr. Haym and Revis'd by the Author, Engraven at Amsterdam by Stephen Roger, and printed on Royal Paper, Price 20s.'. This may refer to the earlier Roger edition or to a later issue.

The titles which follow of the four Corelli works advertised by Walsh and Hare, Sept.

22–5, 1705, are assumed to be as transcribed here from copies at the BM., some of which are later issues. The identification and dating of copies is difficult, but those having 'her (or 'Her') Matie.' in the imprint are *c.* 1705–14 and 'his (or 'His') Matie.' 1714 or after. Editions after 1720 are not dealt with in this bibliography.

Of the RCM. copies, LVIII. E. 15. is partly from the first editions (No. 181) and partly from the later editions (No. 477); LVIII. E. 14. is later still, and bears the numbers 364–7 of Walsh's numerical series.

Arcangelo Corelli Opera Prima XII Sonatas of three parts for two Violins and a Bass with A Through Bass for ye Organ Harpsicord or Arch Lute Engrav'd from ye Score and Carefully Corected by ye best Italian Masters   Note, there are five Operas of this Author's Engrav'd, (wch. may be had Single or in one Volume) being all that are as yet Publish'd.

London Printed for I. Walsh Servt. to her Matie. at ye Harp & Hoboy in Katherine Street near Somerset House in ye Str^and and I. Hare at the Golden Viol in St Pauls Church yard and at his Shop in Freemans yard near ye Roy^l: Exchange.

> BM. g. 45. (1.)
> Violino Primo has portrait frontispiece: 'H. Howard pinx. W. Sherwin Sculp^t.' (*See* Ill. 15.) The earliest Roger edition has no portrait according to the BM. copy (g. 39. a.), but a later edition, by Roger and Le Cene, *c.* 1730, has a portrait by an unnamed artist, engraved by I. Folkema. (BM. g. 39. c.) Later Walsh editions of Corelli works contain a portrait engraved by Van der Gucht after Howard (BM. g. 45. c. (1.); g. 39. b. (1.)), and editions by Benjamin Cooke and John Johnson have a portrait engraved by I. Cole, similar to that by Folkema.
> Included later in Walsh's numerical series with 'his' in place of 'her' Matie, Hare deleted from the imprint, and 'N°. 364' added to the title-page.
> *See* Nos. 400, 477, and 596.

Arcangelo Corelli Opera Secunda XII Sonatas of three parts for two Violins and a Bass with A Through Bass for y^e. Organ Harpsicord or Arch Lute Engrav'd from ye Score and Carefully Corected by y^e. best Italian Masters Note. there are five Operas of this Author Engrav'd wch. may be had Single or in one Volume being all that are as yet Publishd.

London Printed for I Walsh Servt. to her Matie. at ye Harp & Hoboy in Katherine Street near Somerset House in ye Str^and.

> BM. g. 45. (2.); g. 45. k. (3.) Violone o Cimbalo part only.
> Included later in Walsh's numerical series, with 'his' in place of 'her' Matie. and 'N°. 365' added to the title-page.
> *See* Nos. 129, 400, 477, and 596.

Arcangelo Corelli Opera Terza XII Sonatas of three parts for two Violins and a Bass with A Through Bass for ye Organ Harpsicord or Arch Lute Engrav'd from ye Score and Carefully Corected by ye best Italian Masters Note, there are five Operas of this Author's Engrav'd, (w^ch: may be had Single, or in one Volume) being all that are as yet Publishd.

London Printed for I Walsh Servt. to Her Matie. at the Harp and Hoboy in Katherine Street near Somerset House in ye Strand.

> BM. g. 45. k. (4.) Violoncello part only.
> Included later in Walsh's numerical series, with 'His' in place of 'Her' Matie. and 'N°. 366' added to the title-page.
> *See* Nos. 400, 477, and 596.

Arcangelo Corelli Opera Quarta XII Sonatas of three parts for two Violins and a Bass with A Through Bass for y^e. Organ Harpsicord or Arch Lute Engrav'd from ye Score and Carefully Corected by ye best Italian Masters Note there are five Operas of this Author Engrav'd wch. may be had Single or in one Volume being all that are as yet Publish'd.

London Printed for I Walsh Servt. to her Matie. at y^e. Harp & Hoboy in Katherine Street near Somerset House in ye Str^{and}.

> BM. g. 45. (4.); g. 45. k. (6.) Violone o Cimbalo part only.
> Included later in Walsh's numerical series, with 'his' in place of 'her' Matie. and 'N°. 367' added to the title-page.
> *See* Nos. 76, 400, 477, and 596.
> For complete list of Corelli items consult index.

182. The Fifth Book of the New Flute Master Containing The most Perfect Rules and Easiest Directions for Learners on the Flute yet Extant, together wth an Extraordinary Collection of Aires both Italian and English Perticularly the most celibrated Arietts in the New Opera of Arsinoe Queen of Cyprus, and severall other Excellent Tunes never before Printed. To which is added a Scale shewing how to transpose any Tune to the Flute that is made for the Violin or Voice, the whole fairly Engraven. Price. 1^s. 6^d: 1706.

London Printed for I Walsh . . . at the Harp and Hoboy . . . and I. Hare at the Golden Viol . . . and . . . in Freemans yard, &c.

Oct. 18–20, 1705, *Post Man.*

> BM. a. 242.
> *See* Nos. 20b, 33, 113, 305, 39^c, 486, 510, 563, and 578 for other books and works with similar titles. No details of the third, sixth, and eighth books of the early series finishing with No. 486 have been traced.

183. An Overture and Airs for the Harpsicord, Composed by a Person of Quality, pr. 1s. 6d.

Printed for J. Walsh . . . at the Golden Harp and Hautboy . . . and J. Hare, at the Golden Viol . . . and . . . in Freeman's Yard, &c.

Oct. 18–20, 1705, *Post Man.*

> The composer was probably William Byron, Fourth Baron Byron, and the work that subsequently advertised as: 'Ld. Birons Lessons.' (No. 498.)
> *See* Nos. 80, 171, 211, 498, and 601.

184. The First Part of The Division Flute Containing a Collection of Divisions upon Several Excellent Grounds for the Flute being Very Improveing and Delight-

full to all Lovers of that Instrument The whole Fairly Engraven. price 2ˢ. 6ᵈ. 1706.

> London Printed for I. Walsh . . . at the Golden Harp and Hautboy . . . and I. Hare at the Golden Viol . . . and . . . in Freemans yard &c.
>
> Nov. 6–8, 1705, *Post Man.*

>> BM. h. 250. c. (1.)
>> Walsh Cat. *c.* 1721, Ill. 28, as: 'First Division Flute. 2s. 6d.'
>> *See* No. 278.

185. The 1st and 2d parts of the Division Violin, consisting of the most celebrated Grounds and Divisions for the Violin. These Editions are enlarged with Additions of the newest Grounds, Chacoons, Allemands, Preludes and choice Cibels, compos'd by the best Masters of the Age, pr. 2s. 6d each.

> Printed for J. Walsh . . . at the Golden Harp and Hautboy . . . and J. Hare, at the Golden Viol . . . and . . . in Freeman's Yard, &c.
>
> Nov. 6–8, 1705, *Post Man.*

>> Presumably a re-advertisement of Nos. 167 and 174.

186. A Collection of Preludes for the Violin by all the eminent Masters in Europe, pr. 2s. 6d.

> Printed for J. Walsh . . . at the Golden Harp and Hautboy . . . and J. Hare, at the Golden Viol . . . and . . . in Freeman's Yard, &c.
>
> Nov. 6–8, 1705, *Post Man.*

>> Presumably a re-advertisement of No. 166.

187. The Second Book of the Ladys Banquet being A Choice Collection of the Newest and most Airy Lessons for the Harpsicord or Spinnett together with the most Noted Minuets Jiggs and French Dances perform'd at Court the Theatre's and Publick Balls the whole fitted to yᵉ Harpsicord and Spinnett being a most delightfull Collection and proper for Schollers as well as yᵉ Best Performers— all Fairly Engraved. price 2ˢ. 6ᵈ. 1706.

> London Printed for I. Walsh . . . at the Harp and Hoboy . . . and I. Hare at the Golden Viol . . . and . . . in Freemans yard, &c.
>
> Nov. 20–2, 1705, *Post Man.*

>> BM. c. 60. a.
>> *See* Nos. 151 and 593.
>> A new series of six books was issued 1730–5, of which the first two were entirely different from Nos. 151 and 187 in this bibliography.

188. The Monthly Mask of vocal Musick . . . for . . . 1705, price 5s.

> Printed for J. Walsh . . . at the Golden Harp and Hautboy . . . and J. Hare at the Golden Viol . . . and . . . in Freeman's Yard, &c.
>
> Nov. 29–Dec. 1, 1705, *Post Man.*

BM. H. 313. a. Imperfect.
RCM. II. A. 15. Imperfect.
Presumably issued with the collective title-page from the Collins plate (No. 15, *see* Ill. 3) as used for 1703 (No. 140) and other years:
  The Whole Volume Compleat Intituled The Monthly Masks of Vocal Musick . . . for the Year 1705 [i.e. Nov. 1704–Oct. 1705], &c.
  See Nos. 103, 109, 140, 160, 223, 258, 282*a*, 331, 370, and 517.

189. The Musick in 4 parts perform'd in the Comedy [by Sir John Vanbrugh] called the Confederacy. Compos'd by Mr. J. Eccles, Master of her Majesty's Musick.
  Printed for J. Walsh . . . at the Golden Harp and Hautboy . . . and J. Hare, at the Golden Viol . . . and . . . in Freeman's Yard, &c.
  Dec. 20–2, 1705, *Post Man.*

190. Rules for playing a Thorough Bass. By the late Mr. G. Keller.
  Printed for J. Walsh . . . at the Golden Harp and Hautboy . . . and J. Hare, at the Golden Viol . . . and . . . in Freeman's Yard, &c.
  Dec. 20–2, 1705, *Post Man.*

  John Cullen's edition of Keller's 'A Compleat Method For Attaining to Play a Thorough Bass', &c. (Jan. 1707) has been generally considered to be the earliest edition of this work. (BM. K. 2. i. 22.)
  See Nos. 230, 235, 277*c*, and 511.

191. The Musick in 4 parts perform'd in the Comedy [by Thomas Baker] called Hamstead Heath. Composed by Mr. J. Barret.
  Printed for J. Walsh . . . at the Golden Harp and Hautboy . . . and J. Hare, at the Golden Viol . . . and . . . in Freeman's Yard, &c.
  Dec. 20–2, 1705, *Post Man.*

192. Twenty four new Country Dances for the Year 1706, with Directions to each dance, all fairly engraven and carefully corrected, pr. 6d.
  Printed for J. Walsh . . . at the Golden Harp and Hautboy . . . and J. Hare at the Golden Viol . . . and . . . in Freeman's Yard, &c.
  Jan. 15–17, 1706. *Post Man.*

193. The New Country Dancing Master, containing a choice Collection of the newest Country Dances performed at Court, the Theatre and publick Balls, with Directions to each Dance, the Tunes airy and pleasant for the Violin or Hautboy, most of them within compass of the Flute, all fairly engraven, pr. 1s. 6d.
  Printed for J. Walsh . . . at the Golden Harp and Hautboy . . . and J. Hare at the Golden Viol . . . and . . . in Freeman's Yard, &c.
  Jan. 15–17, 1706. *Post Man.*
  See Nos. 260, 333, 371, 394, 441, and 489.

194. Mr. D. Purcell's Musick in 4 parts, in the Comedy [by Susannah Centlivre] called the Basset Table. pr. 1s. 6d.

Printed for J. Walsh . . . at the Golden Harp and Hautboy . . . and J. Hare at the Golden Violin . . . and . . . in Freeman's Yard, &c.

Jan. 22–4, 1706, *Post Man.*

195. The Dancing Master: Or Directions for Dancing Country Dances, with the Tunes to each Dance, for the Treble Violin, The 13th Edition, containing above 360 of the choicest Old and New Tunes now used at Court, and other Publick Places. The whole Work Revis'd and done in the New Ty'd Note, and much more Correct than any former Edition. Most of them within the Compass of the Flute.

Printed for J. Walsh . . . at the Golden Harp and Hautboy . . . and J. Hare, at the Golden Viol . . . and . . . in Freemans Yard, &c.

Jan. 29–31, 1706, *Post Boy.*

No copy of this work with Walsh and Hare imprint has been traced. The earlier editions were by John and Henry Playford and the later ones by W. Pearson and John Young. The latter in conjunction with J. Cullen advertised (Jan. 10–12, 1706, *Post Man*): 'Newly published the 13th Edition of The Dancing Master, or Directions for Dancing Country Dances, with the Tunes to each Dance for the Treble Violin, containing above 360 of the choicest old and new Tunes. . . . Sold by John Young . . . and J. Cullen. . . . Price 3s. 6d.'

This appears to be a similar work in all respects to that advertised by Walsh and Hare, for whom Young and Cullen may have been acting as selling agents, or Walsh and Hare may have been acting for Young and Cullen. Both advertisements refer to a work printed from type.

196. The Britannia. Mr. Isack's new Dance performed before her Majesty on her Birth-day, 1706. The Tune by Mr. Paisible. To which is added all the new Minuets, Riggadoons and French Dances, danced at Balls and publick Entertainments, engraven, pr. 6d.

Printed for J. Walsh . . . at the Golden Harp and Hautboy . . . and J. Hare at the Golden Viol . . . and . . . in Freeman's Yard, &c.

Feb. 9–12, 1706, *Post Man.*

See Nos. 207, 374, and 406.

197. The French Dancing-Master is now published containing all the French Dances for 3 years past. pr. 1s. 6d.

Printed for J. Walsh . . . at the Golden Harp and Hautboy . . . and J. Hare at the Golden Viol . . . and . . . in Freeman's Yard, &c.

Feb. 9–12, 1706, *Post Man.*

See Nos. 34 and 70.

198. A Collection of Several Excellent Overtures Symphonys and Aires for a Flute and a Bass Compos'd by the most Eminent Masters to which is added that Incomperable Sonata for a Flute a Violin and a Bass Perform'd at Court and often

at the Theatre by M^r. Paisible and M^r. Gasperini the whole fairly Engraven price 3^s. Musick for Flutes lately Publishs'd. the Division Flute . . . M^r. Topham's Solos for a Flute and a Bass. [Ten lines of advertisements.]

London Printed for I. Walsh . . . at ye Harp & Hoboy . . . & I. Hare at the Golden Viol . . . and . . . in Freemans yard, &c.

Mar. 21–3, 1706, *Post Man.*

> BM. h. 17. (5.)
> Mr. Gasperini was presumably Gasparo Visconti, not Giovanni Gasparini.
> Walsh Cat., *c.* 1721, Ill. 28, as: 'Overtures & Aires, for a Flute & a Bass. 3s. od.'
> Included later in Walsh's numerical series with 'No. 128' added in MS. to the title-page.
> *See* Ill. 16.

199. M^r. Corbetts Musick in the Opera call'd the British Inchanters or no Magick like Love. [Words by George Granville, Lord Lansdowne.]

[J. Walsh and J. Hare.]

In four parts.

Mar. 21–3, 1706, *Post Man.*

> BM. d. 24. (22.) Imperfect.
> Presumably included in an unidentified collection of *Harmonia Anglicana.*
> *See* Nos. 48, 75, 90, 106, and 121.

200. [Vacant. *See* Introduction p. xii.]

201. A Collection of Songs and Ariets in the new Opera call'd Camilla [Words translated from the Italian of Silvio Stampiglia by Owen MacSwiney. Music by Marco Antonio Bononcini], as they are performed at the Theatre Royal, pr. 2s. 6d.

Printed for J. Walsh . . . at the Golden Harp and Hautboy . . . and J. Hare, at the Golden Viol . . . and . . . in Freeman's-Yard, &c.

Mar. 30–Apr. 2, 1706, *Post Man.*

> Elkin Mathews, 1947.
> This is the first collection of the Songs in Camilla, with title:
> Songs In The New Opera, Call'd Camilla as they are perform'd at the Theatre Royall.
> Sold by I: Walsh Musicall Instrument maker in Or=/=dinary to her Majesty, at the Golden Harpe and Ho=boy, in Catherine=Street near Sommerset House in the Strand.
> The title-page from the plate previously used for No. 29 (*see* Ill. 1), the words 'Camilla . . . Royall' from a supplementary plate, and with 'her' Majesty in the imprint.
> *See* Nos. 204, 206, 209, 221, 238, 298, 402, 560, and 565.

202. A Song in the Opera of Arsinoe, Sung by Mrs Toft, Sett by Mr Th^o Clayton. Within the Compass of the Flute. (O Love, I have gain'd a victory.)

[J. Walsh. *c.* 1706.]

> BM. G. 305. (81.)
> From a plate afterwards used in No. 220, where it has the pagination 20 added to it.
> *See* Nos. 203, 219, 220, 238, and 600.

203. Songs In The New Opera, Call'd Arsinoe Queen of Cyprus [Words from the Italian of Tomaso Stanzani] Compos'd by M^r. Tho: Clayton.

Sold by I: Walsh Musicall Instrument maker in Or=/=dinary to her Majesty, at the Golden Harpe and Ho=boy, in Catherine=Street near Sommerset House in the Strand.

Mar. 30–Apr. 2, 1706, *Post Man*. (Songs in the last new Opera call'd Arsinoe Queen of Cyprus, pr. 3s.)

RM. 15. c. 12. (2.)

This is the first collection of the Songs in Arsinoe, consisting of sixteen unpaginated numbers from the three acts, some of the numbers having appeared previously in *The Monthly Mask of Vocal Music*, May–Oct. 1705. One copy is recorded as having nineteen numbers. (Elkin Mathews, 1947.)

Thomas Clayton is supposed to have arranged, rather than composed, the music.

The title-page from the plate, previously used for No. 29 (*see* Ill. 1), the words 'Arsinoe . . . Clayton' being supplied from a supplementary plate and with 'her' Majesty in the imprint.

See Nos. 202, 219, 220, 238, and 600.

204. A Second Collection of the Songs and Ariets in the last new Opera, call'd Camilla [Words translated from the Italian of Silvio Stampiglia by Owen Mac-Swiney. Music by Marco Antonio Bononcini], as they are perform'd at the Theatre Royal, price 2s. 6d.

Printed for J. Walsh . . . at the Golden Harp and Hautboy, &c.

Apr. 17, 1706, *Daily Courant*.

Elkin Mathews, 1947.

With title:

Songs In The New Opera, Call'd Camilla as they are perform'd at the Theatre Royall The 2ᵈ Collection.

Sold by I: Walsh Musicall Instrument maker in Or=/=dinary to her Majesty, at the Golden Harpe and Ho=boy, in Catherine=Street near Sommerset House in the Strand.

The title-page from the plate used for No. 201 and previously for No. 29 (*see* Ill. 1), with the words 'Camilla . . . Collection' from a supplementary plate.

See Nos. 201, 206, 209, 221, 238, 298, 402, 560, and 565.

205. 6 Sonata's and 6 Solo's by Arcangelo Corelli transpos'd for Flutes.

A New Edition of all Corelli's Works for Violins curiously engraved, which for Beauty and Exactness far exceed all other Editions.

Printed for J. Walsh . . . at the Golden Harp and Hautboy . . . and J. Hare at the Golden Viol . . . and . . . in Freeman's Yard, &c.

Apr. 18–20, 1706, *Post Man*.

May be other editions or re-advertisements of Nos. 85, 107, and 181.

For complete list of Corelli items consult index.

April 18–20, 1706 is the last notice of Hare 'at the Golden Viol in St. Paul's Church-yard and at his shop in Freeman's yard near the Royal Exchange'. From May 2–4, 1706, onwards he is given as 'at the Golden Viol and Flute in Cornhill near the Royal Exchange' or 'at the Viol and Flute' or 'Violin and Flute', &c. These forms existed for a few years, after which the word 'Golden' was dropped, as Kidson points out, probably

*because the 'gilding on the emblems outside the shop must have got worn off or dirty', as
in the case of similar changes made in the addresses of Walsh, Bremner, and others.*

---

206. A third Collection of the Songs and Ariets in the new Opera call'd Camilla
[Words translated from the Italian of Silvio Stampiglia by Owen MacSwiney.
Music by Marco Antonio Bononcini], which together with the 1st and 2d Collec-
tions compleats all the Songs in that Opera as they are perform'd at the Theatre
Royal, the 3d Collection 3s.

    Printed for J. Walsh . . . at the Golden Harp and Hautboy, &c.

    Apr. 30, 1706, *Daily Courant.*

    May 2–4, 1706, *Post Man.* (Printed for J. Walsh . . . at the Golden Harp
and Hautboy . . . and J. Hare, at the Golden Viol and Flute in Cornhill near the
Royal Exchange.)

       This is the earliest notice traced giving Hare a new and only address at the Golden Viol
and Flute.

       The RCM. copy (XXXII. A. 1. (1.)) of the complete work (No. 221) has two title-
pages, one of which is that issued for the Third Collection of the Songs:

       Songs In The New Opera, Call'd Camilla as they are perform'd at the Theatre Royall
The 3d. Collection.

       Sold by I: Walsh Musicall Instrument maker in Or=/=dinary to her Majesty . . . and I.
Hare Musick Instrument maker at ye Golden Viol and Flute in Cornhill near ye Royal
Exchange.

       This title-page adapted from the plate previously used for Nos. 201 and 204 (*see* Ill. 1),
with the words 'Camilla . . . Collection' from a supplementary plate and Hare added to the
imprint. The first edition of this collection was probably without Hare's name in the
imprint, and included 'A Table of all the Songs in the Opera of Camilla, in order as they
are sung'.

       See Nos. 201, 204, 209, 221, 238, 402, 560, and 565.

207. The Britannia a New Dance Compos'd by Mr. Isaac Perform'd at Court on
Her Majesties Birth day Febr: ye 6th 17[06].

    London Printed for I. Walsh Servt to Her Matie at ye Harp & Hoboy . . . I. Hare
. . . at ye Golden Viol & Flute in Cornhill &c.

    [*c.* May 1706.]

       The title-page was afterwards used for a later edition with P. Randall added to the
imprint (No. 374) and also for another dance 'The Marlborough'. (No. 375.)

       The Britannia Compos'd by Mr. Isaac 1706.

       BM. 785. k. 7. (3.)

       This work is assumed to be the same as that listed above, but wanting the outer title-page.
No. 406 is a later edition, from the same plates.

       See Nos. 196, 374, and 406.

208. The Temple Musick: or, an Essay Concerning the Method of Singing the
Psalms of David, in the Temple, Before the Babylonish Captivity. Wherein, The
Musick of our Cathedrals is Vindicated . . . By Arthur Bedford, &c.

    London, Printed and Sold by H. Mortlock, at the Phœnix in St. Paul's Church-

Yard; J. Walsh in Catherine street . . . and Anth. Piesly near St. Mary's Church in Oxford. 1706.

> TC. III. 501. [May] 1706.
> BM. 701. b. 23. (2.)
> This work was not engraved; Walsh probably only acting as selling agent. He is not mentioned on the 1712 edition. (BM. 4515. aa. 6.)

209. The Songs and Ariets in the last new Opera, call'd Camilla [Words translated from the Italian of Silvio Stampiglia by Owen MacSwiney. Music by Marco Antonio Bononcini], as they are perform'd at the Theatre Royal.
Printed for J. Walsh . . . at the Golden Harp and Hautboy . . . and J. Hare Instrument-Maker at the Golden Viol and Flute in Cornhill, near the Royal Exchange.
May 16, 1706, *Daily Courant*; May 16–18, 1706, *Post Man*.

> A re-advertisement of the three previously published collections of Songs in Camilla (Nos. 201, 204, and 206), or the first notice of the collections issued in one volume as the complete work. (No. 221.)
> *See also* Nos. 238, 298, 402, 560, and 565.

210. The Overture and Aires in Four parts perform'd in the Comedy [by George Farquhar] call'd the Recruiting Officer, price 1s. 6d.
Printed for J. Walsh . . . at the Harp and Hoboy . . . and J. Hare at the Golden Viol and Flute, &c.
June 5, 1706, *Daily Courant*.

210a. Airs and Lessons for the Harpsicord by several Masters.
[J. Walsh and J. Hare. *c.* 1706 or earlier.]

> Advertised on No. 211.
> Presumably the work in Walsh Cat., *c.* 1721, Ill. 27, as: 'Lessons by several Masters, for ye Harpsichord, Spinnet or Organ. 1s. 6d.'

211. A Collection of the Song Tunes and Ariets in the Opera of Camilla [by Marco Antonio Bononcini] Contriv'd and Fitted to the Harpsicord or Spinnett by Mr. Ramondon . . . price. 3s. Books for ye Harpsicord Spinnet and Organ lately Printed Dr. Blow's Lessons for the Harpsicord, Dr. Blow's Psalm's for the Organ, The first & second Books of the Lady's Banquet containing all the new and Airy Lessons in use, My Lord Byron's Overtures and Airs for the Harpsicord, Airs and Lessons for the Harpsicord by several Masters, Mr. Dupar's Lessons for the Harpsicord, Mr. Keller's Rules for a Through Bass on the Harpsicord or Organ.
London Printed for I. Walsh Servt. to Her Matie at ye Harp & Hoboy in Katherine street near Somerset House in ye Strand, and I. Hare Instrument-maker at the Golden Viol & Flute in Cornhill near ye Royal Exchange.
July 22, 1706, *Daily Courant*. (Next week will be publish'd.)
July 27–30, 1706, *Post Man*. (New Musick published. A Collection of the Songs, Tunes and Ariets, &c.)

Rowe collection, King's College, Cambridge.

Walsh Cat., *c.* 1721, Ill. 27, as: 'The Opera of Camilla for the Harpsicord. 3s. 0d.'

The Rowe copy is of a later issue as it has 'N⁰. 176' of Walsh's numerical series at the bottom of the contents page.

All of the works listed on the title-page are recorded in the bibliography. (*See* Nos. 162, 130, 151, 187, 183, 210*a*, 179, and 190 respectively.) See also No. 217.

212. The Songs and Dialogues in the Opera call'd Wonders in the Sun, or the Kingdom of the Birds, pr. 1s. 6d. [Words by Thomas D'Urfey. Music by John Smith.]

Printed for J. Walsh . . . at the Harp and Hoboy . . . and J. Hare Instrument-maker at the Golden Viol and Flute, &c.

In four parts for Violins.

Aug. 7, 1706, *Daily Courant.*

See No. 215.

213. A Collection of Easy and Familiar Aires for Two Flutes without a Bass to which is added an Overture and Passacaille for Three Flutes without a Bass the whole Compos'd by M^r. Iames Kremberg one of the Gentlemen of Her Majestys Musick.

Printed for I. Walsh . . . and I. Hare Instrument maker at the Golden Viol and Flute in Cornhill, &c.

Aug. 7, 1706, *Daily Courant* (Next Week will be publish'd.)

Aug. 14, 1706, *Daily Courant.*

BM. b. 2.

Walsh Cat., *c.* 1721, Ill. 28, as: 'Krembergs Aires, for two Flutes. 2s. 0d.'

214. A Collection of Original Scotch tunes for the Violin all pleasant and comical, and full of the Highland humours. pr. 1s.

Printed for J. Walsh . . . and J. Hare . . . at the Golden Viol and Flute &c.

Aug. 17–20, 1706, *Post Man.*

Walsh Cat., *c.* 1721, Ill. 27, as: 'Scotch tunes for ye Violin. 1s. 0d.' H. Playford published a work with a similar title in 1701. (BM. K. 4. b. 18.)

See No. 65, a similar work for the Flute.

215. M^r. In⁰. Smiths Musick in the Opera call'd [Wonders in the Sun, or] the Kingdom of the Birds. [Words by Thomas D'Urfey.]

[J. Walsh and J. Hare. 1706.]

Aug. 27–9, 1706, *Post Man.* (The Overtures and Aires in 4 parts for Violins perform'd in the Comick Opera call'd the Kingdom of Birds . . . pr. 1s. 6d.)

BM. g. 15. (3.)

See No. 212, which appears to be an earlier announcement of the same work.

216. A Collection of the Song-Tunes, Duets and Ariets in the Opera of Camilla [Music by Marco Antonio Bononcini], contriv'd and fitted for two Flutes and a Bass, by Mr. Ramondon.

Printed for J. Walsh . . . and J. Hare . . . at the Golden Viol and Flute, &c. Sept. 5, 1706, *Daily Courant*.

Walsh Cat., *c.* 1721, Ill. 28, as: 'Aires in Camilla, for 2 Flutes & a Bass. 3s. od.'

217. The Songs and Ariets in the Opera of Camilla [Music by Marco Antonio Bononcini] contriv'd and fitted to the Harpsichord or Spinnet by Ramondon, price 3s. Printed for J. Walsh . . . and J. Hare . . . at the Golden Viol and Flute, &c. Sept. 26–8, 1706, *Post Man*.

See No. 211, an earlier announcement, with a transcript of the title-page.

218. The Ariets and Duets in the Opera of Camilla [Music by Marco Antonio Bononcini] for a Flute and a Bass. Printed for J. Walsh . . . and J. Hare . . . at the Golden Viol and Flute, &c. Sept. 26–8, 1706, *Post Man*.

Probably the First Flute and Bass parts of No. 216.

219. A 2d. Collection of the Songs in the Opera call'd Arsinoe [Words from the Italian of Tomaso Stanzani. Music by Thomas Clayton] which together with the first part contains all the Overtures, Airiets and Duets in that Opera, price of the 2d part 4s. The whole Opera 7s. Printed for J. Walsh . . . at the Golden Harp and Hautboy . . . and J. Hare Instrument maker, at the Golden Viol and Flute, &c. Oct. 3–5, 1706, *Post Man*.

This collection may have had title-page from the plate used for the first collection. (No. 203. *See* Ill. 1.) It contains numbers from the three acts, some having appeared previously in *The Monthly Mask of Vocal Music,* May–Oct. 1705. See Nos. 202, 203, 220, 238, and 600.

220. Songs in the Opera Call'd Arsinoe Queen of Cyprus. [Words from the Italian of Tomaso Stanzani. Music by Thomas Clayton.] London Printed for & Sould by I: Walsh Musicall Instrument maker in Ordinary to her Majesty at the Golden Harp & Ho=boy in Catherine=street near Summerset=house in yᵉ strand. Oct. 3–5, 1706, *Post Man*.

BM. H. 124. (1.)
Thomas Clayton was responsible for the music which he is supposed to have arranged rather than composed. His name does not appear engraved on the title-page of the work, but most of the numbers are headed 'Sett by Mʳ Thᵒ Clayton', and the BM. copy has his name added in MS. to the title-page: 'By Thomas Clayton. 1705.' The title-page is from the Collins plate. (No. 15. *See* Ill. 3.) This edition consists of the first and second collections of the Songs (Nos. 203 and 219) arranged in the correct order, paginated, some numbers of which had previously appeared separately, or in *The Monthly Mask of Vocal Music,* May–Oct. 1705, and were subsequently issued separately from the plates as used for *The Monthly Mask of Vocal Music,* or with the pagination of this edition. (BM. G. 316. g. (17.); G. 316. g. (50.); G. 305. (81.)) The work includes the Overture. Copies were also issued with an inner title-page: Songs In The New Opera, &c., as used for No. 203. (*See* Ill. 1.) See Nos. 202, 203, 219, 238, and 600.

221. Songs In The New Opera, Call'd Camilla [Words translated from the Italian of Silvio Stampiglia by Owen MacSwiney. Music by Marco Antonio Bononcini] as they are perform'd at the Theatre Royall.

Sold by I: Walsh Musicall Instrument maker in Or=/=dinary to her Majesty, at the Golden Harpe and Ho=boy, in Catherine=Street near Sommerset House in the Strand and I. Hare Musick Instrument maker at yᵉ Golden Viol and Flute in Cornhill near yᵉ Royal Exchange.

Oct. 18, 1706, *Daily Courant.*

> BM. I. 354.
> RCM. XXXII. A. 1. (1.)
> The title-page from the plate previously used for No. 203 (*see* Ill. 1), the words 'Camilla . . . Royall' being supplied from a supplementary plate, and Hare being added to the imprint.
> This edition of fifty-one numbers does not contain the Overture, but has 'A Table of all the Songs in the Opera of Camilla, in order as they are sung', which is a different order from the contents of the three collections as previously issued.
> The BM. copy has also an outer illustrated title-page from the plate (Berchet–Hulsbergh) first used for No. 156 (*see* Ill. 13), with the title 'Songs in the Opera of Camilla' inserted in the medallion in place of the Eccles title, and with the original imprint of that work: London Printed for I. Walsh, &c.
> The RCM. copy has similar title-pages to the BM. copy, but with the words 'The 3ᵈ. Collection' added after 'Royall' to the plate of the inner title-page, as used previously for No. 206.
> John Cullen also issued an edition, probably pirated, of 'Songs in the New Opera of Camilla . . . Fairly Ingrav'd on Copper Plates and more Correct than the former Edition', &c. (June 3–5, 1707, *Post Boy.* BM. I. 354. d.)
> *See* Nos. 201, 204, 206, 209, 238, 298, 402, 560, and 565; and Ill. 33.

222. Songs In The New Opera, Call'd The Temple of Love [Words by Peter Anthony Motteux] Compos'd by Signʳ: Gioseppe Fedelli Saggione.

Sold by I: Walsh Musicall Instrument maker in Or=/=dinary to her Majesty, at the Golden Harpe and Ho=boy, in Catherine=Street near Sommerset House in the Strand and I. Hare Musick Instrument maker at yᵉ Golden Viol and Flute in Cornhill near yᵉ Royal Exchange.

Oct. 18, 1706, *Daily Courant.*

> BM. H. 124. (2.)
> RCM. XXXII. A. 2. (2.)
> The title-page adapted from the plate previously used for No. 221 (*see* Ill. 1), the words 'The Temple of Love . . . Saggione' being supplied from a supplementary plate. The BM. copy has also an outer illustrated title-page from the plate (Van der Gucht) previously used for Nos. 89 and 102 (*see* Ill. 10), with the title, 'The Temple of Love' at the top, and 'Songs in the Opera Call'd the Temple of Love' in the medallion at the bottom, in place of the original titles, and with the original imprint retained.
> In order to suit this plate to the opera by Saggione, a temple was engraved on the plate in the background immediately above the figures. (*See* Ill. 17.)
> *See* No. 238.

223. The Whole Volume Compleat Intituled The Monthly Masks of Vocal Musick Containing all the Choisest Songs by the Best Masters made for the Play-houses Publick Consorts and other Occasions for the Year 1706 [i.e. Nov. 1705–Oct. 1706] with a Through Bass to Each Song and most of them with in the Composs of the Flute price 5ˢ.

London Printed for & Sould by I: Walsh Musicall Instrument maker in Ordinary to her Majesty, &c.

Nov. 11, 1706, *Daily Courant.* (There is now compleat the whole Volume of Monthly Collections of Vocal Musick . . . Printed for J. Walsh . . . and J. Hare.)

> Title-page from the Collins plate (No. 15, *see* Ill. 3) as used for the annual volumes for 1703, 1704, and other years. The details given are from the RCM. volume for 1707 which has the 1706 title-page altered in MS. to 1707.
> *See* Nos. 103, 109, 140, 160, 188, 258, 282a, 331, 370, and 517.

224. Six Select Solos for a Violin and a thorough Bass, Collected out of the Choicest Works of Six Eminent Masters, viz Signior Martino Betty [i.e. Bitti], Mr. Nicola [Matteis], Jun. Signior Corelli, Signior Torelli, Signior Carlo Ambrogio, and Mr. Pepusch; the first Collection Engraven and carefully Corrected, price 3s.

Printed for J. Walsh . . . and J. Hare . . . at the Golden Viol and Flute, &c.

Nov. 23, 1706, *Daily Courant.*

> Presumably a collected edition of the Violin Solos that appeared in Nos. 150, 149, 150b, 165, 150c, and 150a.
> Walsh Cat., *c.* 1721, Ill. 27, as: '6 Solos by Several Masters, for a Violin & a Bass. 4s. od.'

No. 225. [Vacant. *See* Introduction p. xii.]

The advertisement of The Monthly Mask of Vocal Musick *for November 1706* (Daily Courant, *Nov. 28, 1706*) appears to be the first notice containing the name of P. Randall, No. 227 *being the earliest work with P. Randall in the imprint.*

The address is given as:

The Violin and Lute by Pauls grave Hand (or Head) Court without Temple Bar in the Strand.

---

226. The Monthly Mask of Vocal Musick; or The newest Songs made for the Theatres and other Occasions, for November, price 6d.

Printed for J. Walsh Servant to her Majesty at the Harp and Hoboy in Katherine street near Somerset House in the Strand, J. Hare Instrument-maker at the Golden Viol and Flute in Cornhill near the Royal Exchange, and P. Randall at the Violin and Lute by Paulgrave Hand Court without Temple Bar in the Strand.

Nov. 28, 1706, *Daily Courant.*

> This advertisement appears to be the earliest mentioning Randall, but the work itself only gives Walsh and Hare in the imprint.
> *See* No. 258, the annual volume for 1707, which includes this number for November, 1706.

227. Six Sonatas or Solos for the Flute with a Through Bass for the Harpsicord Compos'd by Wᵐ. Topham. A.M. Opera Secunda.

London Printed for I. Walsh . . . at the Harp and Hoboy . . . I. Hare . . . at the Golden Viol and Flute . . . and P. Randall Instrument seller at yᵉ Violin and Lute by Pauls grave head Court with out Temple Barr in the Strand—

Dec. 11, 1706, *Daily Courant.*

> BM. c. 105. a. (6.)
> Walsh Cat., *c.* 1721, Ill. 28, as: 'Topham's 2ᵈ Solos, for a Flute & a Bass. 3s. 0d.'

228. Twenty Four new Country Dances for the Year 1707, with directions how to dance each dance, the whole fairly Engraven, pr. 6d.

Printed for J. Walsh . . . at the Harp and Hoboy . . . J. Hare . . . at the Golden Viol and Flute . . . and P. Randall . . . at the Violin and Lute by Paulgrave-head Court without Temple-Bar.

Dec. 16, 1706, *Daily Courant.*

229. Mʳ. Gilliers Musick Made for the Queens Theatre.

[J. Walsh, J. Hare and P. Randall.]

In four parts.

Dec. 16, 1706, *Daily Courant.*

> BM. g. 15. (2.)
> Part of an unidentified series.
> *See* 169.

From January 1707, *P. Randall's address is sometimes given in the shortened form: At the Violin and Lute without Temple Bar, and occasionally as: At the Viol and Lute by Pauls grave (Paulgrave) head Court, &c.*

---

230. All Mr. Kellers Rules for a Through Bass, the same which himself intended to publish before his death . . . and sold for 1s. 6d.

Printed for J. Walsh . . . J. Hare at the Viol and Flute . . . and P. Randall at the Violin and Lute by Paulsgreve-hand Court without Temple Bar.

Jan. 18–21, 1707, *Post Man.* (Next week will be published.)

> John Cullen announced, Jan. 14, 1707, *Daily Courant*: 'A compleat Method for attaining to Play a Thorough Bass . . . By the late famous Mr. Godfry Keller.' (BM. K. 2. i. 22.) Walsh issued his first edition Dec. 1705.
> *See* Nos. 190, 235, 277*c*, and 511.

231. Sonate da Camera or Chamber Musick Consisting of Several Sutes of Overtures and Aires for two Flutes and a Bass Compos'd by Signʳ. Christophor Pez Parté Prima.

London Printed for I. Walsh . . . at the Harp and Hoboy . . . I. Hare . . . at yᵉ

Golden Viol and Flute . . . and P. Randall . . . at the Viol and Lute by Pauls grave head Court with out Temple Barr in the Strand—

    Jan. 25–8, 1707, *Post Man.*

> BM. d. 150. (4.)
> Walsh Cat., *c.* 1721, Ill. 28, as: 'Pez 1st Collection, for 2 Flutes & a Bass. 3s. od.'
> *See* No. 242.

232. 6 Solos for a Flute and a Bass, by Mr. Pepusch.

    Printed for J. Walsh . . . at the Harp and Hoboy . . . J. Hare at the Viol and Flute . . . and P. Randal at the Violin and Lute by Paulsgrave head Court without Temple Bar.

    Jan. 25–8, 1707, *Post Man.*

> Walsh Cat., *c.* 1721, Ill. 28, as: 'Pepusch 1st Solos, for a Flute & a Bass. 4s. od.'
> *See* No. 335.

233. Six Select Suites of Lessons for the Harpsicord: in six severall Keys. Consisting of Preludes: Allemans: Corrants: Sarabands: Arietts: Minuetts: and Jiggs Composed by Sign^r: Giovani Baptista Draghi.

    Printed for J. Walsh . . . J. Hare . . . and P. Randall, &c.

    Feb. 4–6, 1707, *Post Man.*

> BM. g. 18. With title as above in MS., no imprint.
> Walsh advertised the work in No. 501, and Walsh Cat., *c.* 1721, Ill. 27, as: 'Sig^r. Baptist Lessons.' Eitner (Quellen-Lexikon) gives: 'Six selected Suites of Lessons', &c.

234. The Union a New Dance Compos'd by M^r. Isaac Perform'd at Court on Her Majestie's Birth day Feb^r: ye 6th. 1707. and writt down in Characters by Iohn Weaver. H. Hulsbergh Schulp^t.

    Feb. 6, 1707, *Daily Courant.* (To be had at Mr. Valiant's a Bookseller near Catherine-street in the Strand. Price 5s.)

> BM. 785. k. 7. (2.)
> This work may have been published by Walsh and Hare, and only sold by Vaillant. A later edition of it from the same plates, with an inner title-page as given above, without imprint, and with an outer title-page bearing the names of Walsh and Hare, was published *c.* 1712. (No. 405.)
> The list of 'Books of Instrumental and Vocal Musick Printed in ye Year 1707 for I. Walsh' issued with the yearly volume of *The Monthly Mask*, &c. for 1707 (No. 258) includes an item 'The Court Dances or Union for 1707', which may be the work recorded above or a Walsh edition of it. .

235. A Compleat Method for attaining to play Thorough Bass upon either Organ, Harpsicord or Theorbo–Lute, by the late famous Mr. Godfry Keller, with variety of proper Lessons and Fuges, explaining the several Rules throughout the whole Work, and a Scale for Tuning the Harpsicord or Spinnet; all taken from his own Copies which he did design to print. In this work, for the Ease of Practitioners, the Chords are explain'd both with figures and Notes over the Bass. Note. The

many faults in the late Edition of Mr. Kellers Rules are corrected in this new edition. The Whole fairly engraven price 1s. 6d.

Printed for J. Walsh . . . at the Harp and Hoboy . . . J. Hare at the Viol and Flute . . . and P. Randal at the Violin and Lute in Paulgrave head Court without Temple-Bar.

Feb. 13–15, 1707, *Post Man*.

An advance notice of this work appears under No. 230. An earlier edition was advertised by Walsh and Hare Dec. 20–2, 1705, *Post Man* (No. 190), and John Cullen issued an edition Jan. 14, 1707, *Daily Courant*. No copy of the Walsh edition of 1707 has been traced, but later editions which may have been from the same plates, with a minor modification of the imprints, have contents, pagination, and layout similar to Cullen's 1707 edition. (BM. K. 2. i. 22.)

See Nos. 190, 230, 277c, and 511.

236. The 4th Book of the Compleat Flute Master: or, the whole Art of Playing on the Flute, laid down in such plain and easie Directions, that by them every Capacity may attain to perfection on that Instrument; with a Collection of the newest Airs, viz. Rigadoons, Horn Pipes, Minuets, Jiggs &c. and choice Song Tunes compos'd by the most able Masters viz. Mr. Akeroyd, Mr. Weldon, Mr. Barret, Mr. Graves, Mr. Leveridge, Mr. Whichello: To which is added, a plain Scale for the transporting of any tune from the Violin or Voice to the Flute; as also an excellent Solo, by Mr. Edw. Keen, never before published.

Printed for J. Hare . . . at the Viol and Flute . . . J. Walsh at the Harp in Catherine street, and P. Randal at the Violin and Lute without Temple Bar. Price 1s. 6d.

Feb. 15–18, 1707, *Post Man*.

See Nos. 2, 3, 9, 240, 421, and 423. No details of the third book have been traced.

237. Songs in the new Opera call'd Rosamond [Words by Joseph Addison], as they are perform'd at the Theatre Royal, compos'd by Mr. Tho. Clayton.

Printed for J. Walsh . . . at the Harp and Hoboy . . . J. Hare at the Viol and Flute . . . and P. Randall at the Violin and Lute by Paulgrave-head Court without Temple Bar.

Mar. 10, 1707, *Daily Courant*.

This was the first collection of the Songs.

See Nos. 245 and 247.

238. The Opera's of Camilla, Arsinoe, and the Temple of Love, the 2d Edition, each Opera may be had single or the 3 in one Volume.

Printed for J. Walsh . . . at the Harp and Hoboy . . . J. Hare at the Viol and Flute . . . and P. Randall at the Violin and Lute by Paulgrave-head Court without Temple Bar.

Mar. 10, 1707, *Daily Courant*.

These particular editions cannot be identified.

See Nos. 220, 221, and 222.

239. Mr. Dan¹. Purcells Musick in yᵉ reviv'd Play [by Sir John Vanbrugh] call'd Vertue in Danger.
[J. Walsh, J. Hare and P. Randall.]
In four parts.
Mar. 22, 1707, *Daily Courant.*
> BM. g. 15. (6.)
> The correct title of the play is: 'The Relapse or Virtue in Danger.'

240. The 4th Book of the Gentlemans Companion, being a choice Collection of the newest Tunes for the Flute, viz Rigadoons, Horn-pipes, Minuets, Jiggs, &c. with admirable Song-Tunes, compos'd by the best Masters, viz. Mr. Akeroyd, Mr. Weldon, Mr. Barret, Mr. Graves, Mr. Leveridge, Mr. Wichello: To which is added, an excellent Solo by Mr. Edw. Keen never before published.
Printed for J. Hare . . . at the Viol and Flute . . . J. Walsh at the Harp in Catherine-street and P. Randal at the Violin and Lute without Temple Bar. Price 1s.
Mar. 29–Apr. 1, 1707, *Post Man.*
> This may have been a separate edition of part of No. 236. No details of the third book have been traced.
> *See* Nos. 83, 236, 421, and 423.

241. The Symphony or Overture in the Opera call'd Camilla [Music by Marco Antonio Bononcini], as it's performed at the Theatre-Royal price 6d engrav'd.
Printed for J. Walsh . . . at the Harp and Hoboy . . . J. Hare at the Viol and Flute . . . and P. Randal at the Violin and Lute by Paulgrave-head Court without Temple Bar.
Apr. 2, 1707, *Daily Courant.*
> This was in score and was included in the later issues of the opera.
> *See* Nos. 298 and 402.

242. A 1st and 2d Collection of Airs and Sonata's for 2 Flutes and a Bass, by Sig. Pez. To the latter is added some of Correlli's great Solo's for a Flute and a Bass. Illustrated throughout with proper Graces, by an eminent Master.
Printed for J. Walsh . . . [J. Hare . . . and P. Randall], &c.
Apr. 12–15, 1707, *Post Man.* Paper mutilated.
> The first collection appeared as: 'Sonate da Camera or Chamber Musick . . . Parté Prima.' (No. 231.)
> The details of the title-page &c. of the second collection have not been traced.
> Walsh Cat., *c.* 1721, Ill. 28, as: 'Pez 2ᵈ. Collection, for 2 Flutes & a Bass. 3s. od.'

243. 6 Sutes of Correlli's Aires for 2 Flutes and a Bass. There is likewise a 2d Collection of 6 Suits of Airs for 2 Flutes and a Bass by the same Author, which will be shortly published.
Printed for J. Walsh . . . [J. Hare . . . and P. Randal], &c.
Apr. 12–15, 1707, *Post Man.* Paper mutilated.

The first work is assumed to be: 'Six Setts of Airs for two Flutes and a Bass &c.' (No. 107.) The second collection was advertised as: 'Six Sonata's for 2 Flutes and a Bass.' (No. 255.)

244. Six Sonata's for a Flute and a Bass, by Wm Corbet.
Printed for J. Walsh . . . [J. Hare . . . and P. Randal], &c.
Apr. 12–15, 1707, *Post Man.* Paper mutilated.

Probably the work in Walsh Cat., *c.* 1721, Ill. 28, as: 'Corbets Sonatas for ye German Flute 3s. od', under 'Musick for 2 Flutes & a Bass', and in the Catalogue, 'Apollo's Feast,' third book, *c.* 1729 (W^m. C. Smith copy), as: 'Corbets Sonatas for two German Flutes & a Bass,' although the latter may refer to another work. (*See* No. 172.)

245. A 2d Part of the Songs in the new Opera call'd Rosamond &c. [Words by Joseph Addison. Composed by Thomas Clayton.]
[J. Walsh, J. Hare and P. Randall.]
Apr. 19–22, 1707, *Post Man.* Paper mutilated.

See Nos. 237 and 247.

246. Songs in the New Opera Call'd Thomyris [Words by Peter Anthony Motteux] Collected out of the Works of the most Celebrated Itallian Autors viz Scarlatti Bononcini and other great Masters Perform'd at the Theatre Royall These Songs are Contriv'd so that theire Symphonys may be perform'd with them. Note there are 4 other Operas after ye Itallian mañer lately printed viz Camilla, Arsinoe, the Temple of Love, and Rosamond, which may be had were this is sold.
London Printed for I. Walsh . . . and P. Randall at ye Violin & Lute, &c.
Apr. 26–9, 1707, *Post Man.* (J. Walsh . . . J. Hare . . . and P. Randal.)

BM. H. 114. (4.)
This edition contains a selection of 17 unpaginated numbers from the three acts, without the Overture. The BM. copy has a label pasted over the imprint: 'Sold by Mickepher Rawlins next door to the half-Moon and Greye[?]hound Tavern in the Strand near Charing Cross. London.'
This selection is earlier than the three acts of the complete work, being unpaginated and having corrections made on the title-page which were afterwards altered on the plate 'Autors' to 'Authors', 'theire Symphonys', to 'their Symphonys', 'were' to 'where', and the dash over maner.
See Nos. 251, 253, 254, 274, 299, 560, and 565.

247. Songs in the New Opera Call'd Rosamond [Words by Joseph Addison] as they are perform'd at the Theatre Royall Compos'd by M^r. Tho. Clayton.
London Printed for I. Walsh Servt. to Her Matie. at ye Harp & Hoboy in Katherine Streed . . . and P. Randall at ye Violin & Lute by Paulsgrave head Court without Temple Barr.
[1707.]

BM. H. 105.
RCM. XXXII. A. 2. (1.) With the order of the title-pages reversed.

With a finely illustrated inner title-page: W: Sykes Iunior Inventor. H: Hulsbergh Fecit. (See Ill. 18.) With title 'Songs in the New Opera Called Rosamond Compos'd by Mʳ. Tho: Clayton', and similar imprint to the outer title-page with the exception of 'Street' in place of 'Streed'. Newspaper notice not traced, but the work was advertised on No. 246.

See Nos. 237 and 245.

248. Te Deum et Jubilate, for Voices and Instruments, Perform'd before the Queen, Lords, and Commons, at the Cathedral-Church of St. Paul, on the Thanks-giving-Day, for the Glorious Successes of Her Majesty's Army the last Campaign. Compos'd By the late Famous Mr. Henry Purcel. The Second Edition.

London. Sold by J. Walsh . . . at the Harp and Hoboy . . . J. Hare . . . at the Golden Viol and Flute in Cornhill . . . and P. Randall . . . at the Violin and Lute, &c.

Apr. 28, 1707, *Daily Courant.* (Price 2s.)

BM. G. 99.
RM. 15. c. 13. (1.)
A reissue of the original edition of 1697 printed from type by J. Heptinstall (BM. Add. MSS. 31, 444.), including dedication by Mrs. Purcell to the Bishop of Durham, and with the original title-page following the Walsh one:

Te Deum & Jubilate for Voices and Instruments, Made for Sᵗ. Cæcilia's Day, 1694. By the late Mr. Henry Purcell.

London, Printed by J. Heptinstall, for the Author's Widow, and are to be Sold by Henry Playford, at his Shop in the Temple-Change in Fleetstreet, 1697.

The RM. copy has only the Walsh title-page and is without the dedication.

An earlier notice (Dec. 10–12, 1702, *Post Man*) refers to what appears to be an earlier issue by Walsh not identified. (No. 108.)

About 1707, or soon after the death of Mrs. Purcell in Feb. 1706, Walsh must have acquired a number of Purcell's works in their original editions, as in the notice of Apr. 28, 1707, *Daily Courant*, he also advertises, 'The following Compositions by the same Author may be had where these are sold, viz. Orpheus Britanicus 1st and 2d Books, all Mr. Henry Purcel's Aires, being 14 Sets, his Opera of Dioclesian, his book of Harpsicord Lessons, and his first and second Sets of Sonatas.'

The notice of Apr. 28, 1707, gives: 'J. Walsh . . . J. Hare . . . and P. Randal . . . and J. Young at the Dolphin and Crown in St. Paul's Church-yard', as the sellers of all the works mentioned, including the *Te Deum & Jubilate*. The annual volume of *The Monthly Mask of Vocal Music* for 1707 (No. 258) also advertises these Purcell works.

Walsh Cat., *c.* 1721, Ill. 27, gives the following Purcell items:

Henʳ. Purcells Sonatas, under Sonatas and Concertos for 2 Violins & a Bass.
Henʳ. Purcells Aires, under Sonatas and Concertos for 2 Violins & a Bass.
Henʳ. Purcells Lessons, for yᵉ Harpsicord, &c.
Opera of Dioclesian.
Henʳ. Purcells Orpheus.

No copies of contemporary or earlier Walsh editions of any of these works, except the *Te Deum et Jubilate* have been identified. It must be assumed, therefore, that Walsh was only listing editions by other publishers, which he had taken over.

See Nos. 108, 276, and 595.

249. The Symphonys or Instrumental Parts in the Opera Call'd Camilla [Music by Marco Antonio Bononcini] as they are Perform'd at the Theatre Royal.

London Printed for I. Walsh . . . at yᵉ Harp & Hoboy . . . and P. Randall . . . at yᵉ Viol and Lute, &c.

May 20–2, 1707, *Post Man.* (Pr. 4s.)

BM. I. 354. c.
The advertisement gives Hare as well as Walsh and Randal, and the Second Treble and Bass parts of the BM. copy have a later imprint pasted on: 'London Printed for I. Walsh . . . and I. Hare . . . at the Golden Viol and Flute', &c.
The work may have been issued earlier than the date of the advertisement.
See No. 250.

250. The Symphonys or Instrumental Parts in the Opera Call'd Camilla [Music by Marco Antonio Bononcini] as they are Perform'd at the Theatre Royal.

London Printed for I. Walsh . . . I. Hare at the Viol and Flute . . . and P. Randall at the Violin and Lute without Temple Barr in the Strand.

[c. 1707.]

BM. h. 17. a. (1.) First Treble part only.
Another edition of the preceding, from the same plates but with imprint altered by erasion and re-engraving.

251. The 1st Part of the new Opera call'd Thomyris [Words by Peter Anthony Motteux. Music by Alessandro Scarlatti, Giovanni Battista Bononcini, &c.] being of late spuriously Copied, these are to acquaint all Lovers of Musick that the original Songs in the 1st Part of that Opera are now Sold at 1s the Book or the Songs single for 1d a piece, all carefully Corrected according to the original Score.

Printed for and Sold by J. Walsh . . . at the Harp and Hoboy . . . J. Hare at the Golden Viol and Flute . . . and P. Randal at the Violin and Lute by Paulsgrave head Court without Temple Bar.

May 31, 1707, *Daily Courant.*

The spurious edition was that published by J. Cullen (BM. H. 113. a.), advertised June 3–5, 1707, *Post Boy*; and an edition by Pippard and Cullen was referred to by Walsh, May 2, 1709, *Daily Courant.*
See Nos. 246, 253, 254, 274, 299, 560, and 565.

252. A Collection of new Songs, For One and Two Voices: with a Thorow-Bass to Each Song. Compos'd by Mr. Anthony Young, Organist of St. Clement Danes. Several of the Songs that are not in the Compass, are Transpos'd for the Flute, at the End of the Book.

London Printed by William Pearson, for the Author; And Sold by J. Walsh, and M. Rawlins in the Strand, J. Young at the Dolphin in St. Pauls-Church-Yard, J. Hare in Cornhill, and J. Cullen at the Buck in Fleet-street 1707.

June 3–5, 1707, *Post Boy.*

RCM. II. A. 20. (30.)

253. The Songs in the 2d and 3d Acts of the new Opera call'd Thomyris [Words by Peter Anthony Motteux] which together with the first part contains all the

Ariets and Duets in that Opera. Compos'd by the most celebrated Authors, viz. Scarlatti, Bononcini, and other great Masters, the 2d and 3d Acts. 6s.

 Printed for John Walsh . . . J. Hare at the Violin and Flute . . . and P. Randal, &c. June 5-7, 1707, *Post Man.*

  See Nos. 246, 251, 254, 274, 299, 560, and 565.

254. Songs in the New Opera Call'd Thomyris [Words by Peter Anthony Motteux] Collected out of the Works of the most Celebrated Itallian Authors viz Scarlatti Bononcini and other great Masters Perform'd at the Theatre Royall These Songs are Contriv'd so that their Symphonys may be perform'd with them. Note there are 4 other Operas after ye Itallian mañer lately printed viz Camilla, Arsinoe, the Temple of Love, and Rosamond, which may be had where this is sold.

 London Printed for I. Walsh . . . and P. Randall at ye Violin & Lute, &c.

 June 17-19, 1707, *Post Man.* (The Overture or first Symphony, also the 1st, 2d and 3d Acts of the last new opera call'd Thomyris. Printed for John Walsh . . . J. Hare at the Violin and Flute . . . and P. Randal.)

  BM. H. 113.
  RCM. XXXIII. A. 3. (4.) Imperfect.
  The title-page is from the same plate as No. 246, but with corrections made on the plate before printing and not by hand on the title-page after printing.
  The BM. copy of this first edition of the complete work includes the overture which is not in the RCM. copy. Some copies were issued with the Collins title-page. (No. 15. *See* Ill. 3.)
  See Nos. 246, 251, 253, 274, 299, 560, and 565.

255. Six Sonata's for 2 Flutes and a Bass, by Arcangelo Corelli, collected out of the choicest of his Works, and carefully Transpos'd and Contriv'd for 2 Flutes and a Bass, the 2d Collection, price 3s.

 Printed for John Walsh . . . J. Hare at the Violin and Flute . . . and P. Randal, &c. June 21-4, 1707, *Post Man.*

  See No. 243, preliminary notice as: '6 Suits of Airs', &c. Walsh Cat., *c.* 1721, Ill. 28, as: 'Corellis 2^d Collection, for 2 Flutes & a Bass. 3s. od.'
  See also Nos. 107 and 205.

256. The Symphonys or Instrumental Parts in the Opera Call'd Thomyris [Music by Alessandro Scarlatti, Giovanni Battista Bononcini, &c.] as they are Perform'd at the Theatre Royal.

 London Printed for I. Walsh . . . at ye Harp & Hoboy . . . I. Hare . . . at ye Golden Viol & Flute . . . and P. Randall at ye Violin and Lute by Paulsgrave head Court without Temple Barr in ye Strand.

 Sept. 25-7, 1707, *Post Man.* (Next week will be published.)

 Sept. 30-Oct. 1, 1707, *Post Man.*

  The title as given partly supplied from a later edition (No. 337) and from *Love's Triumph* (No. 273), and may be open to correction.

257. Harmonia Mundi Consisting of Six Favourite Sonata's Collected out of the Choisest Works of Six most Eminent Authors viz Sign^r. Torelli . . . M^r. H. Purcell . . . Sign^r. Bassani . . . M^r. Pepusch . . . Sign^r. Albinoni . . . Sign^r. Pez . . . the first Collection Engraven & Carefully Corected.

London Printed for I. Walsh . . . at ye Harp & Hoboy . . . and I. Hare . . . at ye Golden Viol and Flute . . . and P. Randall . . . at ye Violin & Lute, &c.

[1707.]
Advertised in No. 258.

> BM. g. 419.
> The Randall portion of the imprint is in smaller lettering than the rest, which suggests that it may have been added to the plate after an edition had been published without Randall's name. The First Violin part of the BM. copy has John Young's imprint on a separate label pasted over the original Walsh imprint. The work is for two Violins and Bass, and one number at least (Sonata in F, Golden Sonata, by H. Purcell) had been previously published from the same plates, as part of a monthly series of instrumental music (No. 149), and other numbers also may have appeared previously in the same series. (No. 143, &c.)
> The second set of *Harmonia Mundi* was published in 1710. (No. 364.)
> Walsh and Joseph Hare issued in 1728 another work entitled *Harmonia Mundi The 2^d collection Being VI Concertos in Six Parts For Violins and other Instruments*, &c. (BM. g. 419. a.) The first collection of this work has not been traced.

258. The Whole Volume Compleat Intituled The Monthly Masks of Vocal Musick Containing all the Choisest Songs by the Best Masters made for the Play-houses Publick Consorts and other Occasions for the Year 1707 [i.e. Nov. 1706–Oct. 1707] with a Through Bass to Each Song and most of them with in the Composs of the Flute price 5^s.

London Printed for & Sould by I: Walsh Musicall Instrument maker in Ordinary to her Majesty, &c.

[c. Nov. 1707.]

> BM. H. 313. b. Without the collective title-page.
> RCM. II. A. 15.
> The title-page of the RCM. copy is from the Collins plate (No. 15, *see* Ill. 3) as used for the volume for 1706 (No. 223), with 1706 altered in MS. to 1707.
> The annual volume has a leaf containing 'A Table of the Songs in the Monthly Masks for the Year 1707 Printed for I Walsh' followed by a list of 'Books of Instrumental and Vocal Musick Printed in ye Year 1707 for I Walsh.' The list is transcribed here, with slight modifications in capitals, &c. and with the reference numbers to the entries in the bibliography added in order to aid identification:
> Mr Gilliers Musick for the Queens Theatre. (No. 229.)
> The 24 Country Dances for ye Year 1707. (No. 228.)
> The Court Dances or Union for 1707. (No. 234.)
> Mr Tophams Flute Solos. (No. 227.)
> Mr Pepusch Flute Solos. (No. 232.)
> Pez Sonatas for two Flutes and a Bass. 1st Set. (No. 231.)
> Pez Sonatas for two Flutes and a Bass. 2^d Set. (No. 242.)

Corellis 2d Six Sonatas for two Flutes & a Bass. (No. 255.)
Signr Baptist Six Sutes of Lessons for ye Harpsicord. (No. 233.)
Six Solos for Violins by Six Masters. (No. 224.)
Harmonia Mundi Six Sonatas in 4 Parts by 6 Masters. (No. 257.)
All Mr Henr Purcells Musick in four Parts Consisting of fourteen Sets of Tunes or Aires
(No. 248.)
    Mr Henr Purcells First & Second Sets of Sonatas. (No. 248.)
    Mr Purcells Opera of Dioclesian all ye Vocall Musick. (No. 248.)
    Mr Purcells Te Deum Et Jubilate. (No. 248.)
    Mr Purcells 1st & 2d Books of Orpheus Britanicus. (No. 248.)
    Mr Purcells Book of Harpsicord Lessons. (No. 248.)
    The Opera of Rosamond. (No. 247.)
    Mr Danl Purcells Tunes in Virtue in Danger. (No. 239.)
    All the Symphonys in the Opera of Camilla. (No. 250.)
    Songs in the Opera call'd Thomyris. (No. 254.)
    See Nos. 103, 109, 140, 160, 188, 223, 282a, 331, 370, and 517; and Ill. 34.

259. 24 New Country Dances for the Year 1708, with proper Tunes, and new
Figures, or Directions to each Dance. engraven, pr. 6d.
    Printed for J. Walsh . . . J. Hare, &c.
    Nov. 18–20, 1707, *Post Man.*

260. The New Country Dancing Master is published; containing the Country
Dances for 3 years past, engraven, pr. 1s. 6d.
    Printed for J. Walsh . . . J. Hare, &c.
    Nov. 18–20, 1707, *Post Man.*

      Presumably the work advertised in No. 282a as: 'The Books of Country Dances for
    3 years.'
      See Nos. 193, 333, 371, 394, 441, and 489.

261. Mr Gilliers Musick in the Play call'd the Stratagem.
    [J. Walsh and J. Hare.]
    In four parts.
Nov. 18–20, 1707, *Post Man.* (The Overture and Ayres in 4 parts, performed in
the Play called the Stratagem.)

      BM. g. 15. (7.)
      Part of an unidentified series.
      The play was presumably 'The Beaux' Stratagem', by George Farquhar.
      See No. 169.

262. A Choice Collection of Airs or Ariett's for two Flutes with the Overture
of Camilla & Arsinoe also Arietts & Duetts in ye Opera of Thomyris Contrived
and fitted for two Flutes to which is added a New Sonata for two Flutes Compos'd
by Mr. Daniel Purcell the whole fairly Engraven.
    London Printed for I. Walsh . . . at ye Harp & Hoboy . . . and I. Hare . . . at ye
Golden Viol and Flute, &c.
    Nov. 19, 1707, *Daily Courant.* (Price 1s. 6d. Printed for and sold by P. Randall

... at the Sign of the Lute and Violin the corner of Paulsgrave Head Court without Temple Bar.)

> BM. b. 171. a. (2.)
> Only Randall is mentioned in the advertisement, but the work gives Walsh and Hare. Walsh Cat., *c.* 1721, Ill. 28, as: 'Overtures in Camilla, &c. for two Flutes. 2s. od.'
> *See* No. 435.

263. Mercurius Musicus; or, A Monthly Entertainment of Musick . . . Which will be continued Monthly for the year 1708. Publish'd for November. Price 6d.
   Printed for J. Walsh . . . at the Harp and Hautboy . . . J. Hare . . . at the Golden Viol and Flute, &c.
   Dec. 2–4, 1707, *Post Man.*

> Henry Playford published an earlier work with the title: 'Mercurius Musicus: or the Monthly Collection of new Teaching Songs', 1699–1702. (BM. K. 1. c. 6; G. 92; RCM. I. F. 5; II. A. 14. (1.))
> Advertisements of later numbers of the Walsh work have been traced as follows:
> Mercurius Musicus . . . Publish'd for December. Price 6d. J. Walsh and J. Hare.
> Dec. 22, 1707, *Daily Courant.*
> Mercurius Musicus; or A Monthly Entertainment of Musick for the Harpsichord or Spinnet, consisting of Preludes, Tocatas, Aires, Lessons, and the most favourite Song Tunes in the new Operas, publish'd for May, price 6d. J. Walsh, J. Hare and P. Randal.
> June 3, 1708, *Daily Courant.*
> Mercurius Musicus; or A Monthly Entertainment of Musick . . . publish'd for September. J. Walsh, P. Randall and J. Hare.
> Oct. 4, 1708, *Daily Courant.*
> Mercurius Musicus . . . for October. Price 6d. J. Walsh, P. Randal and J. Hare.
> Oct. 28, 1708, *Daily Courant.*
> The list of musical works printed in the year 1708, advertised in No. 282a, includes 'A Table of the Preludes Aires and Tocatas for ye Harpsicord in ye mercurys for ye Year 1708'.

264. Mr. Isom's [i.e. John Isham or Isum] new Musick, in 4 Parts, for Violins made for the Tragedy [by Nicholas Rowe] call'd The Royal Convert, price 1s 6d.
   Printed for and Sold by J. Walsh . . . and J. Hare, &c.
   Dec. 22, 1707, *Daily Courant.*

264a. XXIV Solos for a Violin with a Through Bass for the Harpsicord or Bass Violin Compos'd by Sign^r. Pepusch.
   London Printed for I. Walsh Servt. in ordinari to Her Matie at the Harp and Hoboy, &c.
   [*c.* 1707–8.]
   Advertised in No. 282a.

> BM. e. 15. b.
> RCM. XXIX. c. 4.
> With an inner title-page:
> Solos for a Violin with a Through Bass for the Harpsicord or Bass Violin Compos'd by Sign^r. Pepusch.

London Printed for I: Walsh . . . I. Hare at yᵉ Golden Viol and Flute, &c.

This title-page is repeated again from the same plate before Solo No. 13, with the addition of 'Parti Secunda'.

The outer illustrated title-page in the Collins style (*see* Ill. 19) was from the plate originally used for, '*A Second Booke of Songs. . . . Composed by R King*', &c. (*See* No. 15. BM. C. 411; Day and Murrie. Fig. 31.), and afterwards by Walsh for No. 119. The Pepusch title was from a supplementary plate.

There is some reason for assuming that the first edition of the work may have had only the illustrated title-page, and the title-page to the 'Parti Secunda', as these words appear to have been erased from the impressions of the plate used for the first part of the work in the BM. and RCM. copies. The Walsh edition may have appeared at any time between Nov. 1707 and Oct. 1708. The Amsterdam edition by Roger: 'Sonates à un Violon Seul & une Basse Continue', &c., containing sixteen solos (BM. e. 15.) was advertised in London by I. Vaillant, Jan. 14–16, 1707, *Post Man*, but it was probably issued a little earlier and the Walsh edition taken from it. Roger issued more complete editions a few years later. (BM. e. 15. c. 1–3.)

265. Tibaldi's Sonata's or Chamber Aires in three Parts for two Violins and a Through Bass Compos'd by Gio. Battista Tibaldi Opera Prima.

London Printed for I. Walsh . . . I. Hare . . . and P Randall at yᵉ Violin and Lute by Paulsgrave head Court without Temple Barr in the Strand.

[*c.* 1708.]

Advertised in No. 282*a*.

> BM. h. 22.
> RCM. LXI. E. 11. (8.) Wanting title-page.
> *See* No. 483.

266. Bomporti's Sonata's or Chamber Aires in three Parts for two Violins and a Through Bass Compos'd by Francisco Antonio Bomporti Opera Seconda.

London Printed for I. Walsh Servᵗ. to Her Maᵗⁱᵉ. . . . I. Hare . . . and P. Randall, &c.

[*c.* 1708.]

Advertised in No. 282*a*.

> Title as given is from a later edition (No. 482), the plate of which had been used previously for *Opera Quarto*, and is assumed to have been used for the first edition of *Opera Seconda*.
> *See* No. 482.

267. Bomporti's Sonata's or Chamber Aires in three Parts for two Violins and a Through Bass Compos'd by Francisco Antonio Bomporti Opera Quarto.

London. Printed for I. Walsh Servᵗ. to Her Maᵗⁱᵉ. . . . I. Hare . . . at yᵉ Golden Viol & Flute . . . and P. Randall at yᵉ Violin and Lute by Paulsgrave head Court without Temple Barr in the Strand.

[*c.* 1708.]

Advertised in No. 282*a*.

> BM. g. 407.

268. The Opera of Thomyris; or The Royal Amazon . . . the Opera of Camilla, the Opera of Arsinoe, the Opera of Rosamond, the Opera of the Temple of Love. Likewise the Opera of Dioclesian, Compos'd by the late Mr. Henry Purcell. Note, Each of these Operas may be had single or the whole in one Volume.

Printed for J. Walsh . . . and J. Hare, &c.

Jan. 15, 1708, *Daily Courant*.

There is no evidence that Walsh published a new edition of Purcell's *Dioclesian*; the probability is that the edition he was offering for sale was the original Heptinstall edition of 1691 (BM. H. 101. d.), with or without an outer Walsh title-page.

See Nos. 248 and 258, for earlier references to *Dioclesian,* and see index for editions of the other operas.

269. The Saltarella, Mr. Isaac's New Dance, made for her Majesty's Birthday 1708, the tune by Mr. Paisible. To which is added all the new Minuets, Rigadons, and French Dances, Danc'd at Schools and Publick Entertainments. The whole fairly Engraven, Price 6d.

Sold by J. Walsh . . . and J. Hare . . . and at most Musick-Shops in Town.

Feb. 11, 1708, *Daily Courant*.

A different edition from No. 270.

270. The Saltarella M^r. Isaac's New Dance made for Her Majesty's BirthDay 1708 The Tune by M^r. Paisible Engraven in Characters and Figures for the use of Masters The Characters writ by M^r. de la Garde Dancing Master belonging to ye Operas at ye Queens Theatre, and Revis'd by ye Author.

Sold by J. Walsh . . . and J. Hare, &c.

Feb. 11, 1708, *Daily Courant*. (Next Week will be Publish'd.)

BM. h. 993. (7.)

A different edition from No. 269.

A mutilated copy of No. 270, or of another edition, is at BM. 785. k. 7. (11.)

271. Songs In The New Opera, Call'd Love's Triumph as they are Perform'd at the Queens Theatre. [Words adapted from the Italian of Cardinal Ottoboni by Peter Anthony Motteux. Music by Carlo Francesco Cesarini, Francesco Gasparini, and others.]

Sold by I: Walsh . . . at the Golden Harpe and Ho=boy . . . and I. Hare . . . at y^e Golden Viol and Flute in Cornhill near y^e Royal Exchange.

Mar. 12, 1708, *Daily Courant*.

The advertisement reads: 'The Songs set to Musick in the new Opera call'd Love's Triumph . . . Price 3s.' and is assumed to refer to the First Act only, with title-page as above from the plate previously used for No. 222 and earlier works (*see* Ill. 1), with 'Love's Triumph . . . Queens Theatre' from a supplementary plate.

See Nos. 272 and 450.

272. Songs In The New Opera, Call'd Love's Triumph as they are Perform'd at the Queens Theatre. [Words adapted from the Italian of Cardinal Ottoboni by

Peter Anthony Motteux. Music by Carlo Francesco Cesarini, Francesco Gasparini and others.]

Sold by I: Walsh . . . at the Golden Harpe and Ho=boy . . . and I. Hare . . . at yᵉ Golden Viol and Flute in Cornhill near yᵉ Royal Exchange.

Apr. 28, 1708, *Daily Courant.*

The advertisement reads: 'The 2d and 3d Acts of the last new Opera call'd Love's Triumph', &c., and the work is assumed to have had title-page as above from the plate as previously used for the first Act. (No. 271. *See* Ill. 1.) The three acts were also issued together as a complete work, with an additional outer illustrated title-page from the plate used for No. 82a, afterwards adapted for No. 293 and other works (*see* Ills. 8 and 20), including the later edition of No. 272.

See Nos. 271 and 450.

273. The Symphonys or Instrumental Parts in the Opera Call'd Love's Triumph [Music by Carlo Francesco Cesarini, Francesco Gasparini and others] as they are Perform'd at the Queens Theatre.

London Printed for I. Walsh Servᵗ. to Her Maᵗⁱᵉ. at yᵉ Harp & Hoboy . . . I. Hare . . . at yᵉ Golden Viol & Flute . . . and P. Randall at yᵉ Violin and Lute by Paulsgrave head Court without Temple Barr in yᵉ Strand.

May 12, 1708, *Daily Courant.*

BM. h. 17. a. (5.) First Treble part only.

Title-page from plate first used presumably for No. 256, with 'Love's Triumph . . . Queens Theatre' from a supplementary plate.

274. The Overture and Chacone belonging to the 1st 2d and 3d Musick of the Opera of Thomyris, consisting of 4 Parts for Violins, Trumpet and Hoboys. Compos'd by Mr. Dupar [i.e. Charles Dieupart], never before publish'd, price 3s.

Printed for J. Walsh . . . and J. Hare . . . and P. Randal, &c.

June 3, 1708, *Daily Courant.*

Probably the work advertised in No. 282a as: 'The Act Tunes in Thomyris.'

Dieupart's association with the opera is unrecorded elsewhere. Presumably the overture is the same as that given in No. 254.

275. The Lady's Entertainment; or, Banquet of Musick. Being a choice Collection of the newest and most Airy Lessons for the Harpsicord or Spinnet. Together with several excellent Preludes, Tocatas, and the most Favourite Song Tunes in the Operas; all fairly Engraven, price 2s 6d. Note These Lessons are likewise proper for the Lute, Harp or Organ.

Printed for J. Walsh . . . at the Harp and Hoboy . . . and J. Hare . . . at the Golden Viol and Flute . . . and P. Randal at the Violin and Lute, &c.

June 12, 1708, *Daily Courant.*

The work may have been issued with an outer illustrated title-page from the plate used for No. 82a, afterwards adapted for No. 293 (*see* Ills. 8 and 20), and for the later edition of 'The 3ᵈ Book of the Ladys Entertainment.' (No. 484.)

See Nos. 282, 308, 484, and 501.

276. Te Deum & Jubilate, for Voices and Instruments, the same that is appointed to be perform'd at the Cathedral Church of St. Paul's on the Thanksgiving Day being the 19th Instant, occasion'd by the late Glorious Victory obtain'd over the French near Audenarde, to be perform'd by the Gentlemen of her Majesty's Chappel Royal, as also the private Musick, compos'd by the late Mr. Henry Purcel. Price 2s.

Printed for J. Walsh . . . at the Harp and Hoboy . . . J. Hare . . . at the Golden Viol and Flute . . . and P. Randal at the Violin and Lute, &c.

Aug. 17, 1708, *Daily Courant.*

> A re-advertisement or a reissue of No. 248.
> *See* Nos. 108, 248, and 595.

277. Sonatas or Chamber Aires for two Violins and a Through Bass. Composed by the late Mr. Ravenscroft Opera Seconda. Engraven in a better Caracter and more corect then the former Edition.

I. Walsh servant to Her Majesty . . . I. Hare . . . P. Randall at ye Violin and Lute. [*c.* 1708.]

Advertised in No. 282a.

> No copy available, the location of the one from which these particulars were taken is not known.
> Presumably the work advertised in the Walsh Cat., *c.* 1721, Ill. 27, as: 'Ravenscrofts Sonatas, for 2 Violins & a Bass. 5s. 0d.'
> About 1708, I. Vaillant was selling: 'Sonate di Camera . . . Giovanni Ravenscroft. Op. 2', which was probably the edition by Roger of Amsterdam, who also issued: 'Sonate a Tre . . . Opera Prima', by Ravenscroft (RCM. LXI. D. 1. (4.)), the first edition of which was issued in Rome, 1695. (BM. K. 3. m. 15.)
> Walsh Cat., 'Apollo's Feast', third Book, *c.* 1729 (W^m. C. Smith copy), only gives one work by Ravenscroft: 'Sonatas for two Violins & a Bass'.

277a. Musick in the Ladys last Stake. [Play by Colley Cibber.]
[J. Walsh, P. Randall, and J. Hare. 1708.]
Advertised in No. 282a.

277b. Mr John Allnotts Musick made for ye Play [by Edmund Smith] call'd Phædra & Hyppolitus.
[J. Walsh, P. Randall, and J. Hare. 1708.]
In four parts.
Advertised in No. 282a.

> BM. g. 15. (4.)
> Part of an unidentified series.
> *See* No. 169.

277c. Mr Kellers new Edition of Rules for a through Bass.
[J. Walsh, P. Randall, and J. Hare. 1708.]
Advertised in No. 282a.

Presumably a reprint or new edition of No. 235.
See No. 511.

277d. 10 Solos by Bomporti for a Violin and a Bass.
[J. Walsh, P. Randall, and J. Hare. 1708.]
Advertised in No. 282a.
See No. 603.

277e. Fingers and Purcells Solos for Violins.
[J. Walsh, P. Randall, and J. Hare. 1708.]
Advertised in No. 282a.
See No. 329.

277f. Fingers and Purcells Solos for Flutes.
[J. Walsh, P. Randall, and J. Hare. 1708.]
Advertised in No. 282a.
See No. 329.

277g. A Collection of familier and noted Tunes for the Flute.
[J. Walsh, P. Randall, and J. Hare. 1708.]
Advertised in No. 282a.

Probably the same work as in Walsh Cat., *c.* 1721, Ill. 28: 'Familiar Aires for yᵉ Flute. 1s. od.'
See Nos. 320 and 608.

277h. A Generall Collection of Catches and Drinking Songs.
[J. Walsh, P. Randall, and J. Hare. 1708.]
Advertised in No. 282a.

May refer to Nos. 303 and 304.

From Oct. 4, 1708, Walsh and Randall advertised as being together 'at the Harp and Hoboy in Catherine-street . . . and the Violin and Lute by Paulsgrave Court,' &c. This continued until July 1709, when the Violin and Lute address was dropped.

---

278. The Second Part of the Division Flute Containing The Newest Divisions upon The Choicest Grounds for the Flute as also Several Excellent Preludes Chacon's and Cibells by The best Masters The whole Fairly Engraven. price 2ˢ. 6ᵈ.
London Printed for I. Walsh . . . I. Hare . . . and P. Randall at yᵉ Violin and Lute, &c.

Oct. 15, 1708, *Daily Courant.*

BM. h. 250. c. (1.)
Walsh Cat., *c.* 1721, Ill. 28, as: 'Second Division Flute. 2s. 6d.'
See No. 184.

279. Ten Sonata's for 2 Flutes and a thorough Bass, compos'd by Signior Romano, Pr, 3s.

J. Walsh and P. Randal at the Harp and Hoboy in Catherine-street near Somerset house in the Strand; and the Violin and Lute by Paulsgrave Court without Temple Bar, and J. Hare at the Golden Viol and Flute, &c.

Oct. 15, 1708, *Daily Courant.*

Walsh Cat., *c.* 1721, Ill. 28, as: 'Romanos Aires, for 2 Flutes & a Bass. 3s. od.'

280. The Dances for several Years Compos'd by Mr. Isaac for Her Majesties Birth Day, engraved in Characters and Figures for the use of Masters or others who desire to improve themselves in the Art of Dancing; the Rules by Monsieur Fivelet [i.e. R. A. Feuillet], done into English by Mr. Wever. [i.e. J. Weaver.] The Dances done in Characters are the Salteralla, the Union, the Britannia, the Spanheim, the Favourite, the Richmond, the Rigadoon and Rondeau, all curiously engraven and sold at reasonable Rates.

Printed for J. Walsh and P. Randal . . . and J. Hare, &c.

Oct. 22, 1708, *Daily Courant.*

This general notice covers some works previously recorded (Nos. 207, 234, and 269) and others, the early editions of which have not been traced; later editions being included in the bibliography. Feuillet's *Rules done into English by Mr. Wever* may refer to a Walsh edition of *Chorégraphie* of which there were two different English editions in 1706. One of these was translated by J. Weaver, and issued by H. Meere, for the Author. (BM. 558*. c. 39.) This work may have been taken over by Walsh, and subsequently advertised as *The Art of Dancing*, &c. (*See* Nos. 343 and 343*a*.) The other English edition of 1706 was by P. Siris, and was sold by the Author, Richard Meares, and Alexander Livingston. (BM. 797. dd. 20.) See Nos. 383, 407, 408, 409, 410, and 411 for separate editions of the dances.

281. A Collection of choice Airs for a Violen, a Flute or Hoboy, consisting of Trumpet Tunes, Marches and Minuets; to which is added several familiar and pleasant Aires in 2 parts, for the several Instruments. Price 6d.

Printed for J. Walsh and P. Randal . . . and J. Hare, &c.

Oct. 22, 1708, *Daily Courant.*

Advertised in No. 282*a* as: 'The Book of Marches and Trumpet Tunes.'

282. The 2ᵈ Book of the Lady's Entertainment or Banquet of Musick, being a choice Collection of the newest and most airy Lessons for the Harpsicord or Spinnet; together with several excellent Preludes, Tocatas, and the most favourite Song Tunes in the Operas, all fairly engraven, pr. 2s. 6d.

Printed for J. Walsh and P. Randal . . . and J. Hare, &c.

Nov. 12, 1708, *Daily Courant.*

The title-page may have been from the plate as issued for the earlier book (No. 275), and the work may have also had an outer illustrated title-page from the plate used for No. 82*a*, afterwards adapted for No. 293 (*see* Ills. 8 and 20) and for the later edition of 'The 3ᵈ Book of the Ladys Entertainment'. (No. 484.)

See Nos. 275, 308, 484, and 501.

282*a*. The Whole Volume Compleat Intituled The Monthly Masks of Vocal Musick Containing all the Choisest Songs by the Best Masters made for the Play-houses Publick Consorts and other Occasions for the Year 1708 [i.e. Nov. 1707–Oct. 1708] with a Through Bass to Each Song and most of them with in the Compass of the Flute price 5ˢ.

London Printed for & Sould by I: Walsh Musicall Instrument maker in Ordinary to her Majesty, &c.

Nov. 12, 1708, *Daily Courant*. (The yearly Collection of Monthly Masks . . . Printed for J. Walsh and P. Randal . . . and J. Hare, &c.)

> BM. H. 313. c. Catalogued as January 1708, but apparently belonging to some other year. RCM. II. A. 15. September 1708 only.
>
> The title-page from the Collins plate (No. 15, *see* Ill. 3) as used for the annual volumes 1703 (No. 140) and other years.
>
> The annual volume has a leaf containing 'A Table of the Songs', and a list of 'Books of Instrumental and Vocal Musick Printed in the Year 1708'. The list is transcribed here, with slight modifications in capitals, &c., and with the reference numbers to the entries in the bibliography added in order to aid identification.
>
> Twenty-four New Country Dances for 1708. (No. 259.)
> The Court Dances or Salterella for 1708. (Nos. 269 and 270.)
> Musick in the Royall Convert. (No. 264.)
> Musick in the Ladys last Stake. (No. 277*a*.)
> Musick in Phædra and Hyppolitus. (No. 277*b*.)
> Musick in the Stratagem. (No. 261.)
> Mr Kellers new Edition of Rules for a through Bass. (No. 277*c*.)
> The Symphonys in Thomyris. (No. 256.)
> Overtures in Camilla Arsinoe & Aires in Thomyris. (No. 262.)
> Tibaldis Sonatas or Aires for 2 Violins and a Bass. (No. 265.)
> Bomportis Sonatas or Aires for 2 Violins & a Bass 2ᵈ. (No. 266.)
> Bomportis Opera Quorto for Violins. (No. 267.)
> Ravenscroft Sonatas or Chamber Aires for Violins. (No. 277.)
> 24 Solos by Mr Pepusch for a Violin and a Bass. (No. 264*a*.)
> 10 Solos by Bomporti for a Violin and a Bass. (No. 277*d*.)
> Songs in the Opera of Loves Triumph. (Nos. 271 and 272.)
> The Symphonys in Loves Triumph. (No. 273.)
> Fingers and Purcells Solos for Violins. (No. 277*e*.)
> Fingers and Purcells Solos for Flutes. (No. 277*f*.)
> Romanos Sonatas for Flutes. (No. 279.)
> The Ladys Entertainment or Banquet of Musick. (No. 275.)
> The Booke of Hyms or Divine Songs. (No. 287.)
> A Table of the Preludes Aires and Tocatas for yᵉ Harpsicord in yᵉ mercurys for yᵉ Year 1708. (No. 263.)
>> Prelude in . . . G♭3.
>> Can you leave Ranging.
>> Ever mery gay and Airy.
>> Never let your heart.
>> What should allarm me.

N

The Act Tunes in Thomyris. (No. 274.)
The 2ᵈ Part of the Division Flute. (No. 278.)
Preludes and Choice Cibells for ye Flute. (No. 283.)
The Ladys Entertainment the 2 Book. (No. 282.)
24 Country Dances for 1709. (No. 284.)
The Books of Country Dances for 3 years. (No. 260.)
The Book of Marches and Trumpet Tunes. (No. 281.)
A Collection of familier and noted Tunes for the Flute. (No. 277g.)
A Generall Collection of Catches and Drinking Songs. (No. 277h.)
See Nos. 103, 109, 140, 160, 188, 223, 258, 331, 370, and 517.

283. Select Preludes and Vollentarys for the Flute being made & Contriv'd for
yᵉ Improvement of yᵉ Hand with Variety of Compositions by all the Eminent
Masters in Europe.
  London Printed for I Walsh and Randal . . . and I. Hare, &c.
  Nov. 18, 1708, *Daily Courant.*

  BM. h. 250. g.
  Probably the work in Walsh Cat., *c.* 1721, Ill. 28, as: 'Preludes & Cibells by the greatest
  Masters in Europe, for a single Flute. 2s. 0d.'
  Advertised in No. 282*a* as: 'Preludes and Choice Cibells for yᵉ Flute.'
  See No. 166, a similar work for the Violin.

284. Twenty four New Country Dances, for the Year 1709, with proper Tunes,
and new Figueres or Directions to each Dance; the whole fairly Engraven, and
carefully Corrected. Pr. 6d.
  Printed for J. Walsh and P. Randal . . . and J. Hare, &c.
  Nov. 26, 1708, *Daily Courant.*

285. Six Sonatas with an Overture and Aires, in 4 Parts, for Violins and Hoboys,
with a Trumpet, Flute de Almain, and a thorough Bass for the Bass Violin Passoon
or Harpsicord. Compos'd by Mr. Wᵐ Corbett.
  Printed for J. Walsh and P. Randal . . . and J. Hare, &c.
  Dec. 8, 1708, *Daily Courant.*

    The work may be the same as that listed Walsh Cat., 'Apollo's Feast', third book, *c.* 1729
  (Wᵐ. C. Smith copy), as: 'Corbets Sonatas for variety of Instruments in 6 Parts.'

285*a*. A new Set of Tunes Compos'd by Mʳ W. Corbett for the Theatre.
  [J. Walsh, P. Randall, and J. Hare.]
  In four parts.
  Dec. 8, 1708, *Daily Courant.*

  BM. g. 15. (5.)
  Issued as part V of an unidentified series. (*See* No. 169.)
  Advertised in No. 331 as: 'Musick in four Parts by Mr. Corbett.'

286. The Flagelet Reviv'd; or, The Bird Fancyer's Delight: Being a new Plain
and easy Introduction to Play on the Flagelet . . . Pr. 1s.

Printed for J. Walsh and P. Randal . . . and J. Hare, &c.

Dec. 15, 1708, *Daily Courant.*

This is the earliest announcement of a Walsh work using the title *The Bird Fancyer's Delight.* It may or may not be an earlier edition of *The Bird Fancier's Delight.* (No. 513.) Advertised in No. 331 as: 'A Book for the Flagelet Gamut way.'

287. Lyra Davidica: or A Collection of Divine Songs and Hymns, partly New Composed, partly Translated from the High-German, and Latin Hymns: And set to easy and pleasant Tunes, for more General Use. The Musick Engrav'd on Copper Plates. Isa. xxiv. &c.

London, Printed for J. Walsh . . . J. Hare . . . and P. Randal at the Violin and Lute . . . 1708.

Dec. 24, 1708, *Daily Courant.* (Newly Publish'd.)

BM. A. 749.

Presumably the work advertised Dec. 24, 1708, as: 'Youth's Introduction to Divine Harmony: Being a Collection of Divine Hymns and Songs, Translated out of several Languages. Together with new Compositions set to the most pleasant Tunes and Airets for the more general use: The Musick Engraven on Copper Plates. Price 1s.'

Probably issued a little earlier than the advertisement. Advertised in No. 282a as: 'The Booke of Hyms or Divine Songs.'

288. The 4th Book of the Musical Recreation; or The whole Art of playing on the Violin unfolded and Practically improved by short and plain Rules: To which is added, a new Collection of Aires, Trumpet-Tunes, Minuets, Giggs and Horn Pipes, compos'd by the most eminent Masters, with several French Dances never before Published.

Printed for and sold by J. Hare . . . and J. Walsh . . . Price 1s. 6d.

Dec. 29, 1708, *Daily Courant.*

See No. 64. No details of the second and third books have been traced.

289. The 3d Book of Nolens Volens; or, The Art of Playing upon the Hautboy improv'd and made familiar to every Capacity by short and plain Rules. Also a Choice Collection of Aires, Marches, Trumpet-Tunes, and Minuets, purposely composed for that Instrument by several able Masters.

Printed for and sold by J. Hare . . . at the Viol and Flute . . . and J. Walsh . . . Price 1s 6d.

Dec. 29, 1708, *Daily Courant.*

No details of the earlier books have been traced.

290. [Vacant. *See* Introduction p. xii.]

291. [Vacant. *See* Introduction p. xii.]

292. All the Songs set to Musick in the last new Opera call'd, Pyrrhus and Demetrius. [Words translated from the Italian of Adriano Morselli by Owen MacSwiney.

Music by Alessandro Scarlatti and N. F. Haym.] The whole being done from the
Original by that Compleat Writer of Musick Mr. Armstrong, and by him Carefully corrected.

Engraved and Printed for J. Walsh and P. Randall . . . and J. Hare, &c.

Jan. 20, 1709, *Daily Courant.*

This first edition, without the Italian words, may have had an inner title-page as follows:
Songs in the New Opera, call'd Pyrrhus and Demetrius. All ye Singing parts being trans-
pos'd into G Cliff and put into such Keys that bring them into ye Compass of Treble or Tenor
Voices. The whole being done from ye Original by that Compleat writer of Musick Mr.
Armstrong, and by him carefully corrected. Walsh, Randall and Hare.

This transcription is from Ellis Catalogue, No. 297, but the exact wording may have been
as that given for No. 293, down to the end of the word 'corrected'.

The title-page was presumably from the same plate as that used for the inner title-
page of the next edition (No. 293, *see* Ill. 1), and the work also had a frontispiece or outer title-
page also used for No. 293. (*See* Ills. 8 and 20.)

Pyrrhus and Demetrius was an English version of Alessandro Scarlatti's *Pirro e Demetrio,*
the musical arrangement of which is usually attributed to N. F. Haym, who contributed the
overture and many musical numbers. Armstrong's part in the work has not been recognized
hitherto, and except as a musician whose name appears in the contemporary records of
Opera in London (*Proceedings of the Royal Musical Association,* 1913–14) he appears to be
otherwise unknown.

See Nos. 293, 297, 302, 342, and 345.

293. Songs In The New Opera, Call'd Pyrrhus and Demetrius [Words translated
from the Italian of Adriano Morselli by Owen Mac Swiney. Music by Alessandro Scarlatti and N. F. Haym]. All yᵉ Singing Parts being transpos'd into yᵉ
G: Cliff & put into such Keys that brings them into yᵉ Compass of Treble or Tenor
Voices. The whole being done from yᵉ Original by that Compleat writer of
Musick Mʳ. Armstrong. and by him carefully corrected. also he hath made words
to 17 of yᵉ Italian Songs. thus mark'd†.

Sold by I: Walsh Musicall Instrument maker in Or=/=dinary to her Majesty, &
P. Randall at the Harp and Ho=boy . . . and I. Hare . . . at yᵉ Golden Viol and
Flute, &c.

Feb. 9, 1709, *Daily Courant.*

BM. H. 109. Imperfect.
RCM. XCV. D. 15. (4.)
Richard Newton, Henley-in-Arden.
With an outer illustrated title-page:
Songs in the Opera Call'd Pyrrhus and Demetrius.
London Printed for & Sold by Iohn Walsh Servant to her Majesty at the Harp and
Hautboy in Katherine Street near Somerset House in the Strand.

This illustrated title-page is from the plate, first used by Walsh for No. 82a (*see* Ills. 8 and
20), with title from a supplementary plate, and with the Arms of Queen Anne substituted
for the Arms of the Earl of Manchester, Baron Kimbolton, in the medallion centre of the
design.

The inner title-page is from the plate used for No. 203 and earlier works (*see* Ill. 1), with

'Pyrrhus and Demetrius . . . mark'd †' from a supplementary plate, and the imprint modified by the introduction of P. Randall.

The BM. copy is without the original title-pages, but titles have been supplied in MS.; and it also wants the chorus at the end, *Live great Thames.*

This second edition was advertised as:

'A Second Edition of the Songs set to Musick in the last new Opera call'd Pyrrhus and Demetrius; with the Addition of the Italian Words to such Songs as are perform'd in that Language. Also at the desire of several Ladies and Gentlemen (who Plays on the Harpsicord) the Violin part is put in to all the Songs that have Symphonys with them.

Printed for and sold by J. Walsh . . . and P. Randall . . . and J. Hare,' &c.

Some numbers were published separately by Walsh and others, and John Cullen announced 'A New Edition of the Songs in the Opera of Pyrrhus and Demetrius'. (June 21–3, 1709, *Post Boy.* BM. I. 355.) This was engraved by T. Cross, junior, and contains the same numbers as Walsh's edition.

See Nos. 292, 297, 302, 342, and 345.

294. The Symphonys or Instrumental Parts in the Opera Call'd Pyrrhus and Demetrius [Music by Alessandro Scarlatti and N. F. Haym] as they are Perform'd at yᵉ Queens Theatre.

London Printed for I. Walsh Servᵗ. to Her Maᵗⁱᵉ. & P. Randall at yᵉ Harp & Hoboy in Catherine street . . . I. Hare . . . at yᵉ Golden Viol & Flute, &c.

Feb. 24, 1709, *Daily Courant.*

BM. h. 17. a. (2.) First Treble part only.

Title-page from plate previously used for No. 273 with 'Pyrrhus and Demetrius . . . Queens Theatre' from a supplementary plate, and with the imprint altered and cut.

295. Choice Italian and English Musick for Two Flutes In which is contain'd the Overture of Pyrrhus and Demetrius as also several new Overtures and Aires with the choicest Ariets, and Duets, out of the last new Opera's of Loves Triumph Pyrrhus and Clotilda to which are added Three excellent new Sonata's and a Chacoone by Corelli Nicolini Haim Torelli and Pez Note. That there are added several Ariets of the new Opera Introduc'd with their Symphonys in this Edition which are not in the former, And the Whole much more Correct All Engrav'd in a fair Character. Price, 1.ˢʰ: 6.ᵈ:

London Printed for I. Walsh . . . and P. Randall . . . and I. Hare, &c.

Mar. 31, 1709, *Daily Courant.* (Next week will be publish'd.)

BM. a. 209. a. (9.) First Flute part only.

Earlier edition not traced; the advertisement is assumed to refer to the copy listed here. Advertised in No. 331, as: 'English & Italian Airs for 2 Flutes'.

Probably the same work as in Walsh Cat., *c.* 1721, Ill. 28, as: 'Overtures in Pyrrhus, &c., for two Flutes. 2ˢ. 0ᵈ.

296. Songs In The New Opera, Call'd Clotilda [Words from the Italian of G. B. Neri. Music by Francesco Conti and others] The Songs done in Italian and English as they are Perform'd at yᵉ Queens Theatre The whole Carefully Corected.

Sold by I: Walsh. Musicall Instrument maker in Or=/=dinary to her Majesty, & P. Randall at the Harp and Ho=boy . . . and I. Hare, &c.

Apr. 11, 1709, *Daily Courant*. (On Thursday next will be Publish'd.)
Apr. 15, 1709, *Daily Courant*.

> BM. H. 328.
> RCM. XCV. D. 15. (1.); XXXII. A. 3. (5.)
> With an outer illustrated title-page:
> Songs in the Opera Call'd Clotilda.
> London Printed for & Sold by Iohn Walsh Servant to her Majesty at the Harp and
> Hautboy in Katherine Street near Somerset House in the Strand.
>
> The inner title-page from the plate used for No. 293 and earlier works (*see* Ill. 1), with
> 'Clotilda . . . Carefully Corected' from a supplementary plate. The outer title-page from a
> plate first used by Walsh for No. 82a (*see* Ill. 8), modified for No. 293 (*see* Ill. 20), with
> the title 'Songs . . . Clotilda' from a supplementary plate.
>
> Walsh accused Luke Pippard of copying his *Opera of Clotilda* in a very imperfect manner.
> (No. 334.)
>
> *See* Nos. 297, 302, and 342.

297. All the Songs set to Musick in the last new Opera call'd Clotilda . . . Also
the following Opera's Reprinted with Additions, viz. Pyrrhus and Demetrius,
Love's Triump[h], Camilla, Thomyris, Arsinoe, Rosamond and the Temple of
Love; being 8 Operas of the Italian manner, which may be had single, or in
2 volumes, neatly bound all engrav'd.

Printed for J. Walsh . . . P. Randall . . . and J. Hare, &c.

Apr. 25, 1709, *Daily Courant*.

> These particular editions, in so far as they differed from earlier ones, cannot be definitely
> identified. What may be assumed to be a contemporary edition of *Camilla* is described in
> the following item, although it may have been issued rather later than 1709.
>
> *See* index for references to other editions.

298. Songs In The New Opera, Call'd Camilla [Words translated from the Italian
of Silvio Stampiglia by Owen MacSwiney. Music by Marco Antonio Bononcini]
as they are perform'd at the Theatre Royall.

Sold by I: Walsh Musicall Instrument maker in Or=/=dinary to her Majesty, at
the Golden Harpe and Ho=boy, in Catherine=Street near Sommerset House in the
Strand.

[*c.* 1709 or later.]

> RM. 11. b. 20. (1.)
>
> The title-page adapted from the plate as used for the earlier edition (No. 221, *see* Ill. 1),
> with the Hare portion of the imprint omitted. With an outer illustrated title-page from
> the plate (Berchet-Hulsbergh) also used in the earlier edition (No. 221, *see* Ill. 13), but with
> the title 'Opera of Camilia by Bononcini' supplied in MS. in the medallion in place of the
> earlier engraved title, with '10–6' added in MS. to the imprint, which is the same as in the
> earlier work: London Printed for I. Walsh, &c.
>
> This edition is mainly from the same plates in the same order as No. 221, some of
> the paginations being in MS. It includes the overture, differently engraved, inserted at the
> beginning and two additional songs at the end. One number formerly sung by 'Mr
> Hughs' in English is given in Italian (S'en vola) as 'Sung by Sig^ra. Margaritta De Lepine'.
>
> The imprint of the inner title-page of RM. 11. b. 20. (1.) suggests that the copy may

have been issued rather earlier than 1709, but as some of the plates (11, 19, 21, &c.) appear to be later it is impossible to definitely date this copy.

Camilla was the most frequently performed of all the Italian operas of the period, and consequently Walsh was frequently issuing copies, which in most cases only differed in the imprints.

One of these issues has the title from the same plate as No. 298 (*see* Ill. 1): 'Songs In The New Opera, Call'd Camilla', &c., but with the imprint: Sold by I: Walsh . . . P. Randall . . . and I. Hare, &c., as in Nos. 296, 344, and other works. This issue, dated *c.* 1709–10, is not entered elsewhere in the bibliography.

See Nos. 201, 204, 206, 209, 221, 238, 402, 560, and 565.

299. There being lately printed a Spurious Edition of the Songs and Symphonys of the Opera of Thomyris, with many faults by Pippard and Cullen, viz. the Songs sold at 5s and the Symphonys at 1s. 6d. This is to give notice to all Lovers of Musick that to discourage such Practices, the Original Songs and Symphonys of the above-nam'd Opera are now sold at 5s together, or the Symphonys or Instrumental Parts only at 1s and the like shall be done for the future on all such Occasions.

Printed for J. Walsh . . . P. Randall . . . and J. Hare, &c.

May 2, 1709, *Daily Courant.*

See No. 251, for an earlier reference to a 'spurious edition'.

300. The Symphonys or Instrumental Parts in the Opera Call'd Clotilda [Music by Francesco Conti and others] as they are Perform'd at the Queens Theatre.

London Printed for I. Walsh Servt. to Her Matie. and P: Randall at y^e. Harp & Hoboy, in Catherine Street near Somerset House in y^e. Strand. I: Hare Instrument-maker, at the golden Viol and Flute in Cornhill near y^e. Royal Exchange.

May 7–10, 1709, *Post Man.*

BM. h. 17. a. (3.) First Treble part only.
Advertised in No. 331, as: 'The Symphony in Clotilda.'
Earliest traced example of this title-page, the plate of which must have been used before as the title 'Clotilda . . . Queens Theatre' is from a supplementary plate.
See No. 302; and Ill. 21.

301. The Monthly Mask of Vocal Musick for April; in which is contain'd the Comical and Diverting Songs in the last new Play call'd The Modern Prophets, made by Mr. Durfey. Price 6d.

Printed for J. Walsh . . . P. Randall . . . and J. Hare, &c.

May 16, 1709, *Daily Courant.*

This, with other numbers in *The Monthly Mask* for May, 1709, and some separate numbers reprinted from *The Monthly Mask*, or which may have been issued only in single sheet form, are all that appear to have been published by Walsh of the music of this play.
See BM. H. 1601. (315.); G. 313. (46.); G. 313. (21.); H. 1601. (515.); G. 313. (23.), all of which are without Walsh imprints.

302. A Second Edition of all the Songs set to Musick in the last new Opera, call'd Clotilda [Music by Francesco Conti and others], both in Italian and English, with

their Symphonies or Instrumental Parts, as they are performed at the Queen's Theatre: also the most Correct Edition of the Opera of Pyrrhus and Demetrius [Music by Alessandro Scarlatti and N. F. Haym] from the Original Score, with the Symphonies introduced in the Songs for the conveniency of the Harpsicord, and the Instrumental Part, separate for the use of Consorts.

All Engraven and Printed for J. Walsh . . . P. Randal . . . and J. Hare, &c.
May 19–21, 1709, *Post Man.*

See Nos. 292, 293, 296, 297, 300, and 342.

303. The Iovial Companions or Merry Club being A Choice Collection of the Newest and most Diverting Catches for three & four Voices Together with the most Celebrated Catches Compos'd by the late Mr. Henr. Purcell & Dr. Blow all fairly Engraven & Carefully Corrected.

London Printed for I. Walsh & P. Randall . . . and I. Hare at the Golden Viol and Flute, &c.
May 20, 1709, *Daily Courant.*

BM. G. 108.
Advertised in No. 331 and Walsh Cat., *c.* 1721, Ill. 27, as: 'A Book of Catches', &c.
J. Young advertised Sep. 15–17, 1709, *Post Man*, 'The pleasant Musical Companion or Merry Club . . . Songs and Catches . . . by Dr Blow and the late Mr Henry Purcel', &c.
See No. 277*h.*

304. The Bottle Companions or Bacchanalian Club being A choice Collecttion of merry Drinking Songs and Healths Consisting, of Loyalty Love, and good Fellowship; the Compositions by the most Ingenious Masters all fairly Engraven and carefully Corrected.

London Printed for I: Walsh and P: Randall . . . and I: Hare, &c.
May 24–6, 1709, *Post Man.*

BM. H. 34.
Advertised in No. 331 as: 'A Collection of Drinking Songs'.
Walsh Cat., *c.* 1721, Ill. 27, as: 'Drinking Songs. 2s. 6d.'
See No. 277*h.*

305. The new Flute Master 7th Book; containing the most perfect Rules and Directions for Learners on the Flute, together with the newest and choicest Aires, both of Italian and English: As also the most Favourite Song Tunes in the last new Operas of Pyrrhus and Clotilda; Likewise a set of extraordinary Lessons for a single Flute. By Signior Pepusch, and Preludes to introduce the following Aires, in their several Keys. All fairly engraven. pr. 1s 6d.

Printed for J. Walsh . . . P. Randal . . . and J. Hare, &c.
June 9–11, 1709, *Post Man.*

Advertised in No. 331 as: 'A New Flute Book 7th Flute Master'.
See Nos. 20*b*, 33, 113, 182, 390, 486, 510, 563, and 578, for other books and works with

similar titles. No details of the third, sixth and eighth books of the early series finishing with No. 486 have been traced.

From July 1709 Walsh and Randall advertised together at the one address 'the Harp and Hoboy in Catherine-street'; the Paulsgrave Court address having been given up.

---

306. The 4 Books of Nolens Volens, or the Art of Playing on the Violin; being an Introduction for learners on that Instrument in a more plain and easy method than any yet extant. Together with an extraordinary Collection of Tunes and Aires, by Mr. Crofts, Mr. Barret, and Mr. Corbet, and particularly all the favourite Aires in the Operas of Pyrrhus and Clotilda.

Printed for J. Walsh Servant in Ordinary to her Majesty, and P. Randal, at the Harp and Hoboy in Catherine street . . . and J. Hare at the Golden Viol and Flute, &c.

June 30–July 2, 1709, *Post Man.*

> This includes the first notice of the fourth book, which was advertised in No. 331 as: 'A New Violin Book 4th Nolens Volens.'
> See Nos. 72, 158, 424, 442, 472, and 487 for other books. No details of the first book have been traced.

307. Mr Pepusch's Aires for two Violins Made on Purpose for the Improvement of Practitioners in Consort The whole Fairly Engraven and Carefully Corected.

London Printed for J. Walsh Servant in Ordinary to her Majesty and P. Randall . . . and J. Hare, &c.

June 30–July 2, 1709, *Post Man.* (An Excellent Set of Aires made on purpose for two Violins . . . Compos'd by Mr. Pepusch . . . pr. 1s. 6d.)

> The title as given partly supplied from the later edition. (No. 460.)
> See Nos. 327 and 460.

308. The 3ᵈ Book of the Ladys Entertainment or Banquet of Musick being A Choice Collection of the most Celebrated Aires & Duets In the Opera's of Pyrrhus & Clotilda: Curiously Set and Fitted to the Harpsicord or Spinnet: With their Symphonys introduc'd in a Compleat manʳ. by Mʳ: Wᵐ: Babel.

London, Printed for J. Walsh Servant in Ordinary to her Majesty, and P. Randall . . . & J. Hare, &c.

Oct. 22–5, 1709, *Tatler.*

> The title as given is from the later edition (No. 484), with 'In the Opera's . . . Clotilda', from a supplementary plate. The work may have had an outer illustrated title-page from the plate used for No. 296, and earlier works (see Ills. 8 and 20), with the title: 'The 3ᵈ Ladys Entertainment or Banquet of Musick', &c. as in No. 484.
> Included later in Walsh's numerical series, with modified title-page and with 'Nᵒ. 169' added.
> See Nos. 275, 282, 484, and 501.

o   97

309. Minuets for the Royall Portuguise.
   [J. Walsh, P. Randall, and J. Hare. 1709.]
   Advertised in No. 331.

310. Minuets for the Brawl of Audenard.
   [J. Walsh, P. Randall, and J. Hare. 1709.]
   Advertised in No. 331.

311. The Portuguise Figure dance. [The Royall Portuguez.]
   [J. Walsh, P. Randall, and J. Hare. 1709.]
   Advertised in No. 331.

312. Mr Barretts Musick in the Comedy calld the Ladys fine Aires for Violins
and Hoboys.
   [J. Walsh, P. Randall, and J. Hare. 1709.]
   In four parts.
      BM. g. 15. (8.)
      Issued as part of an unidentified series.
      Advertised in No. 331 as: 'Musick in the Ladys Fine Aires.'
      See No. 169.

313. [Vacant. *See* Introduction p. xii.]

314. Musick in Perollo and Isadora. [i.e. Perolla and Izadora, by Colley Cibber.]
   [J. Walsh, P. Randall, and J. Hare. 1709.]
   Advertised in No. 331.

315. A Cantata by Mr Purcell.
   [J. Walsh, P. Randall, and J. Hare. 1709.]
   Advertised in No. 331.
      The work not identified; probably by Daniel Purcell.

316. A Cantata by Mr Eccles.
   [J. Walsh, P. Randall, and J. Hare. 1709.]
   Advertised in No. 331.
      The work not identified.

317. A Cantata by Mr Pepusch.
   [J. Walsh, P. Randall, and J. Hare. 1709.]
   Advertised in No. 331.
      The work not identified.

318. A Collection of Scotch Songs.
   [J. Walsh, P. Randall, and J. Hare. 1709.]
   Advertised in No. 331.

Probably the first edition of the work that was afterwards published with modifications and with the title: 'A Collection of new Songs With a Through Bass to each Song for the Harpsicord Compos'd by Several Masters' (No. 464), although it may have been another edition of No. 37.

319. A Collection of Comicall Songs.
[J. Walsh, P. Randall, and J. Hare. 1709.]
Advertised in No. 331.

Presumably the work in Walsh Cat. *c*. 1721, Ill. 27, as: 'A Book of Comical Songs. 2s. 6d.'

320. A Book of Familiar and Noted Tunes &c.
[J. Walsh, P. Randall, and J. Hare. 1709.]
Advertised in No. 331.

The work not identified; probably for Violin or Flute.
See Nos. 277*g* and 608.

321. Select Lessons for a Single Flute.
[J. Walsh, P. Randall, and J. Hare. 1709.]
Advertised in No. 331.

Walsh Cat. *c*. 1721, Ill. 28, as: 'Select Lessons 1st book. 1s. 6d.' Walsh Cat. also includes: 'Select Lessons 2d book. 1s. 6d.', which has not been traced and cannot be dated.

322. A 2d Book Select Lessons for a Violin.
[J. Walsh, P. Randall, and J. Hare. 1709.]
Advertised in No. 331.

Walsh Cat. *c*. 1721, Ill. 27, as: 'Select Lessons 2d book. 1s. 6d.'
See No. 93.

323. The Court dances for three Last Years.
[J. Walsh, P. Randall, and J. Hare. 1709.]
Advertised in No. 331.

Presumably a collection of Court Dances previously published separately.

324. Corbetts Sonatas for two Violins and a Bass.
[J. Walsh, P. Randall, and J. Hare. 1709.]
Advertised in No. 331.

The work not identified, but probably a Violin edition of No. 172, or a Walsh edition of Corbett's: 'Six Sonata's a 3° for Two Violins & Thrõ=bass . . . Opera Quarta Libro Secondo', published by L. Pippard for the Author. (BM. h. 50. (2.))

325. Pyrrhus Aires for two Flutes. [From the Opera by Alessandro Scarlatti and N. F. Haym.]
[J. Walsh, P. Randall, and J. Hare. 1709.]
Advertised in No. 331.

Newspaper notices (*Post Man, Tatler*, Dec. 10–13, 1709, &c.) give:
'The most celebrated Airs and Duets in the Opera's of Pyrrhus and Clotilda. Curiously

fitted and contrived for two Flutes and their Simphonies; introduced in a compleat **Manner**. Price each Set 2s. 6d. Note, Most of them being printed in the Keys they were performed in at the Theatre, renders them as proper for Two Violins, being very sprightly and agreeable to the Instruments. The whole fairly engraven.

Printed for J. Walsh . . . and P. Randall at the Harp and Hautboy . . . and J. Hare,' &c.

The title was presumably similar to that of the Cardiff copy of No. 326.

326. The Most Celebrated Aires & Duets In the Opera of Clotilda [Music by Francesco Conti and others]: Curiously fitted and Contriv'd for two Flutes: With their Symphonys introduc'd in a Compleat manᵣ. The whole fairly Engraven. Note, most of these being here Printed in the same Keys they were Perform'd in at the Theatre, renders them as well proper for two Violins, being very spritely & agreeable to the Instruments.

Printed for J. Walsh Servant in Ordinary to her Majesty, and P. Randall at the Harp & Hoboy . . . & J. Hare, &c.

[1709.]

Cardiff Public Library. Fluto secundo part only.

Advertised in No. 331 as: 'Clotilda Aires for two Flutes.'

The title-page from a plate probably used previously for No. 325, with 'In the Opera of Clotilda', from a supplementary plate.

Newspaper notices (*Post Man, Tatler*, Dec. 10–13, 1709, &c.) give:

'The most celebrated Airs and Duets in the Opera's of Pyrrhus and Clotilda. Curiously fitted and contrived for two Flutes,' &c.

327. Pepush Aires for two Flutes.

[J. Walsh, P. Randall, and J. Hare. 1709.]

Advertised in No. 331.

Presumably: 'Mr Pepusch's Airs for Two Flutes, made on purpose for the Improvement of Practitioners in Consort. The whole fairly engraven.

Engraven and printed for J. Walsh . . . and P. Randall . . . and J. Hare,' &c. (Apr. 15–18, 1710, *Tatler*.)

The title-page may have been from the plate used for No. 307, of which the Flute work may have been simply another edition.

328. Albinonis Concertos in Seven Parts for three Violins Tenors and Bass Violin with a Through Bass for the Harpsicord Compos'd by Tomaso Albinoni Opera Secunda.

London Printed for J. Walsh Servant in Ordinary to her Majesty and P. Randall . . . and J. Hare at the Viol and Flute, &c.

[1709.]

Advertised in No. 331.

BM. g. 671. a.

Walsh Cat., *c.* 1721, Ill. 27, as: 'Albinonis Concertos, for 2 Violins & a Bass. 6s. od.'

See Nos. 366, 524, and 548.

329. Six Sonatas or Solos for the Flute with a Through Bass for the Harpsichord Compos'd by Mᵣ. G. Finger and Mᵣ. D. Purcell.

London Printed for J. Walsh . . . and P. Randall at the Harp and Hoboy . . . and J. Hare, &c.

[1709.]

Advertised in No. 331 as: 'Fingers and Purcells Solos for the Flute.'

BM. h. 17. (2.)

The work was also issued for a Violin and Bass, probably with a title-page adapted from the Flute edition. It was advertised in No. 331 as: 'Fingers and Purcells Solos for the Violin.'

Both editions are listed in Walsh Cat., *c.* 1721, Ills. 27 and 28, as for: 'Violin & a Bass'; 'Flute & a Bass.'

See Nos. 277e and 277f.

330. Mr Manlys Tunes.

[J. Walsh, P. Randall, and J. Hare. 1709.]

Advertised in No. 331.

The work not identified. Composer's name probably Manley, as in the BM. catalogue.

331. The Whole Volume Compleat Intituled The Monthly Masks of Vocal Musick Containing all the Choisest Songs by the Best Masters made for the Play-houses Publick Consorts and other Occasions for the Year 1709 [i.e. Nov. 1708–Oct. 1709] with a Through Bass to Each Song and most of them with in the Compoß of the Flute price 5s.

London Printed for & Sould by I: Walsh Musicall Instrument maker in Ordinary to her Majesty &c.

[*c.* Nov. 1709.]

BM. H. 313. d. Imperfect.

RCM. II. A. 15. Imperfect.

The title-page is from the Collins plate (No. 15, *see* Ill. 3) as used for 1708 (No. 282a) and earlier years. No complete copy with collective title-page being available, the details have been taken from Ellis Cat. 339, No. 237.

The BM. copy has a leaf containing 'A Table of the Songs in the Monthly Mask for the Year 1709 Printed for I Walsh & Randall' and a list of 'Books of Instrumental and Vocal Musick Printed in ye Year 1709.'

The list is transcribed here, with reference numbers to the entries in the bibliography added in order to aid identification:

Twenty four New Country dances 1709. (No. 284.)
Minuets for the Royall Portuguise. (No. 309.)
Minuets for the Brawl of Audenard. (No. 310.)
The Portuguise Figure dance. (No. 311.)
Musick in the Ladys Fine Aires. (No. 312.)
Musick in four Parts by Mr Corbett. (No. 285a.)
Musick in Perollo and Isadora. (No. 314.)
The Opera of Pyrrhus and Demetrius. (No. 292.)
The Symphonys in Pyrrhus. (No. 294.)
The Opera of Clotilda. (No. 296.)
The Symphony in Clotilda. (No. 300.)
English & Italian Aires for 2 Flutes. (No. 295.)
A Book of Catches for 3 and 4 Voices. (No. 303.)

A Collection of Drinking Songs. (No. 304.)
A Cantata by Mr Purcell. (No. 315.)
A Cantata by Mr Eccles. (No. 316.)
A Cantata by Mr Pepusch. (No. 317.)
A Collection of Scotch Songs. (No. 318.)
A Collection of Comicall Songs. (No. 319.)
A New Flute Book 7th Flute Master. (No. 305.)
A New Violin Book 4th Nolens Volens. (No. 306.)
A Book of Familiar and Noted Tunes, &c. (No. 320.)
A Book for the Flagelet Gamut way. (No. 286.)
Select Lessons for a Single Flute. (No. 321.)
A 2d Book Select Lessons for a Violin. (No. 322.)
Country dances for three Last Years. (No. 333.)
The Court dances for three Last Years. (No. 323.)
Corbetts Sonatas for two Violins and a Bass. (No. 324.)
Pyrrhus Aires for two Flutes. (No. 325.)
Clotilda Aires for two Flutes. (No. 326.)
Pepush Aires for two Flutes. (No. 327.)
Pepush 2d sett of Solos for the Flute. (No. 335.)
Albinonis Concertos. (No. 328.)
Pepush Aires for two Violins. (No. 307.)
The 3d Book of the Ladys Entertainment. (No. 308.)
Fingers and Purcells Solos for the Violin. (No. 329.)
Fingers and Purcells Solos for the Flute. (No. 329.)
Mr Manlys Tunes. (No. 330.)
See Nos. 103, 109, 140, 160, 188, 223, 258, 282a, 370, and 517.

332. Twenty four new Country Dances for 1710. With proper tunes, and new Figures or Directions to each Dance. Compos'd by Mr. Kynaston. All fairly engraven. Pr. 6d.

Printed for J. Walsh . . . and P. Randall, at the Harp and Hautboy . . . and J. Hare, &c.

Nov. 1–3, 1709, *Tatler.*

Advertised in No. 370 as: 'Twenty four Country Dances for 1710.'

333. The new Country Dancing-Master is publish'd, containing the Country Dances for the Three last Years.

Printed for J. Walsh . . . and P. Randall, at the Harp and Hautboy . . . and J. Hare, &c.

Nov. 1–3, 1709, *Tatler.*

Advertised in No. 331 as: 'Country dances for three Last Years.'
See Nos. 193, 260, 371, 394, 441, and 489.

334. Six Sonata's Five in Four & a Sixth in 7 Parts Compos'd In Imitation of Archangelo Corelli By Wm: Topham. M:A Opera Terza.

London, Printed for J. Walsh . . . and P. Randall at ye Harp & Hoboy . . . & J. Hare, &c.

Nov. 14, 1709, *Daily Courant.*

BM. g. 171. Organo part only.

This work occasioned the following correspondence in the press. A notice in the *Post Man*, Nov. 17–19 by Wm. Topham, no copy of which is available, was followed by:

'To all Lovers of Musick. Whereas in the *Post-Man* of Saturday last Wm Topham has published in a Scurrillous manner, that I have Printed a Spurious Edition of his Sonatas, and maliciously under sells them; now the only true Reason of my Reprinting those Sonatas is by the way of reprisal on Luke Pippard, who has lately Coppied on me the Opera of Clotilda (tho in a very imperfect manner) therefore to discourage such practices, I do hereby give notice, that I have Reprinted a 2d Edition of the said Sonnats, and sell them for 2s. 6d. the Sett, and are of a finer Character and more Correct than the said Pippard's Edition, which is so ill done that it is Impracticable to perform from them, as has been observed by several Masters, the like Method of Reprisal will be used on the said Luke Pippard, let who will be the Authors of the Musick. Witness my Hand, John Walsh. Sold at my Shop at the Harp in Catherine street,' &c. Nov. 22–4, 1709, *Post Man*.

'To all Lovers of Musick. Whereas John Walsh has impudently publish'd in the *Post Man*, of Thursday last, two notorious falsehoods, viz. That I have in a Scandalous manner informed the World of his Spurious Edition of my Sonatas; and that Luke Pippards impression is (in his own words) so ill done, that it is impracticable to perform from 'em, as has been observed by several Masters. I hereby declare that there is nothing Scandalous in my Advertisement; unless my just endeavours to detect his Piracy can support his Malicious charge; and that the said John Walshs Impression is so far from being more correct than that of Luke Pippards, which is practicable without Equivocation (tho' not to him that can't perform) that he has Printed such mistakes in the Thorough-Base as only he himself, and no Masters could possibly have overlooked, the truth of which I am ready to give occular Demonstration of, at any time and in any place before Competent and Impartial Judges: witness my Hand, Wm Topham.'

'NB. That Mr. Walsh in the *Post-Man* of Thursday last, has with great injustice Taxed me with the Reprinting of Clotilda upon him, as if I were the first Aggressor, whereas he began with me by Reprinting and Underselling the first Musick I ever published, and says he'll spend Thousand Pounds to ruin me, if I do not discontinue Printing, Tho' I served him therein honestly, during my Apprenticeship to him, I hope the Publick will not think it unreasonable for me to Reprint his Copies till he allows me the sole advantage of my own. Luke Pippard.' Nov. 26–9, 1709, *Post Man*.

Walsh also published his protest in *The Tatler*, Nov. 22–4, 1709.

Walsh's edition of Topham's Opera Terza was presumably the work advertised in No. 370, as: 'Tophams Violin Sonatas,' and in Walsh Cat., *c*. 1721, Ill. 27, as: 'Tophams Sonatas, for 2 Violins & a Bass. 3s. od.'

See No. 363.

335. **A Second Set of Solos for the Flute. with A Thorough Bass for the Bassoon, Bass-Flute or Harpsicord, Compos'd by Mr. Pepusch.**

London, Printed for J. Walsh . . . & P. Randall at ye Harp & Hoboy . . . & J. Hare, &c. [With price '3s' in MS.]

Nov. 26–9, 1709, *Post Man*.

BM. h. 250. c. (2.)
Advertised in No. 331 as: 'Pepush 2d sett of Solos for the Flute.'
Walsh Cat., *c*. 1721, Ill. 28, as: 'Pepusch 2d Solos, for a Flute & a Bass. 4s. od.'
See No. 232.

336. The New Violin-Master; or The whole Art of Playing on that Instrument unfolded and practically Improv'd, by short and plain Rules. To which is added A Choice Collection of Ayrs, Trumpet-Tunes and Minuets, with Flourishes, by the most able Masters: Also the new Marches both single and in two Parts never before Publish'd.

Printed for J. Hare . . . J. Walsh . . . and P. Randall at the Harp and Hoboy . . . Price 1s. 6d.

Dec. 21, 1709, *Daily Courant*.

L. Pippard advertised Feb. 4–7, 1710, *Post Man*: 'The 2^d Book of the Violin Master improved', &c., and 'The 3^d Book', &c., April 12–14, 1711, *Post Man*.
See No. 340.

337. The Symphonys or Instrumental Parts in the Opera Call'd Thomyris [Music by Alessandro Scarlatti, Giovanni Battista Bononcini, &c.] as they are Perform'd at the Theatre Royal.

London Printed for I. Walsh . . . & P. Randall . . . I. Hare, &c.

[*c.* 1709.]

BM. h. 17. a. (4.) First Treble part only.
This edition from the same plates as the earlier one (No. 256), but with modified imprint as used for *Pyrrhus and Demetrius*. (No. 294.)

338. Pyrrhus Aires for a single Flute. [From the opera by Alessandro Scarlatti and N. F. Haym.]

[J. Walsh, P. Randall, and J. Hare. *c.* 1709.]

Walsh Cat., *c.* 1721, Ill. 28, as: 'Pyrrhus & Clotilda Aires, for a single Flute. 1s. 6d.' This notice is assumed to refer to separate issues of each opera, which probably consisted of the First Flute parts of the editions for Two Flutes, with new title-pages, details of which as given are uncertain.
See Nos. 325 and 326.

339. Clotilda Aires for a single Flute. [From the Opera by Francesco Conti and others.]

[J. Walsh, P. Randall, and J. Hare. *c.* 1709.]

Walsh Cat., *c.* 1721, Ill. 28, as: 'Pyrrhus & Clotilda Aires, for a single Flute. 1s. 6d.' This notice is assumed to refer to separate issues of each opera, which probably consisted of the First Flute parts of the editions for Two Flutes, with new title-pages, details of which as given are uncertain.
See Nos. 325 and 326.

340. The Gentleman's Companion for the Violin or Hoboy. Being a Choice Collection of the newest and best Tunes, made purposely for either of those Instruments, with Flourishes by the most able Masters, several of them in two Parts. Never before Publish'd.

Printed for J. Hare . . . J. Walsh . . . and P. Randall at the Harp and Hoboy . . . Price 1s. 6d.

Jan. 4, 1710, *Daily Courant.*

This may have been a separate edition of part of No. 336.

341. Fifty two Minuets and Rigadoons, for Violins; Hautboys and Bassoons; Two Airs with them, and a Paspie, One Hornpipe, Two Jiggs, and a Boree. With a Bass to each of them. All fit for Balls and Dancing Schools. Composed by Mr. W. Hills.

Printed for J. Walsh . . . and P. Randall, at the Harp and Hautboy . . . and J. Hare, &c.

Jan. 10–12, 1709 [i.e. 1710], *Tatler.*

Jan. 26–8, 1709 [i.e. 1710], *Tatler.* (A Collection of New Minuets . . . by Mr. William Hills.)

Probably the same person as Mr. Hill. (BM. a. 26. i. (3.))
Advertised in No. 370 as: 'Mr Hills Minuets of two parts.'
Walsh Cat., *c.* 1721, Ill. 27, gives: 'Hills Minuets, for a single Violin. 1s. 0d,' which may or may not refer to the work listed here.

342. A Second Edition of the Songs and Symphonies of the Opera called Clotilda [Words from the Italian of G. B. Neri. Music by Francesco Conti and others]: The Songs done in Italian and English, as they are performed at the Queen's Theatre.

Printed for J. Walsh . . . and P. Randall, at the Harp and Hautboy . . . and J. Hare, &c.

Jan. 31–Feb. 2, 1710, *Tatler.*

Presumably a reprint of the Second Edition. (No. 302.)
The *Tatler*, Feb. 14–16, 1710 gives: 'There is likewise reprinted, the Opera's of Pyrrhus and Clotilda', &c.
See Nos. 296, 297, and 302.

343. The Royal Gailliarde, Mr. Isaac's New Dance made for Her Majesty's Birth Day 1710 The tune by Mr Paisible Engraven in Characters & Figures for ye use of Mars. Writt by Mr. de la Garde Dancing Master. Note these following Dances by Mr. Isaac is Printed. viz The Royall Portuguez. The Saltarella. The Union. The Britannia. The Spanheim. The Favourite. The Richmond. The Rigadoon. The Rondeau. The Princess. The Gloster. The Marlbrough. And ye Art of Dancing, done into English by Mr. Weaver.

London, Printed for J. Walsh & P. Randall at ye Harp & Hoboy in Catherine Street, & J. Hare at ye Viol & Flute in Cornhill.

Feb. 2–4, 1710, *Tatler.* (Tuesday next will be publish'd.)

BM. h. 993. (6.)
Advertised in No. 370 as: 'The Royall Galliard figure dance.'
Some of the dances listed have been previously noted, others have not.

343*a*. Y^e Art of Dancing, done into English by M^r. Weaver.
London, Printed for J. Walsh & P. Randall . . . & J. Hare, &c.
Feb. 2–4, 1710, *Tatler*.

This work advertised on No. 343 and other works, with and without Weaver's name, was presumably an edition of Feuillet's *Chorégraphie*, &c. of which there were two different English editions issued in 1706. One of these, *Orchesography*, &c., translated by J. Weaver and published by 'H Meere, for the Author' (BM. 558*. c. 39.) may have been taken over by Walsh, and was the work referred to above, or Walsh may have issued a separate edition of it. (c. 1708–10.) A second edition was issued by Walsh and John and Joseph Hare as *Orchesography*, &c., in 1722. (BM. 7907. i. 5.) The other English edition of 1706 was by P. Siris, and was sold by the Author, Richard Meares, and Alexander Livingston. (BM. 797. dd. 20.)
See Nos. 280, 343, 348, and 478.

344. Songs In The New Opera, Call'd Almahide. The Songs done in Italian & English as they are Perform'd at y^e Queens Theatre.
Sold by I: Walsh Musicall Instrument maker in Or=/=dinary to her Majesty, & P. Randall at the Harp and Ho=boy . . . and I. Hare, &c.
Jan. 31–Feb. 2, 1710, *Tatler*. (Next week will be published.)
Feb. 14–16, 1710, *Tatler*.

BM. H. 314.
RCM. XCV. D. 15. (2.) With an outer illustrated title-page:
Songs in y^e Opera call'd Almahide.
London Printed for & Sold by Iohn Walsh Servant to her Majesty at the Harp and Hautboy in Katherine Street near Somerset House in the Strand.
The inner title-page, from the plate used for No. 296 and earlier works (*see* Ill. 1), with 'Almahide . . . Queens Theatre' from a supplementary plate.
The outer title-page, from a plate first used by Walsh for No. 82*a* (*see* Ill. 8), modified for No. 293 (*see* Ill. 20), with the title 'Songs . . . Almahide' from a supplementary plate.

345. Songs In The New Opera, Call'd Pyrrhus and Demetrius, &c. [Words translated from the Italian of Adriano Morselli by Owen MacSwiney. Music by Alessandro Scarlatti and N. F. Haym.]
Printed for J. Walsh . . . and P. Randall, at the Harp and Hautboy . . . and J. Hare, &c.
Feb. 14–16, 1710, *Tatler*. (There is likewise reprinted, the Opera's of Pyrrhus and Clotilda.)

Presumably a reprint similar to that advertised Apr. 25, 1709, *Daily Courant* (No. 297); title as given above open to question.
See Nos. 292, 293, and 297.

346. All the Symphonies or Instrumental Parts in the last new Opera called Almahide, as they are performed at the Queen's Theatre. The whole fairly engraven, and carefully corrected.
Printed for J. Walsh . . . and P. Randal at the Harp and Hautboy . . . and J. Hare, &c.
Mar. 11–14, 1710, *Tatler*.

Title-page may have been from the plate used for No. 337: 'The Symphonys', &c.
Advertised in No. 370 as: 'The Symphonys of Almahide.'

347. Mr. Barret's Musick, in 4 Parts, for Violins and Hautboys, performed in the last new Comedy, [by Charles Shadwell] called, The Fair Quaker of Deal. Engraven. Price 1s 6d the Set.

Printed for J. Walsh . . . and P. Randall at the Harp and Hautboy . . . and J. Hare, &c.

Mar. 28–30, 1710, *Tatler.*

Advertised in No. 370 as: 'Mr Barrets tunes in the Quaker of deal.'

348. For the Further Improvement of Dancing, A Treatis of Chorography or yᵉ Art of Dancing Country Dances after A New Character, In which The Figures Steps, & Manner of Performing are describ'd, & yᵉ Rules Demonstrated in an Easie Method adapted to the Meanest Capacity. Translated from the French of Monˢʳ. Feuillet, and Improv'd wᵗʰ. many additions, all fairly Engrav'd on Copper plates, and a new Collection of Country Dances describ'd in yᵉ same Character by Iohn Essex Dancing Master.

London. Sold by I. Walsh & P. Randall . . . I: Hare . . . I. Culen without Temple-barr, & by yᵉ Author at his house in Rude-lane Fanchurch-street, 1710.

Apr. 6–8, 1710, *Post Man.*

BM. 1042. d. 45.
See Nos. 280, 343*a*, and 478.

349. To all Lovers of Dancing. Whereas there is lately printed a Spurious and very Incorrect Edition of Country Dances, done in a common Press. This is to give Notice, That the Originals of the Dances are engraven in a fair Character, and printed for J. Walsh, P. Randal, and J. Hare, and sold very cheap . . . at the Harp and Hoboy . . . and the Golden Viol in Cornhill, &c.

April 11–13, 1710, *Post Man.* Paper mutilated.

350. To all Lovers of Musick. Whereas there is lately published 12[?] Sonatas, 8 of them in Mr. Pepusch's Name done without his [permission?] or knowledge, being spurious and very Incorrect and [arranged?] from the st[ring?] Instruments they were first designed for. This [is to give] Notice, That there is now engraven and will speedily [be publish]ed, a true Copy of the 8 Sonatas above mentioned with [the addi]tion of 4 more by the same Author, done by his own [hand] and corrected by him Engraven in a fair Character &c.

[Printed for] J. Walsh and P. Randal . . . and J. Hare at the Golden V[iol] . . . near the Royal Exchange.

April 13–15, 1710, *Post Man.* Paper mutilated.

The spurious edition referred to was that advertised by L. Pippard (April 8–11, 1710, *Post Man*; April 15–18, 1710, *Tatler*), as:

'Twelve Sonatas in Parts for Violins or Hautboys, with through Basses to each for the

Bassoon, Bass Violin or Harpsicord; 8 Composed by Mr. Pepusch, being all entirely new and carefully Corrected by Mr. Wm Corbet, &c.

   Printed for and engrav'd by L. Pippard Musical Instrument-maker at the Golden Flute and Hautboy . . . Russel-street, Covent Garden.'

   The Walsh edition of the Sonatas has not been identified. It was probably an edition of the work by Roger of Amsterdam: '12 Sonates à 2 V., 2 Hautb. ou 2 Fl. trav. & Bc. Op. 3.' (Eitner. Quellen–Lexikon.)

351. The Airs in the Opera of Almahide for a single Flute.

   Engraven and printed for J. Walsh . . . and P. Randall . . . and J. Hare at the Viol and Flute, &c.

   April 15–18, 1710, *Tatler*.

   Re-advertised May 23–5, 1710, *Post Man*, with a note about a spurious edition:

   'All the Aires in the last new Opera call'd Almahide, curiously contriv'd and fitted for a single Flute. Note there is published a spurious Edition for the Flute, of the Aires of Almahide, with some scraps of Hydaspes: This is to give Notice, that the originals of both Operas, as well of the single Airs as of the Songs and Symphonies, are printed for J. Walsh, P. Randal, and J. Hare, and sold at their Shops at the Harp in Catherine-street, and at the Golden Viol in Cornhil,' &c.

   May 23–5, 1710, *Post Man*.

   The spurious edition referred to was presumably, 'The Book of the Flute Master Improv'd containing . . . Song Tunes in the last Operas of Almahide and Hydaspes . . . Printed and Engrav'd for L. Pippard', &c., and advertised May 20–3, 1710, *Post-Man*.

   The Walsh work was advertised in No. 370 as: 'The single flute book Almahide.'

   See No. 392.

352. For the Flute A Collection of all the Choicest French Dances Perform'd at Court the Theatres and Publick Balls together with the newest & most Cellebrated Minuets Rigadoons & Paspys Several of them Forreign & Danc'd at most of the Princes Courts in Europe, compleatly fitted to the Flute, being the first of the kind for that Instrument. Fairly Engraven & Carefully Corected.

   London. Printed for J. Walsh & P. Randall . . . & J. Hare at the Viol and Flute, &c.

   April 22–5, 1710, *Post Man*.

   BM. a. 26. i. (2.)
   Walsh Cat., *c.* 1721, Ill. 28, as: 'French dances for yᵉ Flute. 1s. 6d.'
   Probably the same work as No. 365.

353. Six English Cantatas Humbly Inscrib'd To the most Noble the Marchioness of Kent Compos'd by Mʳ I: C Pepusch. [Introduction and words by John Hughes.]

   London Printed for J: Walsh Servant in Ordinary to her Majesty, & P: Randall at yᵉ Harp & Hoboy in Katherine street, near Somerset House in yᵉ Strand, & J: Hare at yᵉ Viol & Flute in Cornhill near the Royall Exchange.

   April 25–7, 1710, *Tatler*.

   BM. G. 222. b.
   This was the first appearance of the beautiful title-page (*see* Ill. 22), which Walsh used for Handel's *Rinaldo* and many other works.

Advertised in No. 370, as: 'Mr Pepusch 6 Cantatas.'
See No. 582; and Ill. 35.

354. Songs In The New Opera, Call'd Hydaspes [Music by Francesco Mancini], as they are Perform'd at the Queens Theatre.
    Sold by I: Walsh Musicall Instrument maker in Or=/=dinary to her Majesty, & P. Randall at the Harp and Ho=boy . . . and I. Hare, &c.
    May 27–30, 1710, *Post Man.*

> BM. I. 282.
> RCM. XCV. D. 15. (3.)
> With an outer illustrated title-page:
> Songs in the Opera calld Hydaspes.
> London Printed for & Sold by Iohn Walsh Servant to her Majesty at the Harp and Hautboy in Katherine Street near Somerset House in the Strand.
> The inner title-page is from the plate used for No. 344 and earlier works (*see* Ill. 1), with 'Hydaspes . . . Queens Theatre' from a supplementary plate.
> The outer title-page is from a plate first used by Walsh for No. 82a (*see* Ill. 8), modified for No. 293 (*see* Ill. 20), with the title 'Songs . . . Hydaspes' from a supplementary plate.
> The Peter Murray Hill Catalogue No. 14 lists an edition with Randall omitted from the imprint.
> *See* No. 373.

355. The Symphonys or Instrumental Parts in the Opera Call'd Hydaspes [Music by Francesco Mancini], as they are Perform'd at the Queens Theatre.
    London Printed for I. Walsh Servt. to Her Matie. and P: Randall at y^e. Harp & Hoboy, in Catherine Street near Somerset House in y^e. Strand. I: Hare Instrument-maker, at the golden Viol and Flute in Cornhill near y^e. Royal Exchange.
    May 27–30, 1710. *Post Man; Tatler.*

> BM. I. 282. a. Wanting Bass part.
> Title-page from a plate used for No. 300 (*see* Ill. 21), with 'Hydaspes . . . Queen's Theatre', from a supplementary plate.
> Advertised in No. 370, as: 'The Symphonys Hydaspes.'
> *See* Nos. 520 and 530.

356. All The Song tunes for the Flute In the Last new Opera call'd Hydaspes. [Music by Francesco Mancini.] Fairly Engraven & Carefully Corrected. Price 1^s. 6^d.
    London, Printed for J. Walsh [& P. Randal] . . . & J. Hare, &c.
    June 20–2, 1710, *Tatler.*

> The title from a later edition (No. 436) without Randall's name in the imprint. The title-page from the plate of some previous work not identified, with 'call'd Hydaspes' from a supplementary plate.
> Details as given open to question.
> Advertised in No. 370, as: 'The single flute book Hydaspes.'
> *See* Nos. 392 and 436.

357. A New Set of Tunes Compos'd by an Italian Master in the Play [by Ben Jonson] call'd the Alchimist, price 6d. The whole fairly engraven.

Printed for J. Walsh . . . and P. Randal at the Harp and Hoboy, &c.
July 8–11, 1710, *Post Man.*

 Advertised in No. 370, as: 'A set of tunes in the Alchimist.'

358. A Collection of Comical Songs and Songs of Humour, by Mr. D'Urfey.
Printed for J. Walsh . . . P. Randal . . . and J. Hare, &c.
Aug. 5–8, 1710, *Post Man.* (Lately published.)
Aug. 26–9, 1710, *Post Man.* (A Collection of Songs of various humours, some historical others comical, and some by way of Dialogues most diverting and pleasant by Mr. To. D'urfey.)

 Walsh Cat., *c.* 1721, Ill. 27, as: 'Durfeys Songs. 2s. od.'
 Walsh's work was doubtless put out in competition with L. Pippard's edition of: 'Musa et Musica or Humour & Musick . . . Pleasant and merry humours with Scotch & Love Songs, the words by Mr. D'urfey', &c. (BM. H. 82. (1.); H. 82.*a.*) This was advertised June 10–13, 1710, *Post Man.*

359. Several Dialogues and 2 and 3 Part Songs.
All printed for J. Walsh . . . P. Randal . . . and J. Hare, &c.
Advertised with other lately published works, Aug. 5–8, 1710. *Post Man.*
Not identified.

360. Voluntarys & Fugues Made on purpose for the Organ or Harpsichord by Ziani Pollaroli, Bassani and other Famous Authors, Engraven in a fair Character.
London, Printed for J. Walsh & P. Randall at the Harp & Hoboy . . . & J. Hare, &c.
Aug. 15–17, 1710, *Tatler.*

 BM. g. 57. a.
 Advertised in No. 370, as: 'A book of Vallentarys for the Organ.'
 See Nos. 504 and 564.

361. Several Tocata's and Preludes for the same Instruments. [i.e. Organ or Harpsichord.]
Lately published, engraven and Printed for J. Walsh . . . P. Randal . . . and J. Hare, &c.
Aug. 15–17, 1710, *Tatler.*

 Not identified.

362. The Royall Galliard Minuet Book.
[J. Walsh, P. Randall and J. Hare. 1710.]
Advertised in No. 370.

363. Tophams Violin Sonatas.
[J. Walsh, P. Randall and J. Hare. 1710.]
Advertised in No. 370.

 Presumably the same work as No. 334.

364. The 2ᵈ Set of Harmonia mundi.
[J. Walsh, P. Randall and J. Hare. 1710.]
Advertised in No. 370.

An earlier collection was published in 1707. (No. 257.) Another work entitled *Harmonia Mundi The 2ᵈ. collection Being VI Concertos in Six Parts*, &c., was published by Walsh and Joseph Hare in 1728. (BM. g. 419. a.) The first collection of this work has not been traced.

365. A single flute book of Minuets.
[J. Walsh, P. Randall and J. Hare. 1710.]
Advertised in No. 370.

Probably the same work as No. 352.

366. Sonate da Chiesa a Violino Solo e Violoncello o Basso Conti: da Tomasso Albinoni Note, there is Printed a 1ˢᵗ. & 2ᵈ. Set of Concertos, & a Collection of Aires, of yˢ Authors.
London Printed for J. Walsh Servant to her Majesty & P. Randall at yᵉ Harp & Hoboy . . . & J. Hare at the Viol and Flute, &c. 4ˢ. 6ᵈ. [Price in MS.]
[1710.]
RCM. XXIX. A. 9. (1.)
Advertised in No. 370 as: 'Albinonis Solos, Walsh Cat., *c.* 1721, Ill. 27, as: '6 Solos by Albinoni Opera 4ᵗᵒ, for a Violin & a Bass. 4s. 0d.'
This is a large, finely engraved work superior in style to the usual Walsh productions.
Of the two sets of Concertos advertised on this work only one by Walsh has been traced. (No. 328.) The Collection of Aires is listed under No. 128.

367. Almahide for 2 flutes & a Bass.
[J. Walsh, P. Randall and J. Hare. 1710.]
Advertised in No. 370.

The title-page probably from the plate afterwards used for No. 368, with the title: 'The Most Celebrated Aires and Duets In the Opera of Almahide. Curiously fitted and Contriv'd for two Flutes and a Bass; With their Symphony Introduc'd in a Compleat Manner The whole fairly Engrav'd—
London Printed for I: Walsh Servᵗ. to Her Matⁱᵉ. and P. Randall at yᵉ Harp and Hoboy . . . I. Hare . . . at yᵉ golden Viol and Flute', &c.
Walsh and Hare advertised the work, Dec. 14–16, 1710, *Tatler*; probably a later edition with 'and Randall' obliterated from the imprint.
See No. 392.

368. The Most Celebrated Aires and Duets In the Opera of Hydaspes. [Music by Francesco Mancini.] Curiously fitted and Contriv'd for two Flutes and a Bass; With their Symphony Introduc'd in a Compleat Manner The whole fairly Engrav'd—

London Printed for I: Walsh Servt. to Her Matie. and P. Randall at ye Harp and Hoboy . . . I. Hare . . . at ye golden Viol and Flute, &c.

[1710.]

Advertised in No. 370 as: 'Hydaspes for 2 flutes & a Bass.'

 Cardiff Public Library. Basso part only.

 The title-page from a plate probably used previously for No. 367, with 'In the Opera of Hydaspes', from a supplementary plate'.

 Walsh and Hare advertised the work Dec. 14–16, 1710, *Tatler*; probably a later edition with 'and Randall' obliterated from the imprint.

 See No. 392.

369. A book of famillier tunes for the Violin.

 [J. Walsh, P. Randall and J. Hare. 1710.]

Advertised in No. 370.

 Walsh Cat., *c.* 1721, Ill. 27, as: 'Familiar tunes for y^e Violin. 1s. 6d.'

 See No. 320.

370. The Monthly Mask of Vocal Music or the New=est Songs Made for the Theatre's & other Ocasions Publish'd for October Price 6 pence.

 These Collections will be Continued Monthly for y^e Year 1710 &c.

 London Printed for and sold by I Walsh and I. Hare, &c.

Oct. 31–Nov. 2, 1710, *Post Man.*

 BM. H. 313. e. Imperfect.

 RCM. II. A. 15. Imperfect.

 The annual volume for 1710 [i.e. Nov. 1709–Oct. 1710] of which the above is a transcription of the title-page of the October number only, was advertised Dec. 21–3, 1710, *Tatler* as: 'The whole Volume of Monthly Collections of Vocal Musick . . . in the Year 1710,' &c. It probably had collective title-page from the Collins plate (No. 15, *see* Ill. 3) as used for 1709 (No. 331) and earlier years. The October number contains 'A Table of the Songs in the Monthly Masks for the Year 1710 Printed for I. Walsh & P. Randall' and a list of 'Vocall and Instrumental Musick Printed in the Year 1710' [i.e. Nov. 1709–Oct. 1710]. The list is transcribed here, with reference numbers to the entries in the bibliography added, in order to aid identification:

 Twenty four Country dances for 1710. (No. 332.)

 Mr Hills Minuets of two parts. (No. 341.)

 The Royall Galliard Minuet Book. (No. 362.)

 The Royall Galliard figure dance. (No. 343.)

 Tophams Violin Sonatas. (No. 363.)

 The Opera of Almahide. (No. 344.)

 The Symphonys of Almahide. (No. 346.)

 The single flute book Almahide. (No. 351.)

 The 2^d Set of Harmonia mundi. (No. 364.)

 Mr Barrets tunes in the Quaker of deal. (No. 347.)

 Mr Pepusch 6 Cantatas. (No. 353.)

 A single flute book of Minuets. (No. 365.)

 Albinonis Solos. (No. 366.)

 The Opera of Hydaspes. (No. 354.)

 The Symphonys Hydaspes. (No. 355.)

The single flute book Hydaspes. (No. 356.)
A set of tunes in the Alchimist. (No. 357.)
A book of Vallentarys for the Organ. (No. 360.)
Almahide for 2 flutes & a Bass. (No. 367.)
Hydaspes for 2 flutes & a Bass. (No. 368.)
A book of famillier tunes for the Violin. (No. 369.)
See Nos. 103, 109, 140, 160, 188, 223, 258, 282a, 331, and 517.

371. Twenty Four New Country Dances for the Year: 1711. With proper new Tunes, & Figures, or Directions to each Dance. Humbly Dedicated to ye Honourable Henry Lᵈ. Newport. by his most Obedient, & most faithfull Servant. Nathaniell Kynaston Note, the 1ˢᵗ .. & 2ᵈ. Vollums of ye new Country Dancing Master is reprinted, & may be had where this is Sold.

London, Printed for J. Walsh Servᵗ. to her Majesty, and P. Randall . . . & J. Hare, &c.

Nov. 14–16, 1710, *Tatler*. (Engraven . . . Price 6d.)

BM. a. 10. (3.)

For other editions of *The New Country Dancing Master, see* Nos. 193, 260, 333, 394, 441, and 489.

372. The New Psalm Book, containing proper Tunes intirely new, to all the different Measures of the Psalms in the Old or any of the new versions; with variety of Tunes for the most Common Measure, and may be sung in 2, 3 or 4 parts, with a figur'd Bass for the Organ; also some short Anthems in 4 parts, at the end of the Book, with a Table shewing how to apply each Tune to its proper Psalm, very proper to be used in all Parish Churches, by J. Bishop, Organist of the Colledge, at Whinton. Pr. 1s. 6d.

Printed for J. Walsh . . . P. Randall . . . and J. Hare, &c.

Nov. 16–18, 1710, *Post Man*; Mar. 15–17, 1711, *Post Man*.

The Second Edition with additions of what appears to be the same work, issued Dec. 1722, has title: 'A Sett of New Psalm Tunes, in Four Parts . . . London: Printed by W. Pearson for the Author, and Sold by J. Walsh . . . J. Hare . . . and at Winchester.' (BM. C. 523.)

373. The Additionall Songs In The New Opera, Call'd Hydaspes, as they are Perform'd at the Queens Theatre by Signʳ. Gioseppe Boscchi.

Sold by I: Walsh Musicall Instrument maker in Or=/=dinary to her Majesty, & P. Randall . . . and I. Hare, &c.

[1710.]

BM. H. 114. (3.)

The title-page from the plate used for the inner title of the original edition of the Songs (No. 354, *see* Ill. 1), with 'The Additionall' added to the plate, and with 'Hydaspes . . . Boscchi' from a supplementary plate.

374. The Britannia a New Dance Compos'd by Mʳ. Isaac Perform'd at Court on Her Majesties Birth day Febʳ: ye 6ᵗʰ 17[06].

London Printed for I. Walsh Servt to Her Matie . . . I. Hare . . . and P. Randall at ye Violin and Lute by Paulsgrave head Court, &c.

[*c*. 1710 or earlier.] Probably first issued with this imprint before July 1709.

Particulars as given are from the plate used for 'The Marlborough' (No. 375) and an earlier edition of 'The Britannia', before Randall was added to the imprint.
See Nos. 196, 207, and 406.

375. The Marlborough a New Dance Compos'd by M^r. Isaac Perform'd at Court on Her Majesties Birth day Feb^r: ye 6th 17[05].

London Printed for I. Walsh Servt to Her Matie . . . I. Hare . . . and P. Randall at ye Violin and Lute by Paulsgrave head Court, &c.

[*c*. 1710 or earlier.] Probably first issued with this imprint before July 1709.

BM. h. 993. (17.)
The title-page is from a plate used for 'The Britannia' (No. 374) with 'Marlborough' engraved on a slip pasted over the original title, 'Britannia'.
See No. 170.

From December 1710, Randall's name was omitted from the imprints and notices, only appearing occasionally in reissues or re-advertisements.

376. A new Set of Tunes for Violins and Hautboys, in 4 Parts. Composed for the Theatre. Price 1s. 6d.

Printed for J. Walsh, Servant in Ordinary to Her Majesty, at the Harp and Hautboy . . . and J. Hare at the Viol and Flute, &c.

Dec. 21–3, 1710, *Tatler*.

377. Six Sonata^s. three For two Flutes & a Bass, and three Solos for a Flute and a Bass, Compos'd by M^r: Dan: Purcell. The whole Fairly Engraven & Carefully Corected by ye Author.

London, Printed for J: Walsh Servant in Ordinary to her Majesty . . . & J: Hare at the Viol & Flute . . . nere the Royal Exchange, o^L. 3^s. o^d. [Price in MS.]

[*c*. 1710.]

BM. h. 250. c. (3.)
Walsh Cat., *c*. 1721, Ill. 28, as: 'Purcells Sonatas, for 2 Flutes & a Bass. 4s. od.'

378. Aires & Symphonys for ye Bass Viol being A choice Collection of ye most favorite Song tunes, Aires & Symphonys out of the late Operas, Curiously contriv'd & fitted to the Bass Viol by the best Masters. also some excellent Lessons made purpose for y^t Instrument, as Almands, Corants, Sarabands & Jiggs the whole fairly Engraven and carefully Corrected.

London Printed for J. Walsh . . . & J. Hare, &c.

[*c*. 1710.]

BM. c. 63.
Presumably the work Walsh Cat., *c*. 1721, Ill. 27, as: 'Songs & Aires for ye Viol. 2s. 6d.'

379. A Collection of New Songs set to Musick By Mr Wm: Morley and Mr: Iohn Isum [or Isham] with A Thorough-bass to each Song, All transpos'd for the Flute: and fairly Engraven on Copper Plates.

> [*c.* 1710.]
>
>> BM. G. 117.
>> RCM. I. A. 11. (1.)
>> The BM. copy, which has no imprint, contains 11 vocal numbers and 4 pages for the Flute.
>> The RCM. copy is from the same plates as the BM. copy; but has added to the plate of the title-page:
>> T. Cross Iunr. Sculpt.
>> London, Printed for the Authors, and are to be Sold by John Hare at the Viol & Flute in Cornhill, John Walsh at the Harp & Hoboy in Catherine Street, & John Young at ye Dolphin & Crown in St. Pauls Church Yard, Price 3 Shillings.
>> The RCM. copy, which appears to be imperfect, contains 9 of the numbers of the BM. copy and one not in the latter work, with 4 pages for the Flute.

380. A Song for two Voices Set by Mr. Henry Purcell.

> [J. Walsh and J. Hare. *c.* 1710 or later.]
> (Dulcibella when e'er I sue for a kiss.)
>
>> BM. G. 316. g. (13.)
>> Plates afterwards used in: *Mr Henr. Purcell's Favourite Songs out of his most celebrated Orpheus Brittanicus . . . Printed for Ino. Walsh . . . and Ino. & Ioseph Hare, &c.*, c. 1723–5. (BM. G. 102. a.)

381. A Song in the Play [by John Dryden] call'd Oranzebe [i.e. Aureng-Zebe] Set to Musick by Mr Henr Purcell, Sung by Mrs Alyff.

> [J. Walsh and J. Hare. *c.* 1710 or later.]
> (I see she flyes me.)
>
>> BM. G. 316. g. (27.)
>> Plates afterwards used in: *Mr Henr. Purcell's Favourite Songs out of his most celebrated Orpheus Brittanicus . . . Printed for Ino. Walsh . . . and Ino. & Ioseph Hare, &c.*, c. 1723–5. (BM. G. 102. a.)

382. In Italian and English (Ho un non so che nel cor; 'Tis not yr Wealth) Sung by Sigra. Francesca Vanini Boschi in the Opera of Pyrrhus. Compos'd by Mr. Handell.

> [J. Walsh and J. Hare. *c.* 1710–11.]
>
>> BM. G. 305. (189); G. 312. (9.)
>> RCM. XCV. D. 22. (4.)
>> This song from Handel's *La Resurrezione*, afterwards used by him in *Agrippina* (Venice, 1709), was inserted in Alessandro Scarlatti's *Pirro e Demetrio* for the 1710–11 performances of that work in London, and was probably the first song of Handel's to be sung on the London stage.
>> A number of other editions and adaptations of it were published, mostly without imprints, although Walsh may have been responsible for several of them. It was included by him in *The Monthly Mask of Vocal Musick* for May 1711 (BM. H. 313. f.) headed 'The Famous mock Song, to Ho un non so che nel cor, Sung by Signra Boscchi, in the Opera of Pyrrhus,

Corectly Engrav'd.' It has English words 'Good folks come here', and was a skit on the Italian Opera, Handel, *Rinaldo*, and Nicolini. This version may have been sold also separately. Another popular setting, probably not issued by Walsh, has English words beginning: 'In Kent so fam'd of old'. (BM. H. 1601. (219.))

383. The Rigadoon Royal M^r. Isaac's New Dance made for Her Majestys Birth Day 1711. Engraven in Characters & Figures for ye use of Masters Writ by M^r. de la Garde Dancing Master. Note these following Dances by M^r. Isaac are likewise Printed. Viz The Royal Galliarde. The Royal Portuguez. The Saltarella. The Union. The Brittania. The Spanheim. The Favourite. The Richmond. The Rigadoon. The Rondeau. The Princess. The Gloster. The Marlbrough. The Royal. The Northumberland. And ye Art of Dancing done by M^r. Weaver.
Printed for I. Walsh Servt in Ordinary to Her Majesty . . . & I. Hare, &c.
[1711.]

> BM. h. 993. (5.)
> Another edition, at BM. 785. k. 7. (8.), without outer title-page and imprint, is from the same plates, with the same inner title as No. 383: 'The Rigadoon Royal by M^r. Isaac.'
> All of the dances listed, except 'The Royal' and 'The Northumberland', have been previously noted. *See* No. 343 for a similar list.

384. Songs in the Opera of Etearco as they are Perform'd at ye Queens Theatre.
London Printed for J: Walsh Servant in Ordinary to her Britanick Majesty, at ye Harp & Hoboy in Katherine street, near Somerset House in ye Strand, & J: Hare at ye Viol & Flute in Cornhill near the Royall Exchange.
Mar. 6, 1711, *Daily Courant.*

> BM. I. 354. b.
> RCM. XCV. D. 15. (5.)
> The title-page from the plate first used for No. 353 (*see* Ill. 22), with the title 'Songs in the Opera . . . Queens Theatre' from a supplementary plate, and with the imprint modified and Randall's name omitted. The advertisement states: 'There being now 11 Opera's in Italian and English, most of them with Symphonys or Instrumental Parts, have been lately Reprinted, and some with additional Songs.'
> No separate edition of 'The Symphonys or Instrumental Parts in the Opera Call'd Etearco' has been traced, but such was probably issued, as the Walsh Cat., *c.* 1721, Ill. 27, advertised *Etearco* as one of the operas which 'have Symphonys'.

385. Song's in the Opera of Rinaldo [Italian words by Giacomo Rossi from a sketch by Aaron Hill after Torquato Tasso, English words by Hill] Compos'd by Mr Hendel.
London Printed for J: Walsh Servant in Ordinary to her Britanick Majesty, at ye Harp & Hoboy in Katherine street, near Somerset House in ye Strand, & J: Hare at ye Viol & Flute in Cornhill near the Royall Exchange.
Apr. 24, 1711, *Daily Courant.*

> RM. 7. h. 24.
> RCM. XI. C. 6. (2), without title-page; may be this edition.
> The title-page from the plate first used for No. 353 (*see* Ill. 22), with the title 'Song's . . . by

'Mr Hendel' from a supplementary plate, and with the imprint as modified for No. 384. This first edition has 65 pages of music.

Five principal editions of *Rinaldo* are recorded in the bibliography. The details of other issues, variants, and copies, some differently made up, that exist elsewhere than in the BM., The King's Music Library, and RCM., are omitted.

Walsh issued some numbers of *Rinaldo* separately. (e.g. 'Il tricerbero humiliato', 'The Rover' (Bel piacere), &c.) As in most other similar cases of excerpts from operas the particulars are omitted from the bibliography.

See Nos. 387, 389, 449, and 459.

386. A new Sett of Tunes in three Parts for Violins and Hoboys with a through Base composed by Mr. N. Kynaston for the Play, call'd, The Injured Lover.

Printed for J. Walsh . . . and J. Hare, &c.

May 15, 1711, *Daily Courant.*

The play was presumably, 'The Injur'd Love', produced at Drury Lane, 1711.

387. Arie dell' Opera di Rinaldo Composta dal Signor Hendel Maestro di Capella di Sua Altezza Elettorale d'Hannover. [Italian words by Giacomo Rossi from a sketch by Aaron Hill after Torquato Tasso, English words by Hill.]

London Printed for J: Walsh Servant in Ordinary to her Britanick Majesty . . . & J: Hare, &c.

[*c.* May 1711.]

NLS.

The title-page from the plate as used for the previous edition No. 385 (*see* Ill. 22), but with a new title 'Arie dell' Opera . . . Hannover' from a supplementary plate.

The contents are the same as in the earlier edition except that pp. 63–5 are wanting; but the title-page is the same as that used for the next edition. (No. 389.) It is possible that this is a made-up copy from the two editions and not a definite issue as such by Walsh and Hare.

See Nos. 385, 389, 449, and 459.

388. The Symphonys or Instrumental Parts in the Opera Call'd Rinaldo As they are Perform'd at the Queens Theatre, Compos'd by Mr. Hendel, Chapple Master to ye Elector of Hanover.

London Printed for I. Walsh Servt. to Her Matie - - - - - at ye. Harp & Hoboy, in Catherine Street near Somerset House in ye. Strand. I: Hare Instrument-maker, at the golden Viol and Flute in Cornhill near ye. Royal Exchange.

June 5, 1711, *Daily Courant.*

BM. h. 2681. b. First Treble, Second Treble, and Tenor parts only.

Title-page from a plate used for No. 355 (*see* Ill. 21), with 'Rinaldo . . . Hanover' from a supplementary plate, and with 'and P. Randall' erased from the imprint. Copies are recorded with Randall's name still in the imprint; but as it appears that he ceased to publish with Walsh before June 1711, and the contemporary advertisements only mention Walsh and Hare, it is probable that the retention of Randall's name on some copies was accidental.

389. Arie dell' Opera di Rinaldo Composta dal Signor Hendel Maestro di Capella di Sua Altezza Elettorale d'Hannover. [Italian words by Giacomo Rossi from a sketch by Aaron Hill after Torquato Tasso, English words by Hill.]

London Printed for J: Walsh . . . & J: Hare, &c.

June 19–21, 1711, *Post Man*.

> Wᵐ. C. Smith collection.
> RCM. XCV. D. 15. (6.)
> Title-page from the plate as used for the previous edition, No. 387. (*See* Ill. 22.)
> This edition contains 67 pages of music, two additional pages being added to the aria 'Vo' far guerra' to include the 'Harpsicord Peice Perform'd by Mr Hendel'. Otherwise, except for the alteration in pagination on the pages and in the 'Table', the work is as the previous edition.
> *See* Nos. 385, 387, 449, and 459.

390. The New Flute Master, the 7th Edit. containing the best Directions for Learners on the Flute; together with the newest Aires both of Italian and English, particularly the Favourite Song Tunes in the Opera of Rinaldo, composed by Mr. Hendel with an extraordinary Collection of Trumpet Tunes, Jiggs, Marches and Minuets for the Flute, pr. 1s. 6d.

Printed for J. Walsh . . . and J. Hare, &c.

Sept. 4–6, 1711, *Post Man*.

> *See* Nos. 20b, 33, 113, 182, 305, 486, 510, 563, and 578 for other books and works with similar titles. No details of the third, sixth, and eighth books of the early series finishing with No. 486 have been traced.

391. The Most Celebrated Aires and Duets in the Opera of Rinaldo [by G. F. Handel] Curiously fitted and Contriv'd for two Flutes and a Bass; With their Symphony Introduc'd in a Compleat Manner The whole fairly Engrav'd—

London Printed for I: Walsh Servᵗ. to Her Maᵗⁱᵉ. [space] at yᵉ. Harp and Hoboy . . . I: Hare, &c.

Sept. 13, 1711, *Daily Courant*.

> NLS.
> Cardiff Public Library. Fluto Basso part only.
> Title-page from a plate previously used for some other work or works, probably No. 367 and No. 368, with 'P. Randall' cut out of the imprint after 'Her Maᵗⁱᵉ', and 'in the Opera of Rinaldo' supplied from a supplementary plate.
> Walsh Cat., *c.* 1721, Ill. 28, as: 'Rinaldo Aires, for 2 Flutes & a Bass. 3s. 0d.'
> *See* No. 392.

392. Rinaldo [by G. F. Handel] Curiously fitted & Contriv'd for a single Flute. with their Symphonys Introduc'd in a Compleat maner. the whole fairly Engraven and carefully Corected.

London, [Printed for I: Walsh . . . I: Hare, &c.]

Sept. 13, 1711, *Daily Courant*.

> BM. a. 206. a. (7.)
> The work consists of the 'Fluto Primo' part of the edition for Two Flutes and a Bass (No. 391), with another title-page from some earlier work, but cut down so as to omit all at the top before 'Rinaldo' and all at the bottom after 'London', the music pages being the original folio sheets cut in half, but bound up in correct order giving the music complete.

One other copy exists with 'Rinaldo' also cut from the title-page.

An advertisement by Walsh and Hare Oct. 6–9, 1711, *Post Man*, of *Rinaldo*, *Hydaspes* and *Almahide* for 2 Flutes and a Bass, has a note: 'All the first Trebles may be had for a single Flute.'

See Nos. 351, 356, 367, 368, and 391.

393. Twenty-four new Country Dances for the Year 1712, with proper Tunes and new figures or Directions to each Dance made by several Authors, all fairly engraven, price 6d.

Printed for J. Walsh . . . and J. Hare, &c.

Oct. 16–18, 1711, *Evening Post*.

394. The new Country Dancing-Master is publish'd, containing the Country Dances for the six last years, price 2s.

Printed for J. Walsh . . . and J. Hare, &c.

Oct. 16–18, 1711, *Evening Post*.

See Nos. 193, 260, 333, 371, 441, and 489.

395. Catches. for Flutes or A Collection of the best Catches contriv'd and fitted for 1: 2: 3: or 4 Flutes, to be perform'd in the nature of Catches, which makes a compleat Con=/=sort of Flutes, being yᵉ first of yᵉ kind yet publish'd; & is very entertaining as well as improving to all Lovers of the Instrument. yᵉ whole fairly Engraven and carefully Corrected.

Printed for J. Walsh . . . & J. Hare, &c.

Nov. 13–15, 1711, *Post Man*. (Pr. 1s. 6d.)

BM. b. 171. a. (1.)

Walsh Cat., *c.* 1721, Ill. 28, as: 'Catches for yᵉ Flute 2s. od.'

396. Sonate a due Violino, e Basso Per Suonarsi con Flauto, o' vero Violino del Signor Martino Bitti Sonator di Violino Del Serenissᵐᵒ. Gran Principe di Toscana Solos by Several Authors Publish'd, Corellis 12 Solos with his Graces, Pepusch's 24 Solos, Bomporti's Solos, Gasperini's Solos, Purcells & Fingers Solos, Albinonis Solos.

London, Printed for J. Walsh . . . & J. Hare, &c.

Dec. 11–13, 1711, *Post Man*. (New Solo's for a Violin and Harpsicord; Compos'd by Signior Martino Bitty.)

BM. d. 161. a. (4.)

Another edition, from the same plates, but with a new title-page, 'Solo's for a Flute', &c., was issued about the same time. (No. 401.)

Both works advertised, Feb. 19–21, 1712, *Post Man*, as: 'Eight Solos for a Violin and Bass, or, a Flute and Bass.'

The violin edition in Walsh Cat., *c.* 1721, Ill. 27, as: 'Martino Bittis Solos, for a Violin & a Bass. 4s. od.'

397. A new set of Tunes in 4 Parts, for Violins and Hoboys; Compos'd by Mr. J. Barrett, performed in the last New Play [by Charles Johnson], called the Wife's Relief, or the Husband's Cure. Price 1s. 6d.
> Printed for J. Walsh ... and J. Hare, &c.
> Dec. 11–13, 1711, *Post Man.*

398. Several curious Pieces done for 2 Flutes and a Bass by the best Masters.
> Printed for J. Walsh ... and J. Hare, &c.
> Dec. 11–13, 1711, *Post Man.*
>> This may be a general advertisement covering several works, or may refer to No. 425.

399. An Essay For the further Improvement of Dancing; Being a Collection of Figure Dances, Of several Numbers, Compos'd by the most Eminent Masters; Describ'd in Characters after The newest Manner of Monsieur Feuillet. By E. Pemberton. To which is added, Three Single Dances, viz. A Chacone by Mr. Isaac, A Passacaille by Mr. L'Abbe, And a Jig by Mr. Pecour, Master of the Opera at Paris.
> London Printed and Sold by J. Walsh ... J. Hare ... and at the Author's next the Fire-Office in St. Martin's-Lane, 1711. Price Half a Guinea.
>> BM. 556. e. 16.

400. XII Sonata's or Solo's for a Violin a Bass Violin or Harpsicord Compos'd by Arcangelo Corelli. His fifth Opera. This Edition has ye advantage of haveing ye Graces to all ye Adagio's and other places where the Author thought proper. by Arcangelo Corelli. There is likewise Engraven his first, second, third and fourth Opera's being all the works of that Author yet extant.
> London, J. Walsh, Servt. to her Majesty at ye Harp & Hoboy ... & J. Hare at ye Viol & Flute, &c.
> [c. 1711.]
> Advertised on No. 396.
>> BM. g. 45. g.
>> RCM. LVIII. E. 18.
>> With a second title on p. 62:
>> The Second Part Containing Preludes, Allemands, Corants, Jiggs, Sarabands, Gavots, & ye Follia by Arcangelo Corelli.
>> Printed for J. Walsh.
>> Probably issued in competition with Roger's edition: 'Sonate a Violino e Violone o Cimbalo Di Arcangelo Corelli ... Opera Quinta ... Troisieme Edition,' &c. (BM. g. 41. a.) The BM. copy (g. 45. g.) has the label of John Young pasted over the Walsh and Hare imprint.
>> See Nos. 31, 41, 85, 112, 135, 205, and 519.
>> For complete list of Corelli items consult the index.

401. Solo's for a Flute, with a through Bass for the Harpsicord or Bass Violin. Compos'd by Martino Bitti. Solos for ye Flute by Several Authors Publish'd,

Corelli's Solos, Purcells & Fingers Solos, Pepusch's 1st. & 2d book of Solos, Tophams 1st. & 2d book of Solos, Overtures & Aires for a Flute & a bass.

London, Printed for J. Walsh . . . & J. Hare at ye Viol & Flute, &c. 4s. 6d.
[Price in MS.]

[c. 1711.]

> BM. e. 201. b. (3.)
> From the same plates as No. 396; with a new title-page.
> Both works advertised Feb. 19–21, 1712, *Post Man*, as: 'Eight Solos for a Violin and Bass,
> or a Flute and Bass.'
> The Flute edition, in Walsh Cat., c. 1721, Ill. 28, as: 'Martino Bitti Solos, for a Flute &
> a Bass. 4s. 0d.'

402. The Additionall Songs In The New Opera, Call'd Camilla [Words translated
from the Italian of Silvio Stampiglia by Owen MacSwiney. Music by Marco
Antonio Bononcini] as they are perform'd at the Theatre Royall.

Sold by I: Walsh Musicall Instrument maker in Or=/=dinary to her Majesty
- - - - - - at the Harp and Ho=boy . . . and I. Hare Musick Instrument maker at ye
Golden Viol and Flute in Cornhill near ye Royal Exchange.

[c. 1711.]

> BM. I. 354. a.
> Title-page from the plate used for the original edition of the score of the songs (No.
> 221, *see* Ill. 1) and for 'The Additionall Songs In The New Opera, Call'd Hydaspes' (No.
> 373) and other works, with P. Randall added to the imprint. For this edition of the songs in
> Camilla (No. 402) Randall's name was deleted from the plate. The work consists of the
> songs of the original edition with the addition of the overture in front, and two additional
> songs at the end. The overture, differently engraved, occurs in No. 298, which also includes
> the two additional songs but in reverse order to that of No. 402. The additional songs were
> probably issued together as a separate work with the title as given above, and copies of the
> fuller score containing the overture and all the songs may have been issued c. 1711 with the
> old title: 'Songs In The New Opera, Call'd Camilla', &c., but with the imprint of No. 402.
> This edition is mainly from the plates of No. 221; p. 42 being from a different plate. The
> deletion of Randall's name from the imprint places it after 1710, but there may have been
> an earlier issue.
> *See* Nos. 201, 204, 206, 209, 221, 238, 298, 560, and 565.

---

*The collection of Newspapers at the British Museum is very imperfect for the year
1712, consequently a number of advertisements are omitted from the bibliography.*

---

403. The Harpsicord Master, 4th Book, containing Plain and Easy Instructions for
Learners on the Harpsicord or Spinnet, with a compleat Explanation of Graces,
and the true manner of fingering the Keys; also an exact method of Tuning the
Harpsicord or Spinnet, being of material use to all that Play thereon; together with
a Collection of Airs and Lessons proper for Learners, and the most favourite
Song-Tunes now in use. Price 2s.

Printed for J. Walsh . . . and J. Hare, &c.

R

Jan. 19–22, 1712, *Post Man.*

Daniel Wright issued a work with a title very similar to that of No. 403: 'The Harpsichord Master Book Containing plain & easy Instructions for Learners on the Harpsichord
or Spinnet,' &c. (Bibliothèque Alfred Cortot.)

See Nos. 14, 27, 59, 471, 505, and 566.

404. The Royall Ann M^r. Isaac's New Dance. made for Her Majestys Birth Day
[1712] The Tune by M^r. Paisible. Engraven in Characters & Figures for ye use
of Masters Note these following Dances by M^r. Isaac are likewise Printed. Viz
The Rigadoon Royal . . . The Northumberland. [16 nos. in 2 columns] And ye Art
of Dancing done in Characters.

Printed for I: Walsh Servt. in Ordinary to Her Majesty . . . & I: Hare at ye Viol
& Flute, &c.

[1712.]

BM. h. 993. (4.)

The title-page from a plate used for a number of similar works reissued *c.* 1712, 'Royall
Ann' and the other titles being supplied in MS. on the title-pages in a blank space left on
the plate for this purpose.

405. The Union M^r. Isaac's New Dance. made for Her Majestys Birth Day [1707]
The Tune by M^r. Paisible. Engraven in Characters & Figures for ye use of Masters
Note these following Dances by M^r. Isaac are likewise Printed. Viz The Rigadoon
Royal . . . The Northumberland. [16 nos. in 2 columns] And ye Art of Dancing
done in Characters.

Printed for I: Walsh . . . & I: Hare, &c.

[*c.* 1712.]

BM. h. 993. (8.)

The title-page from a plate used for No. 404 and a number of similar works reissued
c. 1712, with 'Union' in MS. on the title-page in a blank space left on the plate for this
purpose. The work is otherwise from the same plates as No. 234, and has an inner title-page
from that edition, 'The Union a New Dance Compos'd by M^r. Isaac Perform'd at Court
on Her Majestie's Birth day Feb^r: ye 6th. 1707', &c.

See No. 234.

406. The Britannia M^r. Isaac's New Dance. made for Her Majestys Birth Day
[1706] The Tune by M^r. Paisible. Engraven in Characters & Figures for ye use of
Masters Note these following Dances by M^r. Isaac are likewise Printed. Viz The
Rigadoon Royal . . . The Northumberland. [16 nos. in 2 columns] And ye Art of
Dancing done in Characters.

Printed for I: Walsh . . . & I: Hare, &c.

[*c.* 1712.]

BM. h. 993. (9.)

The title-page from a plate used for No. 404 and a number of similar works reissued
c. 1712, with 'Britannia' in MS. on the title-page in a blank space left on the plate for this
purpose.

See Nos. 196, 207, and 374.

407. The Spanheim M^r. Isaac's New Dance. made for Her Majestys Birth Day The Tune by M^r. Paisible. Engraven in Characters & Figures for ye use of Masters Note these following Dances by M^r. Isaac are likewise Printed. Viz The Rigadoon Royal . . . The Northumberland. [16 nos. in 2 columns.] And ye Art of Dancing done in Characters.

Printed for I: Walsh . . . & I: Hare, &c.

[*c.* 1712.]

BM. h. 993. (10.)

The title-page from a plate used for No. 404 and a number of similar works reissued *c.* 1712, with 'Spanhiem' in MS. on the title-page in a blank space left on the plate for this purpose.

See No. 408 for reference to another edition. (BM. 785. k. 7. (5.))

408. The Favorite M^r. Isaac's New Dance. made for Her Majestys Birth Day The Tune by M^r. Paisible. Engraven in Characters & Figures for ye use of Masters Note these following Dances by M^r. Isaac are likewise Printed. Viz The Rigadoon Royal . . . The Northumberland. [16 nos. in 2 columns.] And ye Art of Dancing done in Characters

Printed for I: Walsh . . . & I: Hare, &c.

[*c.* 1712.]

BM. h. 993. (11.)

The title-page from a plate used for No. 404 and a number of similar works reissued *c.* 1712, with 'Favorite' in MS. on the title-page in a blank space left on the plate for this purpose.

Another edition at BM. 785. k. 7. (5.), without outer title-page and imprint, is from the same plates, with the same inner title as No. 408: 'The Favorite A Chaconne Danc'd by her Majesty.' The Favorite is followed by 'The Spanheim'. (*See* No. 407.)

409. The Richmond M^r. Isaac's New Dance. made for Her Majestys Birth Day The Tune by M^r. Paisible. Engraven in Characters & Figures for ye use of Masters Note these following Dances by M^r. Isaac are likewise Printed. Viz The Rigadoon Royal . . . The Northumberland. [16 nos. in 2 columns] And ye Art of Dancing done in Characters.

Printed for I: Walsh . . . & I: Hare, &c.

[*c.* 1712.]

BM. h. 993. (12.)

The title-page from a plate used for No. 404 and a number of similar works reissued *c.* 1712, with 'Richmond' in MS. on the title-page in a blank space left on the plate for this purpose.

Another edition at BM. 785. k. 7. (6.), without outer title-page and imprint, is from the same plates, with the same inner title as No. 409: 'The Richmond'.

410. The Rigadoon M^r. Isaac's New Dance. made for Her Majestys Birth Day The Tune by M^r. Paisible. Engraven in Characters & Figures for ye use of Masters Note these following Dances by M^r. Isaac are likewise Printed. Viz The Rigadoon

Royal . . . The Northumberland. [16 nos. in 2 columns] And yᵉ Art of Dancing done in Characters.

 Printed for I: Walsh . . . & I: Hare, &c.

 [*c.* 1712.]

  BM. h. 993. (13.)
  The title-page from a plate used for No. 404 and a number of similar works reissued *c.* 1712, with 'Rigadoon' in MS. on the title-page in a blank space left on the plate for this purpose.
  Another edition, at BM. 785. k. 7. (4.), without outer title-page and imprint, is from the same plates, with the same inner title as No. 410: 'The Rigadoone Compos'd by Mʳ. Isaac.'

411. The Rondeau Mʳ. Isaac's New Dance. made for Her Majestys Birth Day [1709] The Tune by Mʳ. Paisible. Engraven in Characters & Figures for yᵉ use of Masters Note these following Dances by Mʳ. Isaac are likewise Printed. Viz The Rigadoon Royal . . . The Northumberland. [16 nos. in 2 columns] And yᵉ Art of Dancing done in Characters.

 Printed for I: Walsh . . . & I: Hare, &c.

 [*c.* 1712.]

  BM. h. 993. (14.)
  The title-page from a plate used for No. 404 and a number of similar works reissued *c.* 1712, with 'Rondeau' in MS. on the title-page in a blank space left on the plate for this purpose.
  An imperfect copy of another edition, at BM. 785. k. 7. (7.), without outer title-page and imprint, is from the same plates, with the same inner title as No. 411: 'The Rondeau.'

412. The Princess Mʳ. Isaac's New Dance. made for Her Majestys Birth Day The Tune by Mʳ. Paisible. Engraven in Characters & Figures for yᵉ use of Masters Note these following Dances by Mʳ. Isaac are likewise Printed. Viz The Rigadoon Royal . . . The Northumberland. [16 nos. in 2 columns] And yᵉ Art of Dancing done in Characters.

 Printed for I: Walsh . . . & I: Hare, &c.

 [*c.* 1712.]

  BM. h. 993. (15.)
  The title-page from a plate used for No. 404 and a number of similar works reissued *c.* 1712, with 'Princess' in MS. on the title-page in a blank space left on the plate for this purpose.

413. The Gloucester Mʳ. Isaac's New Dance. made for Her Majestys Birth Day The Tune by Mʳ. Paisible. Engraven in Characters & Figures for yᵉ use of Masters Note these following Dances by Mʳ. Isaac are likewise Printed. Viz The Rigadoon Royal . . . The Northumberland. [16 nos. in 2 columns] And yᵉ Art of Dancing done in Characters.

 Printed for I: Walsh . . . & I: Hare, &c.

 [*c.* 1712.]

BM. h. 993. (16.)

The title-page from a plate used for No. 404 and a number of similar works reissued *c.* 1712, with 'Gloucester' in MS. on the title-page in a blank space left on the plate for this purpose.

414. The Royall M^r. Isaac's New Dance. made for Her Majestys Birth Day The Tune by M^r. Paisible. Engraven in Characters & Figures for ye use of Masters Note these following Dances by M^r. Isaac are likewise Printed. Viz The Rigadoon Royal . . . The Northumberland. [16 nos. in 2 columns] And ye Art of Dancing done in Characters.

Printed for I: Walsh . . . & I: Hare, &c.

[*c.* 1712.]

BM. h. 993. (18.)

The title-page from a plate used for No. 404 and a number of similar works reissued *c.* 1712, with 'Royal' in MS. on the title-page in a blank space left on the plate for this purpose. An earlier edition, advertised on No. 383, has not been identified.

415. The Northumberland M^r. Isaac's New Dance. made for Her Majestys Birth Day The Tune by M^r. Paisible. Engraven in Characters & Figures for ye use of Masters Note these following Dances by M^r. Isaac are likewise Printed. Viz The Rigadoon Royal . . . The Northumberland. [16 nos. in 2 columns] And ye Art of Dancing done in Characters.

Printed for I: Walsh . . . & I: Hare, &c.

[*c.* 1712.]

BM. h. 993. (19.)

Title-page from a plate used for No. 404 and a number of similar works reissued *c.* 1712, with 'Northumberland' in MS. on the title-page in a blank space left on the plate for this purpose. An earlier edition, advertised on No. 383, has not been identified.

416. A Set of Tunes in 3 parts for Violins and Hoboys, in the last new Comedy [by Susannah Centlivre] call'd the Perplex'd Lovers, Composed by Mr. John Barret. pr. 1s. 6d.

Printed for J. Walsh, &c.

Feb. 19–21, 1712, *Post Man.*

417. Songs in the Opera of Antiochus [Words by Apostolo Zeno. Music by Francesco Gasparini] as they are Perform'd at ye Queens Theatre.

London Printed for J: Walsh Servant in Ordinary to her Britanick Majesty . . . & J: Hare, &c.

Feb. 19–21, 1712, *Post Man.*

BM. H. 298.

The title-page from a plate first used for No. 353 (*see* Ill. 22), with the title 'Songs in the Opera . . . Queens Theatre' from a supplementary plate and with the imprint as modified for No. 384.

No separate edition of 'The Symphonys or Instrumental Parts in the Opera Call'd Antiochus' has been traced, but such was probably issued as the Walsh Cat., *c.* 1721, Ill. 27, advertised *Antiochus* as one of the operas which 'have Symphonys'.

418. Six Sets of Airs for two Flutes, by Mr Hen. Simons.
>   Printed for J. Walsh, &c.
>   Feb. 19–21, 1712, *Post Man.*
>>   Walsh Cat., *c.* 1721, Ill. 28, as: 'Simmons Aires, for two Flutes. 2s. od.'
>>   *See* No. 52: 'A Set of Ayres for Two Flut's and a Bass.'

419. XII. Sonatas of three Parts for two Violins & a Bass with a through Bass for yᵉ Organ Harpsicord or arch Lute Compos'd by Mʳ: Valentine at Rome. Opera Prima.
>   London, Printed for J. Walsh . . . & J. Hare, &c.
>   [*c.* 1712.]
>>   BM. h. 11. c. (1); h. 11. Imperfect.

420. A New Edition of 12 Sonatas for 2 Violins, and a through Bass; composed by Mr. Christopher Pez. Note, This Edition far exceeds the former, both in Correctness and Order in the graving.
>   Printed for J. Walsh . . . and J. Hare, &c.
>   Mar. 20–2, 1712, *Post Man.*
>>   No details of the earlier edition have been traced.

421. The Fifth Book of the Compleat Flute-Master. Or the whole Art of Playing on the Flute, in such plain and easie Directions that every Capacity may attain to Perfection on that Instrument, with a Collection of the newest Airs with a flourish in every Key, by Mr. Teno, Sign. Pepush, Mr. Keene, Mr. Graves, Mr. Barrett. To which is added a Plain Scale for the transposing of any Tune from the Violin or Voice to the Flute; as also an excellent Solo by Sign. Pepush for Flute and a Bass, never before Published.
>   Printed for J. Hare . . . and J. Walsh, &c.
>   Apr. 10–12, 1712, *Post Man.*
>>   *See* Nos. 2, 3, 9, 236, 240, and 423. No details of the third book have been traced.

422. Songs in the Opera of Hamlet [Words by Apostolo Zeno. Music by Francesco Gasparini] as they are perform'd at yᵉ Queens Theatre.
>   London Printed for J: Walsh Servant in Ordinary to her Britanick Majesty . . . & J: Hare, &c.
>   Apr. 21, 1712, *Spectator.*
>>   BM. H. 114. (1.)
>>   The title-page from a plate first used for No. 353 (*see* Ill. 22), with the title 'Songs in the Opera . . . Queens Theatre' from a supplementary plate and with the imprint as modified for No. 384.
>>   No separate edition of 'The Symphonys or Instrumental Parts in the Opera Call'd Hamlet' has been traced, but such was probably issued as the Walsh Cat., *c.* 1721, Ill. 27, advertised *Hamlet* as one of the operas which 'have Symphonys'.

423. The 5th Book of the Gentlemans Companion. Being a choice Collection of the newest Tunes for the Flute, viz. Rigadoons, Hornpipes, Minuets, Jiggs

&c. with a Flourish in every Key, by Mr. Teno, and choice Song-Tunes. Composed by the most able Master, viz. Sig. Pepush, Mr. Keene, Mr. Grave, Mr. Barret: To which is added an excellent Solo by Sig Pepush for a Flute and a Base never before Published.

Sold by J. Hare . . . and J. Walsh, &c.

May 13–15, 1712, *Post Man.*

This may have been a separate edition of part of No. 421.
See Nos. 83, 236, 240, and 421. No details of the third book have been traced.

424. Nolens Volens; or the most compleat Tutor to the Violin, being an Introduction to Learners on that Instrument Digested in the most plain and easie Method, yet extent; also a Collection of the favourite Tunes and Aires in the last new Operas, and the choicest Minuets, Rigadoons, Jiggs and Paspies performed at Court and Publick Balls, being easie and delightful to Practitioners; the 5th Edition carefully Corrected.

Printed for J. Walsh . . . and J. Hare, &c.

May 27–9, 1712, *Post Man.*

Presumably the fifth book of the series.
See Nos. 72, 158, 306, 442, 472, and 487 for other books. No details of the first book have been traced.

425. New Aires made on Purpose for two Flutes & a Bass Familiar & Proper for Practitioners in Consort. fairly Engraven.

London Printed for & Sould by I: Walsh Musicall Instrument maker in Ordinary to her Majesty . . . and I: Hare at the Viol and Flute in Cornhill nere the Royall Exchange. 2ˢ–6ᵈ. [Price in MS.]

May 27–9, 1712, *Post Man.*

BM. h. 17. (1.)
Title-page is from the Collins plate (No. 15, *see* Ill. 3), with the title 'New Aires . . . Engraven.' from a supplementary plate and 'I: Hare at the Viol and Flute in Cornhill nere the Royall Exchange' engraved on the plate below the Walsh imprint, and inside the original border.
See No. 398.

426. Songs in the Opera of Calypso & Telemachus as they are Perform'd at the Queens Theatre. Compos'd by Mʳ Galliard. the Words by Mʳ Hughes.

London Printed for J: Walsh Servant in Ordinary to her Britanick Majesty . . . & J: Hare, &c.

[1712.]

BM. G. 223. (1.)
RCM. I. G. 9.
The title-page from a plate first used for No. 353 (*see* Ill. 22), with the title 'Songs in the Opera . . . Mʳ Hughes' from a supplementary plate, and with the imprint as modified for No. 384. No separate edition of 'The Symphonys or Instrumental Parts in the Opera Call'd Calypso & Telemachus' has been traced, but such was probably issued as the Walsh Cat., c. 1721, Ill. 27, advertised *Calypso* as one of the operas which 'have Symphonys'.

427. Twenty Four New Country Dances, for the year 1713. With Proper Tunes, and New Figures or Directions, to each Dance. The Musick proper for the Violin, Hautboy, or Flute. Printed on the New Capital Character of Musick.
London: Printed for John Walsh . . . and J. Hare, &c.
[1712.]
> BM. a. 9. (2.)
> Earlier similar issues were engraven; this was from type.

428. Opera Calypso, for a single Flute. 1s. 6d.
John Walsh.
[c. 1712.]
Walsh Cat., c. 1721, Ill. 28.
> No details of the title-page have been traced. *Calypso and Telemachus* was by Johann Ernst Galliard.
> *See* No. 426.

429. Sonatas or Solos for a Flute with a Through Bass for the Harpsicord or Bass Violin. Compos'd by Jean Luly [i.e. J. B. Loeillet] of Gant. Parte Prima. [Op. 1.]
London, Printed for J. Walsh Servt. to her Britanick Majesty . . . & J. Hare, &c.
[c. 1712.]
> BM. i. 26. (1.)
> Walsh Cat., c. 1721, Ill. 28, as: 'Lullys 1st Solos, for a Flute & a Bass. 6s. od.'
> Included later in Walsh's numerical series with Hare deleted from the imprint and 'No. 116' added to the title-page and, presumably, 'her' altered to 'his' Britanick Majesty.
> *See* Nos. 476 and 556.

430. Solos for a Violin With a Thorough Bass for the Harpsicord or Bass Violin Compos'd by Michele Mascitti Opera Prima [Prima in MS.] Note there are four excellent pieces Consisting of Solos by the same Author extant.
London Printed for I: Walsh Servant in ordinary to Her Brittanick Majesty . . . & I: Hare, &c.
[c. 1712.]
> BM. g. 422. (3.)
> RCM. II. B. 9. (5.)
> The title-page from a plate which was also used for Nos. 431, 432, 433, and for another issue of No. 479.
> *See* No. 470.

431. Solos for a Violin With a Thorough Bass for the Harpsicord or Bass Violin Compos'd by Michele Mascitti Opera 2da [2da in MS.] Note there are four excellent pieces Consisting of Solos by the same Author extant.
London Printed for I: Walsh . . . & I: Hare, &c.
[c. 1712.]
> Arthur F. Hill collection.

Title-page from the plate used for Opera Prima (No. 430), &c.
See No. 470.

432. Solos for a Violin With a Thorough Bass for the Harpsicord or Bass Violin Compos'd by Michele Mascitti Opera Terza [Terza in MS.] Note there are four excellent pieces Consisting of Solos by the same Author extant.
London Printed for I: Walsh . . . & I: Hare, &c.
[*c.* 1712.]

Arthur F. Hill collection.
Title-page from the plate used for Opera Prima (No. 430), &c.
See Nos. 430 and 470.

433. Solos for a Violin With a Thorough Bass for the Harpsicord or Bass Violin Compos'd by Michele Mascitti Opera Quarta [Quarta in MS.] Note there are four excellent pieces Consisting of Solos by the same Author extant.
London Printed for I: Walsh . . . & I: Hare, &c.
[*c.* 1712.]

BM. g. 422. (4.)
The title-page from the plate used for Opera Prima (No. 430), &c.
See No. 470.

434. Sonatas of three Parts, for two Violins & a Bass with a through Bass for yᵉ Organ Harpsicord or arch Lute Compos'd by Michele Mascitti. Opera Quinta.
London, Printed for J. Walsh . . . & J. Hare, &c.
[*c.* 1712.]

BM. g. 672. b.
Walsh Cat., *c.* 1721, Ill. 27, as: 'Mascittis Sonatas, for 2 Violins & a Bass. 5s. od.' The same catalogue also includes: 'Mascittis Opera Quinta, for a Violin & a Bass, 6s. od,' presumably a different work from that published by Roger of Amsterdam (BM. g. 672. e.), and Foucault of Paris in 1714 (BM. h. 197. (1.)) as listed under No. 479.
See No. 470.

435. A Choice Collection of Airs or Ariett's for two Flutes with the Overture of Camilla & Arsinoe also Arietts & Duetts in yᵉ Opera of Thomyris Contrived and fitted for two Flutes to which is added a New Sonata for two Flutes Compos'd by Mʳ. Daniel Purcell the whole fairly Engraven. 1=6. [Price in MS.]
London Printed for I. Walsh . . . and I. Hare, &c.
[*c.* 1712.]

BM. a. 209. a. (8.) Fluto Primo part only.
The title-page is from the same plate as that of the earlier edition (No. 262); but the music is from different plates, with the same pagination and similar layout.

436. All The Song Tunes for the Flute In the Last new Opera call'd Hydaspes. [Music by Francesco Mancini.] Fairly Engraven & Carefully Corrected. Price 1ˢ. 6ᵈ.

London, Printed for J. Walsh - - - - - at yᵉ Harp & Hoboy . . . & J. Hare, &c. [*c.* 1712.]

    BM. a. 209. a. (6.)
    The title-page from the plate of an earlier work not identified, with 'call'd Hydaspes' from a supplementary plate.
    See No. 356.

437. The Song Tunes for yᵉ Flute in the Opera's of Antiochus & Hamlet. [Music by Francesco Gasparini.] Fairly Engraven & Carefully Corected, Price 1ˢ. 6ᵈ.
    London, Printed for J. Walsh Servᵗ. to her Majesty . . . & J. Hare, &c.
    [*c.* 1712.]
        BM. a. 209. a. (7.)

438. The Musick perform'd in the Tragedy [by Thomas Southerne] of Capua [i.e. The Fate of Capua] in Parts for Violins, Trumpets and Hautboys: composed by Mr. John Eccles Master of Her Majesty's Musick.
    Printed for John Walsh . . . and J. Hare, &c.
    May 23–6, 1713, *Post Boy.*

439. The Pastorall Mr. Isaac's New Dance. made for Her Majestys Birth Day 1713 The Tune by Mʳ Paisible. Engraven in Characters & Figures for yᵉ use of Masters Writ by Mʳ. Pemberton. Note these following dances by Mʳ. Isaac are likewise Printed—Viz The Royal Ann . . . The Northumberland. [17 nos. in 2 columns] And the Art of Dancing done by Mʳ. Weaver—
    Printed for I: Walsh Servᵗ. in Ordinary to Her Majesty . . . and I: Hare, &c.
    [1713.]
        BM. h. 993. (3.)

440. Twenty Four New Country Dances For the Year 1714 With proper Tunes and new Figures or Directions to Each Dance Compos'd by Several Authors, all Fairly Engraven Price. 6ᵈ. Note the new Country Dancing Master is publish'd Containing the Country Dances for the ten last Years.
    London Printed for J. Walsh Servant in Ordinary to her Majesty. at yᵉ Harp and Hoboy . . . and J. Hare, &c.
    Nov. 12–14, 1713, *Post Boy.*

        BM. a. 10. (2.)
    The title-page from a plate used for an earlier collection, 'and P. Randall' being deleted after 'her Majesty', and 'ten' substituted for probably 'seven' last years, in the title.

441. The New Country Dancing Master is publish'd Containing the Country Dances for the ten last Years.
    London Printed for J. Walsh . . . and J. Hare, &c.
    Nov. 12–14, 1713, *Post Boy.*

    Advertised on No. 440.
    See Nos. 193, 260, 333, 371, 394, and 489.

442. The 6th Book of Nolens Volens, or the most compleat Tutor to the Violin; being an Introduction to Learners on that Instrument, digested in the most plain and easy Method yet extant, also a Collection of the newest Favourite Tunes and Airs both Italian and English by the best Masters, with Preludes and Flourishes in every Key for the Violin, all fairly engraven and carefully Corrected pr. 1s. 6d.

 Printed for J. Walsh . . . J. Hare, &c.

 Dec. 12–15, 1713, *Post Boy.*

  See Nos. 72, 158, 306, 424, 472, and 487, for other books. No details of the first book have been traced.

443. XII Sonatas or Solos for a Flute with a Through=bass for the Harpsicord or Bass Violin. Compos'd by M^r: Valentine. at Rome Opera II°. [II° in MS.]

 London, Printed for J. Walsh . . . & J. Hare, &c.

 [*c.* 1713.]

  BM. g. 422. (1.)
  The title-page from a plate used for other similar works by Valentine.
  Presumably the work in Walsh Cat., *c.* 1721, Ill. 28, as: 'Valentines 2^d Solos, for a Flute & a Bass. 6s. od.'
  See No. 474.

444. The Godolphin Mr. Isaac's New Dance made for Her Majestys Birth Day 1714 the Tune by M^r. Paisible. Engraven in Characters & Figures for ye use of Masters Writ by M^r. Pemberton. Note these following Dances by M^r. Isaac are likewise Printed—Viz The Pastorall . . . The Northumberland. [18 nos. in 2 columns.] And the Art of Dancing done by M^r. Weaver.

 Printed for I: Walsh Servt. in Ordinary to Her Majesty . . . and I: Hare, &c.

 [1714.]

  BM. h. 993. (2.)

445. The Siciliana, Mr. Seris new Dance for the Year 1714, the Tune intirely New; to which is added several excellent new Minuets, Jiggs, Entries and Stage Dances, perform'd at the Theatre and Publick Entertainments; the Tunes proper for the Violin, Flute or Hautboy, price 6d.

 Printed for J. Walsh . . . and J. Hare, &c.

 Mar. 4, 1714, *The Lover.*

446. Songs in the Opera of Crœsus as they are Perform'd at ye Queens Theatre.

 London Printed for J: Walsh Servant in Ordinary to her Britanick Majesty . . . & J: Hare, &c.

 Apr. 29–May 1, 1714, *Post Boy.* (There are now 16 Operas of Vocal Musick in Italian and English.)

  BM. H. 323.
  RCM. XXXII. B. (10.)
  Title-page from the plate first used for No. 353 (*see* Ill. 22), with the title 'Songs . . Queens Theatre' from a supplementary plate, and with the imprint as modified for No. 384.

447. Songs in the Opera of Arminius. as they are Perform'd at the Queens Theatre.
London Printed for J: Walsh Servant in Ordinary to her Britanick Majesty
. . . & J: Hare, &c.
   May 29–June 1, 1714, *Post Boy.*
      BM. H. 322.
      Title-page from the plate first used for No. 353 (*see* Ill. 22), with the title 'Songs . . . Queen's
Theatre' from a supplementary plate, and with the imprint as modified for No. 384.

448. A Set of Tunes in 3 parts, with a Trumpet, containing an Overture, Sym-
phony and Aires, as they were perform'd in the reviv'd Comedy [by Colley
Cibber], call'd She wou'd and she wou'd not. Price 1s. 6d.
London Printed for J: Walsh Servant in Ordinary to her Britanick Majesty . . .
& J: Hare, &c.
   June 24–6, 1714, *Post Boy.*
      See No. 110, Paisible's music for the 1702 production of this comedy.

449. Arie dell' Opera di Rinaldo Composta dal Signor Hendel Maestro di Capella
di Sua Altezza Elettorale d'Hannover. [Italian words by Giacomo Rossi from a
sketch by Aaron Hill after Torquato Tasso, English words by Hill.]
London Printed for J: Walsh . . . & J: Hare, &c.
   [*c.* 1714.]
      Title-page, contents, and pagination as in the previous edition, No. 389 (*see* Ill. 22), with
the exception that the aria 'Il tricerbero humiliato', on p. 37, has English words commencing,
'Let ye Waiter bring clean Glasses,' added under the Bass stave, and 'in Italian & English'
added at the top of the page. This number became a popular song and was included in
various collections of the period.
      W^m. C. Smith collection.
      RCM. XI. C. 22. (1.)
      See Nos. 385, 387, 389, and 459.

———————

   *After the death of Queen Anne, August 1, 1714, the imprints give 'His Majesty' in
place of 'Her Majesty'.*

———————

450. Songs in the Opera Calld Loves Triumph. [Words adapted from the Italian
of Cardinal Ottoboni by Peter Anthony Motteux. Music by Carlo Francesco
Cesarini, Francesco Gasparini and others.]
London Printed for & Sold by Iohn Walsh Servant to his Majesty at the Harp
and Hautboy in Katherine Street near Somerset House in the Strand.
   [*c.* 1714.]
      BM. H. 227.
      RCM. XXXII. A. 2. (3.)
      The BM. copy has four title-pages. The first, as transcribed above, from the plate first
used by Walsh for No. 82a (*see* Ill. 8), modified for No. 293 (*see* Ill. 20) and other works,

with the imprint altered to 'his' Majesty and with the title 'Songs . . . Loves Triumph' from a supplementary plate.

The second, third, and fourth title-pages of the BM. copy are from another plate used for earlier editions, Nos. 271 and 272 (*see* Ill. 1), with the title in each case: 'Songs In The New Opera, Call'd Love's Triumph as they are Perform'd at the Queens Theatre.'

The imprints of the third and fourth title-pages are as in Nos. 271 and 272. The imprint of the second title-page is from the plate modified for No. 293, by the insertion of 'P. Randall', whose name was erased before using the plate for No. 402. This imprint reads: 'Sold by I: Walsh Musicall Instrument maker in Or=/=dinary to her Majesty - - - - - - at the Harp and Ho=boy, in Catherine=Street near Sommerset House in the Strand and I. Hare', &c.

Supplementary plates were used for the title 'Love's Triumph . . . Queens Theatre' in the second, third, and fourth title-pages, the second and fourth being the same in engraving; the third being different, apparently from the same plate in an earlier state.

The RCM. copy has the same outer illustrated title-page as the BM. copy, but only the second of the inner title-pages.

The first three title-pages of the BM. copy precede the first 25 pages of the opera, with the index of that part; the fourth title-page, followed by the index of the complete work, precedes pp. 26–70 of the music.

See Nos. 271 and 272.

451. A Collection of the newest Minuits, Rigadons and French Dances, perform'd at Court and publick Entertainments, the Tunes proper for the Violin; Hoboy or Flute. pr. 6d.
Printed for J. Walsh, Servant in Ordinary to His Majesty . . . and J. Hare, &c.
Dec. 14–16, 1714, *Evening Post.*

452. 24 new Country Dances for the Year 1715 with proper Tunes, and new Figures to each Dance pr. 6d.
Printed for J. Walsh . . . and J. Hare, &c.
Dec. 14–16, 1714, *Evening Post.*

453. A Collection of all the French Dances of the last 7 Years, as also the Country Dances of the same Date.
Printed for J. Walsh . . . and J. Hare, &c.
Dec. 14–16, 1714, *Evening Post.* (There is lately published.)
Presumably two different works.

454. Opera Crœsus, for two Flutes. 2s. od.
John Walsh. [*c.* 1714.]
Walsh Cat., *c.* 1721, Ill. 28.
Details of the title-page have not been traced.

455. Opera Crœsus, for a single Flute. 1s. 6d.
John Walsh. [*c.* 1714.]
Walsh Cat., *c.* 1721, Ill. 28.
Details of the title-page have not been traced.

456. Opera Arminius, for two Flutes. 2s. od.
  John Walsh. [c. 1714.]
  Walsh Cat., c. 1721, Ill. 28.
   Details of the title-page have not been traced.

457. Opera Arminius for yᵉ flute. 1s. 6d.
  John Walsh. [c. 1714.]
  Walsh Cat., c. 1721, Ill. 28.
   Details of the title-page have not been traced.

458. XII Sonatas or Solos for a Flute with a Through=bass for the Harpsicord or
Bass Violin. Compos'd by Mʳ: Valentine. at Rome Opera Terza. [Terza in MS.]
  London, Printed for J. Walsh . . . & J. Hare, &c.
  [c. 1714.]
   BM. h. 11. a. (2); i. 26. (4.)
   The title-page from a plate used previously for No. 443.
   Presumably the work in Walsh Cat., c. 1721, Ill. 28, as: 'Valentines 3ᵈ Solos, for a Flute
   & a Bass. 6s. od.' E. Roger of Amsterdam issued an edition: 'XII Sonate À Flauto Solo col
   Basso Continuo Di Roberto Valentino Inglese Opera Terza.' (BM. e. 22.)
   See No. 475.

459. Arie dell' Opera di Rinaldo Composta dal Signor Hendel Maestro di Capella
di Sua Altezza Elettorale d'Hannover. [Italian words by Giacomo Rossi from a
sketch by Aaron Hill after Torquato Tasso, English words by Hill.]
  London Printed for J: Walsh Servant in Ordinary to his Britanick Majesty . . .
& J: Hare, &c.
  [c. 1714–16.]
   BM. H. 299. g.
   RCM. XI. C. 8. (1.)
   Similar to the previous edition, No. 449 (*see* Ill. 22), except for the alteration of 'her'
   Britanick Majesty to 'his' Britanick Majesty in the imprint.
   See Nos. 385, 387, 389, and 449.

460. Mʳ Pepusch's Aires for two Violins Made on Purpose for the Improvement
of Practitioners in Consort The whole Fairly Engraven and Carefully Corected.
  London Printed for J. Walsh Servant in Ordinary to his Majesty———at yᵉ
Harp and Hoboy in Katherinᵉ Street near Somerset House in yᵉ Strand and
J. Hare at the Viol and Flute in Corⁿhill near the Royall Exchange.
  [c. 1715.]
   BM. h. 59.
   Title-page from the plate of the earlier edition (No. 307), with the imprint modified and
   Randall's name omitted.
   Included later in Walsh's numerical series, with 'No 429' added to the title-page, and
   Hare deleted from the imprint.
   See No. 307.

134

461. The Princess Royal a new Dance for his Majesty's Birth Day 1715 Compos'd by M^r: L'Abeé The Figure & Characters fairly Engraven.

London Printed for I: Walsh . . . & I: Hare, &c.

[1715.]

> BM. h. 801. (2.)
> Another edition, apparently not by Walsh, 'Writ by Mr. Pemberton', is at BM. h. 801. b. (6.)
> *See* No. 494; and Ill. 36.

462. The Friendship M^r. Isaac's New Dance for the Year 1715 the Tune by M^r. Paisible Engraven in Characters & Figures for ye use of Masters Writ by Mr. Pemberton Note these following Dances by Mr Isaac are likewise Printed—Viz The Godolphin . . . The Princess Royal [20 nos. in 2 columns] And the Art of Dancing done by M^r. Weaver.

Printed for I: Walsh Servt. in Ordinary to His Majesty . . . and I: Hare, &c.

[1715.]

> BM. h. 993. (1.)

463. A Collection of the Choicest Songs & Dialogues Composd By the most Eminent Masters of the Age.

London Printed for & Sould by I: Walsh Musicall Instrument maker in Ordinary to his Majesty at the Golden Harp & Ho=boy in Catherine=street near Summerset=house in y^e strand.

[*c.* 1715 or later.]

> BM. G. 304.; G. 151.
> Two different collections from plates used previously for separate and other issues of the contents.
>   Both with Collins title-page (No. 15, *see* Ill. 3), with the title from a supplementary plate. Walsh probably issued other made-up collections with the same title-page as the above. The title-page of each has the same imprint of Walsh only, but G. 304 has been cropped at the bottom so that it is impossible to say whether this copy had Hare's name as well as Walsh's as in No. 425.
>   *See* No. 142c, an earlier collection, probably with title similar to No. 463.

464. A Collection of new Songs With a Through Bass to each Song for the Harpsicord Compos'd by Several Masters.

London (Printed for &) Sould by I: Walsh Musicall Instrument maker in Ordinary to his Majesty at the Harp and Hoboy in Cathe=/=rine Street, near Summerset House in the Strand and I Hare at the Viol and Flute in Cornhill nere the Royal Exchange.

[*c.* 1715.]

> BM. G. 316. b.
> The title-page is from the plate first used for No. 13 (*see* Ill. 2), and subsequently modified for other works; with 'Several Masters' from a supplementary plate. In this collection of new songs 'Printed for &' are added in MS. to the imprint, the words 'and P. Randal' after

'his Majesty' are crossed out, and the Hare portion of the imprint added. Some earlier unidentified use of the plate with Randall in the imprint was issued *c.* 1706–10.

The contents of this collection are all Scotch Songs, with 'A Table of the Scotch Songs Contain'd in this Book', from some earlier edition, probably that advertised as 'A Collection of Scotch Songs' in No. 331. In the 'Table' of the *c.* 1715 edition two numbers, 'Ah my fickle Jenny' and 'One Sunday after Mass', are deleted in MS. and two new numbers, 'Believe my sighs' and 'Now Jockey & Moggy', substituted, agreeing with the contents of the work, 33 numbers in all. Some of the plates were afterwards used for the Walsh and Joseph Hare later collections of Scotch Songs. (BM. H. 1374. a., &c.)

See No. 318.

465. Six Sonata's of 3 Parts, purposely made and contrived for three Flutes compos'd by Signior Matteison [i.e. Johann Mattheson] Opera Prima, price 3s.
Printed for J. Walsh . . . and J. Hare, &c.
Aug. 4–6, 1715, *Post Man.*

Walsh Cat., *c.* 1721, Ill. 28, as: 'Mattesons for 3 Flutes. 3s. od,' under 'Musick for 2 Flutes & a Bass'.

Included later in Walsh's numerical series, with 'No. 100' added in MS. to the title-page.

466. Concerti Grossi Con duoi Violini, e Violoncello di Concertino obligati, e duoi altri Violini, Viola, e Basso di Concerto Grosso, ad arbitrio che si potranno radoppiare; Da Arcangelo Corelli da Fusignano Opera Sesta. XII Great Concertos, or Sonatas, for two Violins and a Violoncello or for two Violins more, a Tenor, and a Thorough-Bass: which may be doubled at Pleasure. being the Sixth and last work of Arcangelo Corelli. Note all the other Works of this Author may be had where this is sold.
London Printed for I: Walsh, Servant in Ordinary to his Majesty: at the Harp and Hoboy, in Katherine Street, in the Strand: and I: Hare, &c.
Aug. 4–6, 1715, *Post Man.* (A New Edition of Correlli's 12 great Concertos in 7 Parts, pr. 12s.)

No earlier Walsh edition has been traced. Roger and Le Cene previously published the work at Amsterdam (BM. f. 17.), and Henry Ribotteau, the successor to Vaillant (*see* introduction) announced 'XII Concertos by Sig. Archangelo Corelli, for seven Parts. Opera Sesta'. (Dec. 30, 1714–Jan. 1, 1715, *Post Man.*)

The title-page of the Walsh and Hare edition, as transcribed here, is from a later issue by Walsh (BM. g. 45. c. (1.), *c.* 1732) with Hare omitted from the imprint and with 'N°. 370' of Walsh's numerical series added to the title-page. This later issue has a portrait of Corelli: 'H: Howard Pinx. V^{dr}. Gucht Sculp.', which may or may not have appeared in the 1715 edition.

See Nos. 512, 523, 580, and 596.

467. Six Sonatas for one Flute & two Hoboys or two Violins with a Viol Bass and a Thorough Bass for the Harpsicord & Arch Lute Compos'd by M^r. Christian Schickhard.
London Printed for I. Walsh Servant in Ordinary to his Majesty . . . and I. Hare, &c.

Aug. 4–6, 1715, *Post Man.* (Schickards Sonata's for Flutes, Violins or Hautboys, pr. 6s.)

Oct. 6–8, 1715, *Post Man.* (Schickhard's Sonatas. New edition.)

BM. h. 250. c. (4.)
Walsh Cat., *c.* 1721, Ill. 27, as: 'Schickards Sonatas. 6s. od,' amongst the works for 2 Violins and a Bass. In 'Apollo's Feast', third book, *c.* 1729 (Wm. C. Smith copy), as: 'Schickards Sonatas for variety of Instruments in 6 Parts, Opera Quinta'. The BM. copy may be of a later issue.

468. Six Sonata's of two Parts made on purpose for two Flutes Compos'd by Mr: Valentine at Rome Opera Quarta.
London Printed for I: Walsh Servt. in Ordinary to his Majesty . . . and I: Hare, &c.
Oct. 6–8, 1715, *Post Man.*

BM. h. 11. d.
Walsh Cat., *c.* 1721, Ill. 28, as: 'Valentines 1st Sonatas, for two Flutes. 3s. od.'
Included later in Walsh's numerical series with Hare deleted from the imprint and 'No. 58' added to the title-page.
See No. 480, an edition for Two Violins; and Nos. 497 and 555.

469. Vivaldi's most Celebrated Concertos in all their parts for Violins and other Instruments with a Thorough Bass for the Harpsicord Compos'd by Antonia Vivaldi Opera Terza. [Nos. I–VII.]
London Printed for I: Walsh . . . and I: Hare, &c.
Oct. 6–8, 1715, *Post Man.* (New edition.)

BM. h. 43.
RM. 26. a. 9. Violino (i.e. Violone) e Cembalo part only.
This was the first part of 'L'Estro Armonico'. The second part, containing Nos. VIII–XII, was advertised April 9–11, 1717, *Post Man.*
The first part appears to have been issued by Walsh and Hare, in competition with Roger's Amsterdam edition, advertised by Henry Ribotteau, who added to an advertisement of various works, Oct. 14–16, 1714, *Post Man:* 'Beware of Counterfeits, witness Vivaldi Concertos that are done in London and wants half, and may be had very well for a less Price, being not half Compleat.' No Walsh announcement of the work in 1714 has been traced.
The complete work, Walsh Cat., *c.* 1721, Ill. 27, as: 'Vivaldis Concertos, for 2 Violins & a Bass. 15s. od.'
See Nos. 509 and 522.

470. All Mascitti's Solos.
Printed for J. Walsh . . . and J. Hare, &c.
Oct. 6–8, 1715, *Post Man.* (New editions.)
Presumably Op. I–Op. IV. *See* Nos. 430–3.

471. The Harpsicord Master, 5th Book, containing plain and easy Instructions for Learners on the Harpsicord or Spinet, with an exact Method of Tuning, and a

Collection of the choicest Airs and Lessons proper for Learners. Together with the most Favourite Song Tunes now in use, engraven, price 2s.

> Printed for J. Walsh, at the Harp and Hoboy in Katherine Street in the Strand.
> Oct. 27–9, 1715, *Post Man.*
>
> > *See* Nos. 14, 27, 59, 403, 505, and 566.

472. Nolens Volens the 7th Book, or the most compleat Tutor to the Violin, being an Introduction to Learners on that Instrument digested in the most plain an easy Method extant, with a Collection of the newest favourite Tunes and Airs both Italian and English, by the best Masters, with Preludes and Flourishes in every Key for the Violin. pr. 1s. 6d.

> Printed for J: Walsh, at the Harp and Hoboy in Katherine Street in the Strand.
> Oct. 27–9, 1715, *Post Man.*
>
> > *See* Nos. 72, 158, 306, 424, 442, and 487, for other books. No details of the first book have been traced.

473. Demoivrs 3d Book of curious Airs for a single Flute, 1s. 6d.

> Printed for J. Walsh . . . and J. Hare, &c.
> Nov. 29–Dec. 1, 1715, *Post Man.*
>
> > Probably the same as: 'Demoivers Solos for a Flute and a Bass. Opera Terza', listed in the Walsh Cat. in 'Apollo's Feast', third book, *c.* 1729. (W^m. C. Smith copy.)
> > *See* Nos. 53 and 148.

474. Solos for a Flute with a Thorough Bass for the Harpsicord or Bass Violin Compos'd by M^r. Valentine at Rome Opera 2da.

> London Printed for I: Walsh Servant in Ordinary to his Majesty . . . and I: Hare &c.
> Nov. 29–Dec. 1, 1715, *Post Man.* (Valentines 1st Book of Solos for a Flute and a Bass.)
>
> > BM. h. 11. a. (1.)
> > Another edition of No. 443, with a new title-page. The BM. copy has 'N°. 120' in MS. on the title-page, thus incorporating it at a later date in Walsh's numerical series.
> > Presumably the work in Walsh Cat., *c.* 1721, Ill. 28, as: 'Valentines 2^d Solos, for a Flute & a Bass. 6s. od.'

475. Valentine's 2d Book of Solos for a Flute and a Bass.

> Printed for J. Walsh . . . and J. Hare, &c.
> Nov. 29–Dec. 1, 1715, *Post Man.*
>
> > A re-advertisement of No. 458: 'XII Sonatas or Solos . . . Opera Terza.'
> > Presumably the work in Walsh Cat., *c.* 1721, Ill. 28, as: 'Valentines 3^d Solos, for a Flute & a Bass. 6s. od.'

476. XII Sonatas or Solos for a Flute with a Thorough Bass for the Harpsicord or Bass Violin Compos'd by Iean Baptiste Loeillet de Gant Opera 2da. [2da. in MS.]

London Printed for I: Walsh Servant in Ordinary to his Majesty . . . and I: Hare, &c.

Nov. 29–Dec. 1, 1715, *Post Man.*

> BM. i. 26. (2.)
> The title-page from a plate also used for Opera Terza (No. 556), and probably for an edition of Op. 1 not identified.
> Walsh Cat., *c.* 1721, Ill. 28, as: 'Lullys 2d Solos, for a Flute and a Bass. 6s. od.'
> Included later in Walsh's numerical series with Hare deleted from the imprint and 'No. 117' added to the title-page.
> The advertisement above gives: 'Lulliets 1st and 2d Books of Solos for a Flute and a Bass.'
> *See* Nos. 429 and 556.

477. Arcangelo Corelli Opera Prima (–Quarta) XII Sonatas of three parts, &c.
London Printed for I. Walsh Servt. to his(His) Matie. at the Harp and Hoboy, &c.
[*c.* 1715 or later.]

> BM. g. 45. (3.) Imperfect.
> RCM. LVIII. E. 15. Imperfect.
> Later issues of No. 181, with Hare omitted from the imprints, 'her' (or 'Her') altered to 'his (or 'His') Matie.' and the numbers 2, 3, and 4 added to the bottom of the plates of Opera Secunda–Quarta, respectively.
> The BM. copy consists of Opera Terza only, and the RCM. copy of the Violino Primo part of Opera Prima–Quarta; the other parts of that set belonging to the earlier edition. (No. 181.)
> The four works were subsequently included in Walsh's numerical series as Nos. 364–7.
> *See* Nos. 181, 400, and 596.
> For complete list of Corelli items consult index.

478. For the Further Improvement of Dancing A Treatise of Chorography, or the Art of Dancing Country Dances after a new Character In which The Figures, Steps, and Manner of performing are Describ'd, and the Rules Demonstrated in an Easie Method, adapted to the meanest Capacity, Translated from the French of Monr: Feuillet, and Improv'd with many Additions. All fairly Engrav'd on Copper Plates. with a Collection Of Country Dances, and a New French Dance Call'd the Princess's Passpied Compos'd and Writt in Characters by John Essex.
London Sold by I: Walsh Servt. to his Majesty at the Harp and Hoboy in Catherine Street in the Strand. I: Hare Instrument-maker, at the Viol & Flute in Cornhill near the Royal Exchange. and by the Author at his House in Roode Lane, in Fanchurch Street, where are taught all the Ball Dances of the English and French Court.
[*c.* 1715.]

> BM. 60. h. 28.
> A large folio edition of No. 348 which is octavo. One of the finest Walsh items (*see* Ill. 23), with no evidence as to who was responsible for the engraving. The plates of No. 348 were used for No. 478; but printed off four to the folio page, followed by some additional full-page dances. No. 348 has dedication to the Duchess of Bolton; No. 478 to the Princess of Wales.
> *See* No. 494 for an advertisement of this work.

479. Solos for a Violin With a Thorough Bass for the Harpsicord or Bass Violin Compos'd by Michele Mascitti Opera Sexta [Sexta in MS.] Note there are four excellent pieces Consisting of Solos by the same Author extant which may be had where these are sold.

London Printed for I: Walsh Servt. in Ordinary to his Majesty . . . and I. Hare, &c.

[c. 1715.]

> BM. g. 672.
> The title-page from a plate used for other works by Mascitti, not identified.
> This is a Walsh edition of the work published as Opera Quinta by Roger of Amsterdam: 'XII Sonate a Violino Solo e Basso Continuo . . . da Michele Mascitti, Napolitano' (BM. g. 672. e.), and by Foucault of Paris in 1714: 'Sonate A Violino Solo e Basso . . . da Michele Mascitti Napolitano'. (BM. h. 197. (1.))
> See Nos. 430–4, and 543.

480. Six Sonata's of two Parts for Two Violins Compos'd by M^r. Valentine at Rome Opera Quarta.

London Printed for I: Walsh . . . and I: Hare, &c.

[c. 1715.]

> BM. h. 11. e. Violino Primo part only.
> Walsh Cat., c. 1721, Ill. 27, as: 'Valentines Aires, for two Violins. 3s. od.'
> Included later in Walsh's numerical series with Hare deleted from the imprint and 'N°. 442' added to the title-page.
> The original edition for Two Flutes was advertised Oct. 6–8, 1715, *Post Man*. (No. 468.)
> Daniel Wright published an edition for Two Violins, Hoboys or Flutes and a Bass (BM. h. 11. f.), probably pirated from Walsh and Hare.

481. A Compleat Suite of Lessons for the Harpsicord as Overture, Allemand, Saraband, Corant, Gavott, Chacoon, Jigg & Minuett. Compos'd by Mr Alexander Maas = Mann Prusse.

London Printed for I: Walsh Servant in Ordinary to his Majesty . . . and I: Hare, &c.

[c. 1715 or later.]

Advertised on No. 539.

> BM. g. 16.
> Walsh Cat., c. 1721, Ill. 27, as: 'Maasmans Lessons, for y^e Harpsicord Spinnet or Organ. 2s. od.'

482. Bomporti's Sonata's or Chamber Aires in three Parts for two Violins and a Through Bass Compos'd by Francisco Antonio Bomporti Opera Seconda. [Seconda in MS.]

London Printed for I. Walsh Servt. to His Matie. . . . . I. Hare, &c.

[c. 1715.]

> BM. g. 407. a. Imperfect.

The title-page from the plate probably used for an earlier edition with 'Her Matie'. in the imprint and containing the name of Randall as well as Walsh and Hare.
See No. 266.

483. Tibaldi's Sonatas in Three parts for two Violins and a Through Bass Compos'd by Gio Battista Tibaldi Opera 2^d. [2^d in MS.]
London Printed for I: Walsh Servt. in Ordinary to his Majesty . . . and I: Hare, &c.
[*c.* 1715.]

> BM. i. 85.
> The title-page from a plate probably also used for a contemporary edition of Tibaldi's 'Sonatas . . . Opera Prima', an earlier edition of which (No. 265) has a different title-page.

484. The 3^d Book of the Ladys Entertainment or Banquet of Musick being A Choice Collection of the most Celebrated Aires & Duets In the Opera's of Pyrrhus & Clotilda: Curiously Set and Fitted to the Harpsicord or Spinnet: With their Symphonys introduc'd in a Compleat man^r. by M^r: W^m: Babel.
London, Printed for J. Walsh Servant in Ordinary to his Majesty . . . & J. Hare, &c.
[*c.* 1715.]

> BM. h. 18. (1.)
> The title-page presumably from the plate of the earlier edition (No. 308), with 'In the Opera's . . . Clotilda', from a supplementary plate, and with Randall omitted from the imprint. With an outer illustrated title-page from the plate used for No. 450 and earlier works (*see* Ills. 8 and 20), with the title: 'The 3^d Ladys Entertainment or Banquet of Musick Containing Choice Lessons for the Harpsicord or Spinnet', from a supplementary plate, with '3^d' supplied in MS. and with the imprint: 'London Printed for & Sold by Iohn Walsh Servant to his Majesty . . . & I: Hare,' &c.
> Included later in Walsh's numerical series, with modified title-page, and with 'N°. 169' added.
> See Nos. 275, 282, 308, and 501.

485. The Merry Musician; or, a Cure for the Spleen: Being A Collection of the most diverting Songs and pleasant Ballads, set to Musick; adapted to every Taste and Humour. Together with a curious Compound of State Pills, to allay the Malady of Malecontents.

> Here Mirth and Musick both appear,
> And Songs diverting, new and rare;
> Biting Satyr, smooth, tho' keen,
> The surest Physick for the Spleen,
> By which, both Age and Youth may be
> From Indolence and Vapours free.

Part I.
London, Printed by H. Meere, for J. Walsh (Servant in ordinary to his Majesty)

in Catherine-street in the Strand, J. Hare at the Viol in Cornhill, A Bettesworth in Pater-Noster-Row, and J. Brown without Temple-Bar. 1716. Price bound 2s. 6d.

> BM. B. 353.
>
> Contemporary newspaper advertisement not traced; a later advertisement, Aug. 24–6, 1721, *Post Boy.*
>
> Vol. II was issued in Sept. 1729; Vol. III June, 1731; Vol. IV Aug. 1733. Vol. I was from type, the other volumes from engraved plates.

486. The new Flute Master, the 9th Book, containing the newest Aires and Lessons, with the best Instructions for Learners on the Flute, 1s. 6d.

Printed for John Walsh . . . and J. Hare, &c.

Feb. 2–4, 1716, *Post Man.*

> *See* Nos. 20*b*, 33, 113, 182, 305, 390, 510, 563, and 578 for other books and works with similar titles. No details of the third, sixth, and eighth books of the early series finishing with No. 486 have been traced.

487. Nolens Volens the 8th Book, containing the newest Aires and Lessons, with the best Rules and Instructions for Learners on the Violin, pr. 1s. 6d.

Printed for John Walsh . . . and J. Hare, &c.

Feb. 2–4, 1716, *Post Man.*

> See Nos. 72, 158, 306, 424, 442, and 472 for other books. No details of the first book have been traced.

488. Twenty Four New Country Dances for the Year 1716 With New Tunes and New Figures or Directions to each Dance Humbly dedicated to Walkin Williams Esq[r]. by his most Obediant and most humble Servant Nat[l]. Kynaston. Note the New Country Dancing Master is Publish'd Containing the Country Dances of the last Ten Years.

London Printed for I: Walsh . . . and I: Hare, &c.

Feb. 2–4, 1716, *Post Man.*

> BM. a. 10. (4.)

489. The New Country Dancing Master is Publish'd Containing the Country Dances of the last Ten Years.

London Printed for I: Walsh . . . and I. Hare, &c.

[1716.]

Advertised on No. 488.

> *See* Nos. 193, 260, 333, 371, 394, and 441.

490. All the new Minuets, Rigadoons with the new Morris and Shepherds French Dances for 1716. price 6d.

Printed for John Walsh . . . and J. Hare, &c.

Feb. 2–4, 1716, *Post Man.*

491. Divine Harmony Six Select Anthems For a Voice a lone With a Thorow Bass for the Organ, Harpsicord or Arch-Lute Compos'd on several Occasions by M^r: In^o: Weldon Organist of his Majestys Chappell Royal and there Performed by the late Famous M^r: Richard Elford Very proper not only in private Devotion, but also for Choirs, where they may be Sung either by a Treble or Tenor. [A poem: 'Here Musick shows her Art Divine', &c.]

London Printed for I: Walsh . . . and I: Hare, &c.

Mar. 6–8, 1716, *Post Man.*

> BM. H. 820.
> RCM. XVIII. B. 13; I. A. 16. (2.)
> With an illustrated frontispiece with the heading 'The Sacred Choire' and with the Walsh and Hare imprint at the bottom. (*See* Ill. 24.) This illustration is said, by some writers, to show the interior of the Chapel Royal (Banqueting House), Whitehall, but the Walsh engraving has little in common with the illustration in Walford's *Old and New London*, vol. iii, p. 366, which is much more in agreement with what is known of the appearance of the Chapel at the time.
> Walsh Cat., *c.* 1721, Ill. 27, as: 'Welldons Anthems. 4s. 0d.'
> Included later in Walsh's numerical series with 'No. 206' added to the title-page, and Hare's name deleted from the imprint in some copies. (RCM. I. A. 17. (4.); VI. c. 5. (3.))
> *See* No. 531.

492. The Songs and Symphony's in the Masque of Venus & Adonis [Words by Colley Cibber] as they are Perform'd at the Theatre Royal Compos'd by D^r: Pepusch. Fairly Engraven and Carefully Corected by the Author.

London Printed for J: Walsh Servant in Ordinary to his Britanick Majesty . . . & J: Hare, &c.

May 8–10, 1716, *Post Man.*

> BM. G. 222. (4.)
> RCM. XXXII. B. 20. (3.)
> Title-page from the plate first used for No. 353 (*see* Ill. 22), with the title from a supplementary plate and the imprint as in No. 459.
> The BM. copy has the label of John Young pasted over the Walsh and Hare imprint.
> The work was re-advertised, May 28–31, 1720, *Post Boy.*

493. The Songs and Symphonies made for His Majesty's Birth Day, performed at the Royal Palace of St. James's, composed by Mr. John Eccles, Master of his Majesty's Musick, price 2s.

Printed for J. Walsh . . . and J. Hare, &c.

June 9–12, 1716, *Post Man.*

494. The Princess Anna M^r: L'Abee's New Dance for his Majesty's Birth Day 1716. Engraven in Characters & Figures for the use of Masters Note the Princess Royal M^r. L'Abee's Court Dance for 1715 is likewise Publish'd, as also ye Art of Dancing Demonstrated by Characters and Figures.

London Printed for I: Walsh . . . and I: Hare, &c.

June 9–12, 1716, *Post Man*.

> BM. h. 801. a. (1.)
> The two works advertised on the title-page are Nos. 461 and 478.

495. Six English Cantatas After the Italian Manner Compos'd by M^r: Galliard. [Words by John Hughes, William Congreve and Matthew Prior.]
  London Printed for J: Walsh Servant in Ordinary to his Britanick Majesty . . . & J: Hare, &c.

Nov. 27–9, 1716, *Post Man*.

> BM. H. 117. b.
> RCM. XCV. D. 23; II. F. 27.
> Title-page from the plate first used for No. 353 (*see* Ill. 22), with Galliard's title from a supplementary plate, and with imprint as in No. 492. With dedication to Lady Rich.
> Included later in Walsh's numerical series, with Hare deleted from the imprint and 'No. 291' added to the plate of the title-page at the end of the title.
> The RCM. copy II. F. 27 has the label of Mickepher Rawlins pasted over the imprint.

496. A New Set of Tunes or Aires in 3 Parts for two Violins and a Bass, composed by Mr. Vallentine at Rome. price 1s 6d.
  Printed for J. Walsh . . . and J. Hare, &c.

Nov. 27–9, 1716, *Post Man*.

> This work not identified, presumably by Robert Valentine.

497. Six Sonata's for 2 Flutes by the same Author. [i.e. Robert Valentine.] Price 3s.
  Printed for J. Walsh . . . and J. Hare, &c.

Nov. 27–9, 1716, *Post Man*.

> Probably a re-advertisement of Valentine's Op. 4. (No. 468.)

498. Ld Birons Lessons. 1s. 6d.
  [J. Walsh and J. Hare. *c.* 1716 or earlier.]
  Advertised in No. 501.

> The work was for the Harpsicord, and the composer was William Byron, 4th Baron Byron.
> An earlier notice of the work is listed as No. 183: 'An Overture and Airs for the Harpsicord, Composed by a Person of Quality.'
> See Nos. 80, 171, 183, and 601.

499. Mr Hen^r Purcells Lessons with Instructions for the Harpsicord.
  [J. Walsh and J. Hare. *c.* 1716 or earlier.]
  Advertised in No. 501.

> Presumably a Walsh edition or issue of *A Choice Collection of Lessons for the Harpsichord or Spinnet Composed by ye late Mr. Henry Purcell, &c.*, originally issued in 1696 by Mrs. Frances Purcell, and sold by Henry Playford. (BM. K. 1. c. 5.)
> Walsh apparently took over this work with others in their original editions after the death

of Mrs. Purcell in February 1706, and continued to sell some of them with their original title-pages, issuing Walsh editions of others. No copy of a Walsh edition of the Harpsicord Lessons has been traced. (*See* Nos. 108, 248, and 258.)

The Harpsicord Master issued by Walsh and Hare in 1698, contained 'Instructions for Learners on the Spinnet or Harpsicord; written by the late famous Mr. H. Purcell'. (*See* No. 14.)

John Young advertised Feb. 12–15, 1715, *Post-Boy*: 'Newly Revived. A Choice Collection of Lessons, being excellently Set to the Harpsichord or Spinnet, by the two Great Masters Dr. Blow and Mr. Henry Purcel. Price 2s.' (*See* No. 162.)

500. [Vacant. *See* Introduction p. xii.]

501. The 4th. Book of the Ladys Entertainment or Banquet of Musick Being a Choice Collection of ye most Celebrated Aires & Duets in the Operas of Hydaspes & Almahide Curiously Set and fitted to the Harpsicord or Spinnet With their Symphonys introduc'd in a Compleat manner by Mr: Wm: Babell.
London Printed for I: Walsh Servt. to his Majesty . . . and I: Hare, &c.
[*c.* 1716–17.]

> BM. h. 18. (2.)
> The work advertises (reference numbers to the bibliography added):
> Signr Baptist Lessons. (No. 233.)
> Mr Henr Purcells Lessons with Instructions for the Harpsicord. (No. 499.)
> Dr Blows Psalms. (No. 130)
> Dr Blows Lessons. (No. 162.)
> The Opera of Camilla for the Harpsicord. (No. 211.)
> The 1st Book of the Ladys Banquet. (No. 151.)
> The 2d Book of The Ladys Banquet. (No. 187.)
> Dupars Lessons for the Harpsicord. (No. 179.)
> Ld. Birons Lessons. (Nos. 183 and 498.)
> Aires and Lessons by Severall Masters. (No. 210a.)
> Kellers rules for a Through Bass. (No. 190.)
> The 1st Book of the Ladys Entertainment. (No. 275.)
> The 2d & 3d Books of ye Ladys Entertainment. (Nos. 282 and 308.)
> Included later in Walsh's numerical series with No. 170 added to the title-page, and Hare omitted from the imprint.
> *See* Nos. 275, 282, 308, and 484.

502. Twenty four new Country Dances, with new Tunes and new figures to each Dance, composed by Mr. Nathaniel Kynaston. Price 6d.
Printed for John Walsh . . . and J. Hare, &c.
Jan. 1–3, 1717, *Post Man.*

503. A Collection of the most celebrated Song Tunes, with their Symphonies taken out of the choicest Opera's and fitted to the Violin for the improvement of Practitioners on that Instrument, by Mr. John Banister. price 1s. 6d.
Printed for J. Walsh . . . and J. Hare, &c.
Jan. 29–31, 1717, *Post Man.*

U

Title as given in Peter Murray Hill Cat. No. 14:

A Collection of the most Celebrated Song Tunes, with their Symphonys taken out of the Choicest Operas and Fitted to the Violin for the Improvement of Practitioners on that Instrument.

Printed for I. Walsh and I. Hare.

Presumably the work in Walsh Cat., c. 1721, Ill. 27, as: 'Banisters Choice Opera Aires, for a single Violin. 1s. 6d.'

Re-advertised amongst 'new editions of musick', June 20–2, 1717, *Post Boy*.

See No. 526.

504. **Vollentarys for the Organ by the best M**^{r}**. [i.e. Masters.]**
[**J. Walsh and J. Hare.** *c.* 1717.]
Advertised in No. 505.

Presumably a re-advertisement of No. 360: 'Voluntarys & Fugues . . . by Ziani Pollaroli, Bassani and other Famous Authors.'

See No. 564.

505. **Suits of the most Celebrated Lessons Collected and Fitted to the Harpsicord or Spinnet by M**^{r}**: W**^{m}**: Babell with Variety of Passages by the Author. Note there are two precedent books for y**^{e} **Harpsicord by y**^{e} **same hand.**
London Printed for I: Walsh Servt**. to his Majesty . . . and I: Hare.**
Jan. 29–31, 1717, *Post Man.* **(Next Week will be published.)**

Details as given are from a later Walsh issue with Hare omitted from the imprint and 'N°. 174' of Walsh's numerical series added to the plate. (BM. g. 908. a.) Copies also exist with the 'No. 174' in MS. on the title-page.

The work advertises (reference numbers to the bibliography added):

M^r. Babells 3^d. and 4th. Ladys Entertainment. (Nos. 308 and 501.)

Maasmans Lessons. (No. 481.)

Dupars Lessons. (No. 179.)

L^d. Birons Lessons. (Nos. 183 and 498.)

Kellers rules with the Art of tuning. (No. 190.)

Vollentarys for the Organ by the best M^r. (No. 504.)

Sign^r. Baptist Lessons. (No. 233.)

M^r. Henry Purcells Lessons. (No. 499.)

Aires and Lessons by Severall Masters. (No. 210a.)

D^r. Blows Lessons. (No. 162.)

D^r. Blows Psalms. (No. 130.)

The Opera of Camilla finely Set. (No. 211.)

The 1st. and 2^d. Ladys Banquet. (Nos. 151 and 187.)

The 4th. and 5th. Books of Instructions. (Harpsicord Master. Nos. 403 and 471.)

The two precedent books referred to on the title-page are the third and fourth books of 'The Ladys Entertainment.' (Nos. 308, 484, and 501.)

The earliest issue was by Walsh and Hare and not by Walsh only, the two issues having been hitherto placed in the wrong order. (*See* Quaritch Cat., 355, 447, and W^m. C. Smith, *Rinaldo* article, *Musical Times*, Aug. 1935.)

Richard Meares published an edition (BM. f. 39.) in 1718 in competition with Walsh and Hare's, which produced the following advertisement by Walsh in *The Daily Courant*, Dec. 19 and 22, 1718:

'To all Lovers of Musick. Whereas there has lately been printed (in Prejudice to my

Property) a very Imperfect and Spurious Edition of Mr. Babell's great Book of Harpsicord Lessons, (that the Publick may not be impos'd on) This is to give Notice, the Original one (curiously printed and corrected by the Author) is now sold for 3s. 6d. by me at the Harp in Catherine-street in the Strand, and at the Viol in Cornhill near the Royal Exchange. N.B. In Justice to myself, and for the Advantage of the Publick, the like Fall in Price will be made on all Musick that shall hereafter be printed upon me, John Walsh.'

It must be assumed that the reduction in price of the Walsh and Hare edition was only continued for a time, as the work is listed at 7s. od. (presumably the original price) in the Walsh Cat., *c.* 1721, Ill. 27, as: 'Babells great book of Lessons', and in later Walsh catalogues at 5s. od.

See No. 536.

506. The Royal George, Mr. Labee's new Dance for the Princess's Birthday 1717. The Tune by Mr. Paisible. To which is added, the newest French Dances perform'd at Court and Publick Entertainments, particularly those of the new Masquerade. price 6d.

Printed for J. Walsh . . . and J. Hare, &c.

Mar. 23–6, 1717, *Post Man.*

Another edition, apparently not by Walsh, 'Writ by Mr Pemberton', is at BM. 801. b. (4.)

507. A Set of Tunes in 4 Parts for Violins and Hoboys, in the Comedy [by William Taverner] call'd the Artful Husband, compos'd by Mr. Turner. price 1s 6d.

Printed for J. Walsh . . . and J. Hare, &c.

Mar. 30–Apr. 2, 1717, *Post Man.*

508. Six Sonatas or Solos made on purpose for a Flute and a through Bass by Mr. Dieupar.

Printed for J. Walsh . . . and J. Hare, &c.

Apr. 9–11, 1717, *Post Man.*

Walsh Cat., *c.* 1721, Ill. 28, as: 'Dieuparts Solos', for a Flute & a Bass. 5s. od.'

509. The Second Part of Vivaldi's most Celebrated Concerto's in all their Parts for Violins and other Instruments with a Thorough Bass for the Harpsicord Compos'd by Antonia Vivaldi parti 2d. Note the 1st. part may be had where these are Sold.

London Printed for I: Walsh . . . and I: Hare, &c.

Apr. 9–11, 1717, *Post Man.*

BM. h. 43.
RM. 26. a. 9. Violone e Cembalo part only.
Containing Concertos. Nos. VIII–XII of 'L'Estro Armonico'. The first part was advertised Oct. 6–8, 1715, *Post Man.*
See Nos. 469 and 522.

510. The new Flute Master, containing the most compleat Rules and Directions for Learners on the Flute. Together with a curious Collection of the newest and most celebrated Song Tunes, Airs, Marches and Minuets with Scotch and Highland

Tunes, and the newest French Dances, as Minuets and Rigadoons, perform'd at Court on the Princess's Birthday and at the Masquerade at the Kings Theatre, also Prelude to introduce the following Aires in their several Keys. The whole done by the best Masters. All fairly engraven and carefully corrected. price 1s. 6d.

Printed for J. Walsh . . . and J. Hare, &c.

Apr. 23–5, 1717, *Post Man.*

> Daniel Wright advertised Mar. 23–6, 1717, *Post Man*: 'A New Flute Book, composed by the best of Masters, price 1s. 6d.'
>
> *See* Nos. 20*b*, 33, 113, 182, 305, 390, and 486 for other books and works with similar titles of an earlier series. *See* Nos. 563 and 578 for the later series.

511. Rules Or a Compleat Method for Attaining to Play a Thorough Bass upon the Harpsicord Organ or Arch Lute by the late M^r: Godfry Keller together with Variety of proper Lessons & Fuges and the most Ienuin Examples & Explinations of ye several Rules Throughout the whole Work to which is added an exact Scale for Tuneing the Harpsicord or Spinnet by the same Author.

London Printed for I: Walsh Servt. in Ordinary to His Brittanick Majesty at ye Harp & Hoboy in Catherine street in ye Strand. and I: Hare at ye Viol and Flute in Cornhill nere the Royal Exchange.

June 20–2, 1717, *Post Boy.* (New Editions of Musick.)

> The title-page as given above is from a later issue (BM. K. 2. i. 23.) with 'N° 185' added to the plate, thus including it in Walsh's numerical series. The plate had been used earlier than 1717, as there are signs that 'Her' had been altered to 'His' Brittanick Majesty, suggesting an edition 1714 or earlier, but after No. 235; probably that listed as No. 277*c*.
>
> Richard Meares advertised June 13–15, 1717, *Post Boy*: 'Mr Godfrey Keller's Rules to play a thorow Bass, upon either Organ, Harpsicord, or Spinet', &c.
>
> *See* Nos. 190, 230, 235, and 277*c*.

512. All Corelli's Works, consisting of six Operas, with his great Concertos for Viols and other Instruments, sold at reasonable Rates.

Printed for J. Walsh . . . and J. Hare, &c.

June 20–2, 1717, *Post Boy.* (New Editions of Musick.)

> Similar notices appeared June 25–7, 1717, *Post Man*; Aug. 7–9, 1718, *Post Boy.*
> These various editions not identified.
> For complete list of Corelli items consult index.

513. The Bird Fancier's Delight, with Rules for playing the Flagelet gamut way, and a curious Collection of Tunes for Song-Birds. Price 6d.

Printed for J. Walsh, Servant in Ordinary to his Majesty, at the Harp and Hautboy in Katharine street in the Strand, and J. Hare at the Viol and Flute, &c.

June 20–2, 1717, *Post Boy.* (New Editions of Musick.)

> The copy in the BM. (K. 4. a. 1.) may be of this issue or later like the copies in the Rowe collection, King's College, Cambridge and the Cardiff Public Library. The BM. copy is imperfect, but presumably the title was as follows:
> The Bird Fancyer's Delight Or Choice Observations, And Directions Concerning the

Teaching of all sorts of Singing-Birds, after the Flagelet and Flute when rightly made as to Size and tone, with Lessons properly Compos'd within the Compass and faculty of each Bird, viz for the Canary-Bird, Linnet, Bull-Finch, Wood-Lark, Black-Bird, Throustill, Nightingale and Starling, The whole fairly Engraven and Carefully Corrected. price 1ˢ.

London. Printed for I: Walsh Servᵗ. in Ordinary to his Majesty at the Harp and Hoboy in Catherine street in the Strand, and I: Hare at the Viol and Flute in Cornhill near the Royal Exchange.

The title-page has an illustration of a bird in each top corner, and above the imprint a flagelet.

The Rowe copy has the price altered in pencil to 4ˢ., but the advertisement of June 1717 gives 6ᵈ.

The details of the title-page have been taken from the BM. copy supplemented from the Rowe and Cardiff copies. Owing to the imperfection of the BM. copy it is impossible to say whether it had 'Nᵒ 4' on the title-page, which occurs on the other copies, thus including the work in Walsh's numerical series of a later date.

Walsh, Randall, and Hare published in 1708 an earlier work: 'The Flagelet Reviv'd; or, The Bird Fancyer's Delight . . . Pr. 1ˢ' (*see* No. 286), which may or may not have been an earlier edition of No. 513, of which no earlier advertisement has been traced giving the title exactly as transcribed above.

Richard Meares advertised on May 7–9, June 1–4, 1717, *Post Boy*, a similar work to that of Walsh with the title: 'The Bird Fancyer's Delight or Choice Observations, And Directions Concerning yᵉ Teaching of all Sorts of Singing-birds, after yᵉ Flagelet & Flute, if rightly made as to Size & tone, with a Method of fixing yᵉ wett Air, in a Spung or Cotton, with Lessons properly Composed, within yᵉ Compass & faculty of each Bird, Vizᵗ. for yᵉ Wood-lark, Black-bird, Throustill, House-sparrow, Canary-bird, Black-thorn-Linnet, Garden-Bull-finch, and Starling.

London Printed & Sold by Richard Meares . . . Price 1ˢ. 1717.'

A copy of this work is in the Dayton C. Miller collection (Library of Congress), from which the particulars given here have been taken.

It is impossible to be certain whether Walsh pirated Meares's work or vice versa. In the same advertisements of May 7–9, June 1–4, 1717, *Post Boy*, Meares also announced as being printed at his address, 'the Opera's of Thomyris, Camilla, Pyrrhus and Demetrius, in English, all very correct, and curiously engraved on copper-Plate'. These were all issued earlier by Walsh. It is clear from the advertisements of the various publishers in 1717 that there was competition among them to bring out editions of the same works, and it is not safe to assume that the earliest advertisement traced is definite evidence as to which edition appeared first.

See No. 286.

514. A Collection of the choicest French Dances, consisting of Minuets, Rigadoons, Sarabands, Jiggs, Entries, Paspies, Chacoons, Gavots and Brawls, in all 250: Together with the Birth Day Figure Dances perform'd at Court; as also several of the late Masquerade Dances. Note, The Tunes are proper for the Violin or Hoboy, and most of them in the Compass of the Flute, Second Book, price bound 2s 6d.

Printed for J. Walsh . . . and J. Hare, &c.

June 25–7, 1717, *Post Man*. (New Editions of Musick.)

No details of the first book have been traced. The two books in Walsh Cat., *c.* 1721, Ill. 27, as: 'French dances & Minuets 1ˢᵗ Bk, for a single Violin. 2s. 6d; French dances, &c. 2ᵈ Book.'

515. The Compleat Tutor to the Violin, or the Practical Musician, containing the whole Art of playing on the Violin, improv'd by short and easy Rules for Learners, together with a Collection of the choicest Trumpet Tunes, Aires, Marches and Minuets; as also Jigs, Hornpipes and Things of Humour, with Preludes or Flourishes in all the Keys. The whole composed by the best Masters. To which is added a Scale or Sounding of the Hunting Horn curiously done in Characters, price 1s.

Printed for J. Walsh . . . and J. Hare, &c.

July 4–6, 1717, *Post Man.*

Richard Meares advertised, June 13–15, 1717, *Post Boy*: 'The Practical Musick-Master; or the whole Art of Playing on the Violin unfolded, and practically improved, by short and plain Rules', &c.

See No. 562, third book. No details of the second book have been traced.

516. A Set of Airs or Tunes; in four Parts, for Violins and Hautboys, with a Trumpet-Part; perform'd in the reviv'd Comedy [by William Wycherley], call'd The Plain Dealer: Compos'd by Mr. Turner. Price 1s. 6d.

Printed for J. Walsh . . . and J. Hare . . . and J. Young at the Dolphin and Crown in S. Paul's Church-yard.

July 18–20, 1717, *Post Boy.*

517. The Monthly Mask of Vocal Musick, or the Newest Songs made for the Theatres and other occasions for Iuly, to be Continued Monthly. price 6ᵈ. [Price in MS.]

London Printed for I. Walsh Servᵗ. to His Maᵗⁱᵉ. at the Harp and Hoboy . . . and I: Hare at the Viol and Flute, &c.

July 18–20, 1717, *Post Boy.* (Next week will be publish'd.)

BM. H. 313. g. July–October.

The first of a new series of this periodical which continued until July 1724; the earlier series finishing in 1711.

The title-page from the plate by Van der Gucht used for *The Temple of Love* by Saggione (No. 222, *see* Ills. 10 and 17), with the title of that work retained at the top of the title-page, with 'The Monthly Mask . . . Monthly' supplied from a supplementary plate, and 'Her' altered to 'His' Maᵗⁱᵉ and 'I: Hare at the Viol and Flute in Cornhill, near the Royal Exchange' added below the original Walsh imprint.

Daniel Wright advertised in the *Post Man* July 18–20, 1717, and the *Post Boy*, July 30–Aug. 1, 1717, &c.: 'The Monthly Mask of new Songs, &c. price 6d.'

See Nos. 103, 109, 140, 160, 188, 223, 258, 282a, 331, and 370.

518. Three Cantatas Compos'd by Mᵣ. G: Hayden.

London Printed for & Sold by Iohn Walsh Servant to his Majesty . .   & I: Hare, &c.

Sept. 19–21, 1717, *Post Man.*

Title from a later edition (*c.* 1731. BM. G. 116; G. 116. a.) which has the Hare part of the imprint omitted. The title-page from the plate used for the outer title-page of No. 484 and earlier works (*see* Ills. 8 and 20), with the title from a supplementary plate.

Daniel Wright also advertised July 18–20, 1717, *Post Man*: 'Three Choice Cantatas, composed by Mr. G. Hayden,' presumably with a crude copy of the Walsh title-page which he also used for other works. *See 'Three Songs compos'd by Mr. Marshall, &c.'* (BM. H. 1602.)

519. Corellis 12 Solos with their Graces from the Original, curiously printed on a large thick and white Paper, are now sold only at 2s 6d occasioned by a spurious Edition of Corelli's Solos lately published.

Printed for John Walsh . . . and J. Hare, &c.

Sept. 19–21, 1717, *Post Man*.

This was an issue of Op. V (No. 400) at the very much reduced price of 2s. 6d. (or 2s.) in competition with that of Daniel Wright, advertised at 6s. Sept. 17–19, 1717, *Post Man*, and at 5s. Sept. 28, 1717, *Weekly Journal*.

See Nos. 31, 41, 85, 112, 135, 205, and 400.

520. The Instrumental Musick, in the Opera of Hydaspes [Music by Francesco Mancini], for two Violins, with a thorow Base; the Song Part fitted to a Hautboy, German Flute or Violin; the Hautboy performing the Song-Part, forms a complete Consort, as if a Voice accompany'd.

Printed for J. Walsh . . . and J. Hare, &c.

Sept. 26–8, 1717, *Post Boy*.

Advertised Oct. 3–5, 1717, *Post Boy*, as: 'Concertos; or The Instrumental Musick, in the opera of Hydaspes for two Violins, a Tenor, and thorough Base. The Song-Part fitted to a Hautboy', &c.

Walsh Cat., *c.* 1721, Ill. 27, as: 'Hydaspes Concertos, for 2 Violins & a Bass. 6s. od.'

See Nos. 355 and 530.

521. Camilla Concertos, for 2 Violins and a Bass. 6s. od.

[J. Walsh and J. Hare, *c.* 1717.]

Walsh Cat., *c.* 1721, Ill. 27.

Presumably an arrangement of M. A. Bononcini's opera *Camilla* for instrumental parts, similar to No. 520: 'The Instrumental Musick, in the Opera of Hydaspes', &c.

522. A new Edition of Vivaldis 12 Concerto's . . . neatly printed upon a large thick and white Paper.

Printed for J. Walsh . . . and J. Hare, &c.

Sept. 26–8, 1717, *Post Boy*.

A re-advertisement or new edition of Nos. 469 and 509 together, with both title-pages. Included later in Walsh's numerical series with 'No. 451' added to the title-page. (RCM. LX. C. 17. (26.))

Daniel Wright advertised, Dec. 19–21, 1717, *Post Man*: 'The favourite Concerto, printed single for the violin, composed by Sig. Vivaldi, it being the choicest of all his Works, pr. 1s. which are all engraved.'

523. A new Edition of . . . Corellis 12 Concerto's being his last Work . . . neatly printed upon a large thick and white Paper.

Printed for J. Walsh . . . and J. Hare, &c.

Sept. 26–8, 1717, *Post Boy*.

A re-advertisement or new edition of No. 466.

524. A new Edition of . . . Albinonis Concerto's . . . neatly printed upon a large thick and white Paper.
     Printed for J. Walsh . . . and J. Hare, &c.
     Sept. 26–8, 1717, *Post Boy*.
        A re-advertisement or new edition of No. 328. *See* also No. 548.

525. A Collection of Trumpet Airs; containing six Setts in five Parts, for two Violins, and a Base, a Tenour, and a Trumpet, composed by Mr. Paisible, Mr. Barrett, Mr. Corbet, and Mr. Turner. Price 6s.
     Printed for J. Walsh . . . and J. Hare, &c.
     Oct. 3–5, 1717, *Post Boy*.
        Advertised Oct. 24–6, 1717, *Post Boy*, as: 'Six Setts of Aires for Violins, Hautboys and a Trumpet', &c. Walsh Cat., *c.* 1721, Ill. 27, as: '6 Sets of Trumpet Tunes, for 2 Violins & a Bass. 6s. od.'

526. A Second Collection of the most celebrated Song Tunes, with their Symphonies, taken out of the choicest Opera's, and fitted to the Violin, for the Improvement of Practitioners on that Instrument by Mr. J. Banister, price 1s. 6d.
     Printed for J. Walsh . . . J. Hare . . . and J. Young at the Dolphin and Crown in St Paul's Churchyard.
     Oct. 15–17, 1717, *Post Man*.
        Walsh Cat., *c.* 1721, Ill. 27, as: 'Banisters 2ᵈ Collection, for a single Violin. 1s. 6d.'
        See No. 503.

527. A Collection of choice Airs and Symphonys for two Violins, out of the most celebrated Operas, and fitted to the Instruments, for the Improvement of Practitioners in concert by the best Masters; Price 2s.
     Printed for J. Walsh . . . and J. Hare, &c.
     Oct. 24–6, 1717, *Post Boy*.
        Walsh Cat., *c.* 1721, Ill. 27, as: 'Opera Aires, for two Violins. 2s. od.'

528. A Collection of Songs set to Musick by Mr. James Graves, price 2s.
     Printed for J. Walsh . . . and J. Hare, &c.
     Oct. 24–6, 1717, *Post Boy*.
        Walsh Cat., *c.* 1721, Ill. 27, as: 'Graves Songs. 2s. od.'
        Daniel Wright advertised, Sept. 17–19, 1717, *Post Man*: 'A Book of twenty new Songs composed by Mr. James Graves, pr. 3s, which has all the Flute Part at the bottom of each Song.'

529. Twelve Setts of Airs by Thomaso Albinoni, price 6s.
     Printed for J. Walsh . . . and J. Hare, &c.
     Oct. 24–6, 1717, *Post Boy*.
        Presumably the same work as No. 540, which appears in Walsh Cat., 'Apollo's Feast', third book, *c.* 1729 (Wᵐ. C. Smith copy), as 'Aires or Ballettis in 3 Parts for two Violins & a Bass, Opera Terza.'

530. A new Edition of the Symphony's or Instrumental Musick in the Opera of Hydaspes [Music by Francesco Mancini], for two Violins, a Tenor and a Bass, with the Song part fitted to the Hautboy, &c.

Printed for J. Walsh . . . and J. Hare, &c.

Oct. 24–6, 1717, *Post Boy.*

> A re-advertisement of No. 520.
> *See* No. 355.

531. Divine Harmony The 2ᵈ Collection being Select Anthems for a Voice a lone as also some for 3 and 4 Voices with a Thorough Bass for yᵉ Organ, Harpsicord, or Arch Lute. Compos'd by Several Eminent Authors and perform'd at yᵉ Chappel Royal being very proper not only in private Devotion but also for Choir's. The whole fairly Engraven. Note Mʳ. Weldons Anthems for yᵉ Chappel Royal may be had where these are sold.

London Printed for I: Walsh . . . and I: Hare, &c.

Nov. 5–7, 1717, *Post Boy.*

> RCM. XVIII. B. 13.
> With illustrated frontispiece as No. 491. (*See* Ill. 24.)
> A later edition with Hare omitted from the imprint and 'No. 207' of Walsh's serial numbers added is at BM. H. 820.
> The advertisement also states: 'There is lately publish'd, A New Edition of Mr. Welldons Anthems'. This refers to a reissue of No. 491.
> Re-advertised Nov. 12–14, 1717, *Post Man,* as: 'Printed for J. Walsh . . . J. Hare . . . J. Young at the Dolphin and Crown in St Paul's Church Yard.'
> Walsh Cat., *c.* 1721, Ill. 27, as: 'Anthems by several Authors. 4s. od.'
> *See* No. 587.

532. Solos for a Violin with a Thorough Bass for the Harpsicord or Bass Violin Compos'd by the late Mʳ. Viner of Dublin. Note there is lately Printed for Violins Schickhardts Solos, Dʳ. Pe=/pusch Solos, Mascitti's Solos, Corellis Solos, Albinonis Solos, Martinis Solos, Bomportis Solos, Gasperinis Solos Finger & Purcells Solos.

Printed for I: Walsh . . . & I: Hare, &c.

Dec. 10–12, 1717, *Post Man.*

> BM. g. 1084.
> All of the works advertised on the title-page are included earlier in the bibliography as Solos or Sonatas. For Martini's Solos *see* No. 396: 'Martino Bittis Solos.'
> *See* No. 544.

533. The Compleat Country Dancing-Master: containing Great Variety of Dances, both Old and New; particularly Those perform'd at the several Masquerades: Together with All the Choicest and most Noted Country-Dances, Perform'd at Court, the Theatres, and Publick Balls; With their Proper Tunes, and Figures (or Directions) to each Dance: The Tunes fitted to the Violin, or Haut-boy, and most of 'em within the Compass of the Flute. Note, There is contain'd in this Volume, all the Dances generally us'd, and more correct than the former Editions;

printed in the London Capital Character, far exceeding any other of the Common Press.

London, Printed by H. Meere, for J. Walsh, Servant in Ordinary to his Majesty, at the Harp and Hautboy . . . and J. Hare . . . 1718. Price bound 3s. 6d.

> BM. a. 4. (1.)
> Advertised on No. 534 as: 'A new Edition of the Great Dance Book containing 364 Country Dances,' &c.
> Walsh Cat., *c.* 1721, Ill. 27, as: '1st Great book of Country dances, for a single Violin. 3s. 6d.'
> Printed from type. Earlier edition not identified.
> Haas, Cat. 23, 1946, lists an earlier edition dated 1718, with a similar title-page to the above, but the differences between the two editions are not recorded.
> *See* No. 558.

534. Twenty Four New Country Dances for the Year 1718 With New Tunes and Figures to each Dance Humbly dedicated to Richard Waringe Esqr. at ye Keyes in ye County of Salop, by his Most Obedient humble Servt. Nat^l. Kynaston Note there is lately Publish'd a new Edition of the Great Dance book Containing 364 Country Dances in a New Character and more Correct then the former Editions——

London Printed for I: Walsh . . . & I: Hare, &c.

[*c.* 1718.]

> BM. a. 10. (1.)

535. A Collection of the newest Minuets, Rigadoons, and French Dances, perform'd at Balls, Masquerades, and publick Entertainments; the Tunes proper for the Violin, Hautboy, or Flute. Price 6d.

Printed for, and sold by J. Walsh . . . and J. Hare, &c.

Feb. 20–2, 1718, *Post Boy.*

536. Several Suits of the most celebrated Lessons collected and fitted to the Harpsichord or Spinnet, with Variety of curious Passages. By Mr. William Babell, being his 3d Vol.

Engraven and Printed for John Walsh . . . and J. Hare, &c.

May 1–3, 1718, *Post Man.*

> Presumably a re-advertisement of No. 505. Babell's first two volumes were the third and fourth books of 'The Lady's Entertainment'. (Nos. 308, 484, and 501.)
> Daniel Wright advertised April 26–9, 1718, *Post Man:* 'A choice Collection of new Tunes for the Harpsicord. By Mr. Babel, and other Masters. To which is added, all the Psalm Tunes given out, and with their Interludes. By the late Mr Purcel, late Organist at St. Andrew Holborn . . . Price 2s. 6d.' This advertisement probably referred to 'The Harpsicord Master Improved, containing the most perfect Rules', &c. (BM. b. 26.) The work appears to have been issued in competition with the Walsh items Nos. 536, 537, and 539.

537. A Book containing the Psalm Tunes for the Organ or Harpsichord. By Dr. Blow, Mr. Purcel, &c. proper for Organists to perform in Churches or Chappels. Price 1s. 6d.

Engraven and Printed for John Walsh . . . and J. Hare, &c.
May 1–3, 1718, *Post Man.*

The notice may cover Blow's Psalms (Nos. 130 and 176) and D. Purcell's Psalms. (No. 539.)
See No. 536 for work issued by Daniel Wright.

538. The Princess Amelia, Mr. L'Abees new Dance made for his Majesty's Birth Day 1718. The Tune by Mr. Paisible. To which is added the newest Minuets, Rigadoons, and French Dances perform'd at Court, the Masquerades, and Publick Entertainments. The Tunes proper for the Violin, Flute or Hoboy, Price 6d.

Printed for and Sold by J. Walsh . . . and J. Hare, &c.
May 27–9, 1718, *Post Man.*

539. The Psalms Set full for the Organ or Harpsicord as they are Plaid in Churches and Chappels in the mãner given out; as also with their Interludes of great Variety by Mr: Danl: Purcell. late Organist of St: Andrew's Holbourn. 1s. 6d. Note there are New Editions of severall Curious Pieces for the Organ, Harpsicord and Spinnet which may be had where these are Sold.

London Printed for I: Walsh, Servt. in Ordinary to his Majesty . . . and I: Hare, &c.
July 8–10, 1718, *Post Boy.*

The BM. (c. 20.) and RCM. (XCV. B. 21.) are of a later issue with Hare deleted from the imprint and with 'No. 178' added to the title-page, thus incorporating the work in Walsh's numerical series. The works advertised on p. 15 are as follows: 'Note the following Pieces for the Harpsicord and Organ may be had where these are Sold Mr Babels 3 Books of Lessons The 1st and 2d Lady's Entertainment The Opera of Camilla Maasmanns Lessons Dieupart's Lessons Ld Birons Lessons Kellers rules for a through Bass Voluntarys for the Organ by Several Masters Signr Baptist's Lessons Mr Henry Purcell's Lessons Aires and Lessons by Several Masters Dr Blows Psalms Dr Blows Lessons The 1st and 2d Ladys Banquet and Books of Instructions.' These works all appear earlier in the bibliography.

The work has a frontispiece of a figure playing the Organ, with an imprint: Musick for the Organ and Harpsicord, Printed for I: Walsh and I: Hare. (See Ill. 25.) This illustrated frontispiece was adapted from the upper half of the plate engraved by T. Cross for the title-page of Daniel Purcell's *Six Cantatas For a Voice, with a Through Bass,* &c., printed for J. Cullen. (BM. H. 94.)

See No. 536 for work issued by Daniel Wright; and No. 537.

540. Albinoni's Ballettis in 3 Parts for two Violins and a Thorow Bass Consisting of Preludes, Alemands, Sarabands, Corants, Gavots and Jiggs. Compos'd by Thomaso Albinoni Opera Terza.

London Printed for I: Walsh Servt. in Ordinary to his Majesty . . . and I: Hare, &c.
[c. 1718 or earlier.]

Advertised on No. 541 as lately printed.

> The title transcribed above is from a later edition (BM. h. 24. (1.), *c.* 1732) which has Hare's name deleted from the imprint.
>> See No. 529.

541. Trattenimenti Armonici Per Camera Divisi in Dodici Sonata [altered in MS. to Sonatæ] A Violino Violine E Cembalo Da Thomaso Albinoni Opera Sexto [altered in MS. to Sexta]. An Entertainment of Harmony Containing Twelve Solos or Sonatas for a Violin with a Through Bass for the Harpsicord or Bass Violin Compos'd by Thomaso Albinoni Opera Sexta Note. there are of this Authors Several Curious Pieces lately Printed as Concertos, Ballettis and Solos, which may be had where these are Sold.

> London: Printed for I: Walsh . . . and I: Hare, &c.

> July 8–10, 1718, *Post Boy.* (An Entertainment of Harmony; containing 12 Sonatas or Solos, &c.)

>> BM. h. 24. (2.)
>> Re-advertised Aug. 7–9, 1718, *Post Boy,* as: 'Twelve Solos for a Violin and a thorough Base; by Thomas Albinoni; being his sixth and last great Work.'
>> Walsh Cat., *c.* 1721, Ill. 27, as: 'Albinonis 12 Grand Solos, for a Violin & a Bass. 6s. od.'

542. Solos for a German Flute a Hoboy or Violin with a Thorough Bass for the Harpsicord or Bass Violin Compos'd by M^r. Christian Schick^{h}ardt 20 Overage Note there is lately Printed for Violins M^r. Viners Solos, D^r. Pepusch Solos, Mascittis Solos, Albinonis Solos, Corellis Solos, Gasperinis Solos, Martinis Solos, Bomportis Solos, Finger & Purcells Solos.

> London Printed for I: Walsh . . . & I: Hare, &c.

> Aug. 7–9, 1718, *Post Boy.* (New Editions of Musick just publish'd . . . Six Solos for a German Flute, a Hautboy, or Violin; by Christian Schickart; price 4s.)

>> BM. h. 3055. (2.); g. 1090. (3.)
>> Walsh Cat., *c.* 1721, Ill. 27, as: 'Schickhards 20th Opera, for a Violin & a Bass. 4s. od.'
>> The works advertised on the title-page all appear earlier in the bibliography.

543. Twelve Solos for a Violin and a through Base; by Michele Mascith; being his sixth Opera. price 6s.

> Printed for and sold by J. Walsh . . . and J. Hare, &c.

> Aug. 7–9, 1718, *Post Boy.* (New Editions of Musick just publish'd.)

>> See No. 479.

544. Six Solos for a Violin and a through Base; by Mr. Viner. price 4s.

> Printed for and sold by J. Walsh . . . and J. Hare, &c.

> Aug. 7–9, 1718, *Post Boy.* (New Editions of Musick just publish'd.)

>> See No. 532.

545. Six Setts of Choice Opera Songs or Arietts With their Symphonys fitted for 2 Flutes The Second parts, being Compleat and Airy as the First, not thin and

heavy as second Trebles us^ually are, in both parts there are proper Variations for the Humour of the Flute price 2^s. Note there are lately Publish'd several curious pieces, as Solos for a Flute and a Bass, Sona=/tas & Aires for 2 Flutes, as also for 2 Flutes & a Bass, and all the newest Aires, Song Tunes and Symphonys for a single Flute may be had where these are sold——

London Printed for I: Walsh . . . and I: Hare, &c.

Oct. 30–Nov. 1, 1718, *Post Man.*

> BM. a. 209. Flauto Secondo part only.
> RCM. I. F. 15.
> Walsh Cat., *c.* 1721, Ill. 28, as: 'Opera Aires with Symph:, for two Flutes. 2s. 0d.'

546. Alberti's Concerto's for three Violins an Alto Viola and a Through Bass for the Harpsicord or Bass Violin Compos'd by Giuseppe Matteo Alberti Opera Prima.

London Printed for I: Walsh . . . & I. Hare, &c.

Nov. 6–8, 1718, *Post Man.* (A New Edition.)

> BM. g. 900.
> RCM. II. B. 10.
> No earlier edition by Walsh and Hare has been traced.
> The new edition was presumably in competition with that of Roger of Amsterdam. (BM. g. 900. b.)
> Walsh Cat., *c.* 1721, Ill. 27, as: 'Albertis Concertos, for 2 Violins and a Bass. 9s. 0d.'

547. Venturini's New Concertos for all Instruments.

Sold by John Walsh . . . and J. Hare, &c.

Nov. 6–8, 1718, *Post Man.*

> No Walsh edition has been traced. May refer to Roger's Amsterdam edition of Francesco Venturini's 'Concerti di Camera a 4. 5. 6. 7. 8. & 9 Instromenti . . . Opera Prima' (BM. g. 1082.); Walsh and Hare acting as Roger's selling agents.

548. Albinonis Concertos.

Sold by John Walsh . . . and J. Hare, &c.

Nov. 6–8, 1718. *Post Man.*

> *See* Nos. 328 and 524.

549. Valentini's Concertos.

Sold by John Walsh . . . and J. Hare, &c.

Nov. 6–8, 1718. *Post Man.*

> No Walsh edition has been traced. May refer to Giuseppe Valentini's 'Concerti Grossi', Op. 6 or Op. 7, published by Roger and Le Cene at Amsterdam; Walsh and Hare acting as their selling agents.

550. Vivaldi, Bitti & Torelli's Concertos.

Sold by John Walsh . . . and J. Hare &c.

Nov. 6–8, 1718, *Post Man.*

> No Walsh edition has been traced. Probably refers to Roger's Amsterdam edition of 'Concerts à, 5, 6 & 7 Instrumens . . . Composez par Messieurs Bitti, Vivaldi & Torelli' &c. (BM. h. 917.); Walsh and Hare acting as Roger's selling agents.

551. Corellis Posthumous Works.
   Sold by John Walsh . . . and J. Hare, &c.
   Nov. 6–8, 1718, *Post Man.*

> Not definitely identified. May refer to:
> (*a*) Roger's Amsterdam edition of 'Sonate a Tre, Due Violini col Basso par l'organo di Arcangelo Corelli . . . Ouvrage Posthume' (BM. g. 420. (2.)); Walsh and Hare acting as Roger's selling agents.
> (*b*) 'Sonatos for two Violins; a Violoncello and thro' Bass . . . 7th Opera.' (No. 561.)

552. Six Setts of Aires and a Chacoon for two Flutes & a Bass Compos'd by M^r: Valentine at Rome Note there are several Curious Pieces as Solos and Sonatas for Flutes Com=/pos'd by this Author, which may be had where these are Sold.
   London Printed for I: Walsh . . . and I: Hare, &c.
   Nov. 18–20, 1718, *Post Boy.*

> BM. h. 250. c. (6.)
> Presumably Op. 8.
> Walsh Cat., *c.* 1721, Ill. 28, as: 'Valentines Aires, for 2 Flutes & a Bass. 3s. 0d.'
> Included later in Walsh's numerical series, with 'No. 90' added in MS. to the title-page.

553. Six Solos for a Flute With a Thorough Bass for the Harpsicord or Violoncello Humbly Dedicated to the Right Honble: the Earle of Carnarvan By his most Obediant and Devoted Humble Servant Luis Mercy.
   London Printed for I: Walsh . . . and I: Hare, &c.
   Nov. 29–Dec. 2, 1718, *Post Man.*

> BM. g. 524.
> The BM. copy has 'N^o: 112' added in MS. to the title-page, thus incorporating the work at a later date in Walsh's numerical series.
> The advertisement adds: 'in which are Variety of double Stops, with examples and Directions how to perform the same upon the Flute. Never before made publick'.
> Walsh Cat., *c.* 1721, Ill. 28, as: 'Mercys 1st Solos, for a Flute & a Bass. 4s. 0d.'
> *See* No. 613.

554. XII Sonatas or Solos for a Flute with a Through Bass for the Harpsicord or Bass Violin Compos'd by M^r: Valentine at Rome Opera Quinta.
   London Printed for I: Walsh . . . & I: Hare, &c.
   Dec. 6–9, 1718, *Post Boy.*

> BM. h. 11. a. (3.)
> Walsh Cat., *c.* 1721, Ill. 28, as: 'Valentines 5th (Solos), for a Flute & a Bass. 6s. 0d.'

555. Six new Sonatas for two Flutes and a Bass, by the same Author. [i.e. Mr. Valentine at Rome.]
   Printed for J. Walsh . . . and J. Hare, &c.
   Dec. 6–9, 1718, *Post Boy.*

> May refer to No. 468 or No. 572, Wright editions of which have a Bass part.

556. XII Sonatas or Solos for a Flute with a Thorough Bass for the Harpsicord or Bass Violin Compos'd by Iean Baptiste Loeillet de Gant Opera Terza. [Terza in MS.]

London Printed for I: Walsh . . . and I: Hare, &c.

Dec. 20–3, 1718, *Post Man.*

> BM. i. 26. (3.)
> The title-page from a plate also used for Opera 2da. (No. 476.)
> The advertisement above gives: 'All Mr. Lully's Solos for a Flute and a Bass', presumably Op. 1, Op. 2, and Op. 3.
> Walsh Cat., c. 1721, Ill. 28, as: 'Lullys 3d Solos, for a Flute & a Bass. 6s. od.'
> Included later in Walsh's numerical series, with Hare deleted from the imprint, and 'No. 118' added to the title-page.
> *See* Nos. 429 and 476.

557. Twenty Four New Country Dances for the Year 1719, with New Tunes and New Figures or Directions to each Dance. The Dances perform'd at the most Publick Places, as Epsom, Richmond, Tunbridge and Bath, at the Balls and Masquerades. Engraven and carefully corrected. Price 6d.

London Printed for and sold by J. Walsh . . . and J. Hare, &c.

Jan. 13–15, 1719, *Post Man.*

558. The Second Book of the Compleat Country Dancing-Master: containing Great Variety of Dances, both Old and New; particularly Those perform'd at the several Masquerades: Together with All the Choicest and most Noted Country-Dances, Perform'd at Court, the Theatres, and publick Balls; With their proper Tunes, and Figures (or Directions) to each Dance: The Tunes fitted to the Violin, or Hautboy, and most of 'em within the Compass of the Flute. Note, In this, and the first Book, are contain'd all the Dances generally used and more correct than the former Editions; printed in the London Capital Character, far exceeding any other of the Common Press.

London, Printed by H. Meere, for J. Walsh . . . and J. Hare . . . 1719. Price bound 3s. 6d.

Jan. 13–15, 1719, *Post Man.* (A new Edition of the 2d great Book of Country Dances.)

> BM. a. 4. (2.); a. 4. b.
> Walsh Cat., c. 1721, Ill. 27, as: '2d Great book of Country dances, for a single Violin. 3s. 6d.'
> Printed from type. Earlier edition not identified.
> *See* No. 533.

559. A Collection of the newest Minuets, Rigadoons and French Dances perform'd at Balls, Masquerades and Publick Entertainments, never before published. The Tunes proper for the Violin, Flute or Hoboy. Price 6d.

Printed and sold by J. Walsh . . . and J. Hare at the Viol, &c.

Jan. 27–9, 1719, *Post Man.*

Some advertisements about this time give Hare's address as 'at the Viol in Cornhill', &c.

---

560. The Opera of Camilla [Music by Marco Antonio Bononcini], and the Opera of Thomyris [Music by Alessandro Scarlatti, Giovanni Battista Bononcini, &c.] with all their Songs, Symphonys, and Instrumental Musick, as they are perform'd at the Theatre.

Printed for and sold by John Walsh, Servant in Ordinary to His Majesty, at the Harp in Catherine street in the Strand, and J. Hare at the Viol in Cornhill near the Royal Exchange.

Feb. 26–8, 1719, *Post Man.*

> Re-advertisements, or unidentified editions.
> See Nos. 209 and 254.

561. Sonatos for two Violins; a Violoncello and thro' Bass; by Arcangelo Corelli; being his Posthumous Work, or 7th Opera; price 6s.

Printed for, and sold by J. Walsh . . . at the Harp . . . and J. Hare at the Viol, &c.

Feb. 26–8, 1719, *Post Boy.* (New Musick lately publish'd . . . Likewise new Editions of all the Works of that Author. [i.e. Arcangelo Corelli.])

> Walsh Cat., c. 1721, Ill. 27, as: 'Corellis Posthumous Works, for 2 Violins & a Bass. 6s. od.'
> See No. 551.

562. The Compleat Tutor to the Violin, 3d Book, or the Practical Musician, containing the most Compleat Rules and Directions for learning on the Violin, together with great Variety of the newest and choicest Tunes and Airs. Price 1s 6d.

London Printed for and sold by J. Walsh . . . at the Harp and Hoboy . . . and J. Hare at the Viol and Flute, &c.

Mar. 24–6, 1719, *Post Man.*

> See 515, first book; no details of the second book have been traced.

563. The New Flute Master, 3d Book, containing the best Instructions for learning on the Flute; also a Collection of the newest Songs, Tunes, Aires, Jiggs and Minuets, with great Variety of things of Humour. price 1s 6d.

London Printed for and sold by J. Walsh . . . and J. Hare, &c.

Mar. 24–6, 1719, *Post Man.*

> See Nos. 510 and 578.
> No details of the second book have been traced.

564. A Second Collection of Toccates Vollentarys and Fugues made on Purpose for the Organ & Harpsicord Compos'd by Pasquini, Polietti and others The most Eminent Foreign Authors Engraven & Carefully Corrected. N.B. there are lately Published several excellent Pieces as Psalms Interludes & Lessons for yᵉ Organ Harpsicord or Spinnet wich may be had where these are sold.

London Printed for and Sold by I: Walsh . . . and I: Hare, &c.
April 14–16, 1719, *Post Man.*

> BM. g. 56.
> The BM. copy has 'No. 181' added in MS. to the title-page, thus incorporating the work
> at a later date in Walsh's numerical series.
> Walsh Cat., *c.* 1721, Ill. 27, as: 'Pasquinis (Volentarys) for yᵉ Organ. 2ᵈ book. 5s. od.'
> The Psalms, &c. mentioned on the title-page refer to editions of Blow and D. Purcell.
> (Nos. 537 and 539.)
> 'A Third Collection of Toccates, Vollentarys and Fugues', &c., by D. Zipoli, was issued
> by Walsh and Hare, *c.* 1722, or later, of which the BM. has an issue, *c.* 1731. (BM. h. 21.)
> *See* Nos. 360 and 504; and Ill. 37.

565. The Additional Songs in the Opera's of Thomyris & Camilla as they are
Perform'd at the New Theatre Compos'd by Dʳ. Pepusch Note. the Following
Operas from the Original may be had where these are Sold English Operas
Thomyris Camilla Arsinoe Calypso Rosamond Loves Triumph Dioclesian The
Temple of Love Italian Operas Hydaspes Rinaldo Antiochus Almahide Etearco
Pyrrhus Clotilda Hamlet Crœsus Arminius.
London Printed & Sold by I: Walsh . . . and I: Hare, &c.
May 12–14, 1719, *Post Man.* (Price 2s. 6d.)

> BM. H. 2815. j. (1.)
> One number at least: 'How blest is the soldier', from 'Thomyris', was published separately.
> (BM. H. 1601. (200.) &c.)
> *See* Nos. 209 and 254.

566. The 6th Book of the Harpsicord Master: Containing, the best Instructions for
Learners on the Harpsicord or Spinnet with great Variety of the newest Aires and
Lessons by the best Masters, price 2ˢ.
Printed for and sold by J. Walsh . . . and John Hare, &c.
May 23–6, 1719, *Post Man.*

> *See* Nos. 14, 27, 59, 403, and 471.

567. Six Concertos for 4 Flutes, with a thorough Bass for the Harpsichord or Bass
Violin, compos'd by Mr. Christian Schickhard. Price 6d. [i.e. 6s.]
Printed for John Walsh . . . and J. Hare, &c.
May 28–30, 1719, *Post Man.*

> Advertised in 'Apollo's Feast', third book, *c.* 1729 (Wᵐ. C. Smith copy), as: '19th Opera.'
> Walsh Cat., *c.* 1721, Ill. 28, as: 'Schickhards Concertos, for 2 Flutes & a Bass. 6s. od.'

568. The Princess Anne's Chacoone, Mr L'Abee's new Dance for his Majesty's
Birth-Day, 1719. The Tune by Mr. Galliard, to which is added the newest Minuets,
Riggadoons, and French Dances, perform'd at Court and Publick Entertainments.
price 6d.
Printed for John Walsh . . . and J. Hare, &c.
May 28–30, 1719, *Post Man.*

569. Suits of Lessons for the Harpsicord or Spinnet in most of the Keyes with Variety of Passages and Variations Throughout the Work Compos'd by M^r: Anthony Young Organist of S^t: Clements Danes.

London Printed for and Sold by I: Walsh . . . and I: Hare, &c.

June 11–13, 1719, *Post Man.*

> BM. g. 443. b. (31.)
> Walsh Cat., *c.* 1721, Ill. 27, as: 'Mr Youngs Lessons, for ye Harpsicord, Spinnet or Organ. 5s. od.'

570. XII Solo's for a Violin With a Thorough Bass for the Harpsicord or Bass Violin Compos'd by Francesco Geminiani. [Op. 1.]

London Printed for and Sold by I: Walsh . . . & I: Hare, &c.

Sept. 5–8, 1719, *Post Man.* (A new Edition of Mr. Geminianis Solos in a large and fair Character. price 6s.)

> BM. h. 48. b.
> RCM. LXII. B. 14. (4.) Wanting title-page.
> This Walsh and Hare edition was in competition with Richard Meares's edition advertised Aug. 7, 1718, *Daily Courant*, of which there are two issues in the BM. (d. 74.; d. 74. a.), the first without imprint but with dedication dated 28 November 1716, the second from the same plates, with Richard Meare's imprint, and no dedication. Both issues were engraved by Tho: Cross.

571. Six Sonatas for two Hoboys, two Violins or German Flutes; with a Thorough Bass for the Harpsicord, or Bass Violin. Composed by Mr. Christian Schickard. Pr. 2s.

Printed for and sold by John Walsh . . . and J. Hare, &c.

Nov. 3–5, 1719, *Post Boy.*

> Presumably Op. 10.
> Walsh Cat., *c.* 1721, Ill. 27, as: 'Schickhards 10th Opera, for 2 Violins & a Bass. 2s. 6d.'

572. Six Sonatas of two Parts for two Flutes Compos'd by M^r: Valentine at Rome Opera 6ta. [6$^{ta.}$ in MS. on blocked out portion of plate.]

London Printed for I: Walsh . . . & I: Hare, &c.

[*c.* 1720.]

> Title from later edition (BM. g. 71. f. (7.)) with Hare deleted from the imprint and 'No. 61' of Walsh's numerical series added; the plate having been used earlier for No. 575. Daniel Wright and J. Young issued an edition for Two Violins and a Bass. (BM. h. 11. g.(1.))
> Walsh Cat., *c.* 1721, Ill. 28, as: 'Valentines 2^d Sonatas, for two Flutes. 3s. od.'
> *See* No. 555.

573. Twenty four new Country Dances for the Year 1720. With new Tunes and new Figures or Directions to each Dance. The Dances perform'd at the most Publick Places, as Epsom, Richmond, Tunbridge, and Bath, at the Balls and Masquerades. Engraven, price 6d.

Printed for and sold by J. Walsh . . . and J. Hare, &c.

Jan. 23–6, 1720, *Post Boy*.

> Daniel Wright advertised, Mar. 15–17, 1720, *Post Man*: '24 New Country Dances for the Year 1720. Price 6d.'

574. A new Sett of Tunes, in three Parts, for Violins and Hoboys; perform'd in the Comedy [by John Leigh] call'd the Pretenders [i.e. Kensington Gardens, or The Pretenders]; price 1s 6d.
   Printed for and sold by J. Walsh . . . and J. Hare, &c.
   Jan. 28–30, 1720, *Post Boy*.

575. Six Sonatas of two Parts for two Flutes Compos'd by M^r: Valentine at Rome Opera 7ma.
   London Printed for I: Walsh . . . and I: Hare, &c.
   Jan. 28–30, 1720, *Post Boy*.

> BM. h. 11. j.
> Title-page from the same plate as that afterwards used for an edition of Op. 6. (No. 572.)
> Walsh Cat., *c.* 1721, Ill. 28, as: 'Valentines 7th. Opera, for two Flutes.' 3s. od.'
> Walsh and Hare also issued the work for Two Violins, July 1721.
> Daniel Wright put out an edition for Two Flutes (BM. g. 297. (1.)), and for Two Violins, (BM. h. 11. g. (2.)), both presumably in competition with those of Walsh and Hare.

576. A Collection of Minuets, Rigadoons, or French Dances for the Year 1720. Perform'd at the Balls at Court, the Masquerades, and Publick Entertainments. Together with several favourite Minuets and Rigadoons, by Mr. Hendell, Mr. Lature and Mr. Hill. The tunes proper for the Violin or Hautboy, and many of them within the compass of the Flute. price 6d.
   Printed for and sold by J. Walsh . . . and J. Hare, &c.
   Feb. 5, 1720, *Daily Post*.
   Feb. 9–11, *Post Boy*. (A new Book of Minuets, Rigadoons or French Dances.)

> Daniel Wright advertised Mar. 15–17, 1720, *Post Man*: 'Bulkley's 2d Collection of Minuets and Rigadoons, for the Year 1720, being Twenty by Mr. Latoure, and Twenty more by Mr. Fairbank, Mr. Hills, and other Masters for the Balls at the Courts and the Masquerades,' &c.
> *See* No. 579 for reference to a similar work advertised by John Jones.

577. XII Solos for the Violin or Violoncello With a Thorough Bass for the Harpsicord Compos'd by Giuseppe Valentini Opera Octava.
   London Printed for I: Walsh . . . & I: Hare, &c.
   Feb. 9–11, 1720, *Post Boy*. (A new Edition of 12 Solo's for a Violin and Bass by Joseppi Vallentini, Opera Octava. Price 6s.)

> BM. g. 392. a.
> This work was published by Roger of Amsterdam as: 'Allettamenti Per Camera a Violino, e Violoncello, e Cembalo Opera Ottava di Giuseppe Valentini,' &c. (BM. g. 392.)

578. The New Flute-Master for the Year 1720. Containing All the Rules and Directions for Learners on that Instrument; with a fine Collection of the best Minuets and Rigadoons, made for the Balls at Court. Intermix'd with all those fashionable Airs and Songs which are most suitable for the Flute. The whole dispos'd into regular Setts, by proper Keys, and free from that Confusion which is met with in former Books: The Method here being like that of a Sonata, where the Airs succeed each other in a handsome manner, and in different moods. Note, this is the 2d Yearly Book of this sort. Price 1s 6d.

Printed for and sold by J. Walsh . . . and J. Hare, &c.

Mar. 24–6, 1720, *Post Boy.*

> No details of the first yearly book have been traced.
> *See* Nos. 510 and 563.

579. Two Celebrated Concertos the one Commonly call'd the Cuckow and the other Extravaganza Compos'd by Sigʳ: Antonia Vivaldi Note, the rest of this Authors Works may be had where these are sold.

London, Printed for and Sold by I: Walsh . . . and I: Hare, &c.

Apr. 21–3, 1720, *Post Boy.* (Perform'd by Monsieur Duburge at his late Consort. pr. 3s.)

> BM. h. 43. a.
> The work is for 2 Violins, Viola and Violoncello (Organo e Violoncello), but in Walsh Cat., *c.* 1721, Ill. 27, as: 'Vivaldis Cuckoo Concertos, for 2 Violins & a Bass. 3s. od.'
> John Jones advertised, Mar. 15, 21, 1720, *Daily Post*: 'Two celebrated Concerto's, compos'd by Signior Antonio Vivaldi, being his own Favourites; one commonly call'd the Cuckow; and the other, out of his Extravaganza's.
> Printed for and sold by John Jones, Musical Instrument Maker, and Musick Printer, at the Golden Harp in New Street, Covent Garden, near St. Martins-Lane. As also at the same place, a Book of the Masquerades Minuets and Rigadoons, for the Violin.'
> These works, by a hitherto unknown publisher, were clearly issued in competition with Walsh items Nos. 579 and 576. Jones also advertised some other publications Dec. 5, 1719, *Weekly Journal*, and Dec. 8, 1719, *Daily Post.*

580. Six Concertos for two Flutes and a Bass with a Through Bass for the Harpsicord Neatly Transpos'd from yᵉ great Concertos of Arcangelo Corelli Note all the Works of this Author may be had where this is sold.

London Printed for and sold by I: Walsh . . . and I: Hare, &c.

May 10–12, 1720, *Post Boy.* (By an eminent Master.)

> BM. i. 2. a.
> An arrangement of various movements of the Concerti Grossi. Op. 6. (No. 466.)

581. Six English Cantatas for one Voice Four for a Flute and two with a Trumpet and other Instruments Compos'd by I: C: Pepusch Book yᵉ Second. [Words by John Hughes and others.]

London Printed for J: Walsh Servant in Ordinary to his Britanick Majesty . . . & J: Hare, &c.

May 28–31, 1720, *Post Boy.*

RCM. II. A. 17. With dedication to James, Duke of Chandos.
Title-page from the plate first used for the earlier book of Cantatas (No. 353, *see* Ill. 22), with modified imprint, as No. 495, and with title from a supplementary plate.

582. Six English Cantatas Humbly Inscrib'd To the most Noble the Marchioness of Kent Compos'd by Mr I: C Pepusch. [Introduction and words by John Hughes.]
London Printed for J: Walsh Servant in Ordinary to his Britanick Majesty . . . & J: Hare, &c.
May 28–31, 1720, *Post Boy.*

RCM. II. A. 17.
Title-page from the same plate as the earlier edition, No. 353 (*see* Ill. 22), with modified imprint as No. 581.

583. Modern Harmony or a desire to Please Consisting of Vocal and Instrumental Musick as Songs and Arietts for one and two Voices and a Cantata together with a Solo for a Flute & a Bass and a Solo for a Violin & a Bass as also a Set of Lessons for the Harpsicord The whole Compos'd by Mr: Vanbrughe.
London Printed for J: Walsh . . . & J: Hare, &c.
[*c.* 1720.]

BM. H. 1605. (1.)
Title-page from the plate first used for No. 353 (*see* Ill. 22), with imprint as No. 582, and with the title from a supplementary plate.
Assumed to be the work advertised in No. 588 and Walsh Cat., *c.* 1721, Ill. 27, as: 'Vanbrughes Songs. 5s. od.'

584. Cantatas by several Authors.
[J. Walsh and J. Hare. *c.* 1720 or earlier.]
Advertised in No. 588.

Further details and actual date of publication not available. Probably the work advertised in 'Apollo's Feast', third book., *c.* 1729 (Wm. C. Smith copy), as: 'Twelve Cantatas by Several Eminent Authors.'

585. Ramondon's Songs.
[J. Walsh and J. Hare. *c.* 1720 or earlier.]
Advertised in No. 588.

Further details and actual date of publication not available. The composer was Lewis Ramondon.

586. Carey's Songs.
[J. Walsh and J. Hare. *c.* 1720 or earlier.]
Advertised in No. 588.

Further details and actual date of publication not available.

587. Anthems by several Authors.
[J. Walsh and J. Hare. *c.* 1720 or earlier.]
Advertised in No. 588.

Presumably a re-advertisement of: 'Divine Harmony The 2d Collection.' (No. 531.)

588. Songs in the New Opera call'd Numitor [Words by Paolo Antonio Rolli] as they are Perform'd at the Kings Theatre For the Royal Accademy Compos'd by Sig^r: Porta.

   London: Printed for & sold by I: Walsh . . . & I: Hare, &c.

June 16–18, 1720, *Post Boy.*

> BM. H. 297.
> RCM. XXXII. B. 11. (1.)
> With an outer title-page from the Collins plate (No. 15, *see* Ill. 3), with the title from a supplementary plate: 'Songs in the Opera Call'd Numitor', and imprint, 'London Printed for & Sould by I: Walsh . . . and I: Hare,' &c. as in No. 425, but with the word 'His' newly engraved in place of 'her' Majesty.
> The work contains after the table: 'A Catalogue of Vocal Musick of the best Editions which may be had where these are Sold.'
> Particulars of all the works in this catalogue, except four, are duly recorded in the bibliography in their appropriate order, and it is unnecessary to list them here. The four works otherwise unrecorded are entered as Nos. 584, 585, 586, and 587.
>> *See* Ill. 38.

589. The new Minuets and Rigadoons, and French Dances, perform'd at the Ball at Court on his Majesty's Birthday, 1720. Together with the new Dances, and the Minuets and Rigadoons at the late Masquerades.

   Printed for and sold by J. Walsh . . . and J. Hare, &c.

June 16–18, 1720, *Post Boy.*

590. Songs in the New Opera call'd Narcissus [Words by Apostolo Zeno, altered by Paolo Antonio Rolli] as they are perform'd at the Kings Theatre For the Royal Academy Compos'd by Sig^r: Dom^co : Scarlatti With the Additional Songs Compos'd by M^r: Roseingrave.

   London, Printed for & sold by I: Walsh . . . & I: Hare, &c.

Oct. 4–6, 1720, *Post Boy.*

> BM. H. 315.
> With a catalogue similar to that in No. 588.
> *See* Ill. 26.

591. The Aires and Song Tunes With their Symphonys in the Opera of Numitor [Music by Giovanni Porta] for a single Flute. Price 1^s. 6^d. Note: Several of ye other Operas are done in this manner and may be had where these are sold.

   London: Printed for & sold by I: Walsh . . . & I: Hare, &c.

Oct. 13–15, 1720, *Post Boy.*

> BM. a. 209. a. (5.)
> Walsh Cat., *c.* 1721, Ill. 28, as: 'Opera Numitor, for a single Flute. 1s. 6d.'

592. Twenty four New Country Dances for the Year 1721. With new tunes and new Figures to each Dance. Compos'd by Mr. Birkhead of the Theatre Royal. Note, There are lately publish'd great Variety of curious Pieces for the Harpsicord or Spinnet, by the best Masters, &c.

Printed for and sold by J. Walsh . . . and J. Hare, &c.

Nov. 7, 1720, *Daily Courant*; Nov. 8–10, 1720, *Post Boy*.

> The notice is transcribed from the *Post Boy*. The Harpsicord pieces advertised may be an advance notice of No. 593.
>
> *See* No. 599.

593. The 3d Book of the Lady's Banquet, containing great Variety of the most pleasant and airy Lessons for the Harpsichord or Spinnet now in use. Compos'd by several Authors. Price 3s.

Printed for and sold by J. Walsh . . . and J. Hare, &c.

Nov. 29–Dec. 1, 1720, *Post Boy*. (*See* No. 592.)

> This work may have had an almost similar title-page to that of a later edition (*c.* 1733, RM. 7. e. 17. (3.)):
> 'The Ladys Banquet 3^d. Book Being a Choice Collection of the Newest & most Airy Lessons for the Harpsichord or Spinnet Together with the most noted Minuets, Jiggs, and French Dances, Perform'd at Court the Theatre and Publick Entertainments, all Set by the best Masters Price 3^s Note, there is several Curious Pieces for the Harpsicord Spinnet & Organ which may be had where these are sold.
> London. Printed for I: Walsh . . . & I: Hare,' &c.
> The Hare portion of the imprint is omitted from the later edition, and 'N°. 172' added, thus incorporating the work in Walsh's numerical series.
> The volume is of particular interest as it contains Handel items from *Rinaldo, The Water Music, Radamisto,* &c.
> A new series of six books, issued 1730–5, included the third book listed here, but had two entirely new collections as books one and two in place of the works Nos. 151 and 187 in this bibliography.

594. A Collection of Sea Songs on Several Occasions – – Price 1^s: 6^d– –.

London Printed for & Sould by I: Walsh . . . and I: Hare, &c.

Nov. 29–Dec. 1, 1720, *Post Boy*.

> BM. H. 35.
> Title-page from the Collins plate (No. 15, *see* Ill. 3), with the title from a supplementary plate, and the imprint as in No. 588.
> Walsh Cat., *c.* 1721, Ill. 27, as: 'A book of Sea Songs. 1s. 6d.'

595. Te Deum et Jubilate, for Voices and Instruments Perform'd before the Sons of the Clergy at the Cathedral-Church of St. Paul. Compos'd By the late Mr. Henry Purcel Note. Where these are Sold may be had great variety of Church-Musick.

London. Printed for and Sold by Iohn Walsh, &c.

Dec. 3–6, 1720, *Post Boy*. (Sold by . . . J. Walsh . . . and J. Hare . . . Price 3s.)

> RCM. I. A. 17. (1.) Assumed to be the edition advertised in 1720, but it may have been issued earlier.
> The work was printed from plates, not type as was used in the original Heptinstall edition taken over by Walsh probably in 1702.
> *See* Nos. 108, 248, and 276.

596. New Editions of Corelli's Works now publish'd. His 1st, 2d, 3d and 4th Opera's, containing 48 Sonata's, in four Parts for Violins. Engraven from the Originals, and carefully corrected by our most eminent Masters: Twelve Solo's by Arcangelo Correlli, being his 5th Opera, with their Graces or curious manner: Corelli's twelve great Concerto's, in seven Parts, most celebrated for their Harmony, being his 6th Opera: His Posthumous Work, or 7th Opera, in four Parts, for Violins, being all the Works extant of that great Author, whom the Musical World so much esteem'd: The whole Engraven from the Original, and carefully corrected, now sold at very easy Rates.

    Printed for and sold by J. Walsh . . . and J. Hare, &c.

    Dec. 6–8, 1720, *Post Boy.*

    Dec. 29–31, 1720, *Post Boy.* (The 1st, 2d, 3d and 4th Opera's by Arcangelo Corelli . . . now sold at 13s the Sett in Quires.)

> These editions not identified. The notice may be simply a re-advertisement of earlier issues.
> *See* Nos. 31, 181, 400, 466, 477, 561, and index.

597. Six Setts of Aires for two Flutes & a Bass Consisting of Preludes Allmands Corants Sarabands Marches Minuets Gavotts and Jiggs Compos'd by Mr: Paisible Never before Publish'd.

    London: Printed for & sold by I: Walsh . . . & I: Hare, &c.

    Dec. 13–15, 1720, *Post Boy.*

> BM. h. 23.
> Walsh Cat., *c.* 1721, Ill. 28, as: 'Paisibles Aires, for 2 Flutes & a Bass. 4s. 0d.'; 'Apollo's Feast', third book, *c.* 1729 (Wm. C. Smith copy), as: 'Paisibles Sonatas for two Flutes and a Bass, Opera Seconda.'
> Included later in Walsh's numerical series, with 'No. 101' added in MS. to the title-page.

598. The Primrose, a new Dance in Characters, for the Year 1721. Composed by Monsieur Marcelle of Paris. Price 2s 6d.

    Printed for and sold by J. Walsh . . . and J. Hare, &c.

    Dec. 17–20, 1720, *Post Boy.*

599. 24 New Country Dances for the Year 1721. Price 6d.

    Printed for and sold by J. Walsh . . . and J. Hare, &c.

    Dec. 24–7, 1720, *Post Boy.*

> *See* No. 592, which may or may not refer to the same work.

600. Songs in the Opera Call'd Arsinoe Queen of Cyprus. [Words from the Italian of Tomaso Stanzani. Music by Thomas Clayton.]

    London Printed for & Sould by I: Walsh Musicall Instrument maker in Ordinary to His Majesty . . . and I: Hare at the Viol and Flute in Cornhill nere the Royall Exchange.

    [*c.* 1720 or earlier.]

RCM. XXXII. A. 1. (2.)

Title-page from the Collins plate (No. 15, *see* Ill. 3), with the title from a supplementary plate and the Hare imprint engraved on the plate below the Walsh imprint and inside the original border as in No. 588. The date given is speculative and the work may have been issued with this title-page any time between 1714 and 1720.

See Nos. 202, 203, 219, 220, and 238.

Nos. 601–22 are works not previously listed or identified, but issued c. 1720 or earlier. The details as given are from Walsh Catalogue, c. 1721, Ills. 27 and 28, which includes a few items published in 1721, omitted from the bibliography. References to the Walsh Catalogue have been given in the bibliography whenever it has been necessary to indicate variations in the title or advertisement of a work compared with the title as given in the Catalogue.

---

601. Aires by a Person of Quality, for two Flutes. 2s. od.
[J. Walsh.]
Not identified. Date unknown.

Walsh Cat., *c.* 1721, Ill. 28; presumably published 1720 or earlier.
The composer may have been William Byron, Fourth Baron Byron.
See Nos. 4, 80, 171, 183, and 498.

602. Dr. Blows Songs. 15s. od.
[J. Walsh.]
Not identified. Date unknown.

Walsh Cat., *c.* 1721, Ill. 27; and may refer to stock copies of Blow's 'Amphion Anglicus' (Pearson, 1700, BM.G. 106.) or to some Walsh work, published 1720 or earlier.
Proposals for the publication of 'Dr Blow's Collection of 50 Songs', &c., (H. Playford) were announced May 18–22, 1699, *London Gazette.*

603. Bomportis Solos, for a Violin & a Bass. 4s. od.
[J. Walsh.]

Presumably Op. 7: 'Solos for a Violin with Th. Bass for a harps. or Bass Violin consisting of Preludes, Alemands, Sarabands.' (Eitner. Quellen-Lexikon.) Date unknown; probably the same work as No. 277*d.*
Walsh Cat., *c.* 1721, Ill. 27; presumably published 1720 or earlier.

604. Bononcinis Sonatas, for 2 Violins & a Bass. 3s. od.
[J. Walsh.]
Not identified. Date unknown.

Walsh Cat., *c.* 1721, Ill. 27; presumably published 1720 or earlier.
May refer to an edition of G. M. Bononcini's 'Sonate a due Violini con il BC. Op. 6' (Eitner. Quellen-Lexikon) or to some work by G. B. Bononcini.
Walsh confuses the different members of the Bononcini family in the catalogue in 'Apollo's Feast' third book, *c.* 1729. (Wm. C. Smith copy.)

605. A Book of Instructions for the German Flute. 1s. 6d.
    [J. Walsh.]
    Not identified. Date unknown.

    Walsh Cat., *c.* 1721, Ill. 27; presumably published 1720 or earlier.

606. Country dances for yᵉ Flute. 2s. 0d.
    [J. Walsh.]
    Not identified. Date unknown.

    Walsh Cat., *c.* 1721, Ill. 28; presumably published 1720 or earlier.

607. Mr. Cox's Aires, for a Single Flute. 1s. 0d.
    [J. Walsh.]
    Date unknown. Composer probably Robert Cox.

    Walsh Cat., *c.* 1721, Ill. 28; presumably published 1720 or earlier.
    'Apollo's Feast' third book, *c.* 1729 (Wᵐ. C. Smith copy), lists a similar work for the violin: 'Cox's Aires for a Single Violin.'

608. Familiar Aires for yᵉ Flute. 1s. 0d.
    [J. Walsh.]
    Not identified. Date unknown.

    Walsh Cat., *c.* 1721, Ill. 28; presumably published 1720 or earlier.
    See Nos. 277*g* and 320.

609. Fingers Aires, for two Violins. 3s. 0d.
    [J. Walsh.]
    Date unknown.

    Walsh Cat., *c.* 1721, Ill. 27; presumably published 1720 or much earlier.
    See No. 142*a*.

610. Galliards Solos, for a Flute & a Bass. 5s. 0d.
    [J. Walsh.]
    Date unknown.

    Walsh Cat., *c.* 1721, Ill. 28; probably refers to a work issued anonymously by Walsh a few years earlier with the title: 'Sonata A Flauto Solo e Basso Continuo Composees par Monsieur Galliard Opera prima Sur l'Edition d Amsterdam par Etienne Roger.' (BM. g. 280. b. (3.) RCM. LIX. A. 16. a.)
    This work, which has all the appearance of having been engraved for Walsh, has been wrongly attributed to Roger. It was included by Walsh as Nº. 114 in his numerical series of publications, the RCM. copy having 'Nº. 114' added in MS. to the title-page, and BM. g. 422. (2.) having the number engraved on the plate, both copies being without Walsh's imprint.
    An edition, not by Walsh, was engraved by T. Cross and published 1711. (BM. e. 700.)
    If the editions attributed here to Walsh were issued by him, he must have had permission from Roger to publish them or was so sure of his position that he could definitely state the source from which he had copied them.

611. Geminiani & Castrucci, Solos for a Flute & a Bass. 5s. 0d.
[J. Walsh.]
Date unknown.

> Walsh Cat., *c.* 1721, Ill. 28; presumably published 1720 or earlier.
> Title given in 'Apollo's Feast' third book, *c.* 1729 (W^m. C. Smith copy): 'Geminiani & Castruccis Solos for a Flute and a Bass.'
> May refer to an edition of: 'Geminiani e Castrucci: 12 Sonate a Flauto traversi. o Violino o Hautbois e Basso continuo delle Compositioni. Amsterdam a Spesa di Michele Carlo Cene.' (Eitner. Quellen-Lexikon.)
> H. Reeves Catalogue 118, 1936 gives: 'Geminiani and Castrucci, XII Solos for a German Flute, Violin or Harpsichord.
> London. I. Walsh, *c.* 1715.'
> Included later in Walsh's numerical series with 'No. 428' added to the title-page and probably Hare deleted from the imprint.

612. Lullys Sonatas, for two Flutes. 3s. 0d.
[J. Walsh.]
Date unknown. Not identified.

> Walsh Cat., *c.* 1721, Ill. 28; presumably published 1720 or earlier. May refer to a previous edition of: 'Six Sonata's of two Parts Fitted and Contriv'd for two Flute's Compos'd by M^r: Loeillet of Gant.' (BM. g. 71. e. (9.)) This work was advertised by Walsh and Joseph Hare, Jan. 27, 1728, *Mist's Weekly Journal*, and the BM. copy has 'No. 57' of Walsh's numerical series on the title-page.
> 'Apollo's Feast' third book, *c.* 1729 (W^m. C. Smith copy), advertises 'Loeillets Sonatas for two Flutes' and 'Sonatas for 2 German Flutes', the latter being advertised in the *Daily Post,* Aug. 6, 1730.

613. Mercys 2^d Solos, for a Flute & a Bass. 4s. 0d.
[J. Walsh.]
Date unknown.

> Walsh Cat., *c.* 1721, Ill. 28; presumably published 1720 or earlier.
> 'Apollo's Feast' third book, *c.* 1729 (W^m. C. Smith copy), as: 'Mercys Solos for a Flute and a Bass Opera Seconda.'
> *See* No. 553.

614. Oxon Aires, for 2 Flutes & a Bass. 3s. 0d.
[J. Walsh.]
Not identified.

> Walsh Cat., *c.* 1721, Ill. 28; presumably published 1720 or earlier.

615. Rules for playing a Bass on a Violin. 1s. 6d.
[J. Walsh.]
Date unknown.

> Walsh Cat., *c.* 1721, Ill. 27; presumably published 1720 or earlier.

616. XII Sonatas or Solos for a Flute with a Through Bass for the Harpsicord or Bass Violin Compos'd by M^r: Christian Schikhard Opera 17 Note all ye Choisest Works of this Author may be had where these are sold.

London Printed for I: Walsh . . . and I: Hare, &c.

Date unknown.

> BM. h. 250. c. (5.)
> Walsh Cat., *c.* 1721, Ill. 28, as: 'Schickards 17ᵗʰ Opera, Solos for a Flute & a Bass. 6s. od';
> presumably published 1720 or earlier.

617. Thomyris Concertos, for 2 Violins & a Bass. 6s. od.

[J. Walsh.]

Date unknown.

> Walsh Cat., *c.* 1721, Ill. 27; presumably published 1720 or earlier.
> The work was an arrangement for instrumental parts of the opera *Thomyris*, music by
> A. Scarlatti, G. B. Bononcini, &c. (*see* No. 254), similar to No. 520 (*Hydaspes*) and No. 521.
> (*Camilla.*)

618. Books for Learners on the Flagelet Gamut way. 1s. od.

[J. Walsh.]

> Walsh Cat., *c.* 1721, Ill. 28.
> A general notice covering several works not identified, published 1720 or earlier, some
> of which may have been included previously in the bibliography. *See* No. 140 for a similar
> item in an earlier Walsh catalogue.

619. Books for Learners on yᵉ Flute. 1s. 6d.

[J. Walsh.]

> Walsh Cat., *c.* 1721, Ill. 28.
> A general notice covering several works not identified, published 1720 or earlier, some
> of which may have been included previously in the bibliography. *See* No. 140 for a similar
> item in an earlier Walsh catalogue.

620. Books for Learners on yᵉ Hoboy. 1s. 6d.

[J. Walsh.]

> Walsh Cat., *c.* 1721, Ill. 28.
> A general notice covering several works not identified, published 1720 or earlier, some
> of which may have been included previously in the bibliography. *See* No. 140 for a similar
> item in an earlier Walsh catalogue.

621. Books for Learners on yᵉ Violin. 1s. 6d.

[J. Walsh.]

> Walsh Cat., *c.* 1721, Ill. 27.
> A general notice covering several works not identified, published 1720 or earlier, some of
> which may have been included previously in the bibliography. *See* No. 140 for a similar item
> in an earlier Walsh catalogue.

622. Books of Instructions for Learners on yᵉ Harpsicord or Spinnet. 2s. od.

[J. Walsh.]

> Walsh Cat., *c.* 1721, Ill. 27.
> A general notice covering several works not identified, published 1720 or earlier, some
> of which may have been included previously in the bibliography. *See* No. 140 for a similar
> item in an earlier Walsh catalogue; and No. 505 where 'Books of Instructions' is used for
> the fourth and fifth books of 'The Harpsicord Master.'

ILLUSTRATIONS

SONGS

IN THE NEW

OPERA,

Call'd the

WORLD in the MOON

Sould by I: Walsh Musicall Instrument maker in Or=
=dinary to his Majesty, at the Golden Harpe and Ho=boy.
in Catherine=street near Summersett House in the
Strand, and I: Hare Musicall Instrument Seller at y̆
Golden Violl in St: Paules Church yard, and at his
Shopp in Freemans yard in Cornhill 1697

PLATE I

See Nos. 12, 29, 67, 201, 203, 204, 206, 219, 220, 221, 222, 271, 272, 292, 293, 296, 298, 344, 354, 373, 402, and 450

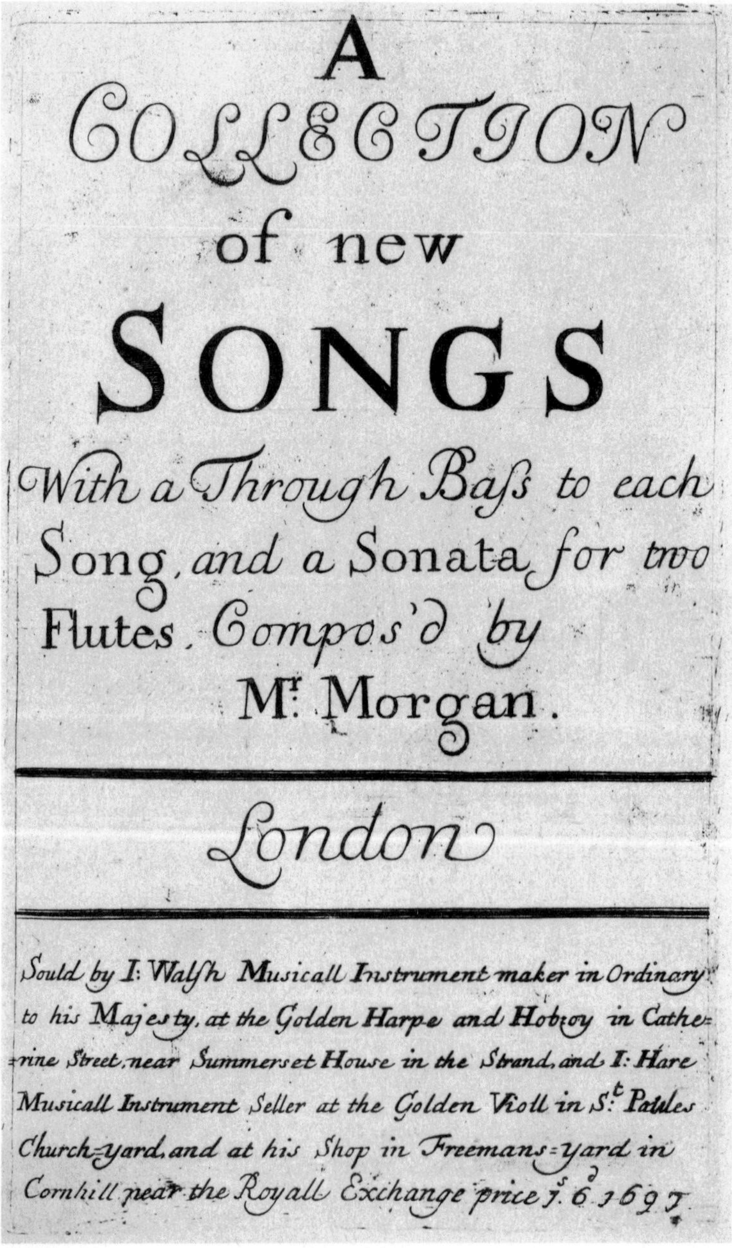

A
COLLECTION
of new
SONGS
With a Through Bass to each
Song, and a Sonata for two
Flutes. Compos'd by
Mr. Morgan.

London

Sould by I. Walsh Musicall Instrument maker in Ordinary
to his Majesty, at the Golden Harpe and Hoboy in Cathe-
rine Street near Summerset House in the Strand, and I. Hare
Musicall Instrument Seller at the Golden Violl in S:t Paules
Church-yard, and at his Shop in Freemans-yard in
Cornhill near the Royall Exchange price 1. 6 1697.

PLATE 2

See Nos. 13, 30, 36, 51, 94, 95, and 464

A

Collection of new Songs,
Set by Mr Nicola, with
A Through Bass to each Song
For the Harpsicord, Theorbo, or
Bass Viol, being all teaching
Songs, made for his Scholars
most of them Transpos'd for the
FLUTE.
The second Book

I: Collins sculp

London Printed for & sould by I: Walsh Musicall Instrument maker in Ordinary to his Majesty at the
Golden Harp & Ho boy in Catherine street near Summerset house in y^e strand

PLATE 3

See Nos. 15, 20, 94, 117, 123, 124, 139, 140, 160, 188, 220, 223, 254, 258, 282a, 331, 370, 425, 463, 588, 594, and 600

SONGS
for
One, Two, and Three
VOICES
Compos'd to a Through
Basse
For ye Organ or Harpsicord
By
R King
Servant to his
Majesty.

T: Collins sculp

PLATE 4

See No. 15

Antonio Meloni Inuent et del.

Girolamo Frezza scul.

PLATE 5

See No. 31

Six SONATA'S or Solos for the FLUTE with a through Bass for the Harpsicord Compos'd by Wm Topham A.M.

Antonio Meloni delt.

P. P. Bouche Sculp.

PLATE 6

See Nos. 31 and 60

The Overtures and Ayrs, in four Parts, made for the OPERA'S, TRAGEDY'S and COMEDY'S of the THEATERS, Printed for I. WALSH.

	s	d
Ayres in the OPERA of the mad Lover, by Mr. I. Eccles --	01	06
Ayres in the OPERA of the fate of Troy, Mr. Finger --	01	06
Ayres in y Tragedy of y Unhapy Penitent, Mr. D. Purcell --	01	06
Ayres in y Tragedy of y Ambitious Stepmother Mr. Lenton	01	06
Ayres in the COMEDY of Loves Stratagem Mr. Peaſable --	01	06
Ayres in the COMEDY of Courtſhip Alamode Mr. Croft --	01	06
Ayres in the COMEDY of Loves at a Loſs Mr. Finger --	01	06
Ayres in the Veſtal Virgin by Mr. O. --	01	06
Ayres in the COMEDY of the Fops Fortune Mr. Finger --	01	06
Ayres in the COMEDY of Sr. Hary Wild Hair, Mr. Finger --	01	06
Ayres in the COMEDY of the Humore of y Age, Mr. Finger --	01	06
Ayres in the OPERA of Alexander the Great, Mr. Finger --	01	06

	s	d
Ayres by Bononcini in three Parts, with a Through Baſs --	03	00
Ayres by Mr. Simons, in three Parts --	01	06
Ayres for two Flutſ and a Baſs by Mr. Simons --	01	06

SONGS made for the Playhouſes and other occaſions, ſold at fourpence the ſheet, and twopence the halfe ſheet.

	s	d
A Collection of Songs by Mr. Leveridge in 2 Books price each --	01	06
A Collection of Songs by Mr. Nicola --	01	06
Songs and Dialogues in the OPERA of the Iſland Princeſs --	03	00
Songs in the OPERA of the Grove, or Loves Pardice --	01	06
A Collection of Songs by Mr John Eccles --	01	06
A Collection of Songs by Mr. Dan. Purcell --	01	06
A Collection of Songs by ſeverall Maſts --	01	06
A Collection of Scotch Songs --	01	06
Songs in the OPERA of Alexander the Great --	01	06
Songs in the Comedy call'd the Pilgrim --	01	06

PLATE 7

See Nos. 60 and 140

VI SONATAS or SOLO'S
Three for a VIOLIN & Three for a FLUTE
wth a Thorough Bass for ye Harpsychord
Most humbly Dedicated
TO THE RIGHT HONOURABLE
CHARLES EARL of MANCHESTER
Vicount Mandevil Baron Kimbolton
and LORD LIEUTENANT of the
county of HUNTINGDON
by ye Author Godfry Finger
London Printed for & Sold by Iohn Walsh Servant to his Majesty at the Harp and Hautboy in Katherine Street
near Somerset House in the Strand

PLATE 8

See Nos. 82*a*, 102, 272, 275, 282, 292, 293, 296, 308, 344, 354, 450, 484, and 518

The Setts of Aires in 4 parts contain'd in ye Several Collections of ye Musick of ye English Stage

The Musick of the TRAGEDYS and COMEDYS contain'd in this First Collection

I   A Set of AIRES made for Mr Banisters Consort by Mr. Orm
II   The COMEDY of Loves Stratagem Mr. Peasable
III   The COMEDY of Courtship Alamode Mr. Croft
IV   The COMEDY of Lover at a Loss Mr. Finger
V   The TRAGEDY of the Ambitious Stepmother Mr. Lenton
VI   The TRAGEDY of the Unhappy Penitent Mr. D: Purcell

The Musick of the OPERA'S TRAGEDYS and COMEDYS contain'd in this 2d. Collection

I   The OPERA of the mad Lover by Mr. John Eccles
II   The OPERA of the Fate of TROY Mr. Finger
III   The COMEDY of the Fops Fortune Mr. Finger
IV   The COMEDY of Sr Harry Wild Aire Mr. Finger
V   The COMEDY of the Humors of the Age Mr. Finger
VI   The OPERA of Alexander ye G. eat Mr. Finger

The Musick of the TRAGEDYS and COMEDYS contain'd in this 3d. Collection

I   The COMEDY call'd the Humors of Sr Ir. Falstaff Mr Peasable
II   The COMEDY call'd the Funeral Mr. Croft
III   The TRAGEDY call'd the Generous Conquerour Mr Barrett
IV   The TRAGEDY call'd Tamerlin Mr Lenton
V   The PLAY call'd the False Friend by Lr. B.
VI   The COMEDY call'd the Inconstant or ye way to win him Mr Purcell

I   The PLAY call'd Edward the Third Mr Peasable
II   The PLAY call'd the Royall Captive Mr Lenton

Note these Aires are Sold att 1-6 the Sett or each Collection at 8 by   J. Walsh.

PLATE 9

See No. 89

PLATE 10

See Nos. 89, 102, 222, *and* 517

THE MONTHLY MASK OF VOCAL MUSIC

or
the New=est
SONGS
Made for the Theatre's & other
Ocations Publish'd
for NOVEMBER
Price 6 pence

Halfbergh Sculp

These Collection's will be Continued Monthly for ye Year 1703.

London Printed for and sold by I. Walsh and I. Hare and may be had at most musick shops in Town.

PLATE II

See Nos. 103 and 109

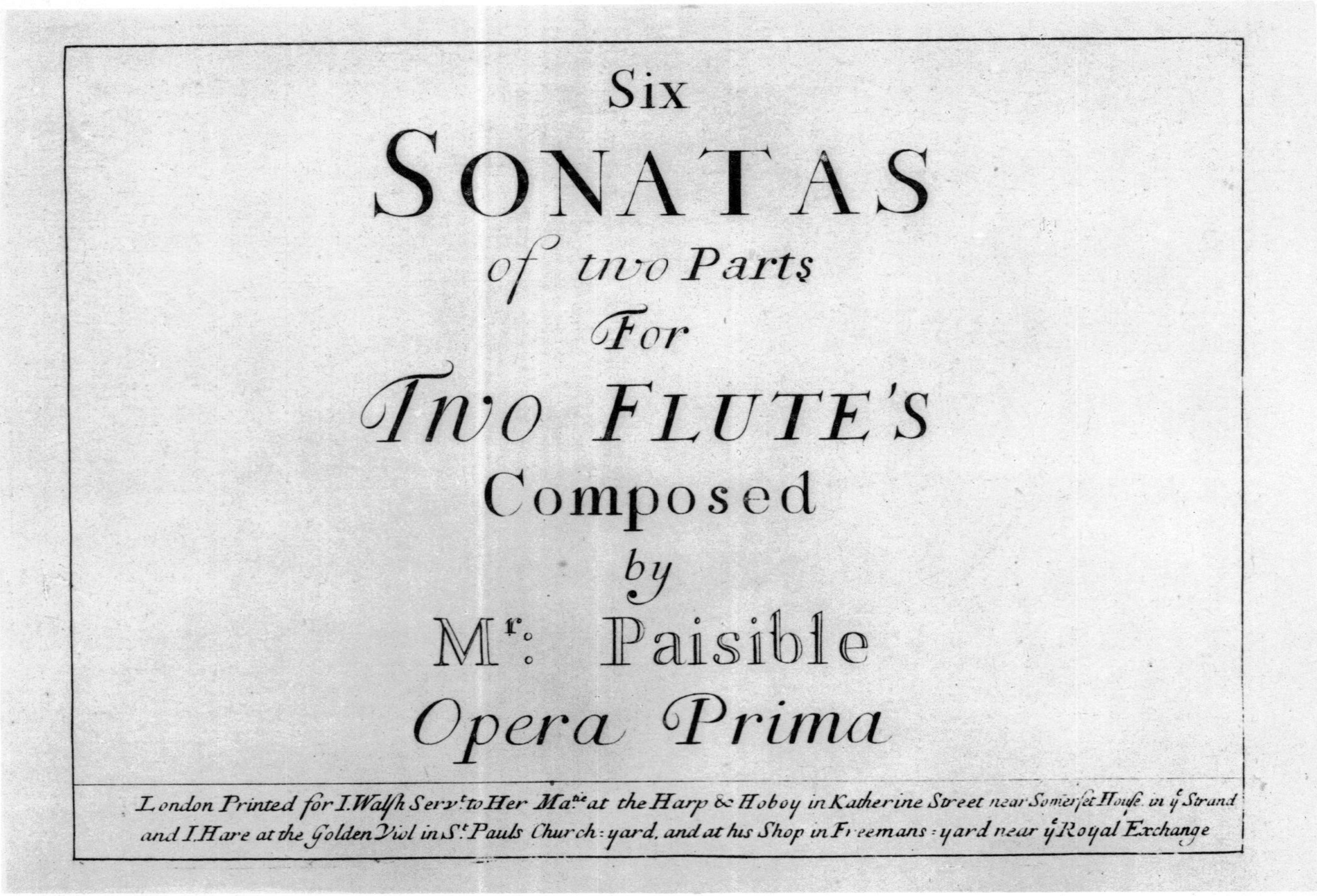

Six

SONATAS

of two Parts

For

Two FLUTE'S

Composed

by

M.r: Paisible

Opera Prima

London Printed for I.Walſh Serv.t to Her Ma.tie at the Harp & Hoboy in Katherine Street near Someſet Houſe in y.e Strand and I.Hare at the Golden Viol in S.t Pauls Church-yard, and at his Shop in Freemans-yard near y.e Royal Exchange

PLATE 12

See No. 142b

Mr.
Inº. Eccles
General Collection
of SONGS

Berchet Inventer.

H. Hulsbergh Sculpsit.

London Printed for I.Walsh Serv: to Her Ma:tie at the Harp and Hoboy in Katherine Street near Somerset House in the Strand.

PLATE 13
See Nos. 156, 221, and 298

Florish in the KEY

Select PRELUDES
or VOLENTARYS for ye VIOLIN
by the most eminent Masters
in Europe
printed for I.Walsh and I.Hare

PLATE 14

See No. 166

ARCANGELUS CORELLIUS de FUSIGNANO dictus BONONIENSIS.

Liquisse Infernas jam Credimus Orphea Sedes | Divinus patet Ipse Orpheus, dum numine digna,
Et terras habitare, hujus sub imagine forma. | Arte modos fingit, vel chordas mulcet utramque
| Agnoscit Laudem, meritosque BRITANNUS honores.

H. Hovard pinx.   W. Sherwin sculp!

PLATE 15

See No. 181

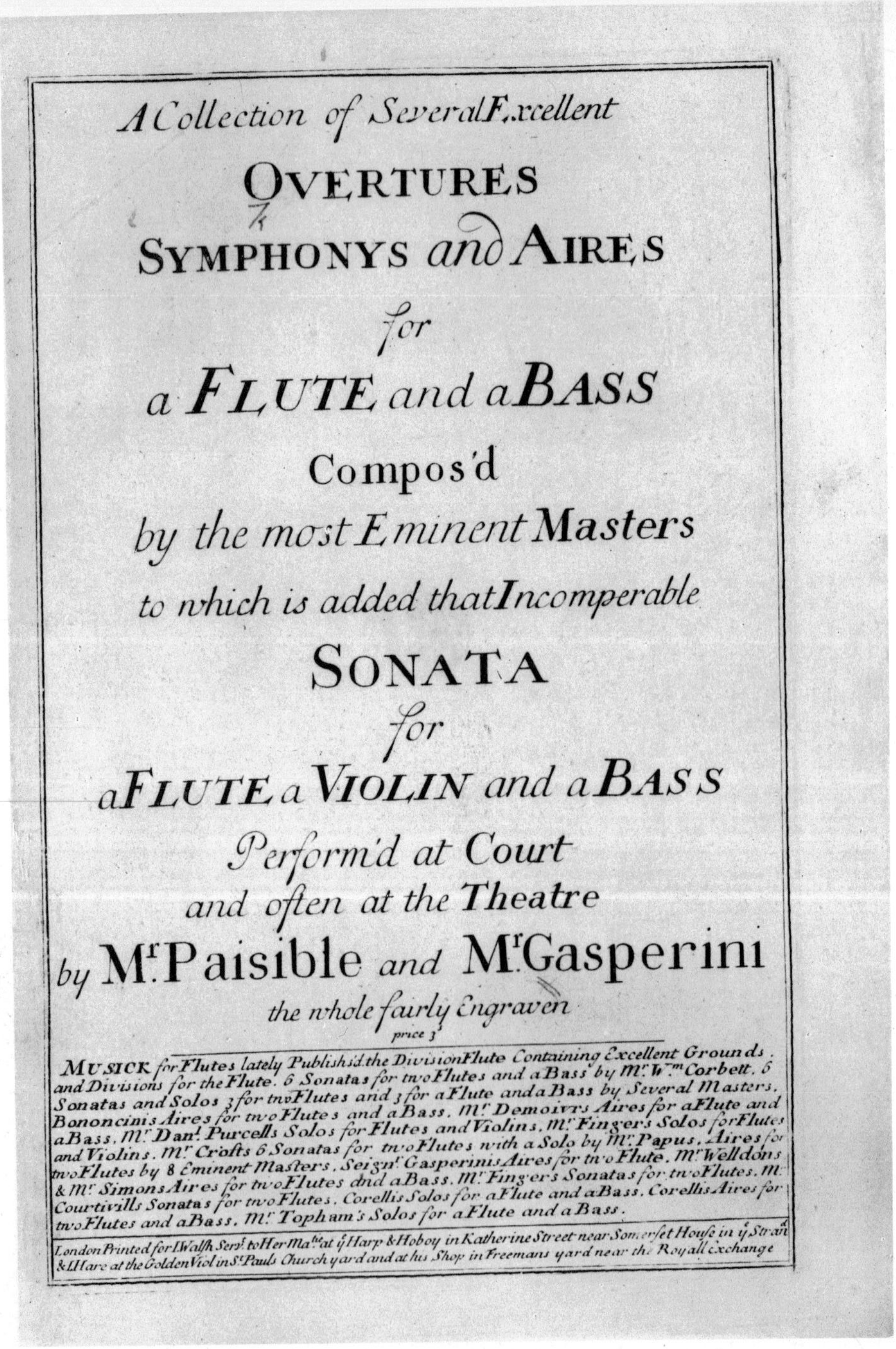

A Collection of Several Excellent

OVERTURES
SYMPHONYS *and* AIRES

for

a FLUTE *and a* BASS

Compos'd

by the most Eminent Masters

to which is added that Incomperable

SONATA
for

a FLUTE a VIOLIN *and a* BASS

Perform'd at Court
and often at the Theatre

by Mr. Paisible *and* Mr. Gasperini

the whole fairly Engraven

price 3

MUSICK *for Flutes lately Publish'd the Division Flute Containing Excellent Grounds and Divisions for the Flute. 6 Sonatas for two Flutes and a Bass by Mr. Wm Corbett. 6 Sonatas and Solos 3 for two Flutes and 3 for a Flute and a Bass by Several Masters. Bononcinis Aires for two Flutes and a Bass. Mr. Demoivrs Aires for a Flute and a Bass. Mr. Danl. Purcells Solos for Flutes and Violins. Mr. Fingers Solos for Flutes and Violins. Mr. Crofts 6 Sonatas for two Flutes with a Solo by Mr. Papus, Aires for two Flutes by 8 Eminent Masters, Seignr. Gasperini Aires for two Flute. Mr. Welldons & Mr. Simons Aires for two Flutes and a Bass. Mr. Fingers Sonatas for two Flutes. Mr. Courtivills Sonatas for two Flutes. Corellis Solos for a Flute and a Bass. Corellis Aires for two Flutes and a Bass. Mr. Topham's Solos for a Flute and a Bass.*

London Printed for I. Walsh Servt. to Her Majt. at ye Harp & Hoboy in Katherine Street near Somerset House in ye Strait & I. Hare at the Golden Viol in St. Pauls Church yard and at his Shop in Freemans yard near the Royall exchange

PLATE 16

See No. 198

THE TEMPLE OF LOVE

SONGS
in the OPERA
Call'd the
TEMPLE of LOVE

M Vander Gucht Sculp

London Printed for I.Walsh Serv.t to Her Ma.tie at the Harp and Hoboy in Katherine Street near Somerset House in ÿ Strand

PLATE 17
See Nos. 222 and 517

SONGS
in the New OPERA Called
ROSAMOND
Compos d by
Mr Tho: Clayton

W: Sykes Iunior Inventor.

H: Hulbergh Fecit.

London Printed for I Walsh Sers.t to Her Ma.tie at ÿ Harp and Hoboy in Katherine Street near Somerset House
in ÿ Strand — and P. Randall at ÿ Violin and Lute by Paulsgrave head Court without Temple Barr 1707

PLATE 18

See No. 247

PLATE 19

See Nos. 15, 119, and 264a

London *Printed for & Sold by* **Iohn Walſh** *Servant to her Majesty at the Harp and Hautboy in Katherine Street near Somerset House in the Strand*

PLATE 20

See Nos. 102, 272, 275, 282, 292, 293, 296, 308, 344, 354, 450, 484, and 518

THE

SYMPHONYS

OR

INSTRUMENTAL PARTS

in the

OPERA

Call'd

CLOTILDA

as they are Perform'd
at the

QUEENS Theatre

3

London Printed for I. Walsh Servt. to Her Matie. and P. Randall at ye Harp & Hoboy, in
Catherine Street near Somerset House in ye Strand. I. Hare Instrument-maker at the
golden Viol and Flute in Cornhill near ye Royal Exchange.

PLATE 21

See Nos. 300, 355, and 388

SIX
ENGLISH
Cantatas
Humbly Inscrib'd
To the most Noble the
Marchioness of KENT

Compos'd by
Mr. J.C. Pepusch

Non ante vulgatas per
artes
Verba loquor Socianda
Chordis citharæ

London Printed for J. Walsh Servant in Ordinary to his Majesty, & P. Randall at ye Harp & Hoboy in Katherine street
near Somerset House in ye Strand, &c J. Hare at ye Viol & Flute in Cornhill near the Royall Exchange.

PLATE 22

See Nos. 353, 384, 385, 387, 389, 417, 422, 426, 446, 447, 449, 459, 492, 495, 581, 582, and 583

For the Further Improvement of Dancing

A Treatise of

Chorography, or the Art of Dancing Country Dances

after a new Character

In which

The Figures, Steps, and Manner of performing are Describ'd, and the Rules Demonstrated in an Easie Method, adapted to the meanest Capacity. Translated from the French of Mon.r Feuillet, and Improv'd with many Additions.

All fairly Engrav'd on Copper Plates.

with a Collection

Of Country Dances, and a New French Dance Call'd the

Princess's Passpied

Compos'd

and Writt in Characters by

John Essex

LONDON

Sold by I. Walsh Serv.t to his Majesty at the Harp and Hoboy in Catherine Street in the Strand. I. Hare Instrument-maker, at the Viol & Flute in Cornhill near the Royal Exchange. and by the Author at his House in Roode Lane, in Fanchurch Street, where are taught all the Ball Dances of the English and French Court.

PLATE 23

See No. 478

London Printed for I Walsh Serv.t in Ordinary to his Majesty at the Harp and Hoboy in Catherine street in the Strand and I Hare at the Viol and Flute in Cornhill near the Royal Exchange.

PLATE 24

See Nos. 491 and 531

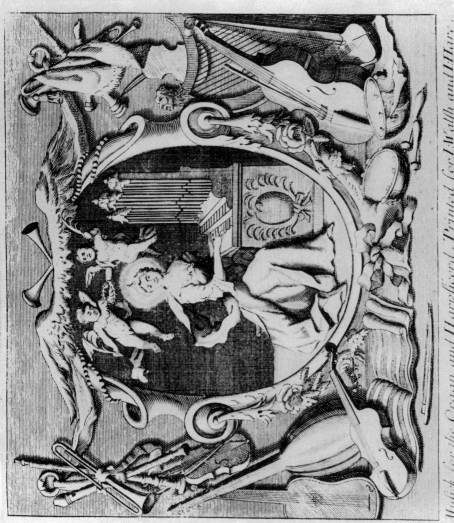

Musick for the Organ and Harpsichord, Printed for I.Walsh and I.Hare.

PLATE 25

See No. 539

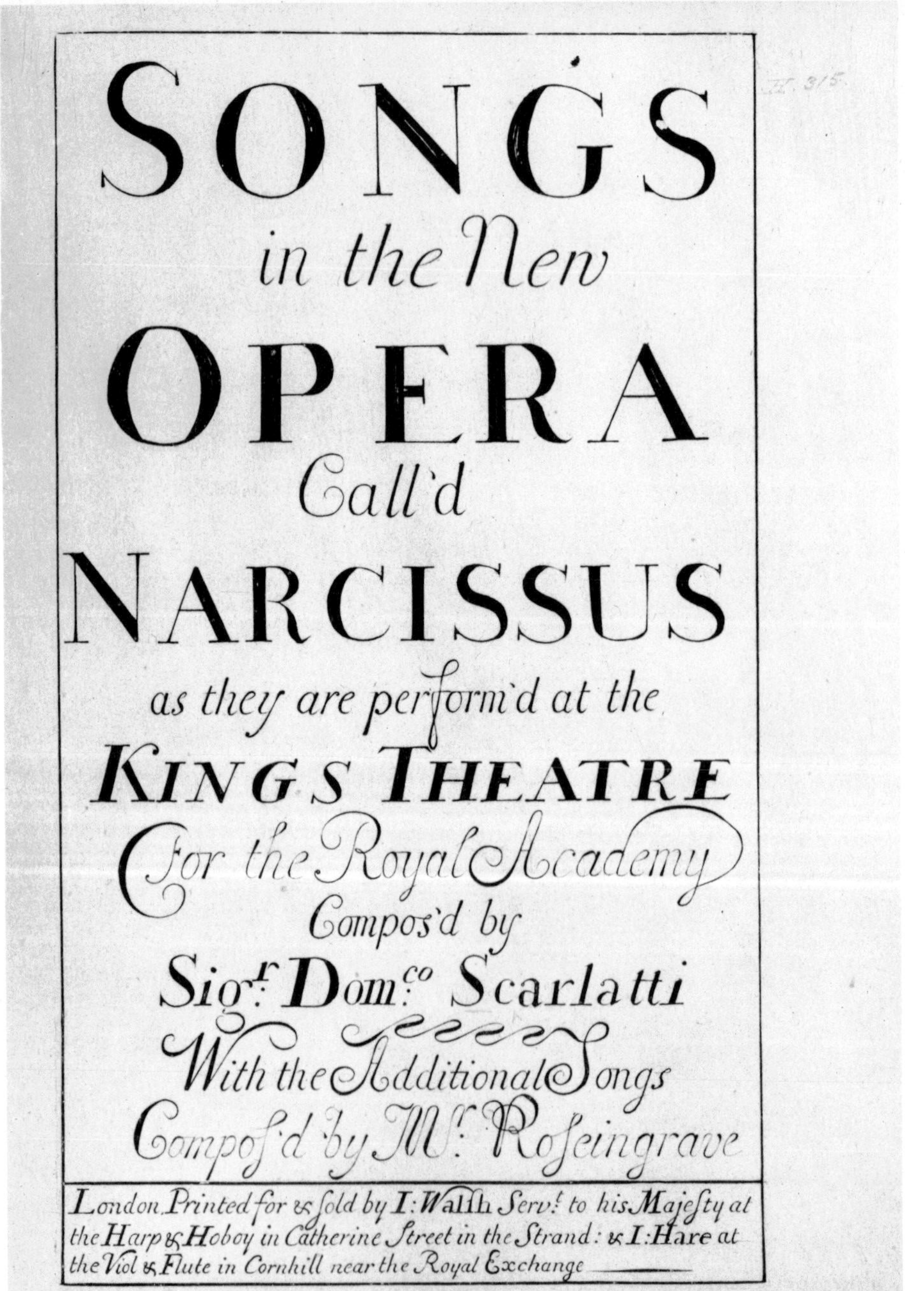

SONGS

in the New

OPERA

Call'd

NARCISSUS

as they are perform'd at the

KINGS THEATRE

for the Royal Academy

Compos'd by

Sigr. Domco. Scarlatti

With the Additional Songs

Compos'd by Mr. Roseingrave

London. Printed for & sold by I: Walsh Servt. to his Majesty at the Harp & Hoboy in Catherine Street in the Strand: & I: Hare at the Viol & Flute in Cornhill near the Royal Exchange _____

PLATE 26

See No. 590

A Catalogue of English & Italian Musick, *Vocal & Instrumental* Printed for Iohn Walsh

Musick for a single Violin

	s d
Books for Learners on $ Violin	1-6
Familiar tunes for $ Violin	1-6
Scotch tunes for $ Violin	1-0
Jiggs & Hornpipes 1st book	1-6
Jiggs & Hornpipes 2d book	1-6
French dances & Minuets 1st B	2-6
French dances &c 2d Book	2-6
1st Great book of Country dances	3-6
2d Great book Country dances	3-6
20 Books of Figure dances by Mr Isaac	1-0-0
Select Lessons 1st book	1-6
Select Lessons 2d book	1-6
Select Preludes by all Mast	2-6
Grounds & Divisions 1st B	2-6
Grounds & Divisions 2d B	2-6
Banisters Choice Opera Aires	1-6
Banisters 2d Collection	1-6
Hills Minuets	1-0
A book of Instructions for the German Flute	1-6

Musick for two Violins

	s d
Dr Pepuschs Aires	3-0
Valentines Aires	3-0
Bononcinis Aires	3-0
Courtivills Aires	3-0
Fingers Aires	3-0
Opera Aires	2-0

Sonatas and Concertos for 2 Violins & a Bass

	s d
Correllis Opera Prima	8-0
Corellis Opera Secunda	6-0
Corellis Opera Terza	8-0
Corellis Opera Quarta	6-0
Corellis 12 Concertos	15-0
Corellis Posthumus works	6-0
Albinonis Concertos	6-0
Vivaldis Concertos	15-0
Albinonis Ballettis	6-0
Tibaldis Opera Prima	4-0
Tibaldis Opera Secunda	4-0
Bomportis Opera Secunda	4-0
Bomportis Opera Quarta	4-0
Zianis Sonatas	4-0
Bonontrinis Sonatas	3-0
Nicola Matice Aires	1-0
Pez 12 Sonatas	3-0
Henr Purcells Sonatas	6-0
Henr Purcells Aires	6-0
Fingers 12 Sonatas	6-0
Ravenscrofts Sonatas	6-0
Harmonia Mundi 1st Coll	5-0
Harmonia Mundi 2d Coll	5-0
Valentines Sonatas	6-0
Schickards Sonatas	6-0
Corellis 4 Operas	1-5-0
Tophams Sonatas	3-0
Mascittis Sonatas	6-0
Hydaspes Concertos	6-0
Thomyris Concertos	6-0
Camilla Concertos	6-0
6 Sets of Trumpet Tunes	6-0
Albertis Concertos	9-0
Schickards 16 Opera	2-6
Vivaldis Cuckoo Concertos	3-0
Valentinis Bizzarias	4-0

Solos for a Violin & a Bass

	s d
12 Solos by Corelli	5-0
Ditto with Graces	5-0
24 Solos by Dr Pepusch	5-0
Mascittis Solos Opera Prima	6-0
Mascittis Opera Secunda	6-0
Mascittis Opera Terza	6-0
Mascittis Opera Quarta	6-0
Mascittis Opera Quinta	6-0
Mascittis Opera Sezta	6-0
Bomportis Solos	4-0
Gasperinis Solos	4-0
6 Solos by Several Masters	4-0
Fingers & Purcells Solos	4-0
Rules for Playing a Bass on a Violin	1-6
6 Solos by Albinoni Opera 4th	4-0
Albinonis 12 Grand Solos	6-0
Martino Bittis Solos	4-0
Viners Solos	4-0
Vivaldis Solos 2d Opera	6-0
Schickards 20th Opera	6-0
12 Solos by Guiseppe Valentini	6-0
Geminianis Solos	6-0

Musick for $ Harpsicord Spinnet or Organ

	s d
Books of Instructions for Learners on $ Harpsicord or Spinnet	2-0
Kellers rules for a Thro-bass	1-6
The Ladys Banquet 1st book	2-6
The Ladys Banquet 2d book	2-6
The Ladys Entertainmt 1st book	2-6
The Ladys Entertainmt 2d book	2-6
The Ladys Entertainmt 3d book	3-0
The Ladys Entertainmt 4th book	4-0
Babells great book of Lessons	7-3
Lessons by several Masters	1-6
1st Birons Lessons	1-6
Dupars Lessons	2-6
The Opera of Camilla for the Harpsicord	5-0
Maasmans Lessons	2-0
Sigr Baptist Lessons	5-0
Henr Purcells Lessons	3-0
Dr Blows Lessons	1-6
Dr Blows Psalms	1-6
Mr Purcells Psalms	1-6
Valentarys for $ Organ 1st book	5-0
Pasquinis for $ Organ 2d book	5-0
Lessons for $ Bass Viol	3-0
Songs & Aires for $ Viol	2-6
Mr Youngs Lessons	5-0
The Ladys Banquet 3 book	3-0

Songs or Vocal Musick

The Operas thus markd + + have Symphonys

	s d
The Opera of Crœsus +	9-0
The Opera of Numitor	9-0
Opera of Arminius	9-0
Opera of Narcissus	9-0
Opera of Calypso +	9-0
Opera of Astartus	
Opera of Camilla +	9-0
Opera of Thomyris +	9-0
Opera of Loves Triumph +	9-0
Opera of Pyrrhus +	9-0
Opera of Clotilda +	9-0
Opera of Arsinoe +	9-0
Opera of Rosamond +	9-0
The Temple of Love +	9-0
Opera of Almahide +	9-0
Opera of Hydaspes +	9-0
Opera of Etearco +	9-0
Opera of Rinaldo +	9-0
Opera of Antiochus +	9-0
Opera of Hamlet +	9-0
Opera of Dioclesion +	9-0

Collections of Songs by Several Authors

	s d
Mr Eccles Songs	15-0
Dr Blows Songs	15-0
Henr Purcells Orpheus	10-0
Mr Weldons Songs	10-0
The Judgment of Paris	7-6
Drinking Songs	2-6
A Book of Catches	2-6
A Book of Scotch Songs	2-6
A Book of Comical Songs	2-6
Ramondons Songs	2-0
Welldops Anthems	4-0
Anthems by several Authors	4-0
The Mask of Venus	
Adonis	5-0
Dr Pepuschs Cantatas	5-0
Galliards Cantatas	2-0
Haydens Cantatas	2-0
Vanbrughes Songs	5-0
Graves Songs	2-0
Careys Songs	2-0
Durleys Songs	2-0
Dr Pepuschs Additional Songs in $ Opera of Thomyris	9-0
Dr Pepuschs 2d Cantatas	5-0
A book of Sea Songs	1-6

PLATE 27

See No. 31 and many other numbers

A Catalogue of English and Italian Musick for Flutes Printed for John Walsh

Musick for a single Flute	s d	Musick for two Flutes	s d	Musick for 2 Flutes & a Bass	s d	Solos for a Flute & a Bass	s d
Books for Learners on ye Flute	1-6	Fingers Sonatas	3-0	Pez 1st Collection	3-0	Correllis Solos	4-0
Books for Learners on the Flagelet Gamut way	1-0	Courtivills Sonatas	3-0	Pez 2d Collection	3-0	Pepusch 1st Solos	4-0
Books for Learners on ye Mock Trumpet 1st 2d 3d & 4th book each	1-0	Dr Crofts Sonatas	3-0	Correllis 1st Collection	3-0	Pepusch 2d Solos	4-0
Books for Learners on ye Hoboy	1-6	Aires by a Person of Quality	2-0	Correllis 2d Collection	3-0	Tophams 1st Solos	3-0
Familiar Aires for ye Flute	1-0	Paisibles Sonatas	3-0	Corbets Sonatas	4-0	Tophams 2d Solos	3-0
Select Lessons 1st book	1-6	Gasperinis Aires	2-0	Ditto for ye German Flute	3-0	Fingers & Purcells Solos	4-0
Select Lessons 2d book	1-6	Six Sonatas three for 2 Flutes & 3 for a Flute & a Bass	3-0	Bononcinis Aires	3-0	Overtures & Aires	3-0
Scotch Aires	1-0	Aires by 8 Masters	2-0	Weldon's & Simmon's	3-0	Demoivers Aires	2-0
Mr Cox's Aires	1-0	Krembergs Aires	2-0	Aires in Camilla	3-0	Martino Bitti Solos	4-0
Demoivers 1st Aires	1-6	Overtures in Camilla &c	2-0	Romanos Aires	3-0	Lullys 1st Solos	6-0
Demoivers 2d Aires	1-6	Overtures in Pyrrhus &c	2-0	Almahide Aires	3-0	Lullys 2d Solos	6-0
Catches for ye Flute	2-0	Pyrrhus Aires	3-0	Hydaspes Aires	3-0	Lullys 3d Solos	6-0
Country dances for ye Flute	2-0	Clotilda Aires	3-0	Rinaldo Aires	3-0	Valentines 2d Solos	6-0
French dances for ye Flute	1-6	Dr Pepuschs Aires	3-0	Oxon Aires	3-0	Valentines 3d	6-0
Preludes & Cibells by the greatest Masters in Europe	2-6	Simmons Aires	2-0	Purcells Sonatas	4-0	Valentines 5th	6-0
First Division Flute	2-6	Opera Arminius	2-0	Mattesons for 3 Flutes	3-0	Dieuparts Solos	5-0
Second Division Flute	2-6	Opera Croesus	2-0	Valentines Aires	3-0	Galliards Solos	5-0
Opera Arminius for ye flute	1-6	Valentines 1st Sonatas	3-0	Schickhards Concertos	6-0	Mercys 1st Solos	4-0
Opera Croesus	1-6	Valentines 2d Sonatas	3-0	Corellis Concertos	4-0	Mercys 2d Solos	4-0
Opera Calypso	1-6	Lullys Sonatas	3-0	Paisibles Aires	4-0	Geminiani & Castrucci	5-0
Opera Almahide	1-6	Opera Aires with Symph:	2-0			Schickards 17th Opera	6-0
Opera Hydaspes	1-6	Valentines ft Opera	3-0				
Opera Rinaldo	1-6						
Pyrrhus & Clotilda Aires	1-6						
Opera Numitor	1-6						

PLATE 28

See No. 21, and many other numbers

A new SONG Sung in the Spanish Frier, set by M.r Henry Purcell Engraven for I. Walsh.

Whilst I with greif did on you look, whilst I with greif did on you look, when Love had

turn . . . . . . d your Brain from you, I.I. the conta . . . . . . gion took, from you

I.I. y.e conta . . . . . . gion took, & for you for you bear . . . . . . the pain; for you for you

bear . . . . . . y.e pain: Mercella, then your Lover prize, and be not, be not, be not

too severe, we well, we well y.e con . . . . . . quest of your eyes for pride, pride, pride has cost

you dear Ambrosio, treats your flames with scorn, and rack . . . . . . s your tender

mind, withdraw your Smiles, withdraw your Smil . . . . . . es and frowns return, and pay him,

pay him, pay him in his kind, and pay him, pay him, pay him in his kind.

PLATE 29

See No. 6

PLATE 30

See No. 12

PLATE 31

See No. 13

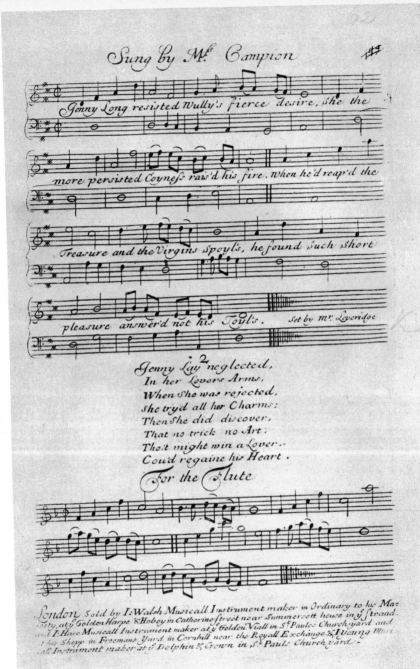

PLATE 32

See No. 35

Sung by Mr Ramondon, in the OPERA call'd Camilla, at the Theatre Royall.

PLATE 33

See No. 221

PLATE 34

See No. 258

PLATE 35

See No. 353

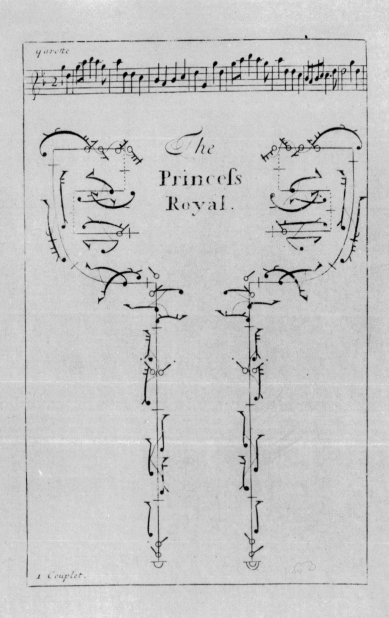

PLATE 36

See No. 461

PLATE 37

See No. 564

(1)

The
Symphony
or
OVERTURE
of
Numitor

Adagio

PLATE 38

See No. 588

INDEX OF TITLES AND WORKS

THE index includes the titles of all the works examined, or as given in the newspaper advertisements, or in Walsh and other catalogues. Although abbreviated in many cases, sufficient information has been given to enable the works to be identified, as a rule, from the index; but the bibliography should be consulted for more exact and complete transcriptions.

The entries are in strictly alphabetical order according to the spelling as given, with a few obvious exceptions. Punctuation has been generally followed, with occasional minor alterations; initial capitals to some unimportant words have been modified; and other words (e.g. Ye, Mr., 1st, 2d, &c.) printed in a uniform way. When the original title includes, but does not begin with, the name of an opera, play, or other distinctive work (e.g. 'Rinaldo', 'The Mad Lover', 'The Division Flute') entries have also been made under such headings; and in some cases, discretionary and made-up titles and cross-references, that will help identification, have been provided. The index is not a subject-index, although it includes a few generic headings (e.g. Country Dances, Minuets), and most of the works appear only once—under the first word of the title (including numerals, whether given in figures or letters, composers' names, &c.) other than an article.

Bass, collected out of the choicest Works of six eminent Masters, 224.

Six select (selected) Suites of Lessons for the Harpsicord in six severall keys . . . Composed by Signr. Giovani Baptista Draghi, 233.

Six Sets of Airs for two Flutes, by Mr. Hen. Simons, 418.

6 Sets of Airs or Italian Arietta's for 2 Flutes and a Bass by Signior Bononcini, 178.

6 Sets of Trumpet Tunes, for 2 Violins & a Bass, 525.

Six Setts of Aires and a Chacoon for two Flutes & a Bass Compos'd by Mr. Valentine at Rome, 552.

Six Setts of Aires for two Flutes & a Bass . . . Compos'd by Mr. Paisible, 597.

Six Setts of Aires for Violins, Hautboys and a Trumpet, &c., 525.

Six Setts of Airs for two Flutes and a Bass. By Archangelo Corelli, 107, 243.

Six Setts of choice Opera Songs or Arietts with their Symphonys fitted for 2 Flutes, 545.

6 Solos by Albinoni, Opera 4to, for a Violin & a Bass, 366.

6 Solos by several Masters, for a Violin & a Bass, 224.

Six Solos for a Flute and a Bass by Archangelo Corelli being the second part of his Fifth Opera, 85.

6 Solos for a Flute and a Bass by Mr. Pepusch, 232.

Six Solos for a Flute with a Thorough Bass for the Harpsicord or Violoncello . . . By . . . Luis Mercy, 553.

Six Solos for a German Flute, a Hautboy, or Violin, by Christian Schickart, 542.

Six Solos for a Violin and a through Base, by Mr. Viner, 544.

Six Solos for Violins by six Masters, 258.

Six Sonatas a 3° for two Violins & Thrŏ=bass . . . Compos'd by William Corbett Opera Quarta. Libro Secondo, 324.

6 Sonata's and 6 Solo's by Arcangelo Corelli transpos'd for Flutes, 205.

Six Sonata's five in four a sixth in 7 parts Compos'd in imitation of Archangelo Corelli by Wm. Topham M.A. Opera Terza, 334.

Six Sonata's for a Flute and a Bass, by Wm. Corbet, 244.

Six Sonatas for one Flute & two Hoboys or two Violins with a Viol Bass and a Thorough Bass for the Harpsicord & Arch Lute Compos'd by Mr. Christian Schickhard, 467.

Six Sonata's for 2 Flutes and a Bass, by Arcangelo Corelli, collected out of the choicest of his Works . . . the 2d Collection, 243, 255.

Six Sonata's for 2 Flutes by the same Author [i.e. Robert Valentine], 497.

Six Sonatas for two Hoboys, two Violins or German Flutes; with a Thorough Bass for the Harpsicord, or Bass Violin. Composed by Mr. Christian Schickard, 571.

Six Sonata's in three parts . . . Composed by William Williams, 126.

Six Sonata's of 3 parts . . . for three Flutes compos'd by Signior Matteison Opera Prima, 465.

Six Sonata's of two parts fitted and contriv'd for two Flute's Compos'd by Mr. Loeillet of Gant, 612.

Six Sonatas of two parts for two Flute's Composed by Mr. Finger Opera Secunda, 99.

Six Sonatas of two parts for two Flute's Composed by Mr. Paisible Opera Prima, 142b, Ill. 12.

Six Sonatas of two parts for two Flutes Compos'd by Mr. Valentine at Rome Opera 6ta, 572.

Six Sonatas of two parts for two Flutes Composed by Mr. Valentine at Rome Opera 7ma, 575.

Six Sonata's of 2 parts for 2 Violins, Composed by Mr. Courtevil, 98.

Six Sonata's of two parts for two Violins Compos'd by Mr. Valentine at Rome Opera Quarta, 480.

Six Sonata's of two parts made on purpose for two Flutes Compos'd by Mr. Valentine at Rome Opera Quarta, 468, 497.

Six Sonata's of two parts purposely contriv'd for two Flutes. Composed by Mr. Rogers, 19.

Six Sonatas of two parts purposely made and contrived for two Flutes Compos'd by Mr. William Croft, &c., 144, 148.

Six Sonatas or Solos for the Flute with a

Index of Titles and Works

GENERAL INDEX

Abell, I., pp. x, xi, xii.

Abell, John, 84.

Addison, Joseph, 237, 245, 247.

Akeroyde, Samuel (Akeroyd, *Mr.*), 236, 240.

Alberti, Giuseppe Matteo, 546.

Albinoni (Albinone), Tommaso, 128, 140, 159, 257, 328, 331, 366, 370, 396, 524, 529, 532, 540, 541, 542, 548.

Allnott, John, 277*b*.

Alyff, *Mrs.*, 381.

Ambrogio, Carlo, 150*c*, 224.

Anne, *Queen*, 82*a*, 88, 108, 113, 116, 117, 139, 140, 145, 154, 170, 196, 207, 234, 248, 269, 270, 280, 293, 343, 374, 375, 383, 404–15, 439, 444, p. xxii.

Arber, Edward, p. xii.

Armstrong, *Mr.*, 292, 293.

Arne, Thomas Augustine, p. vi.

Arnold, Samuel, p. vi.

B., *Lord* [Lord Byron]. *See* Byron, William, *Fourth Baron Byron.*

B., J. [J. Bolton?], 113.

Babell (Babel) William, 308, 484, 501, 505, 536, 539.

Baker, Thomas, 62, 115, 191.

Baloon, *Monsieur*, 34.

Banister, John, 20*b*, 31, 42, Ill. 9, 149, 503, 526.

Banqueting House, Whitehall. *See* Chapel Royal.

Baptist, *Signr. See* Draghi, Giovanni Battista.

Barrett (Barret, Bartet), John, 26, 27, 59, 78, Ill. 9, 96, 106, 109, 115, 140, 146, 151, 175, 191, 236, 240, 306, 312, 347, 370, 397, 416, 421, 423, 525.

Bassani (Basana), Giovanni Battista, 50, 140, 257, 360, 504.

Bedford, Arthur, 208.

Bedford, John, *Duke of*, 160.

Bedford, Wriothesly, *Duke of*, 160.

Beity (Betti, Betty), Martino. *See* Bitti.

Berchet, Pierre, 156, 221, 298.

Bettesworth, Arthur, 485.

Bibliothèque Alfred Cortot, 403.

Bignell, *Mrs.*, 113.

Birchall, Robert, p. xi.

Birkhead (Burket), *Mr.*, 592.

Biron, *Ld. See* Byron, William, *Fourth Baron Byron.*

Bishop, John, 34*a*, 372.

Bishop of Durham. *See* Durham, *Bishop of.*

Bitti (Bitty), Martino, 143, 150, 224, 396, 401, 532, 542, 550.

Blake, *Sir* Richard, p. ix.

Blow, John, 27, 130, 140, 162, 176, 211, 303, 499, 501, 505, 537, 539, 564, 602.

Bodleian Library, Oxford, 140, p. xx.

The Bohemian Woman, 34.

Bolton, *Duchess of*, 478.

Bolton, J. *See* B., J.

Bomporti, Francisco Antonio. *See* Bonporti, Francesco Antonio.

Bononcini, Giovanni Battista, 63, 178, 246, 251, 253, 254, 256, 337, 560, 604, 617, p. vi.

Bononcini, Giovanni Maria, 63, Ill. 7, 140, 178, 604.

Bononcini, Marco Antonio, 201, 204, 206, 209, 211, 216–18, 221, 241, 249, 250, 298, 402, 521, 560.

Bonporti, Francesco Antonio, 266, 267, 277*d*, 282*a*, 396, 482, 532, 542, 603.

Boschi (Boscchi), Francesca Vanini, 382.

Boschi (Boscchi), Giuseppe, 373.

Bouche, Peter Paul, 31, Ill. 6, 60, p. xxiii.

Bound Works, 114, 142*c*, 156, 181, 238, 268, 297, 485, 514, 533, 558, p. xxvii.

Boyce, William, p. vi.

Boyle, Charles, *Earl of Orrery*, 122.

Brandenburg, *Electress of. See* Sophia Charlotte, *Electress of Brandenburg.*

Bray, Thomas, 26*a*.

British Museum (BM.), Department of Printed Books, pp. xii, xiii, xxviii.

—— The King's Music Library (RM.), pp. xii, xiv, xxviii.

Brome, Richard, 180.

Brown, J., 485.

Brydges, James, *Duke of Chandos, Earl of Carnarvon*, 553, 581.

D d

General Index

Handel (Handell, &c.), George Frederick, 156, 166, 353, 382, 385, 387–92, 449, 459, 576, 593, pp. vii, xii, xiv, xv, xvii, xix, xxii, xxxiii.

Hanover, *Elector of. See* George I.

Hare, John, 1–5, 7–16, 18–20, 23–5, 26*a*, 28, 32–9, 42–55, 57–76, 78–88, 90–4, 96–123, 125–38, 140–55, 157–99, 201, 205–7, 209–19, 221–4, 226–46, 248–57, 259–89, 292–312, 314–30, 332–56, 358–415, 417, 419–27, 429–53, 458–70, 473–600, 611, 616, pp. x, xviii, xx, xxiv–xxvi.

— Joseph, 257, 343*a*, 364, 380, 381, 464, 612, pp. ix, x, xxiii, xxvi.

Hartington, William, *Lord Marquiss of*, 140.

Hasse, Johann Adolph, 166, p. vi.

Hawkins, *Sir* John, p. xviii.

Hayden, George, 518.

Haym (Haiam), Niccolò Francesco, 181, 292–5, 302, 325, 338, 345.

Hendel (Hendell, Hendle). *See* Handel, George Frederick.

Henry Watson Library, 82*a*.

Heptinstall, John, 8, 108, 248, 268, 595.

Higgons, Bevill, 78.

Hill, Aaron, 385, 387, 389, 449, 459.

— Arthur F., 431, 432, 479.

— Peter Murray, 354, 503, 575.

Hills (Hill), William, 341, 576.

Hirsch Collection, British Museum, 4, 89, pp. xii, xxxii–xxxiv.

Howard, Hugh, 181, Ill. 15, 466.

Hughes, John, 353, 426, 495, 581, 582.

Hughs, *Mr.* [Francis Hughes?], 298.

Hulsbergh, Henry, 103, Ill. 11, 109, 156, Ill. 13, 160, 221, 234, 247, Ill. 18, 298, p. xxii.

Isaac (Isaack, Isack, Isacks), 116, 145, 170, 196, 207, 234, 269, 270, 280, 343, 374, 375, 383, 399, 404–15, 439, 444, 462.

Isham (Isom, Isum), John, 264, 379.

An Italian Mr. (Master), 28, 357.

John, *Duke of Bedford. See* Bedford.

Johnson, Charles, 397.

— John, 181.

Jones, John, 576, 579.

Jonson, Ben, 357.

Keck, S., 181.

Keen (Keene), Edward, 26, 236, 240, 421, 423.

Keller, Gottfried (Godfry), 190, 211, 230, 235, 277*c*, 282*a*, 501, 505, 511, 539.

Kent, *Marchioness of*, 353, 582.

Kidson, Frank, pp. vi, x, xvi, xviii, xxviii.

Kimbolton, *Baron. See* Charles, *Earl of Manchester.*

King, Robert, 15, Ill. 4, Ill. 19, 20*b*, 31, 119, 264*a*, p. xxi.

King of Spain, The New. *See* Charles, *Archduke of Austria.*

King's College, Cambridge, 15, 82*a*, 513.

— Theatre, Haymarket. *See* Queen's Theatre.

Kremberg, James, 213.

Kynaston, Nathaniel, 332, 371, 386, 488, 502, 534.

L'Abbé (Labee, L'Abee), Anthony, 34, 399, 461, 494, 506, 538, 568.

Labels on title-pages, p. xvii.

Lafayer, *Mr. See* Lefevre.

La Garde, *Mr.* de, 270, 343, 383.

Lampe, Johann Friedrich, p. vi.

Lane, *Mr.*, 170.

Lansdowne, *Lord. See* Granville, George, *Lord Lansdowne.*

La-sac (Le Sac), *Monsieur*, 34.

Latour (Latoure, Lature), *Mr.*, 576.

Le Cene, Michel Charles, 181, 466, 549, 611.

Lee, Nathaniel, 66, 67.

Lefevre (Lafayer?), *Mr.*, 116, 170.

Leigh, John, 574.

Lenton, John, 46, Ill. 7, 79, 87, Ill. 9, 120, 140, 147, 152, 169.

Lepine, *Sigra* Margarita de. *See* Épine, Francesca Margherita de l'.

Leveridge (Leveredge), Richard, 7, 11, 22–4, Ill. 7, 26, 35, Ill. 32, 140, 236, 240, p. vi.

Levingston, *Mr. See* Livingston, Alexander.

Library of Congress, 513.

Lichfield, Leonard, 16.

Lincoln's Inn Fields Theatre (Little Lincoln's Inn Fields Theatre, New Theatre), 29*a*, 159, 565, p. xxi.

Livingston (Levingston), Alexander, 20, 20*a*, 20*b*, 30, 280, 343*a*.

Loeillet (Lulliet, Lully, Luly), Jean Baptiste, 429, 476, 556, 612.

London Gazette, Different issues of, p. xiii.

General Index

Plates:
Changes in, pp. xviii–xx.
Copper, 1, 2, 4, 5, 10, 14, 15, 20a, 29a, 31, 55, 64, 71, 181 (Portrait), 221, 287, 348, 379, 478, 513, pp. xviii, xix.
Engraved, pp. vii, xviii, xix.
Pewter, pp. xviii, xix.
Punched, pp. xviii, xix.
Size of, p. xxvii.
Walsh plates used by Randall and Abell, &c., p. xii.
Playford, Henry, 22, 49, 83, 88, 103, 162, 167, 174, 195, 214, 248, 263, 499, 602.
— John, 167, 174, 195, p. v.
Poglietti (Polietti), Alessandro, 564.
Polaroli (Pollaroli), Carlo Francesco, 360, 504.
Polietti. See Poglietti, Alessandro.
Pollaroli. See Polaroli, Carlo Francesco.
Pope, Alexander, p. xxxiii.
Porta, Giovanni, 588, 591.
Powell [Charles?], Mr., 19a.
Preston, John, p. xii.
— Thomas, p. xii.
Price of Works, p. xv, xxvii.
— reductions in, 251, 299, 334, 505, 519, 596.
Princess of Wales. See Caroline of Anspach.
Prior, Matthew, 495.
Purcell (Purcel), Daniel, 12, Ill. 1, Ill. 30, 15, 22, 26, 29, 30, 47, 51, 58, Ill. 7, 62, 66, 67, 81, 82, 89, Ill. 9, Ill. 10, 97, 102, 103, 105, 106, 114, 140, 180, 194, 239, 258, 262, 277e, 277f, 282a, 315, 329, 331, 377, 396, 401, 435, 532, 536, 537, 539, 542, 564, pp. vi, xxi, xxii.
— Frances (Mrs. Henry), 108, 248, 499.
— (Purcel), Henry. 3, 6, Ill. 29, 14, 59, 108, 140, 149, 248, 257, 258, 268, 276, 303, 315, 331, 380, 381, 499, 501, 505, 539, 595.

Quaritch Catalogues, 505.
Queen's Theatre (King's Theatre), Haymarket, 229, 258, 270–3, 294, 296, 300, 302, 342, 344, 346, 354, 355, 373, 384, 388, 417, 422, 426, 446, 447, 450, 510, 588, 590.
Quires, works issued in, 138, 596, p. xxvii.

Ramondon, Lewis, 211, 216, 217, 585.
Randall, Elizabeth, pp. xi, xii, xxv, xxxiv.
— (Randal), P., 267, 226–33, 235–51, 253–7, 262, 263, 265–7, 273–87, 292–312, 314–75,

384, 388, 391, 402, 436, 440, 450, 460, 464, 482, 484, 513, pp. x, xxiv, xxvi.
Randall, William, pp. x–xii, xiv, xix, xxv, xxxiv.
Ravenscroft, John (Giovanni), 277, 282a.
Rawlins, Mickepher, 246, 252, 495.
Reeves, Harold, Catalogues, 136, 611.
Riboteau (Ribotteau), Henry, 466, 469, p. xvi.
Rich, Lady, 495.
Rimbault, Edward Francis, 82a.
Robart, William, 25.
Roberts, Francis, 15.
Roger, Estienne (Rogers, Stephen), 31, 125, 179, 181, 264a, 277, 350, 400, 434, 458, 466, 469, 479, 546, 547, 549, 550, 551, 577, 610, pp. vi, xvi–xviii.
Rogers (Rodgers), Mr., 19, 140.
Rolli, Paolo Antonio, 588, 590.
Romano, Signior, 279, 282a.
Roseingrave, Thomas, 590.
Rossi, Giacomo, 385, 387, 389, 449, 459.
Rowe Collection, King's College, Cambridge, 15, 211, 513.
Rowe, Nicholas, 46, 79, 120, 161, 264.
Rowley, William, 101.
Royal Academy [of Music], 588, 590.
— College of Music (RCM.), pp. xii, xiii, xxviii.
Royal Musical Association, 292.

The Sacred Choire, 491, Ill. 24, 531.
Saggione, Gioseppe (Giuseppe) Fedelli, 222, 517, p. xxii.
Saint James's Palace, 117, 493.
— Mary le Strand, p. vii, viii.
— Paul's Cathedral, 248, 276, 595.
Salter, Humphrey, 20, 20a, 20b, 30, 34a.
Santa, Gasparo Pietra, p. xxiii.
Scarlatti, Alessandro, 246, 251, 253, 254, 256, 292–4, 302, 325, 337, 338, 345, 382, 560, 617.
— Domenico, 590.
Schenk, Johann (Giovanni), 136, 140.
Schickhard (Schickard, Schickart, Schickhardt, Schikhard), Johann Christian, 467, 532, 542, 567, 571, 616.
Scholes, Percy, p. vi.
Seris, Mr. See Siris, P.
Settle, Elkanah, 12, 54.
Shadwell, Charles, 347.
Shaw, John, p. vii.
Sherwin, William, 181, Ill. 15.

213

PRINTED IN
GREAT BRITAIN
AT THE
UNIVERSITY PRESS
OXFORD
BY
CHARLES BATEY
PRINTER
TO THE
UNIVERSITY